Thomas Carlyle's
OLIVER CROMWELL

After the picture in the National Portrait Gallery. Photo by Walker & Cockerell.

Oliver Cromwell

THE LIFE OF

Oliver Cromwell

With a Selection from his Letters
and Speeches

CARLYLE'S

Fredonia Books
Amsterdam, The Netherlands

Oliver Cromwell:
With a Selection from his
Letters and Speeches

by
Thomas Carlyle

ISBN: 1-58963-735-6

Copyright © 2002 by Fredonia Books

Reprinted from the 1881 edition

Fredonia Books
Amsterdam, the Netherlands
http://www.fredoniabooks.com

All rights reserved, including the right to reproduce this book, or portions thereof, in any form.

In order to make original editions of historical works available to scholars at an economical price, this facsimile of the original edition of 1881 is reproduced from the best available copy and has been digitally enhanced to improve legibility, but the text remains unaltered to retain historical authenticity.

THE LIFE OF OLIVER CROMWELL

INTRODUCTION

CHAPTER I

OF THE CROMWELL KINDRED

OLIVER CROMWELL, afterwards Protector of the Commonwealth of England, was born at Huntingdon, in St. John's Parish there, on the 25th of April 1599. Christened on the 29th of the same month; as the old Parish-registers of that Church still legibly testify.

His Father was Robert Cromwell, younger son of Sir Henry Cromwell, and younger brother of Sir Oliver Cromwell, Knights both; who dwelt successively, in rather sumptuous fashion, at the Mansion of Hinchinbrook hard by. His Mother was Elizabeth Steward, daughter of William Steward, Esquire, in Ely; an opulent man, a kind of hereditary farmer of the Cathedral Tithes and Church lands round that city; in which capacity his son, Sir Thomas Steward, Knight, in due time succeeded him, resident also at Ely. Elizabeth was a young widow when Robert Cromwell married her: the first marriage, to one 'William Lynne, Esquire, of Bassingbourne in Cambridgeshire,' had lasted but a year: husband and only child are buried in Ely Cathedral, where their monument still stands; the date of their deaths, which followed near on one another, is 1589. The exact date of the young widow's marriage to Robert Cromwell is nowhere given; but seems to have been in 1591. Our Oliver was their fifth child; their second boy; but the first soon died. They had ten children in all; of whom seven came to maturity, and Oliver was their only son. I may as well print the little Note, smelted long ago out of huge dross-heaps in Noble's Book, that the reader too may have his small benefit of it.[1]

This Elizabeth Steward, who had now become Mrs. Robert Cromwell, was, say the genealogists, 'indubitably descended from the Royal Stuart Family of Scotland;' and could still count kindred with them. 'From one Walter Steward, who had accompanied Prince James of Scotland,' when our inhospitable politic Henry IV. detained the poor Prince, driven in by stress of weather to him here. Walter did not return with the Prince to Scotland; having 'fought tournaments,'—having made an advantageous marriage-settlement here. One of his descendants, Robert Steward, happened to be Prior of Ely when Henry VIII. dissolved the Monasteries; and proving pliant on that occasion, Robert Steward, last Popish Prior, became the first Protestant Dean of Ely, and—'was remarkably attentive to his family,' says Noble. The profitable Farming of the Tithes at Ely above mentioned; this, and other settlements, and good dotations of Church lands among his nephews, were the fruits of Robert Steward's pliancy on that occasion. The genealogists say, there is no doubt of this pedigree;—and explain in intricate

---

[1] OLIVER CROMWELL'S BROTHERS AND SISTERS.

Oliver's Mother had been a widow (Mrs. *Lynne* of Bassingbourne) before marrying Robert Cromwell; neither her age nor his is discoverable here.

1. *First* child (seemingly), *Joan,* baptized 24th September 1592; she died in 1600 (Noble, i. 88).
2. Elizabeth, 14th October 1593; died unmarried, thinks Noble, in 1672, at Ely.
3. *Henry*, 31st August 1595; died young, 'before 1617.'
4. Catherine, 7th February 1596-7; married to Whitstone, a Parliamentary Officer; then to Colonel Jones.
5. OLIVER, born 25th April 1599.
6. Margaret, 22d February 1600-1; she became Mrs. Wauton, or Walton, Huntingdonshire; her son was killed at Marston Moor,—as we shall see.
7. Anna, 2d January 1602-3; Mrs. Sewster, Huntingdonshire; died 1st November 1646:—her Brother Oliver had just ended the 'first Civil War' then.
8. Jane, 19th January 1605-6; Mrs. Desborow, Cambridgeshire; died, *seemingly*, in 1656.
9. *Robert*, 18th January 1608-9; died same April.
10. Robina, so named for the above Robert: uncertain date: became Mrs. Dr. French; then wife of Bishop Wilkins; her daughter by French, her one child, was married to Archbishop Tillotson.

HINCHINBROOK HOUSE

tables, how Elizabeth Steward, Mother of Oliver Cromwell, was indubitably either the ninth, or the tenth, or some other fractional part of half a cousin to Charles Stuart King of England.

Howsoever related to Charles Stuart or to other parties, Robert Cromwell, younger son of the Knight of Hinchinbrook, brought her home, we see, as his Wife, to Huntingdon, about 1591; and settled with her there, on such portion, with such prospects as a cadet of the House of Hinchinbrook might have. Portion consisting of certain lands and messuages round and in that Town of Huntingdon,—where, in the current name 'Cromwell's Acre,' if not in other names applied to lands and messuages there, some feeble echo of him and his possessions still survives, or seems to survive. These lands he himself farmed: the income in all is guessed or computed to have been about 300*l.* a year, a tolerable fortune in those times; perhaps somewhat like 1000*l.* now. Robert Cromwell's Father, as we said, and then his elder Brother, dwelt successively in good style at Hinchinbrook near by. It was the Father Sir Henry Cromwell, who from his sumptuosity was called the "Golden Knight," that built, or that enlarged, remodelled and as good as built, the Mansion of Hinchinbrook; which had been a Nunnery while Nunneries still were: it was the son, Sir Oliver, likewise an expensive man, that sold it to the Montagues, since Earls of Sandwich, whose seat it still is. A stately pleasant House, among its shady lawns and expanses, on the left bank of the Ouse river, a short half mile west of Huntingdon;—still stands pretty much as Oliver Cromwell's Grandfather left it; rather kept good and defended from the inroads of Time and Accident, than substantially altered. Several Portraits of the Cromwells, and other interesting portraits and memorials of the seventeenth and subsequent centuries, are still there. The Cromwell blazonry 'on the great bay window,' which Noble makes so much of, is now gone, destroyed by fire; has given place to Montague blazonry; and no dull man can bore us with that any more.

Huntingdon itself lies pleasantly along the left bank of the Ouse; sloping pleasantly upwards from Ouse Bridge, which connects it with the old village of Godmanchester; the Town itself consisting mainly of one fair street, which towards the north end of it opens into a kind of irregular market-place, and then contracting again soon terminates. The two churches of All-Saints and St. John's, as you walk up northward from the Bridge, appear successively on your left; the churchyards flanked with shops or other houses. The Ouse, which is of very circular course in this quarter, 'winding as if reluctant to enter the Fen-country,' says one Topographer, has still a respectable drab-colour, gathered from the clays of Bedfordshire; has not yet the Stygian black which in a few miles farther it assumes for good. Huntingdon, as it were, looks over into the Fens; Godmanchester, just across the river, already stands on black bog. The country to the East is all Fen (mostly unreclaimed in Oliver's time, and still of a very dropsical character); to the West it is hard green ground, agreeably broken into little heights, duly fringed with wood, and bearing marks of comfortable long-continued cultivation. Here, on the edge of the firm green land, and looking over into the black marshes with their alder-trees and willow-trees, did Oliver Cromwell pass his young years.

Robert Cromwell, Oliver's father, did Burgh and Quarter-Session duties; was not slack but moderately active as a country-gentleman; sat once in Parliament in his younger years; is found with his elder or other Brothers on various Public Commissions for Draining the Fens of that region, or more properly for inquiring into the possibility of such an operation; a thing much noised of then; which Robert Cromwell, among others, reported to be very feasible, very promising, but did not live to see accomplished, or even attempted. His social rank is sufficiently indicated;—and much flunkeyism, falsity and other carrion ought to be buried! Better than all social rank, he is understood to have been a wise, devout, steadfast and worthy man, and to have lived a modest and manful life in his station there.

CHAPTER II

EVENTS IN OLIVER'S BIOGRAPHY

THE few ascertained, or clearly imaginable, Events in Oliver's Biography may as well be arranged, for our present purpose, in the form of annals.

1603

Early in January of this year, the old Grandfather, Sir Henry, 'the Golden Knight,' at Hinchinbrook, died: our Oliver, not quite four years old, saw funeralia and crapes, saw Father and

Uncles with grave faces, and understood not well what it meant,
—understood only, or tried to understand, that the good old
Grandfather was gone away, and would never pat his head any
more. The maternal Grandfather, at Ely, was yet, and for
above a dozen years more, living.

The same year, four months afterwards, King James, coming
from the North to take possession of the English crown, lodged
two nights at Hinchinbrook ; with royal retinue, with immense
sumptuosities, addressings, knight-makings, ceremonial exhibitions ; which must have been a grand treat for little Oliver.
His Majesty came from the Belvoir-Castle region, 'hunting all
the way,' on the afternoon of Wednesday 27th April 1603 ;
and set off, through Huntingdon and Godmanchester, towards
Royston, on Friday forenoon. The Cambridge Doctors brought
him an Address while here ; Uncle Oliver, besides the ruinously
splendid entertainments, gave him hounds, horses and astonishing
gifts at his departure. In return there were Knights created,
Sir Oliver first of the batch, we may suppose ; King James had
decided that there should be no reflection for the want of Knights
at least. Among the large batches manufactured next year
was Thomas Steward of Ely, henceforth Sir Thomas, Mrs.
Robert Cromwell's Brother, our Oliver's Uncle. Hinchinbrook
got great honour by this and other royal visits ; but found it,
by and by, a dear-bought honour.

Oliver attended the Public School of Huntingdon, which was
then conducted by a worthy Dr. Beard, of whose writing I
possess a Book,[1] of whom we shall hear again : he learned, to
appearance moderately well, what the sons of other gentlemen
were taught in such places ; went through the universal destinies
which conduct all men from childhood to youth, in a way
not particularised in any one point by an authentic record.
Readers of lively imagination can follow him on his bird-

[1] *The Theatre of God's Judgements: By Thomas Beard, Doctor of
Divinity, and Preacher of the Word of God in the Town of Huntingdon:
Third Edition, increased by many new Examples* (' Examples' of God's
Justice vindicating itself openly on Violaters of God's Law,—that is the
purport of the Book): Lond. 1631.—A kindly ingenious little Book ;
still partly readable, almost lovable ; some thin but real vein of
perennial ingenuity and goodness recognisable in it. What one might
call a Set of 'Percy-Anecdotes'; but Anecdotes authentic, solemnly select,
and *with* a purpose : 'Percy-Anecdotes' for a more earnest Century
than ours ! Dedicated to the Mayor and Burgesses of Huntingdon,—
for sundry good reasons ; among others, ' Because, Mr. Mayor, you
were my scholar, and brought up in my house.'

nesting expeditions, to the top of 'Barnabee's big Tree,' and elsewhither, if they choose; on his fen-fowling expeditions, social sports and labours manifold; vacation-visits to his Uncles, to Aunt Hampden and Cousin John among others: all these things must have been; but how they specially were is forever hidden from all men. He had kindred of the sort above specified; parents of the sort above specified, rigorous yet affectionate persons, and very religious, as all rational persons then were. He had two sisters elder, and gradually four younger, the only boy among seven. Readers must fancy his growth there, in the North end of Huntingdon, in the beginning of the Seventeenth Century, as they can.

From the day of his Birth, which is jotted down, as above, in the Parish-register of St. John's Huntingdon, there is no other authentic jotting or direct record concerning Oliver himself to be met with anywhere, till in the Admission-Book of Sidney-Sussex College, Cambridge, we come to this,

1616

'*A Festo Annunciationis ad Festum Sancti Michaelis Archangeli, 1616:*' such (meaning merely, *From New-year's-day or 25th March, to 29th September*) is the general Heading of the List of Scholars, or *Admissi*, for that Term;—and first in order there, stands, '*Oliverius Cromwell Huntingdoniensis admissus ad commeatum Sociorum, Aprilis vicesimo tertio; Tutore Magistro Ricardo Howlet:*' Oliver Cromwell from Huntingdom admitted Fellow Commoner 23d April 1616; Tutor Mr. Richard Howlet.

Curious enough, of all days, on this same day Shakspeare, as his stone monument still testifies, at Stratford-on-Avon, died :

Obiit Anno Domini 1616.
Ætatis 53. Die 23 Apr.

While Oliver Cromwell was entering himself of Sidney-Sussex College, William Shakspeare was taking his farewell of this world. Oliver's Father had, most likely, come with him; it is but some fifteen miles from Huntingdon; you can go and come in a day. Oliver's Father saw Oliver write in the Album at Cambridge: at Stratford, Shakspeare's Ann Hathaway was weeping over his bed. The first world-great thing that remains of English History, the Literature of Shakspeare, was ending; the second world-great thing that remains of English History, the armed Appeal of Puritanism to the Invisible God of Heaven against many very visible Devils, on Earth and Elsewhere, was, so to speak, beginning. They have their exits and their entrances. And one People, in its time, plays many parts.

Chevalier Florian, in his *Life of Cervantes*, has remarked that Shakspeare's death-day, 23rd April 1616, was likewise that of Cervantes at Madrid. 'Twenty-third of April' is, sure enough, the authentic Spanish date: but Chevalier Florian has omitted to notice that the English twenty-third is of *Old Style*. The brave Miguel died ten days before Shakspeare; and already lay buried, smoothed right nobly into his long rest.

1617

In March of this year, 1617, there was another royal visit at Hinchinbrook. But this time, I conceive,' the royal entertainment would be much more moderate; Sir Oliver's purse growing lank. Over in Huntingdon, Robert Cromwell was lying sick, somewhat indifferent to royal progresses.

King James, this time, was returning northward to visit poor old Scotland again, to get his Pretended-Bishops set into activity, if he could. It is well known that he could not, to any satisfactory extent, neither now nor afterwards: his Pretended-Bishops, whom by cunning means he did get instituted, had the name of Bishops, but next to none of the authority, of the respect, or alas, even of the cash, suitable to the reality of that office. They were by the Scotch People derisively called *Tulchan* Bishops.—Did the reader ever see, or fancy in his mind, a Tulchan? A Tulchan is, or rather was, for the thing is long since obsolete, a Calf-skin stuffed into the rude similitude of a Calf,—similar enough to deceive the imperfect perceptive organs of a Cow. At milking-time the Tulchan, with head duly bent, was set as if to suck; the fond cow looking round fancied that her calf was busy, and that all was right, and so gave her milk freely, which the cunning maid was straining in white abundance into her pail all the while! The Scotch milkmaids in those days cried, "Where is the Tulchan; is the Tulchan ready?" So of the Bishops. Scotch Lairds were eager enough to 'milk' the Church Lands and Tithes, to get the rents out of them freely, which was not always easy. They were glad to construct a *Form* of Bishops to please the King and Church, and make the milk come without disturbance

The reader now knows what a Tulchan Bishop was. A piece of mechanism constructed not without difficulty, in Parliament and King's Council, among the Scots; and torn asunder afterwards with dreadful clamour, and scattered to the four winds, so soon as the Cow became awake to it!—

Villiers Buckingham, the new favourite, of whom we say little, was of the royal party here. Dr. Laud, too, King's Chaplain, Archdeacon of Huntingdon, attended the King on this occasion; had once more the pleasure of seeing Huntingdon, the cradle of his promotions, and the birth-place of Oliver. In Scotland, Dr. Laud, much to his regret, found "no religion at all," no surplices, no altars in the east or anywhere; no bowing, no responding; not the smallest regularity of fuglemanship or devotional drill-exercise; in short "no religion at all that I could see,"—which grieved me much.

What to us is greatly more momentous: while these royal things went on in Scotland, in the end of this same June at Huntingdon, Robert Cromwell died. His Will is dated 6th June. His burial-day is marked in the Church of All-Saints, 24th June 1617. For Oliver, the chief mourner, one of the most pregnant epochs. The same year died his old Grandfather Steward, at Ely. Mrs. Robert Cromwell saw herself at once fatherless and a second time widowed, in this year of bereavement. Left with six daughters and an only son; of whom three were come to years.

Oliver was now, therefore, a young heir; his age, eighteen last April. How many of his Sisters, or whether any of them, were yet settled, we do not learn from Noble's confused searching of records or otherwise. Of this Huntingdon household, and its new head, we learn next to nothing by direct evidence; but can decisively enough, by inference, discern several things. 'Oliver returned no more to Cambridge.' It was now fit that he should take his Father's place here at Huntingdon, that he should, by the swiftest method, qualify himself in some degree for that.

The universal very credible tradition is, that he, 'soon after, proceeded to London, to gain some knowledge of Law. 'Soon after' will mean certain months, we know not how many, after July 1617. Noble says, he was entered 'of Lincoln's Inn.' The Books of Lincoln's Inn, of Gray's Inn, of all the Inns of Court have been searched; and there is no Oliver Cromwell found in them. The Books of Gray's Inn contain these Cromwell Names, which are perhaps worth transcribing:

Thomas Cromwell, 1524; Francis Cromwell, 1561;
Gilbert Cromwell, 1609; Henry Cromwell, 1620;
Henry Cromwell, 22nd February 1653.

The first of which seems to me probably or possibly to mean Thomas Cromwell *Malleus Monachorum*, at that time returned from his Italian adventures, and in the service of Cardinal Wolsey;—taking the opportunity of hearing the 'readers,' old Benchers who then actually read, and of learning Law. The Henry Cromwell of February 1653-4 is expressly entered as 'Second sonne to His Highness Oliver, Lord Protector:' an interesting little fact, since it is an indisputable one. For the rest, Henry Cromwell was already a Colonel in the Army in 1651: in 1654, during the spring months he was in Ireland; in the month of June he was at Chippenham in Cambridgeshire with his father-in-law, being already married; and next year he went again on political business to Ireland, where he before long became Lord Deputy: if for a while, in the end of 1654, he did attend in Gray's Inn, it can only have been, like his predecessor the *Malleus*, to gain some inkling of Law for general purposes; and not with any view towards Advocateship, which did not lie in his course at all, and was never very lovely either to his Father or himself. Oliver Cromwell's, as we said, is not a name found in any of the Books in that period.

Whence is to be inferred that Oliver was never of any Inn; that he never meant to be a professional Lawyer; that he had entered himself merely in the chambers of some learned gentleman, with an eye to obtain some tincture of Law, for doing County Magistracy, and the other duties of a gentleman citizen, in a reputable manner. The stories of his wild living while in Town, of his gambling and so forth, rest likewise exclusively on Carrion Heath; and solicit oblivion and Christian burial from all men. We cannot but believe he did go to Town to gain some knowledge of Law. But when he went, how long he stayed, cannot be known except approximately by years; under whom he studied, with what fruit, how he conducted himself as a young man and law-student, cannot be known at all. Of evidence that he ever lived a wild life about Town or elsewhere, there exists no particle. To assert the affirmative was then a great reproach to him; fit for Carrion Heath and others: it would be now, in our present strange condition of the Moral Law, one knows not what.

With a Moral Law gone all to such a state of moonshine; with
the hard Stone-tables, the god-given Precepts and eternal
Penalties, dissolved all in cant and mealy-mouthed official
flourishings,—it might perhaps, with certain parties, be a credit!
The admirers and the censurers of Cromwell have alike no
word to record on the subject.

1620

The Registers of St. Giles's Church, Cripplegate, London,
are written by a third party as usual, and have no autograph
signatures; but in the List of Marriages for 'August 1620,'
stand these words, still to be read *sic*:

'Oliver Cromwell to Elizabeth Bourcher. 22.

Milton's burial-entry is in another Book of the same memorable
Church, '12 Nov. 1674;' where Oliver on the 22nd of August
1620 was married.

Oliver is twenty-one years and four months old on this his
wedding-day. He repaired, speedily or straightway we believe,
to Huntingdon, to his Mother's house, which indeed was now
his. His Law-studies, such as they were, had already ended,
we infer; he had already set up house with his Mother; and
was now bringing a Wife home; the due arrangements for
that end having been completed. Mother and Wife were to
live together; the Sisters had got or were getting married,—
Noble's researches and confused jottings do not say specially
when: the Son, as new head of the house, an inexperienced
head, but a teachable, ever-learning one, was to take his Father's
place; and with a wise Mother and a good Wife, harmonising
tolerably well we shall hope, was to manage as he best might.
Here he continued, unnoticeable but easily imaginable by
History, for almost ten years: farming lands; most probably
attending quarter-sessions; doing the civic, industrial, and social
duties, in the common way;—living as his Father before him
had done. His first child was born here, in October 1621;
a son, Robert, baptised at St. John's Church on the 13th of
the month, of whom nothing farther is known.[1] A second

[1] Date of his burial discovered lately, in the old Parish-Register
of Felsted in Essex; recorded in peculiar terms, and specially in
the then Vicar's hand: '*Robertus Cromwell, Filius honorandi viri
M^{tus}* (Militis) '*Oliveris Cromwell et Elizabethæ Uxoris ejus, sepultus
fuit 31º die Maii 1639. Et Robertus fuit eximiè pius juvenis, Deum*

child, also a son, Oliver, followed, whose baptismal date is 6th February 1623, of whom also we have almost no farther account,—except one that can be proved to be erroneous. The List of his other children shall be given by and by.

It is, we note, in these years, undated by History, that we must place Oliver's clear recognition of Calvinistic Christianity; what he, with unspeakable joy, would name his Conversion; his deliverance from the jaws of Eternal Death. Certainly a grand epoch for a man: properly the one epoch; the turning-point which guides upwards, or guides downwards, him and his activity forevermore. Wilt thou join with the Dragons; wilt thou join with the Gods? Of thee too the question is asked;—whether by a man in Geneva gown, by a man in 'Four surplices at Allhallowtide,' with words very imperfect; or by no man and no words, but only by the Silences, by the Eternities, by the Life everlasting and the Death everlasting. That the 'Sense of difference between Right and Wrong' had filled all Time and all Space for man, and bodied itself forth into a Heaven and Hell for him: this constitutes the grand feature of those Puritan, Old-Christian Ages; this is the element which stamps them as Heroic, and has rendered their works great, manlike, fruitful to all generations. It is by far the memorablest achievement of our Species; without that element, in some form or other, nothing of Heroic had ever been among us.

For many centuries, Catholic Christianity, a fit embodiment of that divine Sense, had been current more or less, making the generations noble: and here in England, in the Century called the Seventeenth, we see the last aspect of it hitherto,— not the last of all, it is to be hoped. Oliver was henceforth a Christian man; believed in God, not on Sundays only, but on all days, in all places, and in all cases.

He naturally consorted henceforth with the Puritan Clergy in preference to the other kind; zealously attended their ministry, when possible;—consorted with Puritans in general, many of whom were Gentry of his own rank, some of them Nobility of much higher rank. A modest devout man, solemnly intent 'to make his calling and his election sure,'

timens suprà multos.' (See Edinburgh Review, No. 209, January 1856, p. 54.) So that Oliver's first great loss in his Family was of this Eldest Son, then in his 18th year; not of a Younger one as was hitherto supposed. (*Note of* 1857.)

to whom, in credible dialect, the Voice of the Highest had spoken. Whose earnestness, sagacity and manful worth gradually made him conspicuous in his circle among such.—The Puritans were already numerous. John Hampden, Oliver's Cousin, was a devout Puritan, John Pym the like; Lord Brook, Lord Say, Lord Montague,—Puritans in the better ranks, and in every rank, abounded. Already either in conscious act, or in clear tendency, the far greater part of the serious Thought and Manhood of England had declared itself Puritan.

1627

A Deed of Sale, dated June 20th 1627, still testifies that Hinchinbrook this year passed out of the hands of the Cromwells into those of the Montagues. The price was 3000*l.*; curiously divided into two parcels, down to shillings and pence,—one of the parcels being already a creditor's. The Purchaser is 'Sir Sidney Montague Knight, of Barnwell, one of his Majesty's 'Masters of the Requests.' Sir Oliver Cromwell, son of the Golden Knight, having now burnt out his splendour, disappeared in this way from Hinchinbrook; retired deeper into the Fens, to a place of his near Ramsey Mere, where he continued still thirty years longer to reside, in an eclipsed manner. It was to this house at Ramsey that Oliver, our Oliver, then Captain Cromwell in the Parliament's service, paid the domiciliary visit much talked of in the old Books. The reduced Knight, his Uncle, was a Royalist or Malignant; and his house had to be searched for arms, for munitions, for furnishings of any sort, which he might be minded to send off to the King, now at York, and evidently intending war. Oliver's dragoons searched with due rigour for the arms; while the Captain respectfully conversed with his Uncle; and even 'insisted' through the interview, say the old Books, 'on standing uncovered': which latter circumstance may be taken as an astonishing hypocrisy in him, say the old blockhead Books. The arms, munitions, furnishings were with all rigour of law, not with more rigour and not with less, carried away; and Oliver parted with his Uncle, for that time, not 'craving his blessing,' I think, as the old blockhead Books say; but hoping he might, one day, either get it or a *better* than it, for what he had now done. Oliver, while in military charge of that country, had probably repeated visits to pay to his Uncle;

and they know little of the man or of the circumstances, who suppose there was any likelihood or need of either insolence or hypocrisy in the course of these.

As for the old Knight, he seems to have been a man of easy temper; given to sumptuosity of hospitality; and averse to severer duties. When his eldest son, who also showed a turn for expense, presented him a schedule of debts, craving aid towards the payment of them, Sir Oliver answered with a bland sigh, "I wish they were paid." Various Cromwells, sons of his, nephews of his, besides the great Oliver, took part in the Civil War, some on this side, some on that, whose indistinct designations in the old Books are apt to occasion mistakes with modern readers. Sir Oliver vanishes now from Hinchinbrook, and all the public business records, into the darker places of the Fens. His name disappears from Willis:— in the next Parliament, the Knight of the Shire for Huntingdon becomes, instead of him, 'Sir Capell Bedall, Baronet.' The purchaser of Hinchinbrook, Sir Sidney Montague, was brother of the first Earl of Manchester, brother of the third Lord Montague of Boughton; and father of 'the valiant Colonel Montague,' valiant General Montague, Admiral Montague, who, in an altered state of circumstances, became first Earl of Sandwich, and perished, with a valour worthy of a better generalissimo than poor James Duke of York, in the Seafight of Solebay (Southwold Bay, on the coast of Suffolk) in 1672.

1628

Sir Oliver Cromwell has faded from the Parliamentary scene into the deep Fen-country, but Oliver Cromwell, Esq. appears there as Member for Huntingdon, at Westminister on 'Monday the 17th of March 1627-8. This was the Third Parliament of Charles: by much the most notable of all Parliaments till Charles's Long Parliament met, which proved his last.

Having sharply, with swift impetuosity and indignation, dismissed two Parliaments, because they would not 'supply' him without taking 'grievances' along with them; and, meanwhile and afterwards, having failed in every operation foreign and domestic, at Cadiz, at Rhé, at Rochelle; and having failed, too, in getting supplies by unparliamentary methods, Charles 'consulted with Sir Robert Cotton what was to be done;' who answered, Summon a Parliament again. So this celebrated Parliament was summoned. It met, as we said, in March 1628.

and continued with one prorogation till March 1629. The two former Parliaments had sat but a few weeks each, till they were indignantly hurled asunder again ; this one continued nearly a year. Wentworth (Strafford) was of this Parliament ; Hampden too, Selden, Pym, Holles, and others known to us : all these had been of former Parliaments as well ; Oliver Cromwell, Member for Huntingdon, sat there for the first time.

It is very evident, King Charles, baffled in all his enterprises, and reduced really to a kind of crisis, wished much this Parliament should succeed ; and took what he must have thought incredible pains for that end. The poor King strives visibly throughout to control himself, to be soft and patient ; inwardly writhing and rustling with royal rage. Unfortunate King, we see him chafing, stamping,—a very fiery steed, but bridled, check-bitted, by innumerable straps and considerations ; struggling much to be composed. Alas ! it would not do. This Parliament was more Puritanic, more intent on rigorous Law and divine Gospel, than any other had ever been. As indeed all these Parliaments grow strangely in Puritanism ; more and ever more earnest rises from the hearts of them all, "O Sacred Majesty, lead us not to Antichrist, to Illegality, to temporal and eternal Perdition !" The Nobility and Gentry of England were then a very strange body of men. The English Squire of the Seventeenth Century clearly appears to have believed in God, not as a figure of speech, but as a very fact, very awful to the heart of the English Squire. 'He wore his Bible-doctrine 'round him,' says one, 'as our Squire wears his shot-belt ; went 'abroad with it, nothing doubting.' King Charles was going on his father's course only with frightful acceleration : he and his respectable Traditions and Notions, clothed in old sheepskin and respectable Church-tippets, were all pulling one way ; England and the Eternal Laws pulling another ;—the rent fast widening till no man could heal it.

This was the celebrated Parliament which framed the Petition of Right, and set London all astir with 'bells and bonfires' at the passing thereof ; and did other feats not to be particularised here. Across the murkiest element in which any great Entity was ever shown to human creatures, it still rises, after much consideration, to the modern man, in a dim but undeniable manner, as a most brave and noble Parliament. The like of which were worth its weight in diamonds even now ;—but has grown very unattainable now, next door to incredible now.

We have to say that this Parliament chastised sycophant Priests, Mainwaring, Sibthorp, and other Arminian sycophants, a disgrace to God's Church ; that it had an eye to other still more elevated Church-Sycophants, as the mainspring of all ; but was cautious to give offence by naming them. That it carefully 'abstained from naming the Duke of Buckingham.' That it decided on giving ample subsidies, but not till there were reasonable discussion of grievances. That in manner it was most gentle, soft-spoken, cautious, reverential ; and in substance most resolute and valiant. Truly with valiant patient energy, in a slow steadfast English manner, it carried, across infinite confused opposition and discouragement, its Petition of Right, and what else it had to carry. Four hundred brave men,—brave men and true, after their sort !

His Majesty saw good to confirm, and ratify beyond shadow of cavil, the invaluable Petition of Right, and thereby produce 'bonfires,' and bob-majors upon all bells. Old London was sonorous ; in a blaze with joy-fires. Soon after which, this Parliament, as London, and England, and it, all still continued somewhat too sonorous, was hastily, with visible royal anger, prorogued till October next,—till January as it proved. Oliver, of course, went home to Huntingdon to his harvest-work ; England continued simmering and sounding as it might.

The day of prorogation was the 26th of June. One day in the latter end of August, John Felton, a short swart Suffolk gentleman of military air, in fact a retired lieutenant of grim serious disposition, went out to walk in the eastern parts of London. Walking on Tower Hill, full of black reflections on his own condition, and on the condition of England, and a Duke of Buckingham holding all England down into the jaws of ruin and disgrace,—John Felton saw, in evil hour, on some cutler's stall there, a broad sharp hunting-knife, price one shilling John Felton, with a wild flash in the dark heart of him, bought the said knife ; rode down to Portsmouth with it, where the great Duke then was ; struck the said knife, with one fell plunge, into the great Duke's heart. This was on Saturday the 23rd of August of this same year.

Felton was tried ; saw that his wild flashing inspiration had been not of God, but of Satan. It is known he repented : when the death-sentence was passed on him, he stretched out his right hand ; craved that this too, as some small expiation, might first be stricken off; which was denied him, as against law. He died at Tyburn ; his body was swinging in chains at Portsmouth ;—and much else had gone awry, when the Parliament reassembled, in January following, and Oliver came up to Town again.

1629

The Parliament Session proved very brief ; but very energetic, very extraordinary. 'Tonnage and Poundage,' what we now call Customhouse Duties, a constant subject of quarrel between Charles and his Parliaments hitherto, had again been levied *without* Parliamentary consent ; in the teeth of old *Tallagio non concedendo*, nay even of the late solemnly confirmed Petition of Right ; and naturally gave rise to Parliamentary consideration. Merchants had been imprisoned for refusing to pay it ; Members of Parliament themselves had been '*supœna'd* :' there was a very ravelled coil to deal with in regard to Tonnage and Poundage. Nay the Petition of Right itself had been altered in the Printing : a very ugly business too.

In regard to Religion also, matters looked equally ill. Sycophant Mainwaring, just censured in Parliament, had been promoted to a fatter living. Sycophant Montague, in the like circumstances, to a Bishopric : Laud was in the act of consecrating him at Croydon, when the news of Buckingham's death came thither. There needed to be a Committee of Religion. The House resolved itself into a Grand Committee of Religion ; and did not want for matter. Bishop Neile of Winchester, Bishop Laud now of London, were a frightfully ceremonial pair of Bishops ; the fountain they of innumerable tendencies to Papistry and the old-clothes of Babylon ! It was in this Committee of Religion, on the 11th day of February 1628-9, that Mr. Cromwell, Member for Huntingdon, stood up and made his first Speech, a fragment of which has found its way into History, and is now known to all mankind. He said, "He "had heard by relation from one Dr. Beard" (his old Schoolmaster at Huntingdon), "that Dr. Alablaster had preached flat "Popery at Paul's Cross ; and that the Bishop of Winchester" (Dr. Neile) "had commanded him as his Diocesan, He should "preach nothing to the contrary. Mainwaring, so justly cen- "sured in this House for his sermons, was by the same Bishop's "means preferred to a rich living. If these are the steps to "Church-preferment, what are we to expect ?"

A new *Remonstrance* behoves to be resolved upon ; Bishops Neile and Laud are even to be *named* there. Whereupon, before they could get well 'named,' perhaps before Dr. Beard had well got up from Huntingdon to testify against them, the King hastily interfered. This Parliament, in a fortnight more, was dissolved; and that under circumstances of the most unparalleled sort. For Speaker Finch, as we have seen, was a Courtier, in constant communication with the King: one day while these high matters were astir, Speaker Finch refused to 'put the question' when ordered by the House! He said he had orders to the contrary; persisted in that;—and at last took to weeping. What was the House to do? Adjourn for two days, and consider what to do! On the second day, which was Wednesday, Speaker Finch signified that by his Majesty's command they were again adjourned till Monday next. On Monday next, Speaker Finch, still recusant, would not put the former nor indeed any question, having the King's order to adjourn *again* instantly. He refused; was reprimanded, menaced; once more took to weeping; then started up to go his ways. But young Mr. Holles, Denzil Holles, the Earl of Clare's second son, he and certain other honourable members were prepared for that movement: they seized Speaker Finch, set him down in his chair, and by main force held him there! A scene of such agitation as was never seen in Parliament before. 'The House was much troubled.' "Let him go," cried certain Privy Councillors, Majesty's Ministers as we should now call them, who in those days sat in front of the Speaker, "Let Mr. Speaker go!" cried they imploringly—"No!" answered Holles; "God's wounds, he shall sit there, till it please the House to rise!" The House, in a decisive though almost distracted manner, with their Speaker thus held down for them, locked their doors; redacted Three emphatic Resolutions, their Protest against Arminianism, against Papistry, against illegal Tonnage and Poundage; and passed the same by acclamation; letting no man out, refusing to let even the King's Usher in; then swiftly vanishing so soon as the resolutions were passed, for they understood the Soldiery was coming. For which surprising procedure, vindicated by Necessity the mother of Invention and supreme of Lawgivers, certain honourable gentlemen, Denzil Holles, Sir John Eliot, William Strode, John Selden, and others less known to us, suffered fine, imprisonment, and much legal tribulation: nay Sir John Eliot, refusing to submit, was kept in the Tower till he died.

This scene fell out on Monday 2nd of March 1629. Directly

on the back of which, we conclude, Mr. Cromwell quitted Town for Huntingdon again;—told Dr. Beard also that he was not wanted now; that he might at leisure go on with his *Theatre of God's Judgements* now. His Majesty dissolved the Parliament by Proclamation: saying something about 'vipers' that had been there.

It was the last Parliament in England for above eleven years. The King had taken his course. The King went on raising supplies without Parliamentary law, by all conceivable devices; of which Shipmoney may be considered the most original, and sale of Monopolies the most universal. The monopoly of 'soap' itself was very grievous to men. Your soap was dear, and it would not wash, but only blister. The ceremonial Bishops, Bishop or Archbishop Laud now chief of them,— they, on their side, went on diligently hunting out 'Lecturers,' erecting 'altars in the east end of churches;' charging all clergymen to have, in good repair and order, 'Four surplices 'at Allhallowtide.' Vexations spiritual and fiscal, beyond what we can well fancy now, afflicted the souls of men. The English Nation was patient; it endured in silence, with prayer that God in justice and mercy would look upon it. The King of England with his chief-priests was going one way; the Nation of England by eternal laws was going another: the split became too wide for healing. Oliver and others seemed now to have done with Parliaments; a royal Proclamation forbade them so much as to speak of such a thing.

1630

In the 'new charter' granted to the Corporation of Huntingdon, and dated 8th July 1630, Oliver Cromwell, Esquire, Thomas Beard, D.D. his old Schoolmaster, and Robert Barnard, Esquire, of whom also we may hear again, are named Justices of the Peace for that Borough. I suppose there was nothing new in this nomination; a mere confirming and continuing of what had already been. But the smallest authentic fact, any undoubted date or circumstance regarding Oliver and his affairs, is to be eagerly laid hold of.

1631

In or soon after 1631, as we laboriously infer from the imbroglio records of poor Noble, Oliver decided on an enlarged sphere of action as a Farmer; sold his properties in Huntingdon, all or some of them; rented certain grazing-lands at St. Ives, five miles down the River, eastward of his native place, and removed thither. The Deed of Sale is dated 7th May 1631; the properties are specified as in the possession of himself or his Mother; the sum they yielded was 1800*l*. With this sum Oliver stocked his Grazing-Farm at St. Ives. The Mother, we infer, continued to reside at Huntingdon, but withdrawn now from active occupation into the retirement befitting a widow up in years. There is even some gleam of evidence to that effect: her properties are sold; but Oliver's children born to him at St. Ives are still christened at Huntingdon, in the Church he was used to; which may mean also that their good Grandmother was still there.

Properly this was no change in Oliver's old activities; it was an enlargement of the sphere of them. His Mother still at Huntingdon, within few miles of him, he could still superintend and protect her existence there, while managing his new operations at St. Ives. He continued here till the summer or spring of 1636. A studious imagination may sufficiently construct the figure of his equable life in those years. Diligent grass-farming, mowing, milking, cattle-marketing: add 'hypochondria,' fits of the blackness of darkness, with glances of the brightness of very Heaven; prayer, religious reading and meditation; household epochs, joys and cares:—we have a solid, substantial, inoffensive Farmer of St. Ives, hoping to walk with integrity and humble devout diligence through this world; and, by his Maker's infinite mercy, to escape destruction, and find eternal salvation in wider Divine Worlds. This latter, this is the grand clause in his Life, which dwarfs all other clauses. Much wider destinies than he anticipated were appointed him on Earth; but that, in comparison to the alternative of Heaven or Hell to all Eternity, was a mighty small matter.

The lands he rented are still there, recognisable to the Tourist; gross boggy lands, fringed with willow-trees, at the east end of the small Town of St. Ives, which is still noted as a cattle-market in those parts. The 'Cromwell Barn,' the pretended 'House of Cromwell,' the &c. &c. are, as is usual in these cases, when you come to try them by the documents, a mere jumble of incredibilities, and oblivious human platitudes, distressing to the mind.

1632.

In January of this year Oliver's seventh child was born to him; a boy, James; who died the day after baptism. There remained six children, of whom one other died young; it is not known at what date. Here subjoined is the List of them, and of those subsequently born; in a Note, elaborated, as before, from the imbroglios of Noble.[1]

[1] OLIVER CROMWELL'S CHILDREN.

(Married to Elizabeth Bourchier, 22d August 1620.)

1. *Robert;* baptised 13 October 1621. Named for his Grandfather. No farther account of him (except, now, *suprà,* p. 10 n.); he died before ripe years.

2. Oliver; baptised 6th February 1622-3; went to Felsted School. 'Captain in Harrison's Regiment,'—no. At Peterborough in 1643 (Noble, i. 133-4). He died, or was killed during the War; date and place not yet discoverable. Noble says it was at Appleby; referring to Whitlocke. Whitlocke (p, 318 of 1st edition, 242 of 2d), on ransacking the old Pamphlets, turns out to be indisputably in error. The Protector on his death-bed alludes to this Oliver's death: "It went to my heart like a dagger, indeed it did."

3. Bridget; baptised 4th August 1624. Married to Ireton, 15th June 1646 (Noble, i. 134, is twice in error); widow, 26th November 1651. Married to Fleetwood (exact date, after long search, remains undiscovered; Noble, ii. 355, says 'before' June 1652,—at random seemingly). Died at Stoke Newington, near London, September 1681.

4. Richard; born 4th October 1626. At Felsted School. 'In Lincoln's Inn, 27th May 1647:' an error? Married, in 1649, Richard Mayor's daughter, of Huisley, Hants. First in Parliament, 1654. Protector, 1658. Dies, poor idle Triviality, at Cheshunt, 12th July 1712.

5. Henry; baptised at All-Saints (the rest are at St. John's), Huntingdon, 20th January 1627-8. Felsted School. In the army at sixteen. Captain, under Harrison I think, in 1647. Colonel in 1649, and in Ireland with his Father. Lord Deputy there in 1657. In 1660, retired to Spinney Abbey, 'near Soham,' nearer Wicken, in Cambridgeshire. Foolish story of Charles II. and the 'stable-fork' there (Noble, i. 212). Died 23d March 1673-4; buried in Wicken Church. A brave man and true: had he been named Protector, there had, most likely, been quite another History of England to write, at present!

6. Elizabeth; baptised 2nd July 1629. Mrs. Claypole, 1645-6. Died at 3 in the morning, Hampton-court, 6th August 1658,—four weeks before her Father. A graceful, brave, and amiable woman. The lamentation about Dr. Hewit and 'bloodshed' (in Clarendon and others) is fudge.

CHAPTER III

OF OLIVER'S LETTERS AND SPEECHES

LETTERS and authentic Utterances of Oliver lie scattered, in print and manuscript, in a hundred repositories, in all varieties of condition and environment. Most of them, all the important of them have already long since been printed and again printed; but we cannot in general say, ever read: too often it is apparent that the very editor of these poor utterances had, if reading means understanding, never *read* them. They stand in their old spelling; mispunctuated, misprinted, unelucidated, unintelligible,—defaced with the dark incrustations too well known to students of that Period. The Speeches above all, as hitherto set forth in *The Somers Tracts*, in *The Milton State-Papers*, in *Burton's Diary*, and other such Books excel human belief: certainly no such agglomerate of opaque confusions, printed and reprinted; of darkness on the back of darkness, thick and threefold; is known to me elsewhere in the history of things spoken or printed by human creatures. Of these Speeches, all except one, which was published by authority at the time, I have to believe myself, not very exultingly, to be the first actual reader for nearly two Centuries past.

Nevertheless these Documents do exist, authentic though defaced; and invite every one who would know that Period, to study them till they become intelligible again. The words of Oliver Cromwell,—the meaning *they* had, must be worth

At St. Ives and Ely:

7. *James;* baptised 8th January 1631-2; died next day.

8. Mary; baptised (at Huntingdon still) 9th February 1636-7. Lady Fauconberg, 18th November 1657. Dean Swift knew her: 'handsome and like her Father.' Died 14th March 1712 (1712-3? is not decided in Noble). Richard died within a few months of her.

9. Frances; baptised (at Ely now) 6th December 1638. 'Charles II. was for marrying her:' not improbable. Married Mr. Rich, Earl of Warwick's grandson, 11th November 1657; he died in three months, 16th February 1657-8. No child by Rich. Married Sir John Russel,—the Checquers Russels. Died 27th January 1720-1.

In all, 5 sons and 4 daughters; of whom 3 sons and all the daughters came to maturity.

The Protector's Widow died at Norborough, her son-in-law Claypole's place (now ruined, patched into a farmhouse; near Market Deeping; it is itself in Northamptonshire), 8th October 1672.

recovering, in that point of view. To collect these Letters and authentic Utterances, as one's reading yielded them, was a comparatively grateful labour; to correct them, elucidate and make them legible again, was a good historical study Surely 'a wise memory' would wish to preserve among men the written and spoken words of such a man;—and as for the 'wise oblivion,' that is already, by Time and Accident, done to our hand. Enough is already lost and destroyed; we need not, in this particular case, omit farther.

Accordingly, whatever words authentically proceeding from Oliver himself I could anywhere find yet surviving, I have here gathered; and will now, with such minimum of annotation as may suit that object, offer them to the reader. That is the purport of this Book. I have ventured to believe that, to certain patient earnest readers, these old dim Letters of a noble English Man might, as they had done to myself, become dimly legible again; might dimly present, better than all other evidence, the noble figure of the Man himself again. Certainly there is Historical instruction in these Letters:—Historical, and perhaps other and better. At least, it is with Heroes and god-inspired men that I, for my part, would far rather converse, in what dialect soever they speak! Great, ever fruitful; profitable for reproof, for encouragement, for building up in manful purposes and works, are the words of those that in their day were men. I will advise serious persons, interested in England past or present, to try if they can read a little in these Letters of Oliver Cromwell, a man once deeply interested in the same object. Heavy as it is, and dim and obsolete, there may be worse reading, for such persons in our time.

For the rest, if each Letter look dim, and have little light, after all study;—yet let the Historical reader reflect, such light as it has cannot be disputed at all. These words, expository of that day and hour, Oliver Cromwell did see fittest to be written down. The Letter hangs there in the dark abysses of the Past: if like a star almost extinct, yet like a real star; fixed; about which there is no cavilling possible. That autograph Letter, it was once all luminous as a burning beacon, every word of it a live coal, in its time, it was once a piece of the general fire and light of Human Life, that Letter! Neither is it yet entirely extinct: well read, there is still in it light enough to exhibit its own *self*; nay to diffuse a faint authentic twilight some distance round it. Heaped embers, which in the daylight looked black,

may still look *red* in the utter darkness. These Letters of
Oliver will convince any man that the Past did exist! By
degrees the combined small twilights may produce a kind of
general feeble twilight, rendering the Past credible, the Ghosts
of the Past in some glimpses of them visible! Such is the effect
of contemporary letters always; and I can very confidently
recommend Oliver's as good of their kind. A man intent to
force for himself some path through that gloomy chaos called
History of the Seventeenth Century, and to look face to face
upon the same, may perhaps try it by this method as hopefully
as by another. Here is an irregular row of beacon-fires, once
all luminous as suns; and with a certain inextinguishable
erubescence still, in the abysses of the dead deep Night. Let
us look here. In shadowy outlines, in dimmer and dimmer
crowding forms, the very figure of the old dead Time itself
may perhaps be faintly discernible here!—

I called these Letters good,—but withal only good of their
kind. No eloquence, elegance, not always even clearness of
expression, is to be looked for in them. They are written with
far other than literary aims; written, most of them, in the very
flame and conflagration of a revolutionary struggle, and with
an eye to the despatch of indispensable pressing business alone:
but it will be found, I conceive, that for such end they are well
written. Superfluity, as if by a natural law of the case, the writer
has had to discard; whatsoever quality *can* be dispensed with
is indifferent to him. With unwieldy movement, yet with a
great solid step he presses through, towards his object; has
marked out very decisively what the real steps towards it are;
discriminating well the essential from the extraneous;—forming
to himself, in short, a true, not an untrue picture of the business
that is to be done. There is in these Letters, as I have said
above, a *silence* still more significant of Oliver to us than any
speech they have. Dimly we discover features of an Intelligence,
and Soul of a Man, greater than any speech. The Intelligence
that can, with full satisfaction to itself, come out in eloquent
speaking, in musical singing, is, after all, a small Intelligence.
He that works and *does* some Poem, not he that merely *says*
one, is worthy of the name of Poet. Cromwell, emblem of
the dumb English, is interesting to me by the very inadequacy
of his speech. Heroic insight, valour and belief, without words,
—how noble is it in comparison to the adroitest flow of words
without heroic insight!—

I have corrected the spelling of these Letters; I have punctuated, and divided them into paragraphs, in the modern manner. The Originals, so far as I have seen such, have in general no paragraphs: if the Letter is short, it is usually found written on the first leaf of the sheet; often with the conclusion, or some postscript, subjoined crosswise on the margin,—indicating that there was no blotting-paper in those days; that the hasty writer was loath to turn the leaf. Oliver's spelling and pointing are of the sort common to educated persons in his time; and readers that so wish may have specimens of him in abundance, and of all due dimness, in many printed Books: but to us, intent here to have the Letters read and understood, it seemed very proper at once and altogether to get rid of that encumbrance. Would the rest were all as easily got rid of! Here and there, to bring out the struggling sense, I have added or rectified a word,—but taken care to point out the same; what words in the Text of the Letters are mine, the reader will find marked off by single commas: it was of course my supreme duty to avoid altering, in any respect, not only the sense, but the smallest feature in the physiognomy, of the Original. And so, a 'minimum of annotation' having been added, what minimum would serve the purpose,—here are the *Letter*s *and Speeches of Oliver Cromwell*; of which the reader, with my best wishes, but not with any very high immediate hope of mine in that particular, is to make what he can.

Surely it is far enough from probable that these Letters of Cromwell, written originally for quite other objects, and selected not by the Genius of History, but by blind Accident which has saved them hitherto and destroyed the rest,—can illuminate for a modern man this Period of our Annals, which for all moderns, we may say, has become a gulf of bottomless darkness! Not so easily will the modern man domesticate himself in a scene of things every way so foreign to him. Nor could any measurable exposition of mine, on this present occasion, do much to illuminate the dead dark world of the Seventeenth Century, into which the reader is about to enter. He will gradually get to understand, as I have said, that the Seventeenth Century did exist; that it was not a waste rubbish-continent of Rushworth-Nalson State-papers, of Philosophical Scepticisms, Dilettantisms, Dryasdust Torpedoisms;—but an actual flesh-and-blood Fact; with colour in its cheeks, with awful august heroic thoughts in its heart, and at last with steel sword in its hand! Theoretically this is a most small postulate, conceded at once by everybody; but practically it is a very large one,

seldom or never conceded; the due practical conceding of it
amounts to much, indeed to the sure promise of all.—I will
venture to give the reader two little pieces of advice, which, if
his experience resemble mine, may prove furthersome to him in
this inquiry: they include the essence of all that I have
discovered respecting it.

The first is, By no means to credit the wide-spread report
that these Seventeenth-Century Puritans were superstitious
crack-brained persons; given up to enthusiasm, the most part
of them; the minor ruling part being cunning men, who knew
how to assume the dialect of the others, and thereby, as skilful
Machiavels, to dupe them. This is a wide-spread report; but
an untrue one. I advise my reader to try precisely the opposite
hypothesis. To consider that his Fathers, who had thought
about this World very seriously indeed, and with very considerable thinking faculty indeed, were not quite so far
behindhand in their conclusions respecting it. That actually
their 'enthusiasms,' if well seen into, were not foolish but
wise. That Machiavelism, Cant, Official Jargon, whereby a
man speaks openly what he does *not* mean, were, surprising
as it may seem, much rarer then than they have ever since
been. Really and truly it may in a manner be said, Cant,
Parliamentary and other Jargon, were still to invent in this
world. O Heavens, one could weep at the contrast! Cant
was not fashionable at all; that stupendous invention of
'Speech for the purpose of concealing Thought'! was not yet
made. A man wagging the tongue of him, as if it were the
clapper of a bell to be rung for economic purposes, and not
so much as attempting to convey any inner thought, if thought
he have, of the matter talked of,—would at that date have
awakened all the horror in men's minds, which at all dates,
and at this date too, is due to him. The accursed thing!
No man as yet dared to do it; all men believing that God
would judge them. In the History of the Civil War far and
wide, I have not fallen in with one such phenomenon. Even
Archbishop Laud and Peter Heylin meant what they say;
through their words you do look direct into the scraggy conviction they have formed:— or if 'lying Peter' do lie, he at
least *knows* that he is lying! Lord Clarendon, a man of
sufficient unveracity of heart, to whom indeed whatsoever has
direct veracity of heart is more or less horrible, speaks
always in official language; a clothed, nay sometimes even
quilted dialect, yet always with some considerable body in the

heart of it, never with none! The use of the human tongue was then other than it now is. I counsel the reader to leave all that of Cant, Dupery, Machiavelism, and so forth, decisively lying at the threshold. He will be wise to believe that these Puritans do mean what they say, and to try unimpeded if he can discover what that is. Gradually a very stupendous phenomenon may rise on his astonished eye. A practical world based on Belief in God; such as many centuries had seen before, but as never any century since has been privileged to see. It was the last glimpse of it in our world, this of English Puritanism: very great, very glorious: tragical enough to all thinking hearts that look on it from these days of ours.

My second advice is, Not to imagine that it was Constitution 'Liberty of the people to tax themselves,' Privilege of Parliament, Triennial or annual Parliaments, or any modification of these sublime Privileges now waxing somewhat faint in our admirations, that mainly animated our Cromwells, Pyms, and Hampdens to the heroic efforts we still admire in retrospect. Not these very measurable 'Privileges,' but a far other and deeper, which could not be measured; of which these, and all grand social improvements whatsoever, are the corollary. Our ancient Puritan Reformers were, as all Reformers that will ever much benefit this Earth are always, inspired by a Heavenly Purpose. To see God's own Law, then universally acknowledged for complete as it stood in the holy Written Book, made good in this world; to see this, or the true unwearied aim and struggle towards this: it was a thing worth living for and dying for! Eternal Justice; that God's Will *be* done on Earth as it is in Heaven: corollaries enough will flow from that, if that be there; if that be not there, no corollary good for much will flow. It was the general spirit of England in the Seventeenth Century. In other somewhat sadly disfigured form, we have seen the same immortal hope take practical shape in the French Revolution, and once more astonish the world. That England should all become a Church, if you like to name it so: a Church presided over not by sham-priests in 'Four surplices at Allhallowtide,' but by true god-consecrated ones, whose hearts the Most High had touched and hallowed with his fire :—this was the prayer of many, it was the godlike hope and effort of some.

Our modern methods of Reform differ somewhat,—as indeed the issue testifies. I will advise my reader to forget the modern

methods of Reform ; not to remember that he has ever heard of
a modern individual called by the name of Reformer, if he
would understand what the old meaning of the word was. The
Cromwells, Pyms, Hampdens, who were understood on the
Royalist side to be firebrands of the Devil, have had still worse
measure from the Dryasdust Philosophies, and sceptical Histories,
of later times. They really did resemble firebrands of the Devil,
if you looked at them through spectacles of a certain colour.
For fire is always fire. But by no spectacles, only by mere
blinders and *wooden-eyed* spectacles, can the flame-girt Heaven's-
messenger pass for a poor mouldy Pedant and Constitution-
monger, such as this would make him out to be!

On the whole, say not, good reader, as is often done, "It was
then all one as now." Good reader, it was considerably different
then from now. Men indolently say, "The Ages are all alike,
"ever the same sorry elements over again, in new vesture ; the
"issue of it always a melancholy farce-tragedy, in one Age as in
"another!" Wherein lies very obviously a truth ; but also in
secret a very sad error withal. Sure enough, the highest Life
touches always, by large sections of it, on the vulgar and
universal: he that expects to see a Hero, or a Heroic Age, step
forth into practice in yellow Drury-lane stage-boots, and speak
in blank verse for itself, will look long in vain. Sure enough, in
the Heroic Century as in the Unheroic, knaves and cowards,
and cunning greedy persons were not wanting,—were, if you
will, extremely abundant. But the question always remains,
Did they lie chained, subordinate in this world's business ;
coerced by steel-whips, or in whatever other effectual way, and
sent whimpering into their due subterranean abodes, to beat
hemp and repent ; a true never-ending attempt going on to
handcuff, to silence and suppress them? Or did they walk
openly abroad, the envy of a general valet-population, and bear
sway ; professing, without universal anathema, almost with
general assent, that they were the Orthodox Party, that they,
even they, were such men as you had right to look for?—

Reader, the Ages differ greatly, even infinitely, from one
another. Considerable tracts of Ages there have been, by far
the majority indeed, wherein the men, unfortunate mortals,
were a set of mimetic creatures rather than men ; without heart-
insight as to this Universe, and its Heights and its Abysses ;
without conviction or belief of their own regarding it, at all ;—
who walked merely by hearsays, traditionary cants, black and
white surplices, and inane confusions ; whose whole Existence

accordingly was a grimace; nothing *original* in it, nothing genuine or sincere but this only. Their greediness of appetite and their faculty of digestion. Such unhappy Ages, too numerous here below, the Genius of Mankind indignantly seizes, as disgraceful to the Family, and with Rhadamanthine ruthlessness—annihilates; tumbles large masses of them swiftly into Eternal Night. These are the Unheroic Ages; which cannot serve, on the general field of Existence, except as *dust*, as inorganic manure. The memory of such Ages fades away forever out of the minds of all men. Why should any memory of *them* continue? The fashion of them has passed away; and as for genuine substance, they never had any. To no heart of a man any more can these Ages become lovely. What melodious loving heart will search into *their* records, will sing of them, or celebrate them? Even torpid Dryasdust is forced to give over at last, all creatures declining to hear him on that subject; whereupon ensues composure and silence, and Oblivion has her own.

Good reader, if you be wise, search not for the secret of Heroic Ages, which have done great things in this Earth, among their falsities, their greedy quackeries and *un*heroisms! It never lies and never will lie there. Knaves and quacks,—alas, we know they abounded: but the Age was Heroic even because it had declared war to the death with these, and would have neither truce nor treaty with these; and went forth, flame-crowned, as with bared sword, and called the Most High to witness that it would not endure these!——

PART I

TO THE BEGINNING OF THE CIVIL WAR

1636—1642

ST. IVES, a small Town of perhaps fifteen hundred souls, stands on the left or Northeastern bank of the River Ouse, in flat grassy country, and is still noted as a Cattle-market in those parts.

The little Town, of somewhat dingy aspect, and very quiescent except on market-days, runs from Northwest to Southeast, parallel to the shore of the Ouse, a short furlong in length : it probably, in Cromwell's time, consisted mainly of a *row* of houses fronting the River ; the now opposite row, which has its back to the River, and still is shorter than the other, still defective at the upper end, was probably built since. In that case, the locality we hear of as the 'Green' of St. Ives would then be the space which is now covered mainly with cattle-pens for market-business, and forms the middle of the *street*. A narrow steep old Bridge, probably the same which Cromwell travelled, leads you over, westward, towards Godmanchester, where you again cross the Ouse, and get into Huntingdon. Eastward out of St. Ives, your route is towards Earith, Ely and the heart of the Fens.

At the upper or Northwestern extremity of the place stands the Church ; Cromwell's old fields being at the opposite extremity. The Church from its Churchyard looks down into the very River, which is fenced from it by a brick wall. The Ouse flows here, you cannot without study tell in which direction, fringed with gross reedy herbage and bushes ; and is of the blackness of Acheron, streaked with foul metallic glitterings and plays of colour. For a short space downwards here, the banks of it are fully visible, the western row of houses being somewhat the shorter, as already hinted : instead of houses here, you have a rough wooden balustrade, and the black Acheron of an Ouse River used as a washing-place or watering-place for cattle. The old Church, suitable for such a population, stands yet as it did in Cromwell's time, except perhaps the steeple and pews ; the flagstones in the interior are worn deep with the pacing of many generations. The steeple is visible from several miles distance ; a sharp high spire, piercing far up from amid the willow-trees. The country hereabouts has all a clammy look, clayey and boggy ; the produce of it, whether bushes and trees, or grass and crops, gives you the notion of something lazy, dropsical, gross. This is St. Ives, a most ancient Cattle-market by the shores of the sable Ouse, on the edge of the Fen-country ; where, among other things that happened, Oliver Cromwell passed five years of his existence as a Farmer and Grazier. Who the primitive *Ives* himself was remains problematic ; Camden says he was 'Ivo a Persian ;'—surely far out of his road here ! From him however, Phantasm as he is (being indeed Nothing,—except an ancient 'stone-coffin,' with bones, and tatters of 'bright cloth' in it, accidentally ploughed up in this spot, and acted on by opaque human wonder, miraculous 'dreams,' and the 'Abbot of Ramsey'), Church and Village indisputably took rise and name ; about the Year 1,000 or later ;—and have stood ever since ; being founded on Cattle-dealing and the firm Earth withal. Ives or Yves, the worthy Frenchman, Bishop of Chartres in the time of our Henry Beauclerk ; neither he nor the other French Yves, Patron Saint of Attorneys, have anything to do with this locality ; but miraculous 'Ivo the Persian Bishop' and that anonymous stone-coffin alone.

Oliver, as we observed, has left hardly any memorial of himself at St. Ives. The ground he farmed is still partly capable of being specified, certain records or leases being still in existence. It lies at the lower or Southeast end of the Town ; a stagnant flat tract of land, extending between the houses or rather kitchen-gardens of St. Ives in that quarter, and the banks of the River, which, very tortuous always, has made a new bend here.

HIS CHILDREN

If well drained, this land looks as if it would produce abundant grass, but naturally it must be little other than a bog. Tall bushy ranges of willow-trees and the like, at present, divide it into fields; the River, not visible till you are close on it, bounding them all to the South. At the top of the fields next to the Town is an ancient massive Barn, still used as such; the people call it 'Cromwell's Barn:—and nobody can prove that it was not his! It was evidently some ancient man's or series of ancient men's.

He had sold His Properties in Huntingdon for 1800*l.*; with the whole or with part of which sum he stocked certain Grazing-Lands on the Estate of Slepe Hall, and farmed the same for a space of some five years. How he lived at St. Ives: how he saluted men on the streets; read Bibles; sold cattle; and walked, with heavy footfall and many thoughts, through the Market Green or old narrow lanes in St. Ives, by the shore of the black Ouse River,—shall be left to the reader's imagination. There is in this man talent for farming; there are thoughts enough, thoughts bounded by the Ouse River, thoughts that go beyond Eternity,—and a great black sea of things that he has never yet been able to *think*.

I count the children he had at this time; and find them six: Four boys and two girls; the eldest a boy of fourteen, the youngest a girl of six; Robert, Oliver, Bridget, Richard, Henry, Elizabeth. Robert and Oliver, I take it, are gone to Felsted School, near Bourchier their Grandfather's in Essex. Sir Thomas Bourchier the worshipful Knight, once of London, lives at Felsted; Sir William Masham, another of the same, lives at Otes, hard by, as we shall see.

LETTER I

OLIVER removed to Ely in 1635. There is a 'receipt for 10*l.*' signed by him, dated 'Ely, 10 June 1636'; and other evidence that he was then resident there. He succeeded to his Uncle's Farming of the Tithes; the Leases of these, and new Leases of some other small lands or fields granted him, are still in existence. He continued here till the time of the Long Parliament; and his Family still after that, till some unascertained date, seemingly about 1647, when it became apparent that the Long Parliament was not like to rise for a great while yet, and it was judged expedient that the whole household should remove to London. His Mother appears to have joined him in Ely; she quitted Huntingdon, returned to her native place, an aged grandmother,—was not, however, to end her days there.

The Second extant Letter of Cromwell's is dated Ely, October 1638. It will be good to introduce, as briefly as possible, a few Historical Dates, to remind the reader what o'clock on the Great Horologe it is, while this small Letter is a-writing. Last year in London there had been a very strange spectacle; and in three weeks after, another in Edinburgh, of still more significance in English History.

On the 30th of June 1637, in Old Palaceyard, three men, gentlemen of education, of good quality, a Barrister, a Physician and a Parish Clergyman of London were set on three Pillories; stood openly, as the scum of malefactors, for certain hours there; and then had their ears cut off,—bare knives, hot branding-irons,—and their cheeks stamped 'S. L.,' Seditious Libeller; in the sight of a great crowd, 'silent' mainly, and looking 'pale.' The men were our old friend William Prynne, —poor Prynne, who had got into new trouble, and here lost his ears a *second* and final time, having had them 'sewed on again' before: William Prynne, Barrister; Dr. John Bastwick; and the Rev. Henry Burton, Minister of Friday-street Church. Their sin was against Laud and his surplices at Allhallowtide, not against any other man or thing. Prynne, speaking to the people, defied all Lambeth, with Rome at the back of it, to argue with him, William Prynne alone, that these practices were according to the Law of England; "and if I fail to prove it," said Prynne, "let them hang my body at the door of that Prison there," the Gate-house Prison. 'Whereat the people gave a great shout,'—somewhat of an ominous one, I think. Bastwick's wife, on the scaffold, received his ears in her lap, and kissed him. Prynne's ears the executioner 'rather sawed than cut.' "Cut me, tear me," cried Prynne; "I fear thee not; I fear the fire of Hell, not thee!" The June sun had shone hot on their faces. Burton, who had discoursed eloquent religion all the while, said, when they carried him, near fainting, into a house in King-street, "It is too hot to last."

Too hot indeed. For at Edinburgh, on Sunday the 23d of July following, Archbishop Laud having now, with great effort and much manipulation, got his Scotch Liturgy and Scotch Pretended-Bishops ready, brought them fairly out to action,—and Jenny Geddes hurled her stool at their head "Let us read the Collect of the Day," said the Pretended-Bishop from amid his tippets;—" De'il *colic* the wame of thee!" answered Jenny, hurling her stool at his head. "Thou foul thief, wilt thou say *mass* at my lug?"[1] I thought we had got done with the mass some time ago;—and here it is again! "A Pape, a Pape!" cried others: "Stane him!"[2]—In fact the service could not go on at all. This passed in St. Giles's Kirk, Edinburgh, on Sunday 23d July 1637. Scotland had endured much in the bishop way for above thirty years bygone, and endeavoured to say nothing, bitterly feeling a great deal. But now, on small signal, the hour was come. All Edinburgh, all Scotland, and behind that all England and Ireland, rose into unappeasable commotion on the flight of this stool of Jenny's; and his Grace of Canterbury, and King Charles himself, and many others had lost their heads before there could be peace again. The Scotch People had sworn their Covenant, not without 'tears;' and were in these very days of October 1638, while Oliver is writing at Ely, busy with their whole might electing their General Assembly, to meet at Glasgow next month. I think the *Tulchan* Apparatus is likely

---

[1]——'No sooner was the Book opened by the Dean of Edinburgh, 'but a number of the meaner sort, with clapping of their hands and 'outcries, made a great uproar; and one of them, called *Jane* or '*Janot Gaddis* (yet living at the writing of this relation), flung a little 'folding-stool, whereon she sat, at the Dean's head, saying, "Out 'thou false thief! dost thou say the mass at my lug?" Which was 'followed with so great a noise,' &c. These words are in the Continuation of *Baker's Chronicle*, by Phillips (Milton's Nephew); fifth edition of *Baker* (London, 1670), p. 478. They are *not* in the fourth edition of *Baker*, 1665, which is the first that contains the Continuation; they follow as here in all the others. Thought to be the first grave mention of Jenny Geddes in Printed History; a heroine still familiar to Tradition everywhere in Scotland.

In a foolish Pamphlet, printed in 1661, entitled *Edinburgh's Joy*, &c.,—Joy for the Blessed Restoration and *Annus Mirabilis*,—there is mention made of 'the immortal Jenet Geddis,' whom the writer represents as rejoicing exceedingly in that miraculous event; she seems to be a well-known person, keeping 'a cabbage-stall at the Tron Kirk,' at that date. Burns, in his Highland Tour, named his mare *Jenny Geddes*. Helen of Troy, for practical importance in Human History, is but a small Heroine to Jenny:—but she has been luckier in the recording!—For these bibliographical notices I am indebted to the friendliness of Mr. David Laing of the Signet Library, Edinburgh.

[2] Rushworth, Kennet, Balfour

to be somewhat sharply dealt with, the Cow having become awake to it! Great events are in the wind; out of Scotland vague news, of unappeasable commotion risen there.

In the end of that same year, too, there had risen all over England huge rumour concerning the Shipmoney Trial at London. On the 6th of November 1637, this important Process of Mr. Hampden's began. Learned Mr. St. John, a dark tough man, of the toughness of leather, spake with irrefragable law-eloquence, law-logic, for three days running, on Mr. Hampden's side; and learned Mr. Holborn for three other days;—preserved yet by Rushworth in acres of typography, unreadable now to all mortals. For other learned gentlemen, tough as leather, spoke on the opposite side; and learned judges animadverted: —at endless length, amid the expectancy of men. With brief pauses, the Trial lasted for three weeks and three days. Mr. Hampden became the most famous man in England,—by accident partly. The sentence was not delivered till April 1638; and then it went against Mr. Hampden: judgment in Exchequer ran to this effect, '*Consideratum est per eosdem Barones quod prædictus Johannes Hampden de iisdem viginti solidis oneretur*,' He must pay the Twenty shillings, '*et inde satisfaciat*.' No hope in Law-Courts, then; Petition of Right and *Tallagio non concedendo* have become an old song. If there be not hope in Jenny Geddes's stool and 'De'il colic the wame of thee,' we are in a bad way!—

During which great public Transactions, there had been in Cromwell's own Fen-country a work of immense local celebrity going on: the actual Drainage of the Fens, so long talked about; the construction, namely, of the great *Bedford Level*, to carry the Ouse River direct into the sea; holding it forcibly aloft in strong embankments, for twenty straight miles or so; not leaving it to meander and stagnate, and in the wet season drown the country, as heretofore. This grand work began, Dryasdust in his bewildered manner knows not when; but it 'went on rapidly,' and had ended in 1637. Or rather had *appeared*, and strongly *endeavoured*, to end in 1637; but was not yet by any means settled and ended; the whole Fen-region clamouring that it could not, and should not, end so. In which wide clamour, against injustice done in high places, Oliver Cromwell, as is well known, though otherwise a most private quiet man, saw good to interfere; to give the universal inarticulate clamour a voice, and gain a remedy for it. He approved himself, as Sir Philip Warwick will testify, 'a man that would

set well at the mark,' that took sure aim, and had a stroke of
some weight in him. We cannot here afford room to disentangle that affair from the dark rubbish-abysses, old and new,
in which it lies deep buried: suffice it to assure the reader that
Oliver did by no means 'oppose' the Draining of the Fens, but
was and had been, as his Father before him, highly favourable
to it; that he opposed the King in Council wishing to do a
public injustice in regard to the Draining of the Fens; and by
a 'great meeting at Huntingdon,' and other good measures,
contrived to put a stop to the same. At a time when, as Old
Palaceyard might testify, that operation of going in the teeth
of the royal will was somewhat more perilous than it would be
now! This was in 1638, according to the good testimony of
Warwick. Cromwell acquired by it a great popularity in the
Fen-country, acquired the name or nickname 'Lord of the
Fens;' and what was much more valuable, had done the duty
of a good citizen, whatever he might acquire by it. The
disastrous public Events which soon followed put a stop to all
farther operations in the Fens, for a good many years.

*To my beloved Cousin Mrs. St. John, at Sir William Mashan
his House called Otes, in Essex : Present these.*

Ely, 13th October 1638.

DEAR COUSIN,
I thankfully acknowledge your love in your kind remembrance of me upon this opportunity. Alas, you do too
highly prize my lines, and my company. I may be ashamed to
own your expressions, considering how unprofitable I am, and
the mean improvement of my talent.

Yet to honour my God by declaring what He hath done for
my soul, in this I am confident, and I will be so. Truly, then,
this I find: That He giveth springs in a dry barren wilderness
where no water is. I live, you know where,—in Meshec,
which they say signifies *Prolonging*; in Kedar, which signifies
Blackness: yet the Lord forsaketh me not. Though He do
prolong, yet He will I trust bring me to His tabernacle, to
His resting place. My soul is with the Congregation of the
Firstborn, my body rests in hope; and if here I may honour
my God either by doing or by suffering, I shall be most
glad.

Truly no poor creature hath more cause to put himself forth
in the cause of his God than I. I have had plentiful wages
beforehand; and I am sure I shall never earn the least mite.

The Lord accept me in His Son, and give me to walk in the light,—and give us to walk in the light, as He is the light ! He it is that enlighteneth our blackness, our darkness. I dare not say, He hideth His face from me. He giveth me to see light in His light. One beam in a dark place hath exceeding much refreshment in it :—blessed be His Name for shining upon so dark a heart as mine ! You know what my manner of life hath been. Oh, I lived in and loved darkness, and hated light ; I was a chief, the chief of sinners. This is true ; I hated godliness, yet God had mercy on me. O the riches of His mercy ; Praise Him for me ;—pray for me, that He who hath begun a good work would perfect it in the day of Christ.

Salute all my friends in that Family whereof you are yet a member. I am much bound unto them for their love. I bless the Lord for them ; and that my Son, by their procurement, is so well. Let him have your prayers, your counsel ; let me have them.

Salute your Husband and Sister from me :—He is not a man of his word ! He promised to write about Mr. Wrath of Epping ; but as yet I receive no letters :—put him in mind to do what with conveniency may be done for the poor Cousin I did solicit him about.

Once more farewell. The Lord be with you : so prayeth
Your truly loving Cousin,
OLIVER CROMWELL.

Reverend Mark Noble, my reverend imbecile friend, discovers in this Letter evidence that Oliver was once a very dissolute man ; that Carrion Heath spake truth in that *Flagellum* Balderdash of his. O my reverend imbecile friend, hadst thou thyself never any moral life, but only a sensitive and digestive ? Thy soul never longed towards the serene heights, all hidden from thee ; and thirsted as the hart in dry places wherein no waters be ? It was never a sorrow for thee that the eternal pole-star had gone out, veiled itself in dark clouds ;—a sorrow only that this or the other noble Patron forgot thee when a living fell vacant ? I have known Christians, Moslems, Methodists,— and, alas, also reverend irreverent Apes by the Dead Sea !

O modern reader, dark as this Letter may seem, I will advise thee to make an attempt towards understanding it. There is in it a 'tradition of humanity' worth all the rest. Indisputable certificate that man once had a soul : that man once walked with

HIS RELIGION REAL

God,—his little Life a sacred island girdled with Eternities and Godhoods. Was it not a time for heroes? Heroes were then possible. I say, thou shalt understand that Letter; thou also, looking out into a too brutish world, wilt then exclaim with Oliver Cromwell,—with Hebrew David, as old Mr. Rouse of Truro, and the Presbyterian populations, still sing him in the Northern Kirks:

> Woe's me that I in Meshec am
> A sojourner so long,
> Or that I in the tents do dwell
> To Kedar that belong!

Yes, there is a tone in the soul of this Oliver that holds of the Perennial. With a noble sorrow, with a noble patience, he longs towards the mark of the prize of the high calling. He, I think, has chosen the better part. The world and its wild tumults,—if they will but let him alone! Yet he too will venture, will do and suffer for God's cause, if the call come. What man with better reason? He hath had plentiful wages beforehand; snatched out of darkness into marvellous light: he will never earn the least mite. Annihilation of self; *Selbsttodtung*, as Novalis calls it; casting yourself at the footstool of God's throne, "To live or to die forever; as Thou wilt, not as I will." Brother, hadst thou never, in any form, such moments in thy history? Thou knowest them not, even by credible rumour? Well, thy earthly path was peaceabler, I suppose. But the Highest was never in thee, the Highest will never come out of thee. Thou shalt at best abide by the stuff; as cherished housedog, guard the stuff,—perhaps with enormous gold-collars and provender: but the battle, and the hero death, and victory's fire-chariot carrying men to the Immortals shall never be thine. I pity thee; brag not, or I shall have to despise thee.

TWO YEARS

SUCH is Oliver's one Letter from Ely. To guide us a little through the void gulf towards his next Letter, we will here intercalate the following small fractions of Chronology.

1639

May—July. The Scots at their Glasgow Assembly had rent their *Tulchan* Apparatus in so rough a way, and otherwise so ill comported themselves, his Majesty saw good, in the beginning of this year, immense negotiation and messaging to and fro having proved so futile, to chastise them with an Army. By unheard-of exertions in the Extra-Parliamentary way, his Majesty got an Army ready; marched with it to Berwick,—is at Newcastle, 8th May 1639. But, alas, the Scots, with a much better Army, already lay encamped on Dunse Law; every nobleman with his tenants there, as a drilled regiment, round him; old Fieldmarshal Lesley for their generalissimo; at every Colonel's tent this pennon flying, *For Christ's Crown and Covenant*: there was no fighting to be thought of. Neither could the Pacification there patched up be of long continuance. The Scots disbanded their soldiers; but kept the officers, mostly Gustavus-Adolphus men, still within sight.

1640

The Scotch Pacification, hastily patched up at Dunse Hill, did not last; discrepancies arose as to the practical meaning of this and the other clause in it. Discrepancies which the farther they were handled, embroiled themselves the more. His Majesty having burnt Scotch paper Declarations 'by the hands of the common hangman,' and almost cut off the poor Scotch Chancellor Loudon's head, and being again resolute to chastise the rebel Scots with an Army, decides on summoning a Parliament for that end, there being no money attainable otherwise. To the great and glad astonishment of England; which, at one time, thought never to have seen another Parliament! Oliver Cromwell sat in this Parliament for Cambridge; recommended by Hampden, say some; not needing any recommendation in those Fen-countries, think others. Oliver's Colleague was a Thomas Meautys, Esquire. This Parliament met, 13th April 1640: it was by no means prompt enough with supplies against the Rebel Scots; the King dismissed it in a huff, 5th May; after a Session of three weeks: Historians call it the *Short Parliament*. His Majesty decides on raising money and an Army 'by other methods;' to which end, Wentworth, now Earl Strafford and Lord Lieutenant of Ireland, who had advised that course in the Council, did himself subscribe 20,000*l*. Archbishop Laud had long ago seen 'a cloud rising' against the Four surplices at Allhallowtide; and now it is covering the whole sky, in a most dismal and really thundery-looking manner.

His Majesty by 'other methods,' commission of array, benvolence, forced-loan, or how he could, got a kind of Army on foot, and set it marching out of the several Counties in the South towards the Scotch Border: but it was a most hopeless Army. The soldiers called the affair a *Bishops' War*; they mutinied against their officers, shot some of their officers: in various Towns on their march, if the Clergyman were reputed Puritan, they went and gave him three cheers; if of Surplice tendency, they sometimes threw his furniture out of window. No fighting against poor Scotch Gospellers was to be hoped for from these men.—Meanwhile the Scots, not to be behindhand, had raised a good Army of their own; and decided on going *into* England with it, this time, 'to present their grievances to the King's Majesty.' On the 20th of August 1640, they cross the Tweed at Coldstream; Montrose wading in the van of them all. They wore uniform of hodden gray, with blue caps; and each man had a moderate haversack of oatmeal on his back.

August 28th. The Scots force their way across the Tyne, at Newburn, some miles above Newcastle; the King's Army making small fight, most of them no fight; hurrying from Newcastle, and all town and country quarters, towards York again, where his Majesty and Strafford were. The *Bishops' War* was at an end. The Scots, striving to be gentle as doves in their behaviour, and publishing boundless brotherly Declarations to all the brethren that loved Christ's Gospel and God's Justice in England,—took possession of Newcastle next day; took possession gradually of all Northumberland and Durham,—and stayed there, in various towns and villages, about a year. The whole body of English Puritans looked upon them as their saviours: some months afterwards, Robert Baillie heard the London ballad-singers, on the streets, singing copiously with strong lungs, "Gramercy, good Master Scot," by way of burden.

His Majesty and Strafford, in a fine frenzy at this turn of affairs, found no refuge, except to summon a 'Council of Peers,' to enter upon a 'Treaty' with the Scots; and alas, at last, summon a New Parliament. Not to be helped in any way. Twelve chief Peers of the summoned 'Council' petitioned for a Parliament; the City of London petitioned for a Parliament, and would not lend money otherwise. A Parliament was appointed for the 3d of November next;—whereupon London cheerfully lent 200,000*l.*; and the treaty with the Scots at Ripon, 1st of October 1640, by and by transferred to London, went peaceably on at a very leisurely pace. The Scotch Army lay quartered at Newcastle, and over Northumberland and Durham, on an allowance of 850*l.* a-day; an Army indispensable for Puritan objects; no haste in finishing its Treaty. The English Army lay across in Yorkshire; without allowance except from the casualties of the King's Exchequer; in a dissatisfied manner, and occasionally getting into 'Army-Plots.'

This Parliament, which met on the 3d of November 1640, has become very celebrated in History by the name of the *Long Parliament*. It accomplished and suffered very singular destinies; suffered a Pride's Purge, a Cromwell's Ejectment; suffered Re-instatements, Re-ejectments; and the *Rump* or Fag-end of it did not finally vanish till 16th March 1659-60. Oliver Cromwell sat again in this Parliament for Cambridge Town; Meautys, his old Colleague, is now changed for 'John Lowry, Esquire,' probably a more Puritanic man. The members for Cambridge University are the same in both Parliaments.

Oliver St. John the Shipmoney Lawyer, now Member for Totness, has lately been made Solicitor-General; on the 2d of February 1640-1, D'Ewes says of him, 'newly created;' a date worth attending to. Strafford's Trial is coming on; to begin on the 22d of March: Strafford and Laud are safe in the Tower long since; Finch and Windebank and other Delinquents in high places, have fled rapidly beyond seas.

IN THE LONG PARLIAMENT

IN D'Ewes's Manuscript are these words, relating to *Monday, 9th November* 1640, the sixth day of the Long Parliament; 'Mr. Cromwell delivered the Petition of John Lilburn,'—young Lilburn, who had once been Prynne's amanuensis, among other things, and whose 'whipping with 200 stripes from Westminster to the Fleet Prison,' had already rendered him conspicuous.

This is the record of D'Ewes. To which let us now annex the
following well-known passage of Sir Philip Warwick; and if
the reader fancy the Speeches on the previous Saturday, and
how the 'whole of this Monday was spent in hearing grievances'
of the like sort, some dim image of a strange old scene may
perhaps rise upon him.

'The first time I ever took notice of Mr. Cromwell,' says
Warwick, 'was in the very beginning of the Parliament held
'in November 1640; when I,' Member for Radnor, 'vainly
'thought myself a courtly young gentleman,—for we courtiers
'valued ourselves much upon our good clothes! I came into
'the House one morning,' Monday morning, 'well clad; and
'perceived a gentleman speaking, whom I knew not,—very
'ordinarily apparelled; for it was a plain cloth suit, which
'seemed to have been made by an ill country-tailor; his linen
'was plain, and not very clean; and I remember a speck or two
'of blood upon his little band, which was not much larger than
'his collar. His hat was without a hatband. His stature was of
'a good size; his sword stuck close to his side : his countenance
'swoln and reddish, his voice sharp and untuneable, and his
'eloquence full of fervour. For the subject matter would not
'bear much of *reason*; it being on behalf of a servant of Mr.
'Prynne's who had dispersed Libels;'—yes, *Libels*, and had
come to Palaceyard for it, as we saw : 'I sincerely profess, it
'lessened much my reverence unto that Great Council, for this
'gentleman was very much hearkened unto;' which was strange,
seeing he had no gold lace to his coat, nor frills to his band;
and otherwise, to me in my poor featherhead, seemed a somewhat unhandy gentleman !

The reader may take what of these Warwick traits he can
along with him, and also omit what he cannot take; for though
Warwick's veracity is undoubted, his memory after many years,
in such an element as his had been, may be questioned. The
'band,' we may remind our readers, is a linen tippet, properly
the shirt-collar of those days, which, when the hair was worn
long, needed to fold itself with a good expanse of washable
linen over the upper-works of the coat, and defend these and
their velvets from harm. The 'specks of blood,' if not fabulous,
we, not without general sympathy, attribute to bad razors : as
for the 'hatband,' one remarks that men did not speak with
their hats *on*, and therefore will, with Sir Philip's leave, *omit* that.
The 'untuneable voice,' or what a poor young gentleman in these
circumstances would consider as such, is very significant to us.

PART II

TO THE END OF THE FIRST CIVIL WAR
1642—1646

1641

Monday, 3d May. Strafford's Trial being ended, but no sentence yet given, Mr. Robert Baillie, Minister of Kilwinning, who was here among the Scotch Commissioners at present, saw in Palaceyard, Westminister, 'some thousands of Citizens and Apprentices' (Miscellaneous Persons and City Shopmen, as we should now call them), who rolled about there 'all day,' bellowing to every Lord as he went in or came out, 'with a loud and hideous voice:' "Justice on Strafford! Justice on Traitors!"—which seemed ominous to the Reverend Mr. Baillie.

In which same hours, amid such echoes from without, the honourable House of Commons within doors, all in great tremor about Army-Plots, Treasons, Death-perils, was busy redacting a 'Protestation;' a kind of solemn Vow, or miniature *Scotch Covenant*, the first of a good many such in those earnest agitated times,—to the effect: "We take the Supreme to "witness that we will stand by one another to the death in "prosecution of our just objects here; in defence of Law, Loyalty "and Gospel here." To this effect; but couched in very mild language, and with a 'Preamble,' in which our Terror of Army-Plots, the moving principle of the affair, is discreetly almost shaded out of sight; it being our object that the House should be 'unanimous' in this Protestation. As accordingly the House was; the House, and to a great extent the Nation.

Hundreds of honourable Members, Mr. Cromwell one of them, sign the Protestation this day; the others on the following days: their names all registered in due succession in the Books. Nay, it is ordered that the whole Nation be invited to sign it; that each honourable Member send it down to his constituents, and invite them to sign it. Which, as we say, the constituents, all the reforming part of them, everywhere in England, did; with 'a feeling of solemnity very strange to the modern mind' Striking terror into all Traitors; quashing down Army-Plots for the present, and the hopes of poor Strafford forever. A Protestation held really sacred; appealed to, henceforth, as a thing from which there was no departing. Cavalcades of Freeholders, coming up from the country to petition the Honourable House,—for instance, the Four-thousand Petitioners from Buckinghamshire, about ten months hence,—rode with this Protestation 'stuck in their hats.' A very great and awe-inspiring matter in those days; till it was displaced by greater of the like kind,—Solemn League and Covenant, and others.

Monday next, 10*th May*, his Majesty accordingly signed sentence on Strafford; who was executed on the Wednesday following. No help for it. A terrible example; the one supremely able man the King had.

On the same Monday, 10th May, his Majesty signed likewise another Bill, That this Parliament should not be dissolved without its own consent. A Bill signed in order that the City might lend him money on good Security of Parliament; money being most pressingly wanted, for our couple of hungry Armies Scotch and English, and other necessary occasions. A Bill which seemed of no great consequence except financial; but which, to a People reverent of Law, and never, in the wildest clash of battle-swords, giving up its religious respect for the constable's baton, proved of infinite consequence. His Majesty's hands are tied; he cannot dismiss this Parliament, as he has done the others;—no, not without its own consent.

November 1st. News came to London, to the reassembled Parliament, that an Irish Rebellion, already grown to be an Irish Massacre, had broken out. An Irish Catholic imitation of the late Scotch Presbyterian achievements in the way of 'religious liberty';—one of the best models, and one of the worst imitations ever seen in this world.

November 22d. The Irish Rebellion blazing up more and

more into an Irish Massacre, to the terror and horror of all
Antipapist men ; and in England, or even in Scotland, except
by the liberal use of *varnish*, nothing yet being satisfactorily
mended, nay all things hanging now, as it seemed, in double and
treble jeopardy,—the Commons had decided on a 'Grand
Petition and Remonstrance,' to set forth what their griefs and
necessities really were, and really would require to have done
for them. The Debate upon it, very celebrated in those times,
came on this day, Monday 22d November. The longest
Debate ever yet known in Parliament ; and the stormiest,—nay,
had it not been for Mr. Hampden's soft management, 'we had
like to have sheathed our swords in each other's bowels,' says
Warwick ; which I find otherwise to be true. The Remonstrance passed by a small majority. It can be read still in
Rushworth, drawn up in precise business order ; the whole 206
Articles of it,—every line of which once thrilled electrically into
all men's hearts, as torpid as it has now grown. 'The chimes
' of Margaret's were striking two in the morning when we came
' out.'—It was on this occasion that Oliver, 'coming down stairs,'
is reported to have said, He would have sold all and gone to
New England, had the Remonstrance not passed ; a vague
report, gathered over dining-tables long after, to which the
reader need not pay more heed than it merits. His Majesty
returned from Scotland on the Thursday following ; and had
from the City a thrice-glorious Civic Entertainment.

December 10*th*.—The Episcopal business, attempted last Spring
in vain, has revived in December, kindled into life by the Remonstrance ; and is raging more fiercely than ever ; crowds of
Citizens petitioning, Corporation 'going in sixty coaches' to
petition ; the Apprentices, or City Shopmen, and miscellaneous
persons, petitioning :—Bishops 'much insulted' in Palaceyard,
as they go in or out. Whereupon hasty Welsh Williams,
Archbishop of York, once Bishop of Lincoln and Lord Keeper,
he with Eleven too hasty Bishops, Smectymnuus Hall, being one
of them, give in a protest, on this 10th of December, That they
cannot get to their place in Parliament ; that all shall be null
and void till they do get there. A rash step ; for which on the
30th of the same month, they are, by the Commons, voted guilty
of Treason ; and 'in a cold evening,' with small ceremony, are
bundled, the whole dozen of them, into the Tower. For there
is again rioting, again are cries 'loud and hideous ; '—Colonel
Lunsford, a truculent one-eyed man, having 'drawn his sword'
upon the Apprentices in Westminster Hall, and truculently

slashed some of them; who of course responded in a loud and
hideous manner, by tongue, by fist, and single stick: nay, on
the morrow, 28th December, they came marching many
thousands strong, with sword and pistol, out of the City, "Slash
"us now! while we wait on the Honourable House for an
"answer to our petition!"—and insulted his Majesty's Guard
at Whitehall. What a Christmas of that old London, of that
old Year! On the 6th of February following, Episcopacy will
be voted down, with blaze of 'bonfires,' and 'ringing' of all
the bells,—very audible to poor old Dr. Laud over in the Tower
yonder.

1642

January 4th. His Majesty seeing these extremities arrive,
and such a conflagration begin to blaze, thought now the time
had come for snatching the main livecoals away, and so quenching the same. Such coals of strife he counts to the number of
Five in the Commons House, and One in the Lords: Pym,
Hampden, Haselrig, with Holles and Strode (who held down
the Speaker fourteen years ago), these are the Five Commons;
Lord Kimbolton, better known to us as Mandevil, Oliver's
friend, of the 'Soke of Somersham,' and Queen's-Court Committee, he is the Lord. His Majesty flatters himself he has
gathered evidence concerning these individual firebrands, That
they 'invited the Scots to invade us' in 1640: he sends, on
Monday 3d January, to demand that they be given to him as
Traitors. Deliberate, slow and, as it were, evasive reply.
Whereupon, on the morrow, he rides down to St. Stephen's
himself, with an armed very miscellaneous force, of Five-hundred
or of Three-hundred truculent braggadocio persons at his back;
enters the House of Commons, the truculent persons looking
in after him from the lobby,—with intent to seize the said
Five Members, five principal hot coals; and trample *them* out,
for one thing. It was the fatallest step this poor King ever
took. The Five Members, timefully warned, were gone into
the City; the whole Parliament removed itself into the City,
'to be safe from armed violence.' From London City, and
from all England, rose one loud voice of lamentation, con-
demnation: Clean against law! Paint an inch thick, there
is, was, or can be, no shadow of law in *this*. Will you grant
us the Militia now; we seem to need it now!—His Majesty's
subsequent stages may be dated with more brevity.

January 10*th*. The King with his Court quits Whitehall; the Five Members and Parliament purposing to return tomorrow, with the whole City in arms round them. He left Whitehall; never saw it again till he came to lay down his head there.

March 9*th*. The King has sent away his Queen from Dover, 'to be in a place of safety,'—and also to pawn the Crown Jewels in Holland, and get him arms. He returns Northward again, avoiding London. Many Messages between the Houses of Parliament and him : "Will your Majesty grant us Power of the Militia ; accept this list of Lord-Lieutenants?" On the 9th of March, still advancing Northward without affirmative response, he has got to Newmarket; where another Message overtakes him, earnestly urges itself upon him: Could not your Majesty please to grant us Power of the Militia for a limited time? "No, by God!" answers his Majesty, "not for an hour!"—On the 19th of March he is at York; where his Hull Magazine, gathered for service against the Scots, is lying near; where a great Earl of Newcastle, and other Northern potentates, will help him; where at least London and its Puritanism, now grown so fierce, is far off.

There we will leave him; attempting Hull Magazine, in vain; exchanging messages with his Parliament ; messages, missives, printed and written Papers without limit :—Lawpleadings of both parties before the great tribunal of the English Nation, each party striving to prove itself right, and within the verge of Law : preserved still in acres of typography, once thrillingly alive in every fibre of them ; now a mere torpor, readable by few creatures, not rememberable by any. It is too clear his Majesty will have to get himself an army, by Commission of Array, by subscriptions of loyal plate, pawning of crown jewels, or how he can. The Parliament by all methods is endeavouring to do the like. London subscribed 'Horses and Plate,' every kind of plate, even to women's thimbles, to an unheard-of amount ; and when it came to actual enlisting, in London alone there were 'Four-thousand enlisted in a day.' Four-thousand, some call it Five-thousand, in a day : the reader may meditate that one fact. Royal messages, Parliamentary messages ; acres of typography thrillingly alive in every fibre of them,—these go on slowly abating, and military preparations go on steadily increasing till the 23d of October next. The King's 'Commission of Array for Leicestershire' came out on the 12th of June, commissions for other counties following as convenient; the Parliament's 'Ordinance for the Militia,' rising cautiously pulse after pulse towards clear emergence, had attained completion the week before. The question puts itself to every English soul, Which of these will you obey?—and in all quarters of English ground, with swords getting out of their scabbards, and yet the constable's baton still struggling to rule supreme, there is a most confused solution of it going on.

Of Oliver in these months we find the following things noted; which the imaginative reader is to spread out into significance for himself the best he can.

February 7th. 'Mr. Cromwell,' among others, 'offers to 'lend Three-hundred Pounds for the service of the Common- 'wealth,'—towards reducing the Irish Rebellion, and relieving the afflicted Protestants there, or here. Rushworth, copying a List of such subscribers, of date 9th April 1642, has Cromwell's name written down for '500*l.*'—seemingly the same transaction; Mr. Cromwell having now mended his offer: or else Mr. Rushworth, who uses the arithmetical cipher in this place, having misprinted. Hampden's subscription there is 1,000*l.* In Mr. Cromwell it is clear there is no backwardness, far from that; his activity in these months notably increases. In the *D'Ewes* MSS. he appears and reappears; suggesting this and the other practical step, on behalf of Ireland oftenest; in all ways zealously urging the work.

July 15th. 'Mr. Cromwell moved that we might make an 'order to allow the Townsmen of Cambridge to raise two 'Companies of Volunteers, and to appoint Captains over them.' On which same day, 15th July, the Commons Clerk writes these words: 'Whereas Mr. Cromwell hath sent down arms 'into the County of Cambridge, for the defence of that County, 'it is this day ordered.'—that he shall have the '100*l.*' expended on that service repaid him by and by. Is Mr. Cromwell aware that there lies a colour of high treason in all this; risk not of one's purse only, but of one's head? Mr. Cromwell is aware of it, and pauses not. The next entry is still stranger.

August 15th. 'Mr. Cromwell in Cambridgeshire has seized 'the Magazine in the Castle at Cambridge; and hath hindered 'the carrying of the Plate from that University; which, as some 'report, was to the value of 20,000*l.* or thereabouts.' So does Sir Philip Stapleton, member for Aldborough, member also of our new 'Committee for Defence of the Kingdom,' report this day. For which let Mr. Cromwell have indemnity.—Mr.

Cromwell has gone down into Cambridgeshire in person, since they began to train there, and assumed the chief management,— to some effect, it would appear.

The like was going on in all shires of England; wherever the Parliament had a zealous member, it sent him down to his shire in these critical months, to take what management he could or durst. The most confused months England ever saw. In every shire, in every parish; in courthouses, alehouses, churches, markets, wheresoever men were gathered together, England, with sorrowful confusion in every fibre, is tearing itself into hostile halves, to carry on the voting by pike and bullet henceforth.

September 14th. Here is a new phasis of the business. In a 'List of the Army under the command of the Earl of Essex,' we find that Robert Earl of Essex is 'Lord General for King *and* Parliament' (to deliver the poor beloved King from traitors, who have misled him, and clouded his fine understanding, and rendered him as it were a beloved Parent fallen *insane*); that Robert Earl of Essex, we say, is Lord General for King and Parliament; that William the new Earl of Bedford is General of the Horse, and has, or is every hour getting to have, 'seventy-five troops of 60 men each;' in every troop a Captain, a Lieutenant, a Cornet and Quartermaster, whose names are all given. In *Troop Sixty-seven*, the Captain is 'Oliver Cromwell,' —honourable member for Cambridge; many honourable members having now taken arms; Mr. Hampden, for example, having become Colonel Hampden,—busy drilling his men in Chalgrove Field at this very time. But moreover, in *Troop Eight* of Earl Bedford's Horse, we find another 'Oliver Cromwell, Cornet;'—and with real thankfulness for this poor flint-spark in the great darkness, recognise him for our honourable member's Son. His eldest Son Oliver, now a stout young man of twenty. "Thou too, Boy Oliver, thou art fit to swing "a sword. If there ever was a battle worth fighting, and to be "called God's battle, it is this; thou too wilt come!" How a staid, most pacific, solid Farmer of three-and-forty decides on girding himself with warlike iron, and fighting, he and his, against principalities and powers, let readers who have formed any notion of this man conceive for themselves.

On *Sunday, 23d October,* was Edgehill Battle, called also Keinton Fight, near Keinton on the south edge of Warwickshire. In which Battle Captain Cromwell *was* present, and did his duty, let angry Denzil say what he will. The fight was indecisive ; victory claimed by both sides. Captain Cromwell told Cousin Hampden, They never would get on with a set of poor tapsters and town-apprentice people fighting against men of honour. To cope with men of honour they must have men of religion. ' Mr. Hampden answered me, It was a good ' notion, if it could be executed.' Oliver himself set about executing a bit of it, his share of it, by and by.

'We all thought one battle would decide it,' says Richard Baxter ;—and we were all much mistaken ! This winter there arise among certain Counties 'Associations' for mutual defence, against Royalism and plunderous Rupertism ; a measure cherished by the Parliament, condemned as treasonable by the King. Of which 'Associations,' countable to the number of five or six, we name only one, that of Norfolk, Suffolk, Essex, Cambridge, Herts ; with Lord Grey of Wark for Commander ; where, and under whom, Oliver was now serving. This 'Eastern Association' is alone worth naming. All the other Associations, no man of emphasis being in the midst of them, fell in few months to pieces ; only this of Cromwell's subsisted, enlarged itself, grew famous ;—and indeed kept its own borders clear of invasion during the whole course of the War. Oliver, in the beginning of 1643, is serving there, under the Lord Grey of Wark. Besides his military duties, Oliver, as natural, was nominated of the Committee for Cambridgeshire in this Association ; he is also of the Committee for Huntingdonshire, which as yet belongs to another ' Association.'

Oliver, in the month of January 1642-3, is present in the Fen-country, and all over the Eastern Association, with his troop or troops ; looking after disaffected persons ; ready to disperse royalist assemblages, to seize royalist plate, to keep down disturbance, and care in every way that the Parliament Cause suffer no damage. A Lieutenant and party have gone to take some survey of Robert Barnard, Esquire ; Robert Barnard, standing on the right of injured innocence, innocent till he be proved guilty, protests : Oliver responds in a very characteristic way.

It was precisely in these weeks, that Oliver from Captain became Colonel : Colonel of a regiment of horse, raised on his own principles so far as might be, in that ' Eastern Association ;' and is henceforth known in the Newspapers as Colonel

Cromwell. Whether on this 23d of January, he was still Captain, or had ceased to be so, no extant accessible record apprises us. On the 2d March 1642-3, I have found him named as 'Col. Cromwell,' and hitherto not earlier. He is getting 'men of religion' to serve in this cause,—or at least would fain get such if he might.

LETTER II

CAMBRIDGE

IN the end of February 1642-3, 'Colonel' Cromwell is at Cambridge; 'great forces from Essex, Norfolk and Suffolk' having joined him, and more still coming in. There has been much alarm and running to and fro, over all those counties. Lord Capel hanging over them with an evident intent to plunder Cambridge, generally to plunder and ravage in this region; as Prince Rupert has cruelly done in Gloucestershire, and is now cruelly doing in Wilts and Hants. Colonel Cromwell, the soul of the whole business, must have had some bestirring of himself; some swift riding and resolving, now here, now there. Some '12,000 men,' however, or say even 23,000 men (for rumour runs very high!) from the Associated Counties, are now at last got together about Cambridge, and Lord Capel has seen good to vanish again. 'He was the first man that rose to complain of Grievances, in this Parliament;' he, while still plain Mr. Capel, member for Herts: but they have made a Lord of him, and the wind sits now in another quarter!—

Lord Capel has vanished; and the 12,000 zealous Volunteers of the Association are dismissed to their counties, with monition to be ready when called for again. Moreover, to avoid like perils in future, it is now resolved to make a Garrison of Cambridge; to add new works to the Castle, and fortify the Town itself. This is now going on in the early spring days of 1643; and Colonel Cromwell and all hands are busy!

A regular Force lies henceforth in Cambridge: Captains Fleetwood, Desborow, Whalley, new soldiers who will become veterans and known to us, are on service here. Of course the Academic stillness is much fluttered by the war-drum, and many a confused brabble springs up between Gown and Garrison;

college tippets, and on occasion still more venerable objects, getting torn by the business ! The truth is, though Cambridge is not so Malignant as Oxford, the Surplices at Allhallow-tide have still much sway there ; and various Heads of Houses are by no means what one could wish : of whom accordingly Oliver has had, and still occasionally has, to send,—by instalments as the cases ripen,—a select batch up to Parliament : Reverend Dr. This and then also Reverend Dr. That ; who are lodged in the Tower, in Ely House, in Lambeth or elsewhere, in a tragic manner, and pass very troublous years.

Cambridge continues henceforth the Bulwark and Metropolis of the Association ; where the Committees sit, where the centre of all business is. 'Colonel Cook,' I think, is Captain of the Garrison ; but the soul of the Garrison, and of the Association generally, is probably another Colonel. Now here, now swiftly there, wherever danger is to be fronted, or prompt work is to be done :—for example, off to Norwich just now, on important businesses ; and, as is too usual, very ill supplied with money.

Huntingdon County soon joined itself with this Eastern Association. Cromwell's next operations, as we shall perceive, were to deliver Lincolnshire, and give it the power of joining, which in September next took effect. Lincoln, Norfolk, Suffolk, Essex, Cambridge, Herts, Hunts : these are thenceforth the 'Seven Associated Counties,' called often the 'Association' simply, which make a great figure in the old Books,—and kept the War wholly out of their own borders, having had a man of due forwardness among them.

The main brunt of the War, during this year 1643, is in the extreme Southwest, between Sir Ralph Hopton and the Earl of Stamford ; and in the North, chiefly in Yorkshire, between the Earl of Newcastle and Lord Fairfax. The Southwest, Cornwall or Devonshire transactions do not much concern us in this place ; but with the Yorkshire we shall by and by have some concern. A considerable flame of War burns conspicuous in those two regions : the rest of England, all in a hot but very dim state, may be rather said to *smoke*, everywhere ready for burning, and incidentally catch fire here and there.

Essex, the Lord General, lies at Windsor, all spring, with the finest Parliamentary Army we have yet had ; but unluckily can undertake almost nothing, till he see. For his Majesty in Oxford is also quiescent mostly ; engaged in a negotiation with his Parliament ; in a Treaty,—of which Colonel Hampden and other knowing men, though my Lord of Essex cannot, already predict the issue. And the Country is all writhing in dim conflict, suffering manifold distress. And from his Majesty's headquarters ever and anon there darts out, now hither now thither, across the dim smoke-element, a swift fierce Prince Rupert, plundering and blazing ; and then suddenly darts in again ;—too like a streak of sudden *fire*, for he plunders, and even *burns*, a good deal! Which state of things Colonel Hampden and others witness with much impatience ; but cannot get the Lord General to undertake anything till he see.

An obscure entangled scene of things ; all manner of War-movements and swift-shooting electric influences crossing one another, with complex action and reaction ;—as happens in a scene of War ; much more of Civil War, where a whole People and its affairs have become *electric*.

LETTER III

A NEW horde of 'Plunderers' is threatening the Association with new infall from the North. The old Newspapers call them 'Camdeners ;' followers of a certain Noel, Viscount Camden, from Rutlandshire ; who has seized Stamford, is driving cattle at a great rate, and fast threatening to become important in those quarters.—'Sir John Burgoyne' is the Burgoyne of Potton in Bedfordshire, chief-Committee-man in that County : Bedford is not in our Association ; but will perhaps lend us help in this common peril.

'*To my honoured Friend Sir John Burgoyne, Baronet : These.*'

'Huntingdon,' 10th April 1643.

SIR,
These Plunderers draw near. I think it will do well if you can afford us any assistance of Dragooners, to help in this great Exigence. We have here about Six or Seven Troops of Horse ; such, I hope, as will fight. It's happy to resist such beginnings betimes.

If you can contribute anything to our aid, let us speedily participate thereof. In the mean time, and ever, command

Your humble servant,
OLIVER CROMWELL.

Cromwell's next achievement is the raising of their Siege of Croyland (in the end of April, exact date not discoverable); concerning which there are large details in loud-spoken Vicars: How the reverend godly Mr. Ram and godly Sergeant Horne, both of Spalding, were 'set upon the walls to be shot at,' when the Spalding people rose to deliver Croyland; how 'Colonel Sir Miles Hobart' and other Colonels rose also to deliver it,—and at last how 'the valiant active Colonel Cromwell' rose, and did actually deliver it.

Cromwell has been at Lynn, he has been at Nottingham, at Peterborough, where the Soldiers were not kind to the Cathedral and its Surplice-furniture: he has been here and then swiftly there; encountering many things. For Lincolnshire is not easy to deliver; dangers, intricate difficulties abound in those quarters and are increasing. Lincolnshire, infested with infalls of Camdeners has its own Malignancies too;—and, much more, is sadly overrun with the Marquis of Newcastle's Northern 'Popish Army' at present. An Army 'full of Papists,' as is currently reported; officered by renegade Scots, 'Sir John Henderson,' and the like unclean creatures. For the Marquis, in spite of the Fairfaxes, has overflowed Yorkshire; flowed across the Humber; has fortified himself in Newark-on-Trent, and is a sore affliction to the well affected thereabouts. By the Queen's interest he is now, from Earl, made Marquis, as we see. For indeed, what is worst of all, the Queen in late months has landed in these Northern parts, with Dutch ammunition purchased by English Crown Jewels; is stirring up all manner of 'Northern Papists' to double animation; tempting Hothams and other waverers to meditate treachery, for which they will pay dear. She is the centre of these new perils. She marches Southward, much agitating the skirts of the Eastern Association; joins the King 'on Keinton field' or Edgehill field, where he fought last autumn. —She was impeached of treason by the Commons. She continued in England till the following summer; then quitted it for long years.

Let the following Letters,—one of which is farther distinguished as the first of Cromwell's ever published in the Newspapers,—testify what progress he is making in the difficult problem of delivering Lincolnshire in this posture of affairs.

LETTER IV

THERE was in those weeks, as we learn from the old Newspapers, a combined plan, of which Cromwell was an element, for capturing Newark; there were several such; but this and all the rest proved abortive, one element or another of the combination always failing. That Cromwell was not the failing element we could already guess, and may now definitely read.

'Lord Grey,' be it remembered, is Lord Grey of Groby, once Military Chief of the Association,—though now I think employed mainly elsewhere, nearer home: a Leicestershire man; as are 'Hastings' and 'Hartop:' well-known all of them in the troubles of that County. Hastings, strong for the King, holds 'Ashby-de-la-Zouch, which is his Father's House, well fortified;' and shows and has shown himself a pushing man. 'His Excellency' is my Lord General Essex. 'Sir John Gell' is Member and Commander for Derbyshire, has Derby Town for Garrison. The Derbyshire forces, the Nottinghamshire forces, the Association forces: if all the 'forces' could but be united! But they never rightly can.

To the Honourable the Committee at Lincoln: These.'

'Lincolnshire,' 3d May 1643.

MY LORDS AND GENTLEMEN,

I must needs be hardly thought on; because I am still the messenger of unhappy tidings and delays concerning you,— though I know my heart is to assist you with all expedition!

My Lord Grey hath now again failed me of the rendezvous at Stamford,—notwithstanding that both he and I received Letters from his Excellency, commanding us both to meet, and, together with Sir John Gell and the Nottingham forces, to join with you. My Lord Grey sent Sir Edward Hartop to me, To let me know he could not meet me at Stamford according to our agreement; fearing the exposing of Leicester to the forces of Mr. Hastings and some other Troops drawing that way.

Believe it, it were better, in my poor opinion, Leicester were not, than that there should not be found an immediate taking of the field by our forces to accomplish the common ends. Wherein I shall deal as freely with him, when I meet him, as you can desire. I perceive Ashby-de-la-Zouch sticks much

with him. I have offered him now another place of meeting;
to come to which I suppose he will not deny me; and that to
be tomorrow. If you shall therefore think fit to send one over
unto us to be with us at night,—you do not know how far we
may prevail with him: To draw speedily to a head, with Sir
John Gell and the other forces, where we may all meet at a
general rendezvous, to the end you know of. And then you
shall receive full satisfaction concerning my integrity; and if no
man shall help you, yet will not I be wanting to do my duty,
God assisting me.

If we could unite those forces 'of theirs;' and with them
speedily make Grantham the general rendezvous, both of yours
and ours, I think it would do well. I shall bend my endeavours
that way. Your concurrence by some able instrument to solicit
this might probably exceedingly hasten it; especially having so
good a foundation to work upon as my Lord General's commands.
Our Norfolk forces, which will not prove so many as
you may imagine by six or seven hundred men, will lie conveniently
at Spalding; and, I am confident, be ready to meet at
Grantham at the general rendezvous.

I have no more to trouble you; but begging of God to take
away the impediments that hinder our conjunction, and to
prosper our designs, take leave.

Your faithful servant,
OLIVER CROMWELL.

Some rendezvous at Grantham does take place, some uniting
of forces, more or fewer; and strenuous endeavour thereupon
As the next Letter will testify.

LETTER V

THIS Letter is the first of Cromwell's ever published in the
Newspapers, 'That valiant soldier Colonel Cromwell' has
written on this occasion to an official Person of name not now
discoverable:

'*To—— ——: These.*'

'Grantham, 13th May 1643.

SIR,
    God hath given us, this evening, a glorious victory over
our enemies. They were, as we are informed, one-and-twenty
colours of horse-troops, and three or four of dragoons.

It was late in the evening when we drew out; they came and faced us within two miles of the town. So soon as we had the alarm, we drew out our forces, consisting of about twelve troops, —whereof some of them so poor and broken, that you shall seldom see worse; with this handful it pleased God to cast the scale. For after we had stood a little, above musket-shot the one body from the other; and the dragooners had fired on both sides, for the space of half an hour or more; they not advancing towards us, we agreed to charge them. And, advancing the body after many shots on both sides, we came on with our troops a pretty round trot; they standing firm to receive us; and our men charging fiercely upon them, by God's providence they were immediately routed, and ran all away, and we had the execution of them two or three miles.

I believe some of our soldiers did kill two or three men apiece in the pursuit; but what the number of dead is we are not certain. We took forty-five Prisoners, besides divers of their horse and arms, and rescued many Prisoners, whom they had lately taken of ours: and we took four or five of their colours. 'I rest.'

* * *

'OLIVER CROMWELL.'

On inquiry at Grantham, there is no vestige of tradition as to the scene of this skirmish; which must have been some two miles out on the Newark road. Thomas May, a veracious intelligent man, but vague as to dates, mentions two notable skirmishes of Cromwell's 'near to Grantham,' in the course of this business; one especially in which 'he defeated a strong 'party of the Newarkers, where the odds of number on their side 'was so great that it seemed almost a miraculous victory:' that probably is the one now in question. Colonel Cromwell, we farther find, was very 'vigilant of all sallies that were made, and 'took many men and colours at several times;' and did what was in Colonel Cromwell;—but could not take Newark at present. One element or other of the combination always fails. Newark, again and again besieged, did not surrender until the end of the War. At present, it is terribly wet weather, for one thing; 'thirteen days of continual rain.'

The King, as we observed, is in Oxford: Treaty, of very slow gestation, came to birth in March last, and was carried on

DEATH OF HAMPDEN

there by Whitlocke and others till the beginning of April; but
ended in absolute nothing. The King still continues in Oxford,
—his headquarters for three years to come. The Lord General
Essex did at one time think of Oxford, but preferred to take
Reading first; is lying now scattered about Thame, and Brick-
hill in Buckinghamshire, much drenched with the unseasonable
rains, in a very dormant, discontented condition. Colonel
Hampden is with him. There is talk of making Colonel
Hampden Lord General. The immediate hopes of the world,
however, are turned on 'that valiant soldier and patriot of his
country,' Sir William Waller, who has marched to discomfit the
Malignants of the West.

On the 4th of this May, Cheapside Cross, Charing Cross, and
other Monuments of Papist Idolatry were torn down by
authority, 'troops of soldiers sounding their trumpets, and all
the people shouting;' the Book of Sports was also burnt upon
the ruins of the same. In which days, too, all the people are
working at the Fortification of London.

'On 21 June 1643, Mr. Pym reports from the Committee of
the Safety of the Kingdom,' our chief authority at present, to
this effect, That Captain Hotham, son of the famed Hull
Hotham, had, as appeared by Letters from Lord Grey and
Colonel Cromwell, now at Nottingham, been behaving very ill;
had plundered divers persons without regard to the side they
were of; had, on one occasion, 'turned two pieces of ordnance
against Colonel Cromwell;' nay, once, when Lord Grey's
quartermaster was in some huff with Lord Grey 'about oats,'
had privily offered to the said quartermaster that they two
should draw out their men, and have a fight for it with Lord
Grey;—not to speak of frequent correspondences with Newark,
with Newcastle, and the Queen now come back from Holland:
wherefore he is arrested there in Nottingham, and locked up for
trial.

This was on the Wednesday, this report of Pym's: and, alas,
while Pym reads it, John Hampden, mortally wounded four
days ago in a skirmish at Chalgrove Field, lies dying at Thame;
—died on the Saturday following!

'On Thursday July the 27th,' on, or shortly before that day,
'news reach London' that Colonel Cromwell has taken
Stamford,—retaken it, I think; at all events taken it. Whereupon the Cavaliers from Newark and Belvoir Castle came
hovering about him: he drove them into Burleigh House, near

by, and laid siege to the same; 'at three in the morning,' battered it with all his shot, and stormed it at last. Which is 'a good help we have had this week.'

On the other hand, at Gainsborough we are suffering siege; indisputably the Newarkers threaten to get the upper hand in that quarter of the County. Here is Cromwell's Letter,— happily now the original itself;—concerning Lord Willoughby of Parham, and the relief of Gainsborough 'with powder and match.'

LETTER VI

To my noble Friends, Sir Edmund Bacon, Knight and Baronet, Sir William Spring, Knight and Baronet, Sir Thomas Barnardiston, Knight, and Maurice Barrow, Esquire: Present these.

Huntingdon, 31st July 1643.

GENTLEMEN,

No man desires more to present you with encouragement than myself, because of the forwardness I find in you,—to your honour be it spoken,—to promote this great Cause. And truly God follows us with encouragements, who is the God of blessings :—and I beseech you let Him not lose His blessings upon us ! They come in season, and with all the advantages of heartening : as if God should say, "Up and be doing, and I will stand by you, and help you !" There is nothing to be feared but our own sin and sloth.

It hath pleased the Lord to give your servant and soldiers a notable victory now at Gainsborough. I marched after the taking of Burleigh House upon Wednesday to Grantham, where I met about 300 horse and dragooners of Nottingham. With these, by agreement, we met the Lincolners at North Scarle, which is about ten miles from Gainsborough, upon Thursday in the evening; where we tarried until two of the clock in the morning; and then with our whole body advanced towards Gainsborough.

About a mile and a half from the Town, we met a forlornhope of the enemy of near 100 horse. Our dragooners laboured to beat them back; but not alighting off their horses, the enemy charged them, and beat some four or five of them off their horses: our horse charged them, and made them retire

VICTORY AT GAINSBOROUGH

unto their main body. We advanced, and came to the bottom of a steep hill : we could not well get up but by some tracks ; which our men essaying to do, a body of the enemy endeavoured to hinder, wherein we prevailed, and got the top of the hill. This was done by the Lincolners, who had the vanguard.

When we all recovered the top of the hill, we saw a great Body of the enemy's horse facing us, at about a musket-shot or less distance ; and a good Reserve of a full regiment of horse behind it. We endeavoured to put our men into as good order as we could. The enemy in the mean time advanced towards us, to take us at disadvantage ; but in such order as we were, we charged their great body, I having the right wing ; we came up horse to horse ; where we disputed it with our swords and pistols a pretty time ; all keeping close order, so that one could not break the other. At last, they a little shrinking, our men perceiving it, pressed in upon them, and immediately routed this whole body ; some flying on one side and others on the other of the enemy's Reserve ; and our men, pursuing them, had chase and execution about five or six miles.

I perceiving this body which was the Reserve standing still unbroken, kept back my Major, Whalley, from the chase ; and with my own troop and the other of my regiment, in all being three troops, we got into a body. In this Reserve stood General Cavendish ; who one while faced me, another while faced four of the Lincoln troops, which was all of ours that stood upon the place, the rest being engaged in the chase. At last General Cavendish charged the Lincolners, and routed them. Immediately I fell on his rear with my three troops ; which did so astonish him, that he gave over the chase, and would fain have delivered himself from me. But I pressing on forced them down a hill, having good execution of them ; and below the hill, drove the General with some of his soldiers into a quagmire ; where my Captain-lieutenant slew him with a thrust under his short ribs. The rest of the body was wholly routed, not one man staying upon the place.

We then, after this defeat which was so total, relieved the Town with such powder and provision as we brought. Which done, we had notice that there were six troops of horse and 300 foot on the other side of the Town, about a mile off us : we desired some foot of my Lord Willoughby's, about 400 ; and, with our horse and these foot, marched towards them : when we came towards the place where their horse stood, we beat back with my troops about two or three troops of the enemy's, who retired into a small village at the bottom of the hill. When we recovered the hill, we saw in the bottom, about a quarter of a mile from us, a regiment of foot; after that another; after that the Marquis of Newcastle's own regiment; consisting in all of about 50 foot colours, and a great body of horse;—which indeed was Newcastle's Army. Which, coming so unexpectedly, put us to new consultations. My Lord Willoughby and I, being in the Town, agreed to call off our foot. I went to bring them off; but before I returned, divers of the foot were engaged; the enemy advancing with his whole body. Our foot retreated in disorder; and with some loss got the Town; where now they are. Our horse also came off with some trouble; being wearied with the long fight, and their horses tired; yet faced the enemy's fresh horse, and by several removes got off without the loss of one man; the enemy following the rear with a great body. The honour of this retreat is due to God, as also all the rest: Major Whalley did in this carry himself with all gallantry becoming a gentleman and a Christian.

Thus you have this true relation, as short as I could. What you are to do upon it, is next to be considered. If I could speak words to pierce your hearts with the sense of our and your condition, I would! If you will raise 2,000 Foot at present to encounter this Army of Newcastle's, to raise the siege, and to enable us to fight him,—we doubt not, by the grace of God, but that we shall be able to relieve the Town, and beat the Enemy on the other side of Trent. Whereas if somewhat be not done in this, you will see Newcastle's Army march up into your bowels; being now, as it is, on this side Trent. I know it will be difficult to raise thus many in so short time: but let me assure you, it's necessary, and therefore to *be* done. At least do what you may, with all possible expedition! I would I had the happiness to speak with one of you:—truly I cannot come over, but must attend my charge; the Enemy is vigilant. The Lord direct you what to do.

Gentlemen, I am
Your faithful servant,
OLIVER CROMWELL

LETTER VII

GAINSBOROUGH was directly taken, after this relief of it; Lord Willoughby could not resist the Newarkers with Newcastle at their head. Gainsborough is lost, Lincoln is lost; unless help come speedily, all is like to be lost. The following Letter, with its enclosure from the Lord Lieutenant Willoughby of Parham, speaks for itself. Read the Enclosure first.

"To my noble Friend Colonel Cromwell at Huntingdon: These."

"Boston, 5th August 1643.

"NOBLE SIR,—Since the business of Gainsborough, the hearts
" of our men have been so deaded that we have lost most
" of them by running away. So that we were forced to leave
" Lincoln upon a sudden;—and if I had not done it then, I
" should have been left alone in it. So that now I am at
" Boston; where we are very poor in strength;—so that without
" some speedy supply, I fear we shall not hold this long
" neither.

"My Lord General, I perceive, hath writ to you, To draw all
" the forces together. I should be glad to see it; for if that will
" not be, there can be no good to be expected. If you will
" endeavour to stop my Lord of Newcastle, you must presently
" draw them to him and fight him! For without we be masters
" of the field we shall be pulled out by the ears, one after
" another.

"The Foot, if they will come on, may march very securely to
" Boston; which, to me, will be very considerable to your
" Association. For if the Enemy get that Town, which is now
" very weak for defence for want of men, I believe they will not
" be long out of Norfolk and Suffolk.

"I can say no more: but desire you to hasten;—and rest,
"Your servant,
"FRANCIS WILLOUGHBY."

*To my honoured Friends the Commissioners at Cambridge:
These present.*

Huntingdon, 6th August, 1643.

GENTLEMEN,
You see by this Enclosed how sadly your affairs stand.
It's no longer Disputing, but Out instantly all you can! Raise

all your Bands ; send them to Huntingdon ;—get up what Volunteers you can ; hasten your Horses.

Send these Letters to Norfolk, Suffolk and Essex, without delay. I beseech you spare not, but be expeditious and industrious ! Almost all our Foot have quitted Stamford : there is nothing to interrupt an Enemy, but our Horse, that is considerable. You must act lively ; do it without distraction. Neglect no means !—I am

Your faithful servant,
OLIVER CROMWELL.

Sir William Waller, whom some called William the Conqueror, has been beaten all to pieces on Lansdown Heath, about three weeks ago. The Fairfaxes too are beaten from the field; glad to get into Hull,—which Hotham the Traitor was about delivering to her Majesty, when vigilant persons laid him fast. And, in the end of May, Earl Stamford was defeated in the Southwest ; and now Bristol has been suddenly surrendered to Prince Rupert,— for which let Colonel Nathaniel Fiennes (says Mr. Prynne, still very zealous) be tried by Court-Martial, and if possible, shot.

In the very hours while Cromwell was storming the sand-hill near Gainsborough 'by some tracks,' honourable gentlemen at St. Stephen's were voting him Governor of the Isle of Ely. Ely in the heart of the Fens, a place of great military capabilities, is much troubled with 'corrupt ministers,' with 'corrupt trainbands,' and understood to be in a perilous state ; wherefore they nominate Cromwell to take charge of it. We understand his own Family to be still resident in Ely.

The Parliament affairs, this Summer, have taken a bad course, and except it be in the Eastern Association, look everywhere declining. They have lost Bristol, their footing in the Southwest and in the North is mostly gone ; Essex's Army has melted away, without any action of mark all Summer, except the *loss* of Hampden in a skirmish. In the beginning of August, the King breaks out from Oxford, very clearly superior in force ; goes to settle Bristol ; and might thence, it was supposed, have marched direct to London, if he had liked. He decides on taking Gloucester with him before he quit those parts. The Parliament, in much extremity, calls upon the Scots for help, who under conditions will consent.

In these circumstances, it was rather thought a piece of

heroism in our old friend Lord Kimbolton, or Mandevil, now become Earl of Manchester, to accept the command of the Eastern Association: he is nominated 'Sergeant-Major of the Associated Counties,' 10th August 1643; is to raise new force, infantry and cavalry; has four Colonels of Horse under him; Colonel Cromwell, who soon became his second in command, is one of them; Colonel Norton, whom we shall meet afterwards, is another. 'The Associated Counties are busy listing,' intimates the old Newspaper; 'and so soon as their harvest 'is over, which for the present much retardeth them, the Earl 'of Manchester will have a very brave and considerable Army, 'to be a terror to the Northern Papists,' Newarkers and Newcastles, 'if they advance Southward.' When specially it was that Cromwell listed his celebrated body of *Ironsides* is of course not to be dated, though some do carelessly date it, as from the very 'beginning of the War;' and in Bates and others are to be found various romantic details on the subject, which deserve no credit. Doubtless Cromwell, all along, in the many changes his body of men underwent, had his eye upon this object of getting good soldiers and dismissing bad; and managed the matter by common practical vigilance, not by theatrical claptraps as Dr. Bates represents. Some months ago, it was said in the Newspapers, of Colonel Cromwell's soldiers, 'not a man swears but he pays his twelvepence;' no plundering, no drinking, disorder, or impiety allowed. We may fancy, in this new levy, as Manchester's Lieutenant and Governor of Ely, when the whole force was again winnowed and sifted, he might complete the process, and see his Thousand Troopers ranked before him, worthy at last of the name of *Ironsides*. They were men that had the fear of God; and gradually lost all other fear. "Truly they were never beaten at all," says he.—Meanwhile:

1643

August 21st. The shops of London are all shut for certain days: Gloucester is in hot siege; nothing but the obdurate valour of a few men there prevents the King, with Prince Rupert, called also Prince Robert and Prince *Robber*, from riding roughshod over us. The City, with much emotion, ranks its Trained Bands under Essex; making up an Army for him, despatches him to relieve Gloucester. He marches on the 26th; steadily along, in spite of rainy weather and

Prince Rupert; westward, westward: on the night of the tenth day, September 5th, the Gloucester people see his signal-fire flame up, amid the dark rain, 'on the top of Presbury Hill;'— and understand that they shall live and not die The King 'fired his huts,' and marched off without delay. He never again had any real chance of prevailing in this War. Essex, having relieved the West, returns steadily home again, the King's forces hanging angrily on his rear; at Newbury in Berkshire, he had to turn round, and give them battle,—*First Newbury Battle*, 20th September 1643,—wherein he came off rather superior. Poor Lord Falkland, in his 'clean shirt,' was killed here. This steady march, to Gloucester and back again, by Essex, was the chief feat he did during the War; a considerable feat, and very characteristic of him, the slow-going, inarticulate, indignant, somewhat elephantine man.

WINCEBY FIGHT

LINCOLNSHIRE, which has now become one of the Associated Seven, and is still much overrun by Newarkers and Northern Papists, shall at last be delivered.

Hull siege still continues, with obstinate sally and onslaught; on the other hand, Lynn siege, which the Earl of Manchester was busy in, has prosperously ended; and the Earl himself with his foot regiments, is now also here; united, in loose quarters, with Cromwell and Fairfax, in the Boston region, and able probably to undertake somewhat. Cromwell and Fairfax with the horse, we perceive, have still the brunt of the work to do. Here, after much marching and skirmishing, is an account of Winceby Fight, their chief exploit in those parts, which cleared the country of the Newarkers, General Kings, and renegade Sir John Hendersons;—as recorded by loud-spoken Vicars. In spite of brevity we must copy the Narrative. Cromwell himself was nearer death in this action than ever in any other; the victory too made its due figure, and 'appeared in the world.'

Winceby, a small upland Hamlet, in the Wolds, not among the Fens of Lincolnshire, is some five miles west of Horncastle. The confused memory of this Fight is still fresh there; the

FIGHT AT WINCEBY

Lane along which the chase went bears ever since the name of '*Slash* Lane,' and poor Tradition maunders about it as she can. Hear Vicars, a poor human soul zealously prophesying as if through the organs of an ass,—in a not mendacious, yet loud-spoken, exaggerative, more or less asinine manner:

* * * 'All that night,' Tuesday, 10th October 1643, 'we were drawing our horse to the appointed rendezvous; and 'the next morning, being Wednesday, my Lord Manchester 'gave order that the whole force, both horse and foot, should 'be drawn up to Bolingbroke Hill, where he would expect the 'enemy, being the only convenient ground to fight with him. 'But Colonel Cromwell was no way satisfied that we should 'fight; our horse being extremely wearied with hard duty 'two or three days together.

'The enemy also drew, that' Wednesday ' morning, their 'whole body of horse and dragooners into the field, being 74 'colours of horse, and 21 colours of dragoons, in all 95 'colours. We had not many more than half so many colours 'of horse and dragooners; but I believe we had as many 'men,—besides our foot, which indeed could not be drawn 'up until it was very late. The enemy's word was "Caven-'dish;"'—he that was killed in the Bog; 'and ours was '"Religion." I believe that as we had no notice of the enemy's 'coming towards us, so they had as little of our preparation to 'fight with them. It was about twelve of the clock ere our 'horse and dragooners were drawn up. After that we marched 'about a mile nearer the enemy; and then we began to descry 'him, by little and little, coming towards us. Until this time 'we did not know we should fight; but so soon as our men 'had knowledge of the enemy's coming, they were very full 'of joy and resolution, thinking it a great mercy that they 'should now fight with him. Our men went on in several 'bodies, singing Psalms. Quarter-master-General Vermuyden 'with five troops had the forlorn-hope, and Colonel Cromwell 'the van, assisted with other of my Lord's troops, and seconded 'by Sir T. Fairfax. Both armies met about Ixbie, if I mistake 'not the Town's name,'—you do mistake, Mr. Vicars; it is Winceby, a mere hamlet and not a town.

'Both they and we had drawn up our dragooners; who gave 'the first charge; and then the horse fell in. Colonel Cromwell 'fell with brave resolution upon the enemy, immediately after 'their dragooners had given him the first volley; yet they were 'so nimble, as that, within half pistol-shot, they gave him

'another: his horse was killed under him at the first charge,
'and fell down upon him; and as he rose up, he was knocked
'down again by the Gentleman who charged him, who 'twas
'conceived was Sir Ingram Hopton: but afterwards he' the
Colonel 'recovered a poor horse in a soldier's hands, and bravely
'mounted himself again. Truly this first charge was so home-
'given, and performed with so much admirable courage and
'resolution by our troops, that the enemy stood not another;
'but were driven back upon their own body, which was to have
'seconded them; and at last put these into a plain disorder;
'and thus, in less than half an hour's fight, they were all quite
'routed, and'—driven along Slash Lane at a terrible rate,
unnecessary to specify. Sir Ingram Hopton, who had been
so near killing Cromwell, was himself killed. 'Above a
hundred of their men were found drowned in ditches,' in
quagmires that would not bear riding; the 'dragooners now
left on foot' were taken prisoners; the chase lasted to
Horncastle or beyond it,—and Henderson the renegade Scot
was never heard of in those parts more. My Lord of
Manchester's foot did not get up till the battle was over.

This very day of Winceby Fight, there has gone on at Hull
a universal sally, tough sullen wrestle in the trenches all day:
with important loss to the Marquis of Newcastle; loss of
ground, loss of lives, loss still more of invaluable guns, brass
drakes, sackers, what not:—and on the morrow morning the
Townsfolk, looking out, discern with emotion that there is now
no Marquis, that the Marquis has marched away under cloud
of night, and given up the siege. Which surely are good
encouragements we have had; two in one day.

This will suffice for Winceby Fight, or Horncastle Fight, of
11th October 1643; and leave the reader to imagine that
Lincolnshire too was now cleared of the 'Papist Army,' as we
violently nickname it,—all but a few Towns on the Western
border, which will be successfully besieged when the Spring
comes.

LETTER VIII

IN the month of January 1643-4, Oliver, as Governor of Ely, is
present for some time in that City; lodges, we suppose, with
his own family there; doing military and other work of

government;—makes a transient appearance in the Cathedral one day; memorable to the Reverend Mr. Hitch and us.

The case was this. Parliament, which, ever since the first meeting of it, had shown a marked disaffection to Surplices at Allhallowtide and 'monuments of Superstition and Idolatry,' and passed Order after Order to put them down,—has in August last come to a decisive Act on the subject, and specifically explained that go they must and shall. Act of Parliament which, like the previous Orders of Parliament, could only have gradual partial execution, according to the humour of the locality; and gave rise to scenes. By the Parliament's directions, the Priest, Churchwardens, and proper officers were to do it, with all decency: failing the proper officers, *im*proper officers, military men passing through the place, these and such like, backed by a Puritan populace, and a Puritan soldiery, had to do it;—not always in the softest manner. As many a *Querela*, Peter Heylin's (lying Peter's) *History*, and *Persecutio Undecima*, still testifies with angry tears. You cannot pull the shirt off a man, the skin off a man, in a way that will please him !—Our Assembly of Divines, sitting earnestly deliberative ever since June last, will direct us what Form of Worship we are to adopt,—some form, it is to be hoped, not grown dramaturgic to us, but still awfully symbolic for us. Meanwhile let all Churches, especially all Cathedrals, be stript of whatever the general soul so much as suspects to be stage-property and prayer by machinery,—a thing we very justly hold in terror and horror, and dare not live beside !—

Ely Cathedral, it appears, had still been overlooked,—Ely, much troubled with scandalous ministers, as well as with disaffected trainbands,—and Mr. Hitch, under the very eyes of Oliver, persists in his Choir-service there. Here accordingly is an official Note, copies of which still sleep in some repositories.

'*To the Reverend Mr. Hitch, at Ely : These.*'

'Ely,' 10th January 1643.

Mr. Hitch,

Lest the Soldiers should in any tumultuary or disorderly way attempt the reformation of the Cathedral Church, I require you to forbear altogether your Choir-service, so unedifying and offensive:—and this as you shall answer it, if any disorder should arise thereupon.

I advise you to catechise, and read and expound the Scripture to the people; not doubting but the Parliament, with the advice of the Assembly of Divines, will direct you farther. I desire your Sermons 'too,' where usually they have been,—but more frequent

Your loving friend,
OLIVER CROMWELL.

Mr. Hitch paid no attention; persisted in his Choir-service: —whereupon enter the Governor of Ely with soldiers, 'with a rabble at his heels,' say the old *Querelas*. With a rabble at his heels, with his hat on, he walks up to the Choir; says audibly: "I am a man under Authority; and am commanded to dismiss this Assembly,"—then draws back a little, that the Assembly may dismiss with decency. Mr. Hitch has paused for a moment; but seeing Oliver draw back, he starts again : " As it was in the beginning"—!—"Leave off your fooling, and come down, Sir !" said Oliver, in a voice still audible to this Editor; which Mr. Hitch did now instantaneously give ear to. And so 'with his whole congregation,' files out, and vanishes from the field of History.

Friday, 19th January. The Scots enter England by Berwick, 21,000 strong: on Wednesday they left Dunbar 'up to the knees in snow'; such a heart of forwardness was in them. Old Lesley, now Earl of Leven, was their General, as before; a Committee of Parliamenteers went with him. They soon drove-in Newcastle's 'Papist Army' within narrower quarters; in May, got Manchester with Cromwell and Fairfax brought across the Humber to join them, and besieged Newcastle himself in York. Which, before long, will bring us to Marston Moor, and another letter.

In this same month of January, 22d day of it, directly after Hitch's business, Colonel Cromwell, now more properly Lieutenant-General Cromwell, Lieutenant to the Earl of Manchester in the Association, transiently appeared in his place in Parliament; complaining much of my Lord Willoughby, as of a backward General, with strangely dissolute people about him, a great sorrow to Lincolnshire;—and craving that my Lord Manchester might be appointed there instead : which, as we see, was done; with good result.

Before the summer the Western Towns of Lincolnshire are all taken; Manchester with Cromwell and Fairfax are across the

Humber, joined with the Scots besieging York, where Major-
General Crawford again distinguishes himself ;—and we are now
at Marston Moor.

LETTER XI

MARSTON MOOR

IN the last days of June 1644, Prince Rupert, with an army of
some 20,000 fierce men, came pouring over the hills from
Lancashire, where he had left harsh traces of himself, to relieve
the Marquis of Newcastle, who was now with a force of 6,000
besieged in York, by the united forces of the Scots under
Leven, the Yorkshiremen under Lord Fairfax, and the Associated Counties under Manchester and Cromwell. On hearing
of his approach, the Parliament Generals raised the Siege; drew
out on the Moor of Long Marston, some four miles off, to
oppose his coming. He avoided them by crossing the river
Ouse; relieved York, Monday, 1st July; and might have
returned successful; but insisted on Newcastle's joining him,
and going out to fight the Roundheads. The Battle of Marston
Moor, fought on the morrow evening, Tuesday, 2d July
1644, from 7 to 10 o'clock, was the result,—entirely disastrous
for him.

Of this Battle, the bloodiest of the whole War, I must leave
the reader to gather details in the King's Pamphlets, *et cetera*;
or to imagine it in general as the most enormous hurlyburly,
of fire and smoke, and steel-flashings and death-tumult, ever
seen in those regions: the end of which, about ten at night,
was 'Four-thousand one-hundred-and-fifty bodies' to be buried,
and total ruin to the King's affairs in those Northern parts

The Armies were not completely drawn up till after five in
the evening; there was a ditch between them; they stood
facing one another, motionless except the exchange of a few
cannon-shots, for an hour-and-half. Newcastle thought there
would be no fighting till the morrow, and had retired to his
carriage for the night. There is some shadow of surmise that
the stray cannon-shot which, as the following Letter indicates,
proved fatal to Oliver's Nephew did also, rousing Oliver's
humour to the charging point, bring on the general Battle.
'The Prince of Plunderers,' invincible hitherto, here first tasted
the steel of Oliver's Ironsides, and did not in the least like it.

'The Scots delivered their fire with such constancy and swift-
'ness, it was as if the whole air had become an element of fire,'—
in the ancient summer gloaming there.

> '*To my loving Brother, Colonel Valentine Walton: These.*'
>
> 'Leaguer before York,' 5th July 1644.

DEAR SIR,
It's our duty to sympathise in all mercies; and to praise the Lord together in chastisements or trials, that so we may sorrow together.

Truly England and the Church of God hath had a great favour from the Lord, in this great Victory given unto us, such as the like never was since this War began. It had all the evidences of an absolute Victory obtained by the Lord's blessing upon the Godly Party principally. We never charged but we routed the enemy. The Left Wing, which I commanded, being our own horse, saving a few Scots in our rear, beat all the Prince's horse. God made them as stubble to our swords. We charged their regiments of foot with our horse, and routed all we charged. The particulars I cannot relate now; but I believe, of Twenty-thousand the Prince hath not Four-thousand left. Give glory, all the glory, to God.—

Sir, God hath taken away your eldest Son by a cannon-shot. It brake his leg. We were necessitated to have it cut off, whereof he died.

Sir, you know my own trials this way:[1] but the Lord supported me with this, That the Lord took him into the happiness we all pant for and live for. There is your precious child full of glory, never to know sin or sorrow any more. He was a gallant young man, exceedingly gracious. God give you His comfort. Before his death he was so full of comfort that to Frank Russel and myself he could not express it, " It was so great above his pain." This he said to us. Indeed it was admirable. A little after, he said, One thing lay upon his

---

[1] I conclude, the poor Boy Oliver has already fallen in these Wars, —none of *us* knows where, though his Father well knew!— — *Note to Third Edition*: In the *Squire Papers* (Fraser's Magazine, December 1847) is this passage; 'Meeting Cromwell again after some absence, 'just on the edge of Marston Battle, Squire says, " I thought he looked 'sad and wearied, for he had had a sad loss; young Oliver got killed 'to death not long before, I heard: it was near Knaresborough, and '30 more got killed."'

spirit. I asked him, What that was? He told me it was, That
God had not suffered him to be any more the executioner of
His enemies. At his fall, his horse being killed with the bullet,
and as I am informed three horses more, I am told he bid them,
Open to the right and left, that he might see the rogues run.
Truly he was exceedingly beloved in the Army, of all that knew
him. But few knew him; for he was a precious young man,
fit for God. You have cause to bless the Lord. He is a
glorious Saint in Heaven; wherein you ought exceedingly to
rejoice. Let this drink up your sorrow; seeing these are not
feigned words to comfort you, but the thing is so real and undoubted a truth. You may do all things by the strength of
Christ. Seek that, and you shall easily bear your trial. Let
this public mercy to the Church of God make you to forget
your private sorrow. The Lord be your strength: so prays
  Your truly faithful and loving brother,
      OLIVER CROMWELL.

My love to your Daughter, and my Cousin Perceval, Sister
Desborow and all friends with you.

Colonel Valentine Walton, already a conspicuous man, and
more so afterwards, is of Great-Staughton, Huntingdonshire, a
neighbour of the Earl of Manchester's; Member for his County,
and a Colonel since the beginning of the War. There had long
been an intimacy between the Cromwell Family and his. His
Wife, the Mother of this slain youth, is Margaret Cromwell,
Oliver's younger Sister, next to him in the family series. 'Frank
Russel' is of Chippenham, Cambridgeshire, eldest Son of the
Baronet there; already a Colonel; soon afterwards Governor
of Ely in Oliver's stead. It was the daughter of this Frank that
Henry Cromwell, some ten years hence, wedded.

York was now captured in a few days. Prince Rupert had
fled across into Lancashire, and so 'south to Shropshire, to
recruit again;' Marquis Newcastle with 'about eighty gentlemen,' disgusted at the turn of affairs, had withdrawn beyond
seas. The Scots moved northward to attend the Siege of Newcastle,—ended it by storm in October next. On the 24th of
which same month, 24th October 1644, the Parliament pro-
mulgated its Rhadamanthine Ordinance, To 'hang any Irish
Papist taken in arms in this country'; a very severe Ordinance,
but not uncalled for by the nature of the 'marauding apparatus'
in question there.

THREE FRAGMENTS OF SPEECHES

SELF-DENYING ORDINANCE

THE following Three small Fragments of Speeches will have to represent for us some six months of occasional loud debating, and continual anxious gestation and manipulation, in the Two Houses, in the Committee of Both Kingdoms, and in many other houses and places;—the ultimate outcome of which was the celebrated 'Self-denying Ordinance,' and 'New Model' of the Parliament's Army; which indeed brings on an entirely New Epoch in the Parliament's Affairs.

Essex and Waller had, for the third or even fourth time, chiefly by the exertions of ever-zealous London, been fitted out with Armies; had marched forth together to subdue the West; —and ended in quite other results than that. The two Generals differed in opinion; did not march long together: Essex, urged by a subordinate, Lord Roberts, who had estates in Cornwall and hoped to get some rents out of them, turned down thitherwards to the left: Waller bending up to the right;—with small issue either way. Waller's last action was an indecisive, rather unsuccessful Fight, or day of skirmishing, with the King, at Cropredy Bridge on the border of Oxford and Northampton Shires, three days before Marston Moor. After which both parties separated: the King to follow Essex, since there was now no hope in the North; Waller to wander Londonwards, and gradually 'lose his Army by desertion,' as the habit of him was. As for the King, he followed Essex into Cornwall with effect; hemmed him in among the hills there, about Bodmin, Lostwithiel, Foy, with continual skirmishing, with evergrowing scarcity of victual; forced poor Essex to escape to Plymouth by the Fleet, and *leave* his Army to shift for itself as best might be: the horse under Balfour to cut their way through; the foot under Skippon to lay down their arms, cease to be soldiers, and march away 'with staves in their hands' into the wide world. This surrender was effected 1st September 1644, two months after Marston Moor. The Parliament's and Cromwell's worst anticipation, in that quarter, is fulfilled.

The Parliament made no complaint of Essex; with a kind of Roman dignity, they rather thanked him. They proceeded to recruit Waller and him, summoned Manchester with Cromwell his Lieutenant-General to join them; by which three bodies,

SECOND BATTLE OF NEWBURY

making again a considerable army, under the command of Manchester and Waller (for Essex lay 'sick,' or seeming to be sick), the King, returning towards Oxford from his victory, was intercepted at Newbury; and there, on Sunday, 27th October 1644, fell out the *Second* Battle of Newbury. Wherein his Majesty, after four hours confused fighting, rather had the worse; yet contrived to march off, unmolested, 'by moonlight at 10 o'clock,' towards Wallingford, and got safe home. Manchester refused to pursue; though urged by Cromwell, and again urged. Nay twelve days after, when the King came back, and openly revictualled Donnington Castle, an important strongplace hard by,—Manchester, in spite of Cromwell's urgency, still refused to interfere.

They in fact came to a quarrel here, these two :—and much else that was represented by them came to a quarrel; Presbytery and Independency, to wit. Manchester was reported to have said, If they lost this Army pursuing the King, they had no other; the King 'might hang them all.' To Cromwell and the thorough-going party, it had become very clear that high Essexes and Manchesters, of limited notions and large estates and anxieties, who besides their fear of being themselves beaten utterly, and forfeited and 'hanged,' were afraid of beating the King too well, would never end this Cause in a good way. Whereupon ensue some six months of very complex manipulation, and public and private consultation, which these Three Fragments of Speeches are here to represent for us.

I. *In the House of Commons, on Monday 25th November 1644, Lieutenant-General Cromwell did, as ordered on the Saturday before, exhibit a charge against the Earl of Manchester, to this effect:*

That the said Earl had always been indisposed and backward to engagements, and the ending of the War by the sword; and 'always' *for* such a Peace as a 'thorough' victory would be a disadvantage to;—and hath declared this by principles express to that purpose, and 'by' a continued series of carriage and actions answerable.

That since the taking of York, as if the Parliament had now advantage fully enough, he hath declined whatsoever tended to farther advantage upon the Enemy; 'hath' neglected and studiously shifted-off opportunities to that purpose, as if he thought the King too low, and the Parliament too high,—especially at Donnington Castle.

That he hath drawn the Army into, and detained them in, such a posture as to give the Enemy fresh advantages ; and this, before his conjunction with the other Armies, by his own absolute will, against or without his Council of War, against many commands of the Committee of Both Kingdoms, and with contempt and vilifying of those commands ;—and, *since* the conjunction, sometimes against the Councils of War, and sometimes by persuading and deluding the Council to neglect one opportunity with pretence of another, and this again of a third, and at last by persuading 'them' that it was not fit to fight at all.

To these heavy charges, Manchester,—furnished with his confused Crawford Documents, and a recriminatory Narrative about the Newbury battle,—makes heavy answer, at great length, about a week after : of which we shall remember only this piece of counter-charge, How his Lordship had once, in those very Newbury days, ordered Cromwell to proceed to some rendezvous with the horse, and Cromwell, very unsuitably for a Lieutenant-General, had answered, The horses were already worn off their feet ; "if your Lordship want to have the *skins* of the horses, this is the way to get them !"—Through which small slit, one looks into large seas of general discrepancy in those old months ! Lieutenant-General Cromwell is also reported to have said, in a moment of irritation surely, "There would never be a good time in England till we had done with Lords." But the most appalling report that now circulates in the world is this, of his saying once, "If he met the King in battle, he would fire his pistol at the King as at another ; "—pistol, at our poor semi-divine misguided Father fallen insane : a thing hardly conceivable to the Presbyterian human mind !

II. *In the House of Commons, on Wednesday 9th December, all sitting in Grand Committee, 'there was a general silence for a good space of time,' one looking upon the other to see who would break the ice, in regard to this delicate point of getting our Essexes and Manchesters softly ousted from the Army ; a very delicate point indeed ;—when Lieutenant-General Cromwell stood up, and spake shortly to this effect :*

It is now a time to speak, or forever hold the tongue. The important occasion now, is no less than To save a Nation, out of a bleeding, nay almost dying condition ; which the long continuance of this War hath already brought it into ; so that

without a more speedy, vigorous and effectual prosecution of
the War,—casting off all lingering proceedings like 'those of'
soldiers-of-fortune beyond sea, to spin out a war,—we shall
make the kingdom weary of us, and hate the name of a Par
liament.

For what do the enemy say? Nay, what do many say
that were friends at the beginning of the Parliament? Even
this, That the Members of both Houses have got great places
and commands, and the sword into their hands ; and, what
by interest in Parliament, what by power in the Army, will
perpetually continue themselves in grandeur, and not permit
the War speedily to end, lest their own power should determine
with it. This 'that' I speak here to our own faces, is but
what others do utter abroad behind our backs. I am far from
reflecting on any. I know the worth of those Commanders,
Members of both Houses, who are yet in power: but if I
may speak my conscience without reflection upon any, I do
conceive if the Army be not put into another method, and
the War more vigorously prosecuted, the People can bear
the War no longer, and will enforce you to a dishonourable
Peace.

But this I would recommend to your prudence, Not to
insist upon any complaint or oversight of any Commander-in-
chief upon any occasion whatsoever ; for as I must acknowledge
myself guilty of oversights, so I know they can rarely be avoided
in military affairs. Therefore waving a strict inquiry into the
causes of these things, let us apply ourselves to the remedy ;
which is most necessary. And I hope we have such true
English hearts, and zealous affections towards the general weal
of our Mother Country, as no Members of either House will
scruple to *deny* themselves, and their own private interests,
for the public good ; nor account it to be a dishonour done to
them, whatever the Parliament shall resolve upon in this weighty
matter.

III. *On the same day, seemingly at a subsequent part of the debate,
Lieutenant-General Cromwell said likewise, as follows:*

Mr. Speaker,—I am not of the mind that the calling of the
Members to sit in Parliament will break, or scatter our Armies.
I can speak this for my own soldiers, that they look not upon
me, but upon you ; and for you they will fight, and live and
die in your Cause ; and if others be of that mind that they are

of, you need not fear them. They do not idolise me, but look
upon the Cause they fight for. You may lay upon them what
commands you please, they will obey your commands in that
Cause they fight for.

To be brief, Mr. Zouch Tate, Member for Northampton,
moved this day a Self-denying Ordinance; which, in a few
days more, was passed in the Commons. It was not so easily
got through the Lords; but there too it had ultimately to pass.
One of the most important clauses was this, introduced not
without difficulty. That religious men might now serve
without taking the Covenant as a *first* preliminary,—perhaps they
might take it by and by. This was a great ease to tender
consciences; and indicates a deep split, which will grow wider
and wider, in our religious affairs. The Scots Commissioners
have sent for Whitlocke and Maynard to the Lord General's,
to ask in judicious Scotch dialect, Whether there be not ground
to prosecute Cromwell as an 'incendiary'? "You ken varry
weel!"—The two learned gentlemen shook their heads.

This Self-denying Ordinance had to pass; it and the New
Model wholly; by the steps indicated below.[1] Essex was
gratified by a splendid Pension,—very little of it ever actually
paid; for indeed he died some two years after: Manchester
was put on the Committee of Both Kingdoms: the Parliament
had its New-Model Army, and soon saw an entirely new epoch
in its affairs.

LETTER X

BEFORE the old Officers laid down their commissions, Waller
with Cromwell and Massey were sent on an expedition into the
West against Goring and Company; concerning which there
is some echo in the old Books and Commons Journals, but no
definite vestige of it, except the following Letter, read in the

---

[1] Self-denying Ordinance *passed* in the Commons 19th December,
and is sent to the Lords; Conference about it, 7th January; *rejected*
by the Lords 15th January,—because "we do not know what *shape*
the Army will now suddenly take." Whereupon, 21st January,
'Fairfax is nominated General;' and on the 19th February, the New
Model is completed and passed: "*This* is the shape the Army is to
take." A second Self-denying Ordinance, now introduced, got itself
finally passed 3d April 1645.

House of Commons, 9th April 1645 ; which D'Ewes happily had given his Clerk to copy. The Expedition itself, which proved successful, is now coming towards an end. Fairfax the new General is at Windsor all April ; full of business, regimenting, discharging, enlisting, new-modelling.

For the Right Honourable Sir Thomas Fairfax, General of the Army: Haste, Haste: These: At Windsor.

'Salisbury,' 9th April (ten o'clock at night) 1645.

SIR,

Upon Sunday last we marched towards Bruton in Somersetshire, which was General Goring's head-quarter : but he would not stand us ; but marched away, upon our appearance, to Wells and Glastonbury. Whither we held it unsafe to follow him ; lest we should engage our Body of Horse too far into that enclosed country, not having foot enough to stand by them ; and partly because we doubted the advance of Prince Rupert with his force to join with Goring ; having some notice from Colonel Massey of the Prince his coming this way.

General Goring hath 'Sir Richard' Greenvil in a near posture to join with him. He hath all their Garrisons in Devon, Dorset and Somersetshire, to make an addition to him. Whereupon, Sir William Waller having a very poor Infantry of about 1,600 men,—lest they, being so inconsiderable, should engage[1] our Horse,—we came from Shaftesbury to Salisbury to secure our Foot ; to prevent our being necessitated to a too unequal engagement, and to be nearer a communication with our friends.

Since our coming hither, we hear Prince Rupert is come to Marshfield, a market-town not far from Trowbridge. If the enemy advance altogether, how far we may be endangered,— that I humbly offer to you ; entreating you to take care of us, and to send us with all speed such an assistance, to Salisbury, as may enable us to keep the field and repel the enemy, if God assist us : at least to secure and countenance us, so as that we be not put to the shame and hazard of a retreat ; which will lose the Parliament many friends in these parts, who will think themselves abandoned on our departure from them. Sir, I beseech you send what Horse and Foot you can spare towards Salisbury, by way of Kingscleere, with what convenient

[1] Entangle or incumber.

expedition may be. Truly we look to be attempted upon every day.

These things being humbly represented to your knowledge and care, I subscribe myself,

Your most humble servant,
OLIVER CROMWELL.

LETTERS XI., ETC.

PRINCE RUPERT had withdrawn without fighting; was now at Worcester with a considerable force, meditating new infall. For which end, we hear, he has sent 2,000 men across the country to his Majesty at Oxford, to convoy 'his Majesty's person and the Artillery over to Worcester to him,'—both of which objects are like to be useful there. The Committee of Both Kingdoms order the said Convoy to be attacked.

'The charge of this service they recommended particularly to 'General Cromwell, who looking on himself now as discharged 'of military employment by the New Ordinance, which was 'to take effect within few days, and to have no longer oppor- 'tunity to serve his country in that way,—was, the night before, 'come to Windsor, from his service in the West, to kiss the 'General's hand and take leave of him: when, in the morning 'ere he was come forth of his chamber, those commands, than 'which he thought of nothing less in all the world, came to 'him from the Committee of Both Kingdoms.'[1]

'The night before' must mean, to all appearance, the 22d of April. How Cromwell instantly took horse; plunged into Oxfordshire, and on the 24th, at Islip Bridge, attacked and routed this said Convoy; and the same day, 'merely by dragoons' and fierce countenance, took Bletchington House, for which poor Colonel Windebank was shot, so angry were they; all this is known from Clarendon, or more authentically from Rushworth; and here now is Cromwell's own account of it:

---

[1] Sprigge's Anglia Rediviva (London, 1647), p. 10. Sprigge was one of Fairfax's Chaplains; his Book, a rather ornate work, gives florid but authentic and sufficient account of this New-Model Army in all its features and operations, by which 'England' had 'come alive again.' A little sparing in dates; but correct where they are given. None of the old Books is better worth reprinting.

LETTER XI

'COMMITTEE of Both Kingdoms,' first set up in February gone a year, when the Scotch Army came to help, has been the Executive in the War-department ever since; a great but now a rapidly declining authority. Sits at Derby House: Four Scotch; Twenty-one English, of whom Six a quorum. Johnston of Warriston is the notablest Scotchman; among the leading English are Philip Lord Wharton and the Younger Vane.

'Watlington' is in the Southeast nook of Oxfordshire; a day's march from Windsor. 'Major-General Browne' commands at Abingdon; a City Wood-merchant once; a zealous soldier of Presbyterian principles, at present. The rendezvous at Watlington took place on Wednesday night; the 25th of April is Friday.

To the Right Honourable the Committee of Both Kingdoms, at Derby House: These.

Bletchington, 25th April 1645.

MY LORDS AND GENTLEMEN,

According to your Lordships' appointment, I have attended your Service in these parts; and have not had so fit an opportunity to give you an account as now.

So soon as I received your commands, I appointed a rendezvous at Watlington. The body being come up, I marched to Wheatley Bridge, having sent before to Major-General Browne for intelligence; and it being market-day at Oxford, from whence I likewise hoped, by some of the market-people, to gain notice where the Enemy was.

Towards night I received certain notice by Major-General Browne, that the Carriages were not stirred, that Prince Maurice was not here; and by some Oxford scholars, that there were Four Carriages and Wagons ready in one place, and in another Five; all, as I conceived, fit for a march.[1]

I received notice also that the Earl of Northampton's Regiment was quartered at Islip; wherefore in the evening I marched that way, hoping to have surprised them; but, by the mistake and failing of the forlorn-hope, they had an alarm there, and to all their quarters, and so escaped me; by means whereof they had time to draw all together.

I kept my body all night at Islip: and, in the morning, a

---

[1] 'March.' out towards Worcester.

party of the Earl of Northampton's Regiment, the Lord Wilmot's and the Queen's, came to make an infall upon me. Sir Thomas Fairfax's Regiment was the first that took the field; the rest drew out with all possible speed. That which is the General's Troop charged a whole squadron of the Enemy, and presently broke it. Our other Troops coming seasonably on, the rest of the Enemy were presently put into confusion; so that we had the chase of them three or four miles; wherein we killed many, and took near Two-hundred prisoners, and about Four-hundred horse.

Many of them escaped towards Oxford and Woodstock, divers were drowned; and others got into a strong House in Bletchington, belonging to Sir Thomas Cogan; wherein Colonel Windebank kept a garrison with near Two-hundred men. Whom I presently summoned; and after a long Treaty, he went out, about twelve at night, with these Terms here enclosed; leaving us between Two and Three-hundred muskets, besides horse-arms, and other ammunition, and about Threescore-and eleven horses more.

This was the mercy of God; and nothing is more due than a real acknowledgment. And though I have had greater mercies, yet none clearer: because, in the first 'place,' God brought them to our hands when we looked not for them; and delivered them out of our hands, when we laid a reasonable design to surprise them, and which we carefully endeavoured. His mercy appears in this also, That I did much doubt the storming of the House, it being strong and well manned, and I havıng few dragoons, and this being not my business;—and yet we got it.

I hope you will pardon me if I say, God is not enough owned. We look too much to men and visible helps: this hath much hindered our success. But I hope God will direct all to acknowledge Him alone in all 'things.'

Your most humble servant,
OLIVER CROMWELL.

Poor Windebank was shot by sudden Court-martial, so enraged were they at Oxford,—for Cromwell had not even foot-soldiers, still less a battering gun. It was his poor young Wife, they said, she and other 'ladies on a visit there,' that had confused poor Windebank: he set his back to the wall of Merton College, and received his death-volley with a soldier's stoicism. The Son of Secretary Windebank, who fled beyond seas long since.

LETTER XII

By letter here following it will be seen that Lieutenant-General Cromwell has never yet resumed his Parliamentary duty. In fact, he is in the Associated Counties, raising force; 'for protection of the Isle of Ely,' and other purposes. To Fairfax and his Officers, to the Parliament, to the Committee of Both Kingdoms, to all persons, it is clear that Cromwell cannot be dispensed with. Fairfax and the Officers petition Parliament that he may be appointed their Lieutenant-General, Commander-in-Chief of the Horse. There is a clear necessity in it. Parliament, the Commons somewhat more readily than the Lords, continue, by instalments of 'forty days,' of 'three months,' his services in the Army; and at length grow to regard him as a constant element there. A few others got similar leave of absence, similar dispensation from the Self-denying Ordinance. Sprigge's words, cited above, are no doubt veracious; yet there is trace of evidence that Cromwell's continuance in the Army had, even by the framers of the Self-denying Ordinance, been considered a thing possible, a thing desirable. As it well might! To Cromwell himself there was no overpowering felicity in getting out to be shot at, except where wanted; he very probably, as Sprigge intimates, did let the matter in silence take its own course.

'*To the Right Honourable Sir Thomas Fairfax, General o, the Parliament's Army: These.*'

Huntingdon, 4th June 1645.

Sir,
    I most humbly beseech you to pardon my long silence. I am conscious of the fault, considering the great obligations lying upon me. But since my coming into these parts, I have been busied to secure that part of the Isle of Ely where I conceived most danger to be.

Truly I found it in a very ill posture: and it is yet but weak; without works, ammunition or men considerable,—and of money least: and then, I hope, you will easily conceive of the defence: and God has preserved us all this while to a miracle. The party under Vermuyden waits the King's Army, and is about Deeping; has a command to join with Sir John Gell, if he commands him. So 'too' the Nottingham Horse. I shall be bold to present you with intelligence as it comes to me.

I am bold to present this as my humble suit: That you would be pleased to make Captain Rawlins, this Bearer, a Captain of Horse. He has been so before; was nominated to the Model; is a most honest man. Colonel Sidney leaving his regiment, if it please you to bestow *his* Troop on him, I am confident he will serve you faithfully. So, by God's assistance, will

Your most humble servant,
OLIVER CROMWELL.

The 'Vermuyden' mentioned here, who became Colonel Vermuyden, is supposed to be a son of the Dutch Engineer who drained the Fens. 'Colonel Sidney' is the celebrated Algernon; he was nominated in the 'Model,' but is 'leaving his regiment;' having been appointed Governor of Chichester. Captain Rawlins does obtain a Company of Horse; under 'Colonel Sir Robert Pye.'—Colonel Montague, afterwards Earl of Sandwich, has a Foot-Regiment here. Hugh Peters is 'Chaplain to the Train.'

LETTER XIII

NASEBY

THE old Hamlet of Naseby stands yet, on its old hill-top, very much as it did in Saxon days, on the Northwestern border of Northamptonshire; some seven or eight miles from Market-Harborough in Leicestershire; nearly on a line, and nearly midway, between that Town and Daventry. A peaceful old Hamlet, of some eight hundred souls; clay cottages for labourers, but neatly thatched and swept; smith's shop, saddler's shop, beer-shop, all in order; forming a kind of square, which leads off Southwards into two long streets: the old Church, with its graves, stands in the centre, the truncated spire finishing itself with a strange old Ball, held up by rods; a 'hollow copper Ball, which came from Boulogne in Henry the Eighth's time,'—which has, like Hudibras's breeches, 'been at the Siege of Bullen.' The ground is upland, moorland, though now growing corn; was not enclosed till the last generation, and is still somewhat bare of wood. It stands nearly in the heart of England: gentle Dulness, taking a turn at etymology, sometimes derives it from *Navel*; 'Navesby, quasi *Navels*by, from being,' &c.: Avon Well, the distinct source of Shakespeare's Avon, is on the Western slope of the high grounds; Nen and

Welland, streams leading towards Cromwell's Fen-country, begin to gather themselves from boggy places on the Eastern side. The grounds, as we say, lie high; and are still, in their new subdivisions, known by the name of 'Hills,' 'Rutput Hill,' 'Mill Hill,' 'Dust Hill,' and the like, precisely as in Rushworth's time: but they are not properly hills at all; they are broad blunt clayey masses, swelling towards and from each other, like indolent waves of a sea, sometimes of miles in extent.

It was on this high moor-ground, in the centre of England, that King Charles, on the 14th of June 1645, fought his last battle; dashed fiercely against the New-Model Army, which he had despised till then; and saw himself shivered utterly to ruin thereby. 'Prince Rupert, on the King's right wing, charged *up* the hill, and carried all before him;' but Lieutenant-General Cromwell charged downhill on the other wing, likewise carrying all before him,—and did *not* gallop off the field to plunder, he. Cromwell, ordered thither by the Parliament, had arrived from the Association two days before, 'amid shouts from the whole Army:' he had the ordering of the Horse this morning. Prince Rupert, on returning from his plunder, finds the King's Infantry a ruin; prepares to charge again with the rallied Cavalry; but the Cavalry too, when it came to the point, 'broke all asunder,'—never to reassemble more. The chase went through Harborough; where the King had already been that morning, when in an evil hour he turned back, to revenge some 'surprise of an outpost at Naseby the night before,' and give the Roundheads battle.

Ample details of this Battle, and of the movements prior and posterior to it, are to be found in Sprigge, or copied with some abridgment into Rushworth; who has also copied a strange old Plan of the Battle; half plan, half picture, which the Sale-Catalogues are very chary of, in the case of Sprigge. By assiduous attention, aided by this Plan, as the old names yet stick to the localities, the Narrative can still be, and has lately been, pretty accurately verified, and the Figure of the old Battle dimly brought back again. The reader shall imagine it, for the present.—On the crown of Naseby Height stands a modern Battle-monument; but, by an unlucky oversight, it is above a mile to the east of where the Battle really was. There are likewise two modern Books about Naseby and its Battle; both of them without value.

The Parliamentary Army stood ranged on the Height still partly called 'Mill Hill,' as in Rushworth's time, a mile and

half from Naseby; the King's Army, on a parallel 'Hill, its back to Harborough;—with the wide table of upland now named *Broad Moor* between them; where indeed the main brunt of the action still clearly enough shows itself to have been. There are hollow spots, of a rank vegetation, scattered over that Broad Moor, which are understood to have once been buried *mounds*;—some of which, one to my knowledge, have been (with more or less of sacrilege) verified as such. A friend of mine has in his cabinet two ancient grinder-teeth, dug lately from that ground,—and waits for an opportunity to rebury them there. Sound effectual grinders, one of them very large; which ate their breakfast on the fourteenth morning of June two hundred years ago, and, except to be clenched once in grim battle, had never work to do more in this world!—
'A stack of dead bodies, perhaps about 100, had been buried 'in this Trench; piled as in a wall, a man's length thick: 'the skeletons lay in courses, the heads of one course to 'the heels of the next; one figure, by the strange position 'of the bones, gave us the hideous notion of its having been 'thrown in *before* death! We did not proceed far:—perhaps 'some half-dozen skeletons. The bones were treated with all 'piety; watched rigorously, over Sunday, till they could be 'covered in again.' Sweet friends, for Jesus' sake forbear!—

At this Battle Mr. John Rushworth, our Historical Rushworth, had, unexpectedly, for some instants, sight of a very famous person. Mr. John is Secretary to Fairfax; and they have placed him today among the Baggage-wagons, near Naseby Hamlet, above a mile from the fighting, where he waits in an anxious manner. It is known how Prince Rupert broke our left wing, while Cromwell was breaking their left. 'A Gentleman of Public Employment in the late Service near Naseby' writes next day, 'Harborough, 15th June, 2 in the morning,' a rough graphic Letter in the Newspapers, wherein is this sentence:

* * 'A party of theirs that broke through the left wing 'of horse, came quite behind the rear to our Train: the 'Leader of them, being a person somewhat in habit like the 'General, in a red montero, as the General had. He came 'as a friend; our commander of the guard of the Train 'went with his hat in his hand, and asked him, How the 'day went? thinking it had been the General: the Cavalier, 'who we since heard was Rupert, asked him and the rest, 'If they would have quarter? They cried No; gave fire,

'and instantly beat them off. It was a happy deliverance,'—
without doubt.

There were taken here a good few 'ladies of quality in
carriages ;'—and above a hundred Irish ladies not of quality,
tattery camp-followers 'with long skean-knives about a foot
in length,' which they well knew how to use ; upon whom I
fear the Ordinance against Papists pressed hard this day. The
King's Carriage was also taken, with a Cabinet and many
Royal Autographs in it, which when printed made a sad
impression against his Majesty,—gave in fact a most melancholy
view of the veracity of his Majesty, "On the word of a King."
All was lost !—

Here is Cromwell's Letter, written from Harborough, or
'Haverbrowe' as he calls it, that same night ; after the hot
Battle and hot chase were over. The original, printed long
since in Rushworth, still lies in the British Museum,—with
'a strong steady signature,' which one could look at with
interest. 'The Letter consists of two leaves ; much worn,
'and now supported by pasting, red seal much defaced ; is
addressed on the second leaf:'

*For the Honourable William Lenthall, Speaker of the Commons
House of Parliament : These.*

Harborough, 14th June 1645.

SIR,

Being commanded by you to this service, I think myself
bound to acquaint you with the good hand of God towards
you and us.

We marched yesterday after the King, who went before us
from Daventry to Harborough ; and quartered about six miles
from him. This day we marched towards him. He drew out
to meet us ; both Armies engaged. We, after three hours fight
very doubtful, at last routed his Army ; killed and took about
5,000,—very many officers, but of what quality we yet know
not. We took also about 200 carriages, all he had ; and all
his guns, being 12 in number, whereof two were demi-cannon,
two demi-culverins, and I think the rest sackers. We pursued
the Enemy from three miles short of Harborough to nine
beyond, even to the sight of Leicester, whither the King fled.

Sir, this is none other but the hand of God ; and to Him
alone belongs the glory, wherein none are to share with Him.
The General served you with all faithfulness and honour :

and the best commendation I can give him is, That I daresay he attributes all to God, and would rather perish than assume to himself. Which is an honest and a thriving way:—and yet as much for bravery may be given to him, in this action, as to a man. Honest men served you faithfully in this action. Sir, they are trusty; I beseech you, in the name of God, not to discourage them. I wish this action may beget thankfulness and humility in all that are concerned in it. He that ventures his life for the liberty of his country, I wish he trust God for the liberty of his conscience, and you for the liberty he fights for. In this he rests, who is

Your most humble servant,
OLIVER CROMWELL.

John Bunyan, I believe, is this night in Leicester,—not yet writing his *Pilgrim's Progress* on paper, but acting it on the face of the Earth, with a brown matchlock on his shoulder. Or rather, *without* the matchlock, just at present; Leicester and he having been taken the other day. 'Harborough Church' is getting 'filled with prisoners' while Oliver writes,—and an immense contemporaneous tumult everywhere going on!

The 'honest men who served you faithfully' on this occasion are the considerable portion of the Army who have not yet succeeded in bringing themselves to take the Covenant. Whom the Presbyterian Party, rigorous for their own formula, call 'Schismatics,' 'Sectaries,' 'Anabaptists,' and other hard names; whom Cromwell, here and elsewhere, earnestly pleads for. To Cromwell, perhaps as much as to another, order was lovely, and disorder hateful; but he discerned better than some others what order and disorder really were. The forest-trees are not in 'order' because they are all clipt into the same shape of Dutch-dragons, and forced to die or grow in that way; but because in each of them there is the same genuine unity of life, from the inmost pith to the outmost leaf, and they do grow according to that!—Cromwell naturally became the head of this Schismatic Party, intent to grow not as Dutch-dragons, but as real trees; a Party which naturally increased with the increasing earnestness of events and of men.—

The King stayed but a few hours in Leicester; he had taken Leicester, as we saw, some days before, and now it was to be retaken from him some days after :—he stayed but a few hours here; rode on, that same night, to Ashby-de-la-Zouch, which he reached 'at daybreak,'—poor wearied King!—then again swiftly

Westward, to Wales, to Ragland Castle, to this place and that ; in the hope of raising some force, and coming to fight again ; which, however, he could never do. Some ten months more of roaming, and he, 'disguised as a groom,' will be riding with Parson Hudson towards the Scots at Newark.

The New-Model Army marched into the Southwest ; very soon 'relieved Colonel Robert Blake' (Admiral Blake), and many others ;—marched to ever new exploits and victories, which excite the pious admiration of Joshua Sprigge ; and very soon swept all its enemies from the field, and brought this War to a close.

LETTER XIV

STORM OF BRISTOL

'ON the Lord's Day, September 21, according to Order of 'Parliament, Lieutenant-General Cromwell's Letter on the 'taking of Bristol was read in the several Congregations about 'London, and thanks returned to Almighty God for the admir-'able and wonderful reducing of that city. The Letter of the 'renowned Commander is well worth observation.' For the Siege itself and what preceded and followed it, see, besides this Letter, Rupert's own account, and the ample details of Sprigge copied with abridgment by Rushworth : Sayer's *History of Bristol* gives Plans, and all manner of local details, though in a rather vague way.

For the Honourable William Lenthall, Speaker of the Commons House of Parliament: These.

Bristol, 14th September 1645.

SIR,

It has pleased the General to give me in charge to represent unto you a particular account of the taking of Bristol ; the which I gladly undertake.

After the finishing of that service at Sherborne, it was disputed at a council of war, Whether we should march into the West or to Bristol ? Amongst other arguments, the leaving so considerable an enemy at our backs, to march into the heart of the Kingdom, the undoing of the country about Bristol, which was 'already' exceedingly harassed by the Prince his being thereabouts but a fortnight ; the correspondency he might hold in Wales ; the possibility of uniting the Enemy's

forces where they pleased, and specially of drawing to an head
the disaffected Clubmen of Somerset, Wilts and Dorset, when
once our backs were toward them : these considerations, together
with 'the hope of' taking so important a place, so advantageous
for the opening of trade to London,—did sway the balance,
and beget that conclusion.

When we came within four miles of the city, we had a
new debate, Whether we should endeavour to block it up, or
make a regular siege ? The latter being overruled, Colonel
Welden with his brigade marched to Pile Hill, on the South
side of the City, being within musket-shot thereof :—where
in a few days they made a good quarter, overlooking the City.
Upon our advance, the enemy fired Bedminster, Clifton, and
some other villages lying near to the City; and would have
fired more, if our unexpected coming had not hindered. The
General caused some Horse and Dragoons under Commissary-
General Ireton to advance over Avon, to keep-in the enemy
on the North side of the Town, till the foot could come up :
and after a day, the General, with Colonel Montague's and
Colonel Rainsborough's Brigades, marched over at Kensham
to Stapleton, where he quartered that night. The next day,
Colonel Montague, having this post assigned with his brigade,
To secure all between the Rivers Froom and Avon ; he came
up to Lawford's Gate, within musket-shot thereof. Colonel
Rainsborough's post was near to Durham Down, whereof the
Dragoons and three regiments of Horse made good a post upon
the Down, between him and the River Avon, on his right
hand. And from Colonel Rainsborough's quarters to Froom
River, on his left, a part of Colonel Birch's, and 'the whole of'
General Skippon's regiment were to maintain that post.

These posts thus settled, our Horse were forced to be upon
exceeding great duty ; to stand by the Foot, lest the Foot,
being so weak in all their posts, might receive an affront. And
truly herein we were very happy, that we should receive so
little loss by sallies ; considering the paucity of our men to
make good the posts, and strength of the enemy within. By
sallies (which were three or four) I know not that we lost
thirty men in all the time of our siege. Of officers of quality,
only Colonel Okey was taken by mistake (going 'of himself'
to the enemy, thinking they had been friends), and Captain
Guilliams slain in a charge. We took Sir Bernard Astley ;
and killed Sir Richard Crane,—one very considerable with
the Prince.

We had a council of war concerning the storming of the
Town, about eight days before we took it; and in that there
appeared great unwillingness to the work, through the unseason-
ableness of the weather, and other apparent difficulties. Some
inducement to bring us thither had been the report of the good
affection of the Townsmen to us; but that did not answer
expectation. Upon a second consideration, it was overruled
for a storm. And all things seemed to favour the design;—
and truly there hath been seldom the like cheerfulness to any
work like to this, after it was once resolved upon. The day
and hour of our storm was appointed to be on Wednesday
morning, the Tenth of September, about one of the clock.
We chose to act it so early because we hoped thereby to surprise
the Enemy. With this resolution also, to avoid confusion
and falling foul one upon another, That when 'once' we
had recovered[1] the Line, and Forts upon it, we should not
advance further till day. The General's signal unto a storm
was to be, The firing of straw, and discharging four pieces
of cannon at Pryor's Hill Fort.

The signal was very well perceived of all;—and truly the
men went on with great resolution; and very presently recovered
the Line, making way for the Horse to enter. Colonel
Montague and Colonel Pickering, who stormed at Lawford's
Gate, where was a double work, well filled with men and
cannon, presently entered; and with great resolution beat the
Enemy from their works, and possessed their cannon. Their
expedition was such that they forced the Enemy from their
advantages, without any considerable loss to themselves. They
laid down the bridges for the Horse to enter;—Major Desborow
commanding the Horse; who very gallantly seconded the Foot.
Then our Foot advanced to the City Walls; where they
possessed the Gate against the Castle Street: whereinto were put
a Hundred men; who made it good. Sir Hardress Waller with
his own and the General's regiment, with no less resolution,
entered on the other side of Lawford's Gate, towards Avon
River; and put themselves into immediate conjunction with the
rest of the brigade.

During this, Colonel Rainsborough and Colonel Hammond
attempted Pryor's Hill Fort, and the Line downwards towards
Froom; and the Major-General's regiment being to storm to-

[1] *recovered* means 'taken,' 'got possession of:' *the Line* is a new
earthen work outside the walls; very deficient in height, according
to Rupert's account.

wards Froom River, Colonel Hammond possessed the Line
immediately, and beating the enemy from it, made way for the
Horse to enter. Colonel Rainsborough, who had the hardest
task of all at Pryor's Hill Fort, attempted it ; and fought near
three hours for it. And indeed there was great despair of
carrying the place ; it being exceeding high, a ladder of thirty
rounds scarcely reaching the top thereof; but his resolution was
such that, notwithstanding the inaccessibleness and difficulty, he
would not give it over. The Enemy had four pieces of cannon
upon it, which they plied with round and case shot upon our
men : his Lieutenant-Colonel Bowen, and others, were two
hours at push of pike, standing upon the palisadoes, but could
not enter. 'But now' Colonel Hammond being entered the
Line (and 'here' Captain Ireton,[1] with a forlorn of Colonel
Rich's regiment, interposing with his Horse between the Enemy's
Horse and Colonel Hammond, received a shot with two pistol
bullets, which broke his arm),—by means of this entrance of
Colonel Hammond they did storm the Fort on that part which
was inward ; 'and so' Colonel Rainsborough's and Colonel
Hammond's men entered the Fort, and immediately put almost
all the men in it to the sword.

And as this was the place of most difficulty, so 'it was' of
most loss to us on that side,—and of very great honour to the
undertaker. The Horse 'too' did second them with great
resolution : both these Colonels do acknowledge that *their*
interposition between the Enemy's Horse and their Foot was
a great means of obtaining of this strong Fort. Without
which all the rest of the Line to Froom River would have
done us little good : and indeed neither Horse nor Foot could
have stood in all that way, in any manner of security, had
not the Fort been taken.—Major Bethel's were the first Horse
that entered the Line; who did behave himself gallantly; and
was shot in the thigh, had one or two shot more, and had
his horse shot under him. Colonel Birch with his men, and
the Major-General's regiment, entered with very good resolution
where their post was ; possessing the Enemy's guns, and turning
them upon them.

By this, all the Line from Pryor's Hill Fort to Avon (which
was a full mile), with all the forts, ordnance and bulwarks, were
possessed by us ;—save one, wherein were about Two-hundred

[1] This is not the famous Ireton; this is his Brother. 'Commissary-General Ireton' is also here; he is not wedded yet.

TAKING OF BRISTOL

and twenty men of the Enemy; which the General summoned, and all the men submitted.

The success on Colonel Weldon's side did not answer with this. And although the Colonels, and other the officers and soldiers both Horse and Foot, testified as much resolution as could be expected,—Colonel Weldon, Colonel Ingoldsby, Colonel Herbert, and the rest of the Colonels and Officers, both of Horse and Foot, doing what could be well looked for from men of honour,—yet what by reason of the height of the works, which proved higher than report made them, and the shortness of the ladders, they were repulsed, with the loss of about a Hundred men. Colonel Fortescue's Lieutenant-Colonel was killed, and Major Cromwell[1] dangerously shot; and two of Colonel Ingoldsby's brothers hurt; with some Officers.

Being possessed of thus much as hath been related, the Town was fired in three places by the Enemy; which we could not put out. Which begat a great trouble in the General, and us all; fearing to see so famous a City burnt to ashes before our faces. Whilst we were viewing so sad a spectacle, and consulting which way to make further advantage of our success, the Prince sent a trumpet to the General to desire a treaty for the surrender of the Town. To which the General agreed; and deputed Colonel Montague, Colonel Rainsborough, and Colonel Pickering for that service; authorising them with instructions to treat and conclude the Articles,—which 'accordingly' are these enclosed. For performance whereof hostages were mutually given.

On Thursday about two of the clock in the afternoon, the Prince marched out; having a convoy of two regiments of Horse from us; and making election of Oxford for the place he would go to, which he had liberty to do by his Articles.

The cannon which we have taken are about a Hundred-and-forty mounted; about a Hundred barrels of powder already come to our hands, with a good quantity of shot, ammunition, and arms. We have found already between Two and Three-thousand muskets. The Royal Fort had victual in it for a Hundred-and-fifty men, for Three-hundred-and-twenty days; the Castle victualled for nearly half so long. The Prince had in Foot of the Garrison, as the Mayor of the City informed me,

---

[1] A cousin.

Two-thousand five-hundred, and about a thousand Horse, besides the Trained Bands of the Town, and Auxiliaries a Thousand, some say a Thousand five-hundred.—I hear but of one man that hath died of the plague in all our Army, although we have quartered amongst and in the midst of infected persons and places. We had not killed of ours in the Storm, nor in all this Siege, Two-hundred men.

Thus I have given you a true, but not a full account of this great business; wherein he that runs may read, That all this is none other than the work of God. He must be a very Atheist that doth not acknowledge it.

It may be thought that some praises are due to those gallant men, of whose valour so much mention is made :—their humble suit to you and all that have an interest in this blessing, is, That in the remembrance of God's praises they be forgotten. It's their joy that they are instruments of God's glory, and their country's good. It's their honour that God vouchsafes to use them. Sir, they that have been employed in this service know, that faith and prayer obtained this City for you: I do not say ours only, but of the people of God with you and all England over, who have wrestled with God for a blessing in this very thing. Our desires are, that God may be glorified by the same spirit of faith by which we ask all our sufficiency, and have received it. It is meet that He have all the praise. Presbyterians, Independents, all have here the same spirit of faith and prayer; the same presence and answer; they agree here, have no names of difference—pity it is it should be otherwise anywhere! All that believe have the real unity, which is most glorious; because inward, and spiritual, in the Body, and to the Head. For being united in forms, commonly called Uniformity, every Christian will for peace-sake study and do, as far as conscience will permit. And for brethren, in things of the mind we look for no compulsion, but that of light and reason. In other things, God hath put the sword in the Parliament's hands,—for the terror of evil-doers, and the praise of them that do well. If any plead exemption from that,—he knows not the Gospel: if any would wring that out of your hands, or steal it from you under what pretence soever, I hope they shall do it without effect. That God may maintain it in your hands, and direct you in the use thereof, is the prayer of

Your humble servant,
OLIVER CROMWELL.

These last paragraphs are, as the old Newspapers say, 'very remarkable.' If modern readers suppose them to be 'cant,' it will turn out an entire mistake. I advise all modern readers not only to believe that Cromwell here means what he says; but even to try how *they*, each for himself in a new dialect, could mean the like or something better!—

Prince Rupert rode out of Bristol amid seas of angry human faces, glooming unutterable things upon him; growling audibly, in spite of his escort, "Why not hang *him!*" For indeed the poor Prince had been necessitated to much plunder; commanding 'the elixir of the Blackguardism of the Three Kingdoms,' with very insufficient funds for most part!—He begged a thousand muskets from Fairfax on this occasion, to assist his escort in protecting him across the country to Oxford; promising, on his honour, to return them after that Service. Fairfax lent the muskets; the Prince did honourably return them, what he had of them,—honourably apologising that so many had 'deserted' on the road, of whom neither man nor musket were recoverable at present.

LETTERS XV., ETC

From Bristol the Army turned Southward again, to deal with the yet remaining force of Royalism in that quarter. Sir Ralph Hopton, with Goring and others under him, made stubborn resistance; but were constantly worsted, at Langport, at Torrington, wheresoever they rallied and made a new attempt. The Parliament Army went steadily and rapidly on; storming Bridgewater, storming all manner of Towns and Castles; clearing the ground before them: till Sir Ralph was driven into Cornwall; and, without resource or escape, saw himself obliged next spring to surrender, and go beyond seas. A brave and honourable man; respected on both sides; and of all the King's Generals the most deserving respect. He lived in retirement abroad; taking no part in Charles Second's businesses; and died in honourable poverty before the Restoration.

The following Two Letters are what remain to us concerning Cromwell's share in that course of victories. He was present in various general or partial Fights from Langport to Bovey Tracey; became especially renowned by his Sieges, and took many Strong Places besides those mentioned here.

'*To the Right Honourable Sir Thomas Fairfax, General of the Parliament's Army: These.*'

'Winchester, 6th October 1645.'

SIR,
  I came to Winchester on the Lord's day, the 28th of September; with Colonel Pickering,—commanding his own, Colonel Montague's, and Sir Hardress Waller's regiments. After some dispute with the Governor, we entered the Town. I summoned the Castle; was denied; whereupon we fell to prepare batteries,—which we could not perfect (some of our guns being out of order) until Friday following. Our battery was six guns; which being finished,—after firing one round, I sent in a second summons for a treaty; which they refused. Whereupon we went on with our work, and made a breach in the wall near the Black Tower; which, after about 200 shot, we thought stormable; and purposed on Monday morning to attempt it. On Sunday night, about ten of the clock, the Governor beat a parley, desiring to treat. I agreed unto it; and sent Colonel Hammond and Major Harrison in to him, who agreed upon these enclosed Articles.

Sir, this is the addition of another mercy. You see God is not weary in doing you good: I confess, Sir, His favour to you is as visible, when He comes by His power upon the hearts of your enemies, making them quit places of strength to you, as when He gives courage to your soldiers to attempt hard things. His goodness in this is much to be acknowledged: for the Castle was well manned with Six-hundred-and-eighty horse and foot, there being near Two-hundred gentlemen, officers, and their servants; well victualled, with fifteen hundred-weight of cheese, very great store of wheat and beer; near twenty barrels of powder, seven pieces of cannon; the works were exceeding good and strong. It's very likely it would have cost much blood to have gained it by storm. We have not lost twelve men: this is repeated to you, that God may have all the praise, for it's all His due.

      Sir, I rest,
        Your most humble servant,
         OLIVER CROMWELL.

'Lieutenant-General Cromwell's Secretary,' who brings this Letter, gets 50*l.* for his good news. By Sprigge's account, he appears to have been 'Mr. Hugh Peters,' this Secretary. Peters

there makes a verbal Narrative of the affair, to Mr. Speaker and
the Commons, which, were not room so scanty, we should be
glad to insert.

It was at this surrender of Winchester that certain of the
captive enemies having complained of being plundered contrary
to Articles, Cromwell had the accused parties, six of his own
soldiers, tried: being all found guilty, one of them by lot
was hanged, and the other five were marched off to Oxford,
to be there disposed of as the Governor saw fit. The Oxford
Governor politely returned the five prisoners, 'with an acknowledgment of the Lieutenant-General's nobleness.'

LETTER XVI

BASING House, Pawlet Marquis of Winchester's Mansion,
stood, as the ruined heaps still testify, at a small distance from
Basingstoke in Hampshire. It had long infested the Parliament
in those quarters; and been especially a great eyesorrow to
the 'Trade of London with the Western Parts.' With
Donnington Castle at Newbury, and this Basing House at
Basingstoke, there was no travelling the western roads, except
with escort, or on sufferance. The two places had often been
attempted; but always in vain. Basing House especially had
stood siege after siege, for four years; ruining poor Colonel
This and then poor Colonel That; the jubilant Royalists
had given it the name of *Basting* House: there was, on the
Parliament side, a kind of passion to have Basing House taken.
The Lieutenant-General, gathering all the artillery he can lay
hold of; firing incessantly, 200 or 500 shot at some given
point till he see a hole made; and then storming like a
fire-flood:—he perhaps may manage it.

To the Honourable William Lenthall, Speaker of the
Commons House of Parliament: These.

Basingstoke 14th October 1645.

SIR,

I thank God, I can give you a good account of Basing.
After our batteries placed, we settled the several posts for
the storm: Colonel Dalbier was to be on the north side of
the House next the Grange; Colonel Pickering on his left
hand, and Sir Hardress Waller's and Colonel Montague's
regiments next him. We stormed, this morning, after six of

the clock: the signal for falling on was the firing four of our cannon; which being done, our men fell on with great resolution and cheerfulness. We took the two Houses without any considerable loss to ourselves. Colonel Pickering stormed the New House, passed through, and got the gate of the Old House; whereupon they summoned a parley, which our men would not hear.

In the mean time Colonel Montague's and Sir Hardress Waller's regiments assaulted the strongest work, where the Enemy kept his Court of Guard;—which, with great resolution, they recovered: beating the Enemy from a whole culverin, and from that work: which having done, they drew their ladders after them, and got over another work, and the house-wall, before they could enter. In this Sir Hardress Waller, performing his duty with honour and diligence, was shot in the arm. but not dangerously.

We have had little loss: many of the Enemy our men put to the sword, and some officers of quality; most of the rest we have prisoners, amongst whom the Marquis 'of Winchester himself,' and Sir Robert Peak, with divers other officers, whom I have ordered to be sent up to you. We have taken about ten pieces of ordnance, with much ammunition, and our soldiers a good encouragement.

I humbly offer to you, to have this place utterly slighted, for these following reasons: It will ask about Eight-hundred men to manage it; it is no frontier; the country is poor about it; the place exceedingly ruined by our batteries and mortar-pieces, and by a fire which fell upon the place since our taking it. If you please to take the Garrison at Farnham, some out of Chichester, and a good part of the foot which were here under Dalbier, and to make a strong Quarter at Newbury with three or four troops of horse,—I dare be confident it would not only be a curb to Donnington, but a security and a frontier to all these parts; inasmuch as Newbury lies upon the River, and will prevent any incursion from Donnington, Wallingford or Farringdon into these parts; and by lying there, will make the trade most secure between Bristol and London for all carriages. And I believe the gentlemen of Sussex and Hampshire will with more cheerfulness contribute to maintain a garrison on the frontier than in their bowels, which will have less safety in it.

Sir, I hope not to delay, but to march towards the West tomorrow; and to be as diligent as I may in my expedition thither. I must speak my judgment to you, That if you intend to have your work carried on, recruits of Foot must be had, and a course taken to pay your Army ; else, believe me, Sir, it may not be able to answer the work you have for it to do.

I entrusted Colonel Hammond to wait upon you, who was taken by a mistake whilst we lay before this Garrison, whom God safely delivered to us, to our great joy ; but to his loss of almost all he had, which the Enemy took from him. The Lord grant that these mercies may be acknowledged with all thankfulness : God exceedingly abounds in His goodness to us, and will not be weary until righteousness and peace meet ; and until He hath brought forth a glorious work for the happiness of this poor Kingdom. Wherein desires to serve God and you, with a faithful heart,

Your most humble servant,
OLIVER CROMWELL.

Colonel Hammond, whom we shall by and by see again, brought this good news to London, and had his reward, of 200*l* ; Mr. Peters also, being requested 'to make a relation to the House of Commons, spake as follows.' The reader will like to hear Mr. Peters for once, a man concerning whom he has heard so many falsehoods, and to see an old grim scene through his eyes. Mr. Peters related :

"That he came into Basing House some time after the storm," on Tuesday 14th of October 1645 ;—" and took a view "first of the works ; which were many, the circumvallation "being above a mile in compass. The Old House had stood "(as it is reported) two or three hundred years, a nest of "Idolatry ; the New House surpassing that, in beauty and state-"liness ; and either of them fit to make an emperor's court.

"The rooms before the storm (it seems), in both Houses, were "all completely furnished ; provisions for some years rather "than months ; 400 quarters of wheat ; bacon divers rooms-full, "containing hundreds of flitches ; cheese proportionable ; with "oatmeal, beef, pork ; beer divers cellars-full, and that very "good,"—Mr. Peters having taken a draught of the same.

"A bed in one room, furnished, which cost 1,300*l*. Popish "books many, with copes, and such utensils. In truth, the "House stood in its full pride ; and the Enemy was persuaded " that it would be the last piece of ground that would be taken " by the Parliament, because they had so often foiled our forces "which had formerly appeared before it. In the several rooms

"and about the House, there were slain, seventy-four, and only
"one woman, the daughter of Dr. Griffith, who by her railing,"
poor lady, "provoked our soldiers (then in heat) into a further
"passion. There lay dead upon the ground, Major Cuffle ;—a
"man of great account amongst them, and a notorious Papist ;
"slain by the hands of Major Harrison, that godly and gallant
"gentleman,"—all men know him ; "and Robinson the Player,
"who, a little before the storm, was known to be mocking and
"scorning the Parliament and our Army. Eight or nine gentle-
"women of rank, running forth together, were entertained by
"the common soldiers somewhat coarsely ;—yet not uncivilly,
"considering the action in hand.

"The plunder of the soldiers continued till Tuesday night :
"one soldier had a Hundred-and-twenty Pieces in gold for his
"share ; others plate, others jewels ;—among the rest, one got
"three bags of silver, which (he being not able to keep his own
"counsel) grew to be common pillage amongst the rest, and the
"fellow had but one half-crown left for himself at last.—The
"soldiers sold the wheat to country-people ; which they held up
"at good rates awhile ; but afterwards the market fell, and there
"were some abatements for haste. After that, they sold the
"household stuff ; whereof there was good store, and the country
"loaded away many carts ; and they continued a great while,
"fetching out all manner of household stuff, till they had
"fetched out all the stools, chairs, and other lumber, all which
"they sold to the country-people by piecemeal.

"In all these great buildings, there was not one iron bar left
"in all the windows (save only what were on fire), before night.
"And the last work of all was the lead ; and by Thursday
"morning, they had hardly left one gutter about the House.
"And what the soldiers left, the fire took hold on ; which made
"more than ordinary haste ; leaving nothing but bare walls and
"chimneys in less than twenty hours ;—being occasioned by
"the neglect of the Enemy in quenching a fire-ball of ours at
first."—What a scene !

"We know not how to give a just accout of the number
"of persons that were within. For we have not quite Three-
"hundred prisoners ; and it may be, have found a Hundred
"slain,—whose bodies, some being covered with rubbish, came
"not at once to our view. Only, riding to the House on
"Tuesday night, we heard divers crying in vaults for quarter ;
"but our men could neither come to them, nor they to us.
"Amongst those that we saw slain, one of their officers lying

"on the ground, seeming so exceeding tall, was measured; and "from his great toe to his crown was 9 feet in length" (*sic*).

"The Marquis being pressed, by Mr. Peters arguing with him," which was not very chivalrous in Mr. Peters, "broke out "and said, 'That if the King had no more ground in England "but Basing House, he would adventure as he did, and so "maintain it to the uttermost;'—meaning with these Papists; "comforting himself in this disaster, 'That Basing House was "called *Loyalty*.' But he was soon silenced in the question "concerning the King and Parliament; and could only hope "'That the King might have a day again.'—And thus the "Lord was pleased in a few hours to show us what mortal seed "all earthly glory grows upon; and how just and righteous "the ways of God are, who takes sinners in their own snares, "and lifteth up the hands of His despised people.

"This is now the Twentieth garrison that hath been taken-"in, this Summer, by this Army;—and, I believe most of them "the answers of the prayers, and trophies of the faith, of some "of God's servants. The Commander of this Brigade," Lieutenant General Cromwell, "had spent much time with God "in prayer the night before the storm;—and seldom fights "without some Text of Scripture to support him. This time "he rested upon that blessed word of God, written in the "Hundred-and-fifteenth Psalm, eighth verse, *They that make them* "*are like unto them; so is every one that trusteth in them.* Which, "with some verses going before, was now accomplished."[1]

'Mr. Peters presented the Marquis's own Colours, which 'he brought from Basing; the Motto of which was, *Donec pax* '*redeat terris*; the very same as King Charles gave upon his 'Coronation-money, when he came to the Crown.'—So Mr. Peters; and then withdrew,—getting by and by 200*l*. a-year settled on him.

---

[1] 'Not unto us, O Lord, not unto us, but unto Thy Name give 'glory; for Thy mercy and for Thy truth's sake. Wherefore should the 'Heathen say, Where is now their God? Our God is in the Heavens: 'he hath done whatsoever He hath pleased!—Their Idols are silver 'and gold; the work of men's hands. They have mouths, but they 'speak not; eyes have they, but they see not: they have ears, but 'they hear not; noses have they, but they smell not; they have hands, 'but they handle not; feet have they, but they walk not: neither 'speak they through their throat! They that make them are like 'unto them; so is every one that trusteth in them.'—These words, awful as the words of very God, were in Oliver Cromwell's heart that night.

This Letter was read in all Pulpits next Sunday, with thanks rendered to Heaven by order of Parliament. Basing House is to be carted away; 'whoever will come for brick or stone shall freely have the same for his pains.'

Among the names of the Prisoners taken here one reads that of *Inigo Jones,*—unfortunate old Inigo. Vertue, on what evidence I know not, asserts farther that Wenceslaus Hollar, with his graving tools, and unrivalled graving talent, was taken here. The Marquis of Winchester had been addicted to the Arts,—to the Upholsteries perhaps still more. A magnificent kind of man; whose 'best bed,' now laid bare to general inspection, excited the wonder of the world.

Basing is black ashes, then; and Langford is ours, the Garrison 'to march forth tomorrow at twelve of the clock, being the 18th instant.'[1] And now the question is, Shall we attack Donnington or not?—

Colonel Dalbier, a man of Dutch birth, well known to readers of the old Books, is with Cromwell at present; his Second in command. It was from Dalbier that Cromwell first of all learned the mechanical part of soldiering; he had Dalbier to help him in drilling his Ironsides; so says Heath, credible on such a point. Donnington Castle was not besieged at present; it surrendered next Spring to Dalbier.[2] Cromwell returned to Fairfax; served through Winter with him in the West, till all ended there.

About the middle of the month of September, the King had appeared again with some remnant of force, got together in Wales; with intent to relieve Chester, which was his key to Ireland: but this force too he saw shattered to pieces on Rowton Heath, near that City.[3] He had also had an eye towards the great Montrose in Scotland, who in these weeks was blazing at his highest there: but him too David Lesley with dragoons, emerging from the mist of the Autumn morning, on Philipshaugh near Selkirk, had, in one fell hour, trampled utterly out. The King had to retire to Wales again, to Oxford and obscurity again.

On the 14th of next March, as we said, Sir Ralph Hopton

[1] Spr.gge, p. 145.
[2] 1st April 1646 (Rushworth, vi. 252).
[3] 24th September 1645 (Rushworth, vi. 117; Lord Digby's account of it, Ormond Papers, ii. 90).

surrendered himself in Cornwall.[1] On the 22d of the same
month, Sir Jacob Astley, another distinguished Royalist General,
the last of them all,—coming towards Oxford with some small
force he had gathered,—was beaten and captured at Stow among
the Wolds of Gloucestershire:[2] surrendering himself, the brave
veteran said, or is reported to have said, "You have now done
"your work, and may go to play,—unless you will fall out
"among yourselves.

On Monday night, towards twelve of the clock, 27th April
1646, the King in disguise rode out of Oxford, somewhat uncertain whitherward,—at length towards Newark and the Scots
Army.[3] On the Wednesday before, Oliver Cromwell had returned to his place in Parliament.[4] Many detached Castles and
Towns still held out, Ragland Castle even till the next August;
scattered fires of an expiring conflagration, that need to be
extinguished with effort and in detail. Of all which victorious
sieges, with their elaborate treaties and moving accidents, the
theme of every tongue during that old Summer, let the following
one brief glimpse, notable on private grounds, suffice us at
present.

Oxford, the Royalist metropolis, a place full of Royalist
dignitaries, and of almost inexpugnable strength, had it not
been so disheartened from without,—was besieged by Fairfax
himself in the first days of May. There was but little fighting,
there was much negotiating, tedious consulting of Parliament
and King; the treaty did not end in surrender till Saturday
20th June. And now, dated on the Monday before, at Holton,
a country Parish in those parts, there is this still legible in the
old Church Register,—intimately interesting to some friends of
ours! 'HENRY IRETON, Commissary-General to Sir Thomas
'Fairfax, and BRIDGET, Daughter to Oliver Cromwell, Lieu-
'tenant-General of the Horse to the said Sir Thomas Fairfax,—
'were married, by Mr. Dell, in the Lady Whorwood her House
'in Holton, 15th June 1646.—ALBAN EALES, Rector.'[5]

Ireton, we are to remark, was one of Fairfax's Commissioners

[1] Hopton's own account of it, Ormond Papers, ii. 109-26.
[2] Rushworth, vi. 139-41.
[3] Ibid, vi. 267; Iter Carolinum.
[4] Cromwelliana, p. 31.
[5] Parish Register of Holton (copied, Oct. 1846) Poor Noble (i. 134)
seems to have copied this same Register, and to have misread his own
Note: giving instead of Holton, *Nalton*, an imaginary place; and
instead of June, *January*, an impossible date.

on the Treaty for surrendering Oxford, and busy under the walls there at present: Holton is some five miles east of the City; Holton House we guess by various indications to have been Fairfax's own quarter. Dell, already and afterwards well known, was the General's Chaplain at this date. Of 'the Lady Whorwood' I have traces, rather in the Royalist direction; her strong moated House, very useful to Fairfax in those weeks, still stands conspicuous in that region, though now under new figure and ownership; drawbridge become *fixed*, deep ditch now dry, moated island changed into a flower-garden;—'rebuilt in 1807.' Fairfax's Lines, we observe, extended, 'from Headington Hill to Marston,' several miles in advance of Holton House, then 'from Marston across the Cherwell, and over from that to the 'Isis on the North side of the City;' southward and elsewhere, the besieged, 'by a dam at St. Clement's Bridge, had laid the 'country all under water:'—in such scene, with the treaty just ending and general Peace like to follow, did Ireton welcome his Bride,—a brave young damsel of twenty-one; escorted, doubtless by her Father among others, to the Lord General's house; and there, by the Rev. Mr. Dell, solemnly handed over to new destinies!

This wedding was on Monday 15th June; on Saturday came the final signing of the treaty; and directly thereupon, on Monday *next*, Prince Rupert and Prince Maurice took the road, with their attendants, and their passes to the sea-coast; a sight for the curious. On Tuesday 'there went about 300 persons mostly of quality;' and on Wednesday all the Royalist force, '3,000' (or say 2,000) 'to the Eastward, 500 to the North;' with 'drums beating, colours flying,' for the last time; all with passes, with agitated thoughts and outlooks: and in sacred Oxford, as poor Wood intimates, the abomination of desolation supervened!—Oxford surrendering with the King's sanction quickened other surrenders; Ragland Castle itself, and the obstinate old Marquis, gave in before the end of August: and the First Civil War, to the last ember of it, was extinct.

The Parliament, in these circumstances, was now getting itself 'recruited,'—its vacancies filled up again. The Royalist Members who had deserted three years ago, had been, without much difficulty, successively 'disabled,' as their crime came to light: but to issue new writs for new elections, while the quarrel with the King still lasted, was a matter of more delicacy; this too, however, had at length been resolved upon, the Parliament Cause now looking so decidedly prosperous, in the Autumn of

1645. Gradually, in the following months, the new Members were elected, above Two-hundred-and-thirty of them in all. These new Members, 'Recruiters,' as Anthony Wood and the Royalist world reproachfully call them, were, by the very fact of their standing candidates in such circumstances, decided Puritans all,—Independents many of them. Colonel, afterwards Admiral Blake (for Taunton), Ludlow, Ireton (for Appleby), Algernon Sidney, Hutchinson known by his Wife's *Memoirs*, were among these new Members. Fairfax, on his Father's death some two years hence, likewise came in.

PART III

BETWEEN THE TWO CIVIL WARS
1646—1648

LETTERS XVII., ETC.

THE conquering of the King had been a difficult operation; but to make a Treaty with him now when he was conquered proved an impossible one. The Scots, to whom he had fled, entreated him, at last, 'with tears' and 'on their knees,' to take the Covenant, and sanction the Presbyterian worship, if he could not adopt it: on that condition they would fight to the last man for him: on no other condition durst or would a man of them fight for him. The English Presbyterians, as yet the dominant party, earnestly entreated to the same effect. In vain, both of them. The King had other schemes: the King, writing privately to Digby before quitting Oxford, when he had some mind to venture privately on London, as he ultimately did on the Scotch Camp, to raise Treaties and Caballings there, had said, "—endeavouring to get to London; "being not without hope that I shall be able so to draw "either the Presbyterians or the Independents to side with me "for extirpating one another, that I shall be really King again." Such a man is not easy to make a Treaty with,—on the word of a King! In fact, his Majesty, though a belligerent party who had not now one soldier on foot, considered himself still a tower of strength; as indeed he was; all men having a to us inconceivable reverence for him, till bitter Necessity and he together drove them away from it. Equivocations, spasmodic obstinacies, and blindness to the real state of facts, must have an end.—

Then comes a period of most intricate negotiation;

negotiations with the Scots, managed manfully on both sides, otherwise it had ended in quarrel; negotiations with the King; infinite public and private negotiations;—which issue at last in the Scots marching home with 200,000*l.* as a 'fair instalment of their arrears,' in their pocket; and the King marching, under escort of Parliamentary Commissioners, to Holmby House in Northamptonshire, to continue in strict though very stately seclusion, ' on 50*l.* a-day,' and await the destinies there.

LETTER XVII

COLONEL IRETON, now Commissary-General Ireton, was wedded, as we saw, to Bridget Cromwell on the 15th of June last. A man 'able with his pen and his sword;' a distinguished man. Once B.A. of Trinity College, Oxford, and Student of the Middle Temple; then a gentleman trooper in my Lord General Essex's Lifeguard; now Colonel of Horse, soon Member of Parliament; rapidly rising. A Nottinghamshire man; has known the Lieutenant-General ever since the Eastern-Association times. Cornbury House, not now conspicuous on the maps, is discoverable in Oxfordshire, disguised as *Blandford Lodge*,—not too far from the Devizes, at which latter Town Fairfax and Ireton have just been, disbanding Massey's Brigade. The following Letter will require no commentary.

*For my beloved Daughter Bridget Ireton, at Cornbury,
General's Quarters: These.*

London, 25th October 1646.

DEAR DAUGHTER,

I write not to thy Husband; partly to avoid trouble, for one line of mine begets many of his, which I doubt makes him sit up too late; partly because I am myself indisposed [1] at this time, having some other considerations.

Your Friends at Ely are well: your Sister Claypole is, I trust in mercy, exercised with some perplexed thoughts. She sees her own vanity and carnal mind; bewailing it: she seeks after (as I hope also) what will satisfy. And thus to be a seeker is to be of the best sect next to a finder; and such an one shall every faithful humble seeker be at the end. Happy seeker, happy finder! Who ever tasted that the Lord is

[1] Not in the mood at this time, having other matters in view.

gracious, without some sense of self, vanity, and badness?
Who ever tasted that graciousness of His, and could go less
in desire,—less than pressing after full enjoyment? Dear
Heart, press on; let not Husband, let not anything cool thy
affections after Christ. I hope[1] he will be an occasion to
inflame them. That which is best worthy of love in thy
Husband is that of the image of Christ he bears. Look on that,
and love it best, and all the rest for that. I pray for thee
and him; do so for me.

My service and dear affections to the General and Generaless.
I hear she is very kind to thee; it adds to all other obligations.

I am

Thy dear Father,
OLIVER CROMWELL.

Bridget Ireton is now Twenty-two. Her Sister Claypole
(Elizabeth Cromwell) is five years younger. They were both
wedded last Spring. 'Your Friends at Ely' will indicate that
the Cromwell Family was still resident in that City; though, I
think, they not long afterwards removed to London. Their
first residence here was King-street, Westminster; Oliver for the
present lodges in Drury Lane: fashionable quarters both, in
those times.

General Fairfax had been in Town only three days before,
attending poor Essex's Funeral: a mournful pageant, consisting
of 'both the Houses, Fairfax and all the Civil and Military
'Officers then in Town, the Forces of the City, a very great
'number of coaches and multitudes of people;' with Mr. Vines
to preach;—regardless of expense, 5,000*l*. being allowed for it.

LETTER XVIII

THE intricate Scotch negotiations have at last ended. The paying of the Scots their first instalment, and getting them to
march away in peace, and leave the King to our disposal, is the
great affair that has occupied Parliament ever since his Majesty
refused the Propositions. Not till Monday the 21st December
could it be got 'perfected' or 'almost perfected.' After a busy
day spent in the Commons House on that affair, Oliver writes
the following Letter to Fairfax. The 'Major-General' is
Skippon. Fairfax, 'since he left Town,' is most likely about
Nottingham, the head-quarters of his Army, which had been

[1] thy Husband.

AFFAIRS IN LONDON

drawing rather Northward, ever since the King appeared among the Scots. Fairfax came to Town 12th November, with great splendour of reception; left it again '18th December.'

On the morrow after that, 19th December 1646, the Londoners presented their Petition, not without tumult; complaining of heavy expenses and other great grievances from the Army; and craving that the same might be, as soon as possible, disbanded, and a good Peace with his Majesty made. The first note of a very loud controversy which arose between the City and the Army, between the Presbyterians and the Independents, on that matter. Indeed the humour of the City seems to be getting high; impatient for 'a just peace' now that the King is reduced. On Saturday 6th December, it was ordered that the Lord Mayor be apprised of tumultuous assemblages which there are, 'to the disturbance of the peace;' and be desired to quench them,—if he can.

For his Excellency Sir Thomas Fairfax, General of the Parliament's Armies: These.

'London,' 21st December 1646.

SIR,

Having this opportunity by the Major-General to present a few lines unto you, I take the boldness to let you know how our affairs go on since you left Town.

We have had a very long Petition from the City: how it strikes at the Army, and what other aims it has, you will see by the contents of it; as also what is the prevailing temper at this present, and what is to be expected from men. But this is our comfort, God is in Heaven, and He doth what pleaseth Him; His and only His counsel shall stand, whatsoever the designs of men, and the fury of the people be.

We have now, I believe, almost perfected all our business for Scotland. I believe Commissioners will speedily be sent down to see agreements performed; it's intended that Major-General Skippon have authority and instructions from your Excellency to command the Northern Forces, as occasion shall be, and that he have a Commission of Martial Law. Truly I hope that the having the Major-General to command this Party will appear to be a good thing, every day more and more.

Here has been a design to steal away the Duke of York from my Lord of Northumberland: one of his own servants, whom he preferred to wait on the Duke, is guilty of it; the Duke

himself confessed so. I believe you will suddenly hear more
of it.

I have no more to trouble you 'with ;' but praying for you,
rest,

    Your Excellency's most humble servant,
          OLIVER CROMWELL.

Skippon, as is well known, carried up the cash, 200,000*l*., to
Newcastle successfully, in a proper number of wagons; got
it all counted there, 'bags of 100*l*., chests of 1000*l*.,' (5th-
16th January 1646-7); after which the Scots marched peaceably
away.

The little Duke of York, entertained in a pet-captive
fashion at St. James's, did not get away at this time; but
managed it, by and by, with help of a certain diligent intriguer
and turncoat called Colonel Bamfield; of whom we may
hear farther.

On Thursday, 11th February 1646-7, on the road between
Mansfield and Nottingham,—road between Newcastle and
Holmby House,—'Sir Thomas Fairfax went and met the King;
'who stopped his horse: Sir Thomas alighted, and kissed the
'King's hand; and afterwards mounted, and discoursed with
'the King as they passed towards Nottingham.' The King
had left Newcastle on the 3d of the month; got to Holmby,
or Holdenby, on the 13th;—and 'there,' says the poor *Iter
Carolinum*, 'during pleasure.'

The troubles of the Parliament and Army are just beginning.
The order for quartering beyond twenty-five miles from London,
and many other 'orders' were sadly violated in the course of
this season. 'Sir W. Massam's House,' 'Otes in Essex,' is a
place known to us since the beginning of these *Letters*.

The Officers ought really to go down to their quarters in the
Eastern Counties; Oliver has sent them off, as many of them as
he 'could well light of.'

The Presbyterian System is now fast getting into action : on
the 20th of May 1647, the Synod of London, with due
Prolocutor or Moderator, met in St. Paul's. In Lancashire
too the System is fairly on foot; but I think in other English
Counties it was somewhat lazy to move, and never came rightly
into action, owing to impediments.—Poor old Laud is condemned of treason, and beheaded, years ago; the Scots, after

Marston Fight, pressing heavy on him ; Prynne too being very
ungrateful. That 'performance' of the Service to the Hyperborean populations in so exquisite a way, has cost the Artist
dear ! He died very gently ; his last scene much the best, for
himself and for us. The two Hothams also, and other traitors,
have died.

ARMY MANIFESTO

OUR next entirely authentic Letter is at six months distance : a
hiatus not unfrequent in this Series ; but here most especially to
be regretted : such a crisis in the affairs of Oliver and of England
transacting itself in the interim. The Quarrel between City and
Army, which we here see begun ; the split of the Parliament
into two clearly hostile Parties of Presbyterians and Independents,
represented by City and Army ; the deadly wrestle of these
two Parties, with victory to the latter, and the former flung on
its back, and its 'Eleven Members' sent beyond Seas : all this
transacts itself in the interim, without autograph note or
indisputably authentic utterance of Oliver's to elucidate it for
us. We part with him labouring to get the Officers sent down
to Saffron Walden ; sorrowful on the Spring Fast-day in
Covent Garden : we find him again at Putney in Autumn ; the
insulted Party now dominant, and he the most important man
in it. One Paper which I find among the many published on
that occasion, and judge pretty confidently, by internal evidence,
to be of his writing, is here introduced ; and there is no other
that I know of.

How this Quarrel between City and Army, no agreement
with the King being for the present possible, went on waxing ;
developing itself more and more visibly into a Quarrel between
Presbyterianism and Independency ; attracting to the respective
sides of it the two great Parties in Parliament and in England
generally : all this the reader must endeavour to imagine for
himself,—very dimly, as matters yet stand. In books, in
Narratives old or new, he will find little satisfaction in regard
to it. The old Narratives, written all by baffled enemies of
Cromwell,[1] are full of mere blind rage, distraction and darkness ;
the new Narratives, believing only in 'Machiavelism,' &c.,
disfigure the matter still more. Common History, old and new,

[1] Holles's Memoirs ; Waller's Vindication of his Character ; Clement
Walker's History of Independency, &c. &c.

represents Cromwell as having underhand,—in a most skilful and indeed prophetic manner,—fomented or originated all this commotion of the elements; steered his way through it by 'hypocrisy,' by 'master-strokes of duplicity,' and such like. As is the habit hitherto of History.

'The fact is,' says a Manuscript already cited from, 'poor 'History, contemporaneous and subsequent, has treated this 'matter in a very sad way. Mistakes, misdates; exaggerations, 'unveracities, distractions; all manner of misseeings and 'misnotings in regard to it, abound. How many grave historical 'statements still circulate in the world, accredited by Bishop 'Burnet and the like, which on examination you will find 'melt away into after-dinner rumours,—gathered from ancient 'red-nosed Presbyterian gentlemen, Harbottle Grimston and 'Company, sitting over claret under a Blessed Restoration, and 'talking to the loosely recipient Bishop in a very loose way! 'Statements generally with some grain of harmless truth, mis-'interpreted by those red-nosed honourable persons; frothed up 'into huge bulk by the loquacious Bishop above mentioned, and 'so set floating on Time's Stream. Not very lovely to us, they, 'nor the red-noses they proceeded from! I do not cite them 'here; I have examined most of them; found not one of them 'fairly believable; wondered to see how already in one 'generation, earnest Puritanism being hung on the gallows or 'thrown out in St. Margaret's Churchyard, the whole History 'of it had grown *mythical*, and men were ready to swallow all 'manner of nonsense concerning it. Ask for dates, ask for 'proofs: Who saw it, heard it; when was it, where? A misdate, 'of itself, will do much. So accurate a man as Mr. Godwin, 'generally very accurate in such matters, makes "a master-'stroke of duplicity" merely by mistake of dating:[1] the thing 'when Oliver did say it, was a credible truth, and no master-'stroke or stroke of any kind!

'"Master-strokes of duplicity;" "false protestations;" "fo-'menting of the Army discontents:" alas, alas! It was not 'Cromwell that raised these discontents; not he, but the 'elemental Powers! Neither was it, I think, "by master-'strokes of duplicity" that Cromwell steered himself victoriously 'across such a devouring chaos; no, but by *continuances* of noble 'manful *simplicity*, I rather think,—by meaning one thing 'before God, and meaning the same before men, not as a weak

[1] Godwin, ii. 300,—citing Walker, p. 31 (should be p. 33).

THE ARMY

'but as a strong man does. By conscientious resolution ; by
'sagacity, and silent wariness and promptitude ; by religious
'valour and veracity,—which, however it may fare with *foxes*,
'are really, after all, the grand source of clearness for a *man* in
'this world !'— —We here close our Manuscript.

Modern readers ought to believe that there was a real
impulse of heavenly Faith at work in this Controversy ; that
on both sides, more especially on the Army's side, here lay the
central element of all ; modifying all other elements and
passions ;—that this Controversy was, in several respects, very
different from the common wrestling of Greek with Greek for
what are called 'Political objects !'—Modern readers, mindful
of the French Revolution, will perhaps compare these Presby
terians and Independents to the Gironde and the Mountain
And there is an analogy ; yet with differences. With a great
difference in the situations ; with the difference, too, between
Englishmen and Frenchmen, which is always considerable
and then with the difference between believers in Jesus Christ
and believers in Jean Jacques, which is still more considerable !

A few dates, and chief summits of events, are all that car
be indicated here, to make our 'Manifesto' legible.

From the beginnings of this year 1647 and earlier, there had
often been question as to what should be done with the Army
The expense of such an Army, between twenty and thirty
thousand men, was great ; the need of it, Royalism being now
subdued, seemed small ; besides it was known that there were
many in it who 'had never taken the Covenant,' and were never
likely to take it. This latter point, at a time when Heresy
seemed rising like a hydra,[1] and the Spiritualism of England was
developing itself in really strange ways, became very important
too,—became gradually most of all important, and the soul of
the whole Controversy.

Early in March, after much debating, it had been got settled
that there should be Twelve-thousand men employed in
Ireland,[2] which was now in sad need of soldiers. The rest
were, in some good way, to be disbanded. The 'way,' how
ever, and whether it might really be a good way, gave rise to
considerations.—Without entering into a sea of troubles, we

[1] See Edwards s *Gangræna* (London, 1646) for many furious details
of it.
[2] 6th March, Commons Journals, v. 107.

may state here in general that the things this Army demanded were strictly their just right : Arrears of pay, 'three-and-forty weeks' of hard-earned pay ; indemnity for acts done in War ; and clear discharge according to contract, not service in Ireland except under known Commanders and conditions,—'our old Commanders,' for example. It is also apparent that the Presbyterian party in Parliament, the leaders of whom were, several of them, Colonels of the *Old* Model, did not love this victorious Army ; that indeed they disliked and grew to hate it, useful as it had been to them. Denzil Holles, Sir William Waller, Harley, Stapleton, these men, all strong for Presbyterianism, were old unsuccessful Colonels or Generals under Essex ; and for very obvious reasons looked askance on this Army, and wished to be, as soon as possible, rid of it. The first rumour of a demur or desire on the part of the Army, rumour of some Petition to Fairfax by his Officers as to the 'way' of their disbanding, was by these Old-Military Parliament men very angrily repressed ; nay, in a moment of fervour they proceeded to decree that whoever had, or might have, a hand in promoting such Petition in the Army was an 'Enemy to the State, and a Disturber of the Public Peace,'—and sent forth the same in a 'Declaration of the 30th of March,' which became very celebrated afterwards. This unlucky 'Declaration,' Waller says, was due to Holles, who smuggled it one evening through a thin House. "Enemies to the State, Disturbers of the Peace :" it was a severe and too proud rebuke ; felt to be unjust, and looked upon as 'a blot of ignominy ;' not to be forgotten, nor easily forgiven, by the parties it was addressed to. So stood matters at the end of March.

At the end of April they stand somewhat thus. Two Parliament Deputations, Sir William Waller at the head of them, have been at Saffron Walden, producing no agreement :[1] five dignitaries of the Army, 'Lieutenant-General Hammond, Colonel Hammond, Lieutenant-Colonel Pride,' and two others, have been summoned to the bar ;[2] some subalterns given into custody ; Ireton himself 'ordered to be examined ;'—and no 'satisfaction to the just desires of the Army ;' on the contrary, the 'blot of ignominy' fixed deeper on it than before. We can conceive a universal sorrow and anger, and all manner of dim schemes and consultations going on at Saffron Walden and the other Army-quarters, in those days. Here is a scene from

[1] Waller, pp. 42-85.
[2] Commons Journals, v. 129 (29th March 1647).

Whitlocke, worth looking at, which takes place in the Honourable House itself; date 30th April 1647:[1]

'Debate upon the Petition and Vindication of the Army. 'Major-General Skippon, in the House, produced a Letter 'presented to him the day before by some Troopers, in behalf 'of Eight Regiments of the Army of Horse. Wherein they 'expressed some reasons, Why they could not engage in the 'service of Ireland under the present Conduct,' under the proposed Commandership, by Skippon and Massey; 'and com-'plained, Of the many scandals and false suggestions which were 'of late raised against the Army and their proceedings; That 'they were taken as enemies; That they saw designs upon 'them, and upon many of the Godly Party in the Kingdom; 'That they could not engage for Ireland till they were satisfied 'in their expectations, and their just desires granted.—Three 'Troopers, Edward Sexby, William Allen, Thomas Sheppard, 'who brought this Letter, were examined in the House, touching 'the drawing and subscribing of it; and, Whether their Officers 'were engaged in it or not? They affirmed, That it was 'drawn up at a Rendezvous of several of those Eight Regiments; 'and afterwards at several meetings by Agents or Agitators, for 'each Regiment; and that few of their Officers knew or took 'notice of it.

'Those Troopers being demanded, Whether they had not 'been Cavaliers?—it was attested by Skippon, that they had 'constantly served the Parliament, and some of them from the 'beginning of the War. Being asked concerning the meaning 'of some expressions in the Petition,' especially concerning "certain men aiming at a *Sovereignty*,"—'they answered, That 'the Letter being a joint act of those Regiments, they could 'not give a punctual answer, being only Agents; but if they 'might have the queries in writing, they would send or carry 'them to those Regiments, and return their own and their 'answers.—They were ordered to attend the House upon 'summons.'

Three sturdy fellows, fit for management of business; let the reader note them. They are 'Agents' to the Army: a class of functionaries called likewise 'Adjutators' and misspelt 'Agitators;' elected by the common men of the Army, to keep

[1] Whitlocke, p. 249; Commons Journals *in die*; and a fuller account in Rushworth, vi. 474. The 'Letter,' immediately referred to, is in Cary's *Memorials* (Selections from the Tanner MSS.; London, 1842), i. 201.

the ranks in unison with the Officers in the present crisis of their affairs. This is their first distinct appearance in the eye of History ; in which, during these months, they play a great part. Evidently the settlement with the Army will be a harder task than was supposed.

During these same months some languid negotiation with the King is going on ; Scots Commissioners come up to help in treating with him ; but as he will not hear of Covenant or Presbytery, there can no result follow. It was an ugly aggravation of the blot of ignominy which the Army smarts under,—the report raised against it, That some of the Leaders had said, "If the King would come to *them*, they would put the crown on his head again."—Cromwell, from his place in Parliament, earnestly watches these occurrences ; waits what the great 'birth of Providence' in them may be ;—'carries himself with much wariness ;' is more and more looked up to by the Independent Party, for his interest with the Soldiers. One day, noticing the 'high carriages' of Holles and Company, he whispers Edmund Ludlow who sat by him, "These men will never leave till the "Army pull them out by the ears !"[1] Holles and Company, who at present rule in Parliament, pass a New Militia Ordinance for London ; put the Armed Force of London into hands more strictly Presbyterian.[2] There have been two London Petitions against the Army, and two London Petitions covertly in favour of it ; the Managers of the latter, we observe, have been put in prison.

May 8th. A new and more promising Deputation, Cromwell at the head of it. 'Cromwell, Ireton, Fleetwood, Skippon,' proceed again to Saffron Walden ; investigate the claims and grievances of the Army ;[3] engage, as they had authority to do, that real justice shall be done them ; and in a fortnight return with what seems an agreement and settlement ; for which Lieutenant-General Cromwell receives the thanks of the House.[4] The House votes what *it* conceives to be justice, 'eight weeks of pay' in ready money, bonds for the rest,—and so forth. Congratulations hereupon ; a Committee of Lords and Commons are ordered to go down to Saffron Walden, to *see* the Army disbanded.

[1] Ludlow, i 189 ; see Whitlocke, p. 252.
[2] 4th May 1647, Commons Journals, v. 160 :—'Thirty-one Persons,' their names given.
[3] Letters from them, in Appendix, No. 9.
[4] May 21st, Commons Journals, v. 131.

THE KING AND CORNET JOYCE 115

May 28th. On arriving at Saffron Walden, they find that their notions of what is justice, and the Army's notions, differ widely. "Eight weeks of pay," say the Army; "we want nearer eight times eight!" Disturbances in several of the quarters :—at Oxford the men seize the disbanding-money as *part* of payment, and will not disband till they get the whole. A meeting of Adjutators, by authority of Fairfax, convenes at Bury St. Edmund's,—a regular Parliament of soldiers, 'each common man paying fourpence to meet the expense:' it is agreed that the Army's quarters shall be 'contracted,' brought closer together; that on Friday next, 4th of June, there shall be a Rendezvous, or General Assembly of all the Soldiers, there to decide on what they will do.[1]

June 4th and 5th. The Newmarket Rendezvous, 'on Kentford Heath,' a little east of Newmarket, is held; a kind of Covenant is entered into, and other important things are done :—but elsewhere in the interim a thing still more important had been done. On Wednesday June 2d, Cornet Joyce,—once a London tailor they say, evidently a very handy active man,—he, and Five-hundred common troopers, a volunteer Party, not expressly commanded by anybody, but doing what they know the whole Army wishes to be done, sally out of Oxford, where things are still somewhat disturbed; proceed to Holmby House, and, after two days of talking, bring 'the King's Person' off with them. To the horror and despair of the Parliament Commissioners in attendance there; but clearly to the satisfaction of his Majesty,—who hopes, in this new shuffle-and-deal, some good card will turn up for him; hopes with some ground, 'the Presbyterians and Independents *may* now be got to extirpate one another.' His Majesty rides willingly; the Parliament Commissioners accompany, wringing their hands; —to Hinchinbrook, that same Friday night; where Colonel Montague receives them with all hospitality, entertains them for two days. Colonel Whalley with a strong party, deputed by Fairfax, had met his Majesty; offered to deliver him from Joyce, back to Holmby and the Parliament; but his Majesty positively declined.—Captain Titus, *quasi* Tighthose, very well known afterwards, arrives at St. Stephen's with the news; has 50*l.* voted him 'to buy a horse,' for his great service; and fills all men with terror and amazement. The Honourable Houses agree to 'sit on the Lord's day;' have Stephen Marshall

[1] Rushworth, pp. 496-510.

to pray for them; never were in such a plight before. The Controversy, at this point, has risen from Economical into Political: Army Parliament in the Eastern Counties, against Civil Parliament in Westminster; and, 'How the Nation shall be settled' between them; whether its growth shall be in the forest-tree fashion, or in the clipt Dutch-dragon fashion?—

Monday, June 7th. All Officers in the House are ordered forthwith to go down to their regiments. Cromwell, without order, not without danger of detention, say some,—has already gone: this same day, 'General Fairfax, Lieutenant-General Cromwell and the chief men of the Army,' have an interview with the King, 'at Childerley House between Huntingdon and Cambridge:' his Majesty will not go back to Holmby; much prefers 'the air' of these parts, the air of Newmarket for instance; and will continue with the Army.[1] Parliament Commissioners, with new Votes of Parliament, are coming down; the Army must have a new Rendezvous, to meet them. New Rendezvous at Royston, more properly on Triploe Heath near Cambridge, is appointed for Thursday; and in the interim a 'Day of Fasting and Humiliation' is held by all the soldiers,—a real Day of Prayer (very inconceivable in these days), For God's enlightenment as to what should now be done.

Here is Whitlocke's account of the celebrated Rendezvous itself—somewhat abridged from Rushworth, and dim enough; wherein, however, by good eyes a strange old Historical Scene may be discerned. The new Votes of Parliament do not appear still to meet 'the just desires' of the Army; meanwhile, let all things be done decently and in order.

'The General had ordered a Rendezvous at Royston;' properly on Triploe Heath, as we said; on Thursday 10th June 1647: the Force assembled was about Twenty-one thousand men, the remarkablest Army that ever wore steel in this world. 'The General and the Commissioners rode to 'each Regiment. They first acquainted the General's Regiment 'with the Votes of the Parliament; and Skippon,' one of the Commissioners, 'spake to them to persuade a compliance. An 'Officer of the Regiment made answer, That the Regiment 'did desire that their answer might be returned *after* perusal 'of the Votes by some select Officers and Agitators, whom 'the Regiment had chosen; and said, This was the motion of 'the Regiment.

---

[1] Rushworth, vi. 549.

PARLIAMENT AND THE ARMY

'He desired the General and Commissioners to give him leav
'to ask the whole Regiment if this *was* their answer. Leave
'being given, they cried, "All." Then he put the question,
'If any man were of a contrary opinion he should say, No;—
'and not one man gave his "No."—The Agitators in behalf
'of the soldiers pressed to have the question put at once,
'Whether the Regiment did acquiesce and were satisfied with
'the Votes?' The Agitators knew well what the answer would
have been!—'But in regard the other way was more orderly,
'and they might after perusal proceed more deliberately, that
'question was laid aside.

'The like was done in the other Regiments; and all
'were very unanimous; and always after the Commissioners
'had done reading the Votes, and speaking to each Regiment,
'and had received their answer, all of them cried out, "Justice,
'Justice!"—not a very musical sound to the Commissioners.

'A Petition was delivered in the field to the General, in the
'name of "many well-affected people in Essex;" desiring, That
'the Army might *not* be disbanded; in regard the Common-
'wealth had many enemies, who watched for such an occasion
'to destroy the good people.'[1]

Such, and still dimmer, is the jotting of dull authentic
Bulstrode,—drowning in official oil, and somnolent natural
pedantry and fat, one of the remarkablest scenes our History
ever had: An Armed Parliament, extra-official, yet not without
a kind of sacredness, and an Oliver Cromwell at the head of it;
demanding with one voice, as deep as ever spake in England,
"Justice, Justice!" under the vault of Heaven.

That same afternoon, the Army moved on to St. Albans,
nearer to London; and from the Rendezvous itself, a joint
Letter was despatched to the Lord Mayor and Aldermen, which
the reader is now at last to see. I judge it, pretty confidently,
by evidence of style alone, to be of Cromwell's own writing.
It differs totally in this respect from any other of those
multitudinous Army-Papers; which were understood, says
Whitlocke, to be drawn up mostly by Ireton, 'who had a
subtle working brain;' or by Lambert, who also had got
some tincture of Law and other learning, and did not want
for brain. They are very able Papers, though now very
dull ones. This is in a far different style; in Oliver's worst style;
his style when he writes in haste,—and not in haste of the

---

[1] Whitlocke, p. 255.

pen merely, for that seems always to have been a most rapid business with him ; but in haste before the matter had matured itself for him, and the real kernels of it got parted from the husks. A style of composition like the structure of a block of oak-root,—as tortuous, unwedgeable, and as strong ! Read attentively, this Letter can be understood, can be believed : the tone of it, the 'voice' of it, reminds us of what Sir Philip Warwick heard ; the voice of a man risen justly into a kind of *chaunt*,—very dangerous for the City of London at present.

To the Right Honourable the Lord Mayor, Aldermen, and Common Council of the City of London : These.

Royston, 10th June 1647.

RIGHT HONOURABLE AND WORTHY FRIENDS,

Having, by our Letters and other Addresses presented by our General to the Honourable House of Commons, endeavoured to give satisfaction of the clearness of our just Demands ; and 'having' also, in Papers published by us remonstrated the grounds of our proceedings in prosecution thereof ;—all of which being published in print, we are confident 'they' have come to your hands, and received at least a charitable construction from you.

The sum of all these our Desires as Soldiers is no other than this : Satisfaction to our undoubted Claims as Soldiers ; and reparation upon those who have, to the utmost, improved all opportunities and advantages, by false suggestions, misrepresentations and otherwise, for the destruction of this Army with a perpetual blot of ignominy upon it. Which 'injury' we should not value, if it singly concerned our own particular 'persons ;' being ready to deny ourselves in this, as we have done in other cases, for the Kingdom's good : but under this pretence, we find, no less is involved than the overthrow of the privileges both of Parliament and People ;—and that rather than they[1] shall fail in their designs, or we receive what in the eyes of all good men is 'our' just right, the Kingdom is endeavoured to be engaged in a new War. 'In a new War,' and this singly by those who, when the truth of these things shall be made to appear, will be found to be the authors of those 'said' evils that are feared ;—and who have no other way to protect *themselves* from question and punishment but by putting the Kingdom

[1] The Presbyterian leaders in Parliament, Holles, Stapleton, Harley, Waller, &c.

into blood, under the pretence of their honour of and their love to the Parliament. As if that were dearer to them than to us; or as if they had given greater proof of their faithfulness to it than we.

But we perceive that, under these veils and pretences, they seek to interest in their design the City of London :—as if that City ought to make good their miscarriages, and should prefer a few self-seeking men before the welfare of the Public. And indeed we have found these men so active to accomplish their designs, and to have such apt instruments for their turn in that City, that we have cause to suspect they may engage many therein upon mistakes,—which are easily swallowed, in times of such prejudice against them[1] that have given (we may speak it without vanity) the most public testimony of their good affections to the Public, and to that City in particular.

'As' for the thing we insist upon as Englishmen,—and surely our being Soldiers hath not stript us of that interest, although our malicious enemies would have it so,—we desire a Settlement of the Peace of the Kingdom and of the Liberties of the Subject, according to the Votes and Declarations of Parliament, which, *before* we took arms, were, by the Parliament, used as arguments and inducements to invite us and divers of our dear friends out; some of whom have lost their lives in this War. Which being now, by God's blessing, finished,—we think we have as much right to demand, and desire to see, a happy Settlement, as we have to our money and 'to' the other common interest of Soldiers which we have insisted upon. We find also the ingenuous and honest People, in almost all parts of the Kingdom where we come, full of the sense of ruin and misery if the Army should be disbanded *before* the Peace of the Kingdom, and those other things before mentioned, have a full and perfect Settlement.

We have said before, and profess it now, We desire no alteration of the Civil Government. As little do we desire to interrupt, or in the least to intermeddle with, the settling of the Presbyterial Government. Nor did we seek to open a way for licentious liberty, under pretence of obtaining ease for tender consciences. We profess, as ever in these things, When once the State has made a Settlement, we have nothing to say but to submit or suffer. Only we could wish that every good citizen, and every man who walks peaceably in a blameless conversation,

---

[1] Oblique for 'us.

and is beneficial to the Commonwealth, might have liberty and encouragement ; this being according to the true policy of all States, and even to justice itself.

These in brief are our Desires, and the things for which we stand ; beyond which we shall not go. And for the obtaining of these things, we are drawing near your City ;[1]—professing sincerely from our hearts, 'That' we intend not evil towards you ; declaring, with all confidence and assurance, That if you appear not against us in these our just desires, to assist that wicked Party which would embroil us and the Kingdom, neither we nor our Soldiers shall give you the least offence. We come not to do any act to prejudice the being of Parliaments, or to the hurt of this 'Parliament' in order to the present Settlement of the Kingdom. We seek the good of all. And we shall wait here, or remove to a farther distance to abide there, if once we be assured that a speedy Settlement of things is in hand,—until it be accomplished. Which done, we shall be most ready, either all of us, or so many of the Army as the Parliament shall think fit,—to disband, or to go for Ireland.

And although you may suppose that a rich City may seem an enticing bait to poor hungry Soldiers to venture far to gain the wealth thereof,—yet, if not provoked by you, we do profess, Rather than any such evil should fall out, the soldiers shall make their way through our blood to effect it. And we can say this for most of them, for your better assurance, That they so little value their pay, in comparison of higher concernments to a Public Good, that rather than they will be unrighted in the matter of their honesty and integrity (which hath suffered by the Men they aim at and desire justice upon), or want the settlement of the Kingdom's Peace, and their 'own' and their fellow-subjects' Liberties,—they will lose all. Which may be a strong assurance to you that it's not your wealth they seek, but the things tending in common to your and their welfare. That they may attain 'these,' you shall do like Fellow-Subjects and Brethren if you solicit the Parliament for them, on their behalf.

If after all this, you, or a considerable part of you, be seduced to take up arms in opposition to, or hindrance of, these our just undertakings,—we hope we have, by this brotherly premonition, to the sincerity of which we call God to witness, freed ourselves from all that ruin which may befall

---

[1] That is the remarkable point !

THE "ELEVEN MEMBERS"

that great and populous City; having thereby washed our hands thereof.

We rest,
Your affectionate Friends to serve you,

THOMAS FAIRFAX.	HENRY IRETON.
OLIVER CROMWELL.	ROBERT LILBURN.
ROBERT HAMMOND.	JOHN DESBOROW.
THOMAS HAMMOND.	THOMAS RAINSBOROW.
HARDRESS WALLER.	JOHN LAMBERT.
NATHANIEL RICH.	THOMAS HARRISON.
THOMAS PRIDE.	

This Letter was read next day in the Commons House,—not without emotion. Most respectful answer went from the Guildhall, 'in three coaches with the due number of outriders.'

On June 16th, the Army, still at St Albans, accuses of treason Eleven Members of the Commons House by name, as chief authors of all these troubles; whom the Honourable House is respectfully required to put upon their Trial, and prevent from voting in the interim. These are the famed Eleven Members; Holles, Waller, Stapleton, Massey are known to us; the whole List, for benefit of historical readers, we subjoin in a Note.[1] They demurred; withdrew; again returned; in fine, had to 'ask leave to retire for six months,' on account of their health, we suppose. They retired swiftly in the end; to France; to deep concealment,—to the Tower otherwise.

The history of these six weeks, till they did retire and the Army had its way, we must request the reader to imagine for himself. Long able Papers, drawn by men of subtle brain and strong sincere heart: the Army retiring always to a safe distance when their Demands are agreed to; straightway advancing if otherwise,—which rapidly produces an agreement. A most remarkable Negotiation; conducted with a method, a gravity and decorous regularity beyond example in such cases. The 'shops' of London were more than once 'shut;' tremor

[1] Denzil Holles (Member for Dorchester), Sir Philip Stapleton (Boroughbridge), Sir William Waller (Andover), Sir William Lewis (Petersfield), Sir John Clotworthy (Malden), Recorder Glynn (Westminster), Mr. Anthony Nichols (Bodmin); these Seven are old Members, from the beginning of the Parliament;—the other Four are 'recruiters,' elected since 1645: Major-General Massey (Wootton Basset), Colonel Walter Long (Ludgershall), Colonel Edward Harley (Herefordshire), Sir John Maynard (Lostwithiel).

occupying all hearts :—but no harm was done. The Parliament regularly paid the Army; the Army lay coiled round London and the Parliament, now advancing, now receding; saying in the most respectful emblematic way, "Settlement with us and the Godly People, or——!"—the King, still with the Army, and treated like a King, endeavoured to play his game, 'in meetings at Woburn' and elsewhere; but the two Parties could not be brought to extirpate one another for his benefit.

Towards the end of July, matters seem as good as settled: the Holles 'Declaration,' that 'blot of ignominy,' being now expunged from the Journals;[1] the Eleven being out; and now at last, the New Militia Ordinance for London (Presbyterian Ordinance brought in by Holles on the 4th of May) being revoked, and matters in that quarter set on their old footing again. The two Parties in Parliament seem pretty equal in numbers; the Presbyterian Party, shorn of its Eleven, is cowed down to the due pitch; and there is now prospect of fair treatment for all the Godly Interest, and such a Settlement with his Majesty as may be the best for that. Towards the end of July, however, London City, torn by factions, but Presbyterian by the great majority, rallies again in a very extraordinary way. Take these glimpses from contemporaneous Whitlocke; and rouse them from their fat somnolency a little.

July 26th. Many young men and Apprentices of London came to the House in a most rude and tumultuous manner; and presented some particular Desires. Desires, That the Eleven may come back; that the Presbyterian Militia Ordinance be *not* revoked,—that the Revocation of it be revoked. Desire, in short, That there be no peace made with Sectaries, but that the London Militia may have a fair chance to fight them!— Drowsy Whitlocke continues; almost as if he were in Paris in the eighteenth century: 'The Apprentices, and many other 'rude boys and mean fellows among them, came into the House 'of Commons, and kept the Door open and their hats on; and 'and called out as they stood, "Vote, Vote!" and in this 'arrogant posture, stood till the votes passed in that way, To 'repeal the Ordinance for change of the Militia, to' &c. 'In 'the evening about seven o'clock, some of the Common Council 'came down to the House:' but finding the Parliament and Speaker already *had* been forced, they, astute Common-Council

---

[1] Asterisks still in the place of it, Commons Journals, 29th March 1647.

men, ordered their Apprentices to go home again, the work they had set them upon being now finished.[1] This disastrous scene fell out on Monday 26th July 1647 : the Houses, on the morrow morning, without farther sitting, adjourned till Friday next.

On Friday next, —— behold, the Two Speakers, 'with the Mace,' and many Members of both Houses, have withdrawn ; and the Army, lately at Bedford, is on quick march towards London ! Alarming pause. 'About noon,' however, the Remainders of the Two Houses, reinforced by the Eleven who reappear for the last time, proceed to elect new Speakers, 'get the City Mace ;' order, above all, that there be a vigorous enlistment of forces under General Massey, General Poyntz, and others. 'St. James's Fields' were most busy all Saturday, all Monday ; shops all shut ; drums beating in all quarters ; a most vigorous enlistment going on. Presbyterianism will die with harness on its back. Alas, news come that the Army is at Colnebrook, advancing towards Hounslow ; news come that they have rendezvoused at Hounslow, and received the Speakers and fugitive Lords and Commons with shouts. Tuesday, 3d August 1647, was such a day as London and the Guildhall never saw before or since ! Southwark declares that it will not fight ; sends to Fairfax for Peace and a 'sweet composure ;' comes to the Guildhall in great crowds petitioning for Peace ;— at which sight, General Poyntz, pressing through for orders about his enlistments, loses his last drop of human patience ; 'draws his sword' on the whining multitudes, 'slashes several persons, whereof some die.' The game is nearly up. Look into the old Guildhall on that old Tuesday night ; the palpitation, tremulous expectation ; wooden Gog and Magog themselves almost sweating cold with terror :

'General Massey sent out scouts to Brentford : but Ten men 'of the Army beat Thirty of his ; and took a flag from a Party 'of the City. The City Militia and Common Council sat late ; 'and a great number of people attended at Guildhall. When 'a scout came in and brought news, That the Army made a 'halt ; or other good intelligence,—they cry, "One and all !" 'But if the scouts reported that the Army was advancing nearer 'them, then they would cry as loud, "Treat, treat, treat !" So 'they spent most part of the night. At last they resolved to 'send the General an humble Letter, beseeching him that there 'might be a way of composure.'

[1] Whitlocke, p. 263.

On Friday morning, was 'a meeting at the Earl of Holland's House in Kensington' (the Holland House that yet stands), and prostrate submission by the Civic Authorities and Parliamentary Remainders ; after which the Army marched 'three deep by Hyde Park' into the heart of the City, 'with boughs of laurel in their hats ;'—and it was all ended. Fair treatment for all the Honest Party : and the Spiritualism of England shall not be forced to grow in the Presbyterian fashion, however it may grow. Here is another entry from somnolent Bulstrode. The Army soon changes its head-quarters to Putney ; one of its outer posts is Hampton Court, where his Majesty, obstinate still, but somewhat despondent now of getting the two Parties to extirpate one another, is lodged.

Saturday, '*September 18th.* After a Sermon in Putney Church 'the General, many great Officers, Field-Officers, inferior Officers 'and Adjutators, met in the Church ; debated the Proposals of 'the Army' towards a Settlement of this bleeding Nation ; 'altered some things in them ;—and were very full of the 'Sermon, which had been preached by Mr. Peters.'

LETTER XIX

THE immeasurable Negotiations with the King, 'Proposals of the Army,' 'Proposals of the Adjutators of the Army,' still occupying tons of printed paper, the subject of intense debatings and considerations in Westminster, in Putney Church, and in every house and hut of England, for many months past,— suddenly contract themselves for us, like a universe of gaseous vapour, into one small point : the issue of them all is failure. The Army Council, the Army Adjutators, and serious England at large, were in earnest about one thing ; the King was not in earnest, except about another thing : there could be no bargain with the King.

Cromwell and the Chief Officers have for some time past ceased frequenting his Majesty or Hampton Court ; such visits being looked upon askance by a party in the Army : they have left the matter to Parliament ; only Colonel Whalley, with due guard, and Parliament Commissioners, keep watch 'for the security of his Majesty.' In the Army, his Majesty's real purpose becoming now apparent, there has arisen a very terrible 'Levelling Party ;' a class of men demanding punishment not only of Delinquents, and Deceptive Persons who have

KING ESCAPES FROM HAMPTON COURT

involved this Nation in blood, but of the 'Chief Delinquent:' minor Delinquents getting punished, how should the Chief Delinquent go free? A class of men dreadfully in earnest;— to whom a King's Cloak is no impenetrable screen; who within the King's Cloak discern that there is a Man, accountable to a God! The Chief Officers, except when officially called, keep distant: hints have fallen that his Majesty is not out of danger.—In the Commons Journals this is what we read:

'*Friday 12th November* 1647. A Letter from Lieutenant- 'General Cromwell, of 11th November, twelve at night, was 'read; signifying the escape of the King; who went away 'about 9 o'clock yesterday' evening.[1]

Cromwell, we suppose, lodging in head-quarters about Putney, had been roused on Thursday night by express That the King was gone; had hastened off to Hampton Court; and there about 'twelve at night' despatched a Letter to Speaker Lenthall. The Letter, which I have some confused recollection of having, somewhere in the Pamphletary Chaos, seen in full, refuses to disclose itself at present except as a Fragment:

'*For the Honourable William Lenthall, Speaker of the House of Commons: These.*'

'Hampton Court, Twelve at night, 11th November 1647.

'SIR,'
                 * * * Majesty * * withdrawn himself * * at nine o'clock.

The manner is variously reported; and we will say little of it at present, but That his Majesty was expected at supper, when the Commissioners and Colonel Whalley missed him; upon which they entered the Room:—they found his Majesty had left his cloak behind him in the Gallery in the Private Way. He passed, by the backstairs and vault, towards the Water-side.

He left some Letters upon the table in his withdrawing room, of his own handwriting; whereof one was to the Commissioners of Parliament attending him, to be communicated to both Houses, 'and is here enclosed.'

                         * * *
                        'OLIVER CROMWELL'[2]

We do not give his Majesty's Letter 'here enclosed': it is that well-known one where he speaks, in very royal style, still every inch a King, Of the restraints and slights put upon

[1] Commons Journals, v. 356.
[2] Rushworth, vii. 871.

him,—men's obedience to their King seeming much abated of late. So soon as *they* return to a just temper, "I shall "instantly break through this cloud of retirement, and show "myself ready to be *Pater Patriæ*,"—as I have hitherto done.

See, among the Old Pamphlets, Letters to the like effect from Royalist Parties: also a Letter of thanks from the King to Whalley;—ending with a desire, 'to send the black-gray bitch to the Duke of Richmond,' on the part of his Majesty: Letters from &c., Letters to &c., in great quantities.[1] For us here this brief notice of one Letter shall suffice:

'Monday 15th November 1647. Letter from Colonel Robert 'Hammond, Governor of the Isle of Wight, *Cowes*, 13° '*Novembris*, signifying that the King is come into the Isle of Wight.'[2] The King, after a night and a day of riding, saw not well whither else to go. He delivered himself to Robert Hammond;[3] came into the Isle of Wight. Robert Hammond is ordered to keep him strictly within Carisbrook Castle and the adjoining grounds, in a vigilant though altogether respectful manner.

Robert Hammond, Governor of the Isle of Wight, who has for the present become so important to England, is a young man 'of good parts and principles:' a Colonel of Foot; served formerly as Captain under Massey in Gloucester;—where, in October 1644, he had the misfortune to kill a brother Officer, one Major Gray, in sudden duel, 'for giving him the lie;' he was tried, but acquitted, the provocation being great. He has since risen to be Colonel, and become well known. Originally of Chertsey, Surrey; his Grandfather, and perhaps his Father, a Physician there.

LETTER XX

For Colonel Robert Hammond

'London,' 6th April 1648.

DEAR ROBIN,

Your business is done in the House: your 10*l*. by the week is made 20*l*.; 1000*l*. given you; and Order to Mr. Lisle to draw up an Ordinance for 500*l*. *per annum* to be settled upon you and your heirs. This was done with smoothness; your

---

[1] Parl. Hist. xvi. 324-30.
[2] Commons Journals, *in die* (v. 359).
[3] Berkley's and Ashburnham's Narratives.

friends were not wanting to you. I know thy burden; this is an addition to it: the Lord direct and sustain thee.

Intelligence came to the hands of a very considerable Person, That the King attempted to get out of his window; and that he had a cord of silk with him whereby to slip down, but his breast was so big the bar would not give him passage. This was done in one of the dark nights about a fortnight ago. A Gentleman with you led him the way, and slipped down. The Guard, that night, had some quantity of wine with them. The same party assures that there is aquafortis gone down from London, to remove that obstacle which hindered; and that the same design is to be put in execution in the next dark nights. He saith that Captain Titus, and some others about the King are not to be trusted. He is a very considerable Person of the Parliament who gave this intelligence, and desired it should be speeded to you.

The Gentleman that came out of the window was Master Firebrace; the Gentlemen doubted are Cresset, Burrowes, and Titus; the time when this attempt of escape was, the 20th of March.

Your servant,
OLIVER CROMWELL.

Henry Firebrace is known to Birch, and his *Narrative* is known. 'He became Clerk of the Kitchen to Charles II.'— The old Books are full of King's Plots for escape, by aquafortis and otherwise. His Majesty could make no agreement with the Parliament, and began now to smell War in the wind. His presence in this or the other locality might have been of clear advantage. But Hammond was too watchful. Titus, with or without his new horse, attends upon his Majesty; James Harrington also (afterwards author of *Oceana*); and 'the Honourable Thomas Herbert,' who has left a pleasing *Narrative* concerning that affair. These, though appointed by the Parliament, are all somewhat in favour with the King. Hammond's Uncle the Chaplain, as *too* favourable, was ordered out of the Island about Christmas last.

PART IV

SECOND CIVIL WAR

1648

About the beginning of May 1648, the general Presbyterian-Royalist discontent announces itself by tumults in Kent, tumults at Colchester, tumults and rumours of tumult far and near; portending, on all sides, that a new Civil War is at hand. The Scotch Army of Forty-thousand is certainly voted; certainly the King is still prisoner at Carisbrook; factious men have yet made no bargain with him: certainly there will and should be a new War? So reasons Presbyterian Royalism everywhere. Headlong discontented Wales in this matter took the lead.

Wales has been full of confused discontent all Spring; this or the other confused Colonel Poyer, full of brandy and Presbyterian texts of Scripture, refusing to disband till his arrears be better paid, or indeed till the King be better treated. To whom other confused Welsh Colonels, as Colonel Powel, Major-General Laughern, join themselves. There have been tumults at Cardiff, tumults here and also there; open shooting and fighting. Drunken Colonel Poyer, a good while ago, in March last, seized Pembroke; flatly refuses to obey the Parliament's Order when Colonel Fleming presents the same.—Poor Fleming, whom we saw some time ago soliciting promotion: he here, attempting to defeat some insurrectionary party of this Poyer's 'at a Pass' (name of the Pass not given), is himself defeated, forced into a Church, and killed. Drunken Poyer, in Pembroke strong Castle, defies the Parliament and the world: new Colonels, Parliamentary and Presbyterian Royalist, are hastening towards him, for and against. Wales smoking with confused discontent

all Spring, has now, by influence of the flaming Scotch comet or
Army of Forty-thousand, burst into a general blaze. 'The
'gentry are all for the King ; the common people understand
'nothing, and follow the gentry.' Chepstow Castle too has been
taken 'by a stratagem.' The country is all up or rising :
'the smiths have all fled, cutting their bellows before they
'went ;' impossible to get a horse shod,—never saw such a
country ! On the whole, Cromwell will have to go. Cromwell,
leave being asked of Fairfax, is on the 1st of May ordered to
go ; marches on Wednesday the 3d. Let him march swiftly !

Horton, one of the Parliamentary Colonels, has already, while
Cromwell is on march, somewhat tamed the Welsh humour, by
a good beating at St. Fagan's : St. Fagan's Fight, near Cardiff,
on the 8th of May, where Laughern, hastening towards Poyer
and Pembroke, is broken in pieces. Cromwell marches by
Monmouth, by Chepstow (11th May) ; takes Chepstow Town ;
attacks the Castle, Castle will not surrender,—he leaves Colonel
Ewer to do the Castle ; who, after four weeks, does it. Cromwell, by Swansea and Carmarthen, advances towards Pembroke ;
quelling disturbance, rallying force, as he goes ; arrives at
Pembroke in some ten days more ; and, for want of artillery, is
like to have a tedious siege of it.

LETTER XXI

HERE is his first Letter from before the place : a rugged rapid
despatch, with some graphic touches in it, and rather more of
hope than the issue realised. Guns of due quality are not to be
had. In the beginning of June, 'Hugh Peters' went across to
Milford Haven, and from the Lion, a Parliament Ship riding
there, got 'two drakes, two demi-culverins, and two whole
culverins,' and safely conveyed them to the Leaguer ; with
which new implements an instantaneous essay was made, and a
'storming' thereupon followed, but without success.—Of 'the
Prince,' Prince Charles and his revolted ships, of the 'victory in
Kent' and what made it needful, we shall have to speak anon.

'*To the Honourable William Lenthall, Esquire, Speaker of the
House of Commons : These.*'

Leaguer before Pembroke, 14th June 1648.

SIR,

All that you can expect from hence is a relation of the
state of this Garrison of Pembroke. Which is briefly thus :

They begin to be in extreme want of provision, so as in all probability they cannot live a fortnight without being starved. But we hear that they mutinied about three days since ; cried out, "Shall we be ruined for two or three men's pleasure ? Better it were we should throw them over the walls." It's certainly reported to us that within four or six days they'll cut Poyer's throat, and come all away to us. Poyer told them, Saturday last, that if relief did not come by Monday night, they should no more believe him, nay they should hang him.

We have not got our Guns and Ammunition from Wallingford as yet ; but, however, we have scraped up a few, which stand us in very good stead. Last night, we got two little guns planted, which in Twenty-four hours will take away their Mills ; and then, as Poyer himself confesses, they are all undone. We made an attempt to storm him, about ten days since ; but our ladders were too short, and the breach so as men could not get over. We lost a few men ; but I am confident the Enemy lost more. Captain Flower, of Colonel Dean's Regiment, was wounded ; and Major Grigg's Lieutenant and Ensign slain ; Captain Burges lies wounded, and very sick. I question not, but within a fortnight we shall have the Town ; 'and' Poyer hath engaged himself to the Officers of the Town, Not to keep the *Castle* longer than the Town can hold out. Neither indeed can he ; for we can take away his water in two days, by beating down a staircase, which goes into a cellar where he hath a well. They allow the men half-a-pound of beef, and as much bread a-day ; but it is almost spent.

We much rejoice at what the Lord hath done for you in Kent. Upon our thanksgiving for that victory, which was both from Sea and Leaguer, Poyer told his men, that it was the Prince, 'Prince Charles and his revolted Ships,' coming with relief. The other night they mutinied in the Town. Last night we fired divers houses ; which 'fire' runs up the Town still : it much frights them. Confident I am, we shall have it in Fourteen days, by starving. I am,

Sir,

Your servant,

OLIVER CROMWELL.

Precisely in about 'Fourteen days' a new attempt was made, not without some promising results, but again ineffectual. 'The Guns are not come from Bristol, for want of wind ;' and against hunger and short scaling-ladders Poyer is stubborn.

LETTER XXII

SINCE Cromwell quitted London, there have arisen wide commotions in that central region too; the hope of the Scotch Army and the certainty of this War in Wales excite all unruly things and persons. At Pembroke lately we heard the cannons fire, both from Leaguer and Ships, for a 'victory in Kent:' concerning which and its origins and issues, take the following indications.

May 16th. Came a celebrated 'Surrey Petition;' highflying armed cavalcade of Freeholders from Surrey, with a Petition craving in very high language that Peace be made with his Majesty: they quarrelled with the Parliament's Guard in Westminster Hall, drew swords, had swords drawn upon them; 'the Miller of Wandsworth was run through with a halbert,' he and others; and the Petitioners went home in a slashed and highly indignant condition. Thereupon, *May 24th*, armed meeting of Kentish-men on Blackheath; armed meeting of Essex-men; several armed meetings, all in communication with the City Presbyterians: Fairfax, ill of the gout, has to mount,—in extremity of haste, as a man that will quench fire among smoking flax.

June 1st. Fairfax, at his utmost speed, smites fiercely against the centre of this Insurrection; drives it from post to post; drives it into Maidstone 'about 7 in the evening,' 'with as hard fighting as I ever saw;' tramples it out there. The centre-flame once trampled out, the other flames, or armed meetings, hover hither and thither; gather at length, in few days, all at Colchester in Essex; where Fairfax is now besieging them, with a very obstinate and fierce resistance from them. This is the victory in Kent, these are the 'glorious successes God has vouchsafed you,' which Oliver alludes to in this Letter.

We are only to notice farther that Lambert is in the North; waiting, in very inadequate strength, to see the Scots arrive Oliver in this Letter signifies that he has reinforced him with some 'horse and dragoons,' sent by 'West Chester,' which we now call Chester, where 'Colonel Dukinfield' is Governor. The Scots are indubitably coming: Sir Marmaduke Langdale (whom Oliver, we may remark, encountered in the King's left wing at *Naseby Fight*) has raised new Yorkshiremen, has seized Berwick, seized Carlisle, and joined the Scots; it is becoming an openly Royalist affair. In Lancashire a certain Sir Richard Tempest, very forward in his Royalism, goes suddenly blazing abroad 'with 1,000 horse and many knights and gentlemen,' threatening huge peril; but is, in those very hours, courageously set upon by Colonel Robert Lilburn with what little compact force there is, and at once extinguished :—an acceptable service on the part of Colonel Robert; for which let him have thanks from Parliament, and reward of 1,000*l*.

Very desirable, of course, that Oliver had done with Pembroke, and were fairly joined with Lambert. But Pembroke is strong; Poyer is stubborn, hopes to surrender 'on conditions;' Oliver equally stubborn, though sadly short of artillery and means, will have him 'at mercy of the Parliament,' so signal a rebel as him. Fairfax's Father, the Lord Ferdinando, died in March last; so that the General's title is now changed:

To his Excellency the Lord Fairfax, General of the Parliament's Army: These.

Before Pembroke, 28th June 1648.

SIR,

I have some few days since despatched horse and dragoons for the North. I sent them by the way of West Chester; thinking it fit to do so in regard of this enclosed Letter which I received from Colonel Dukinfield;—requiring them to give him assistance in the way. And if it should prove that a present help would not serve the turn, then I ordered Captain Pennyfeather's troop to remain with the Governor 'Dukinfield;' and the rest immediately to march towards Leeds,—and to send to the Committee of York, or to him that commands the forces in those parts, for directions whither they should come, and how they shall be disposed of.

The number I sent are six troops: four of horse, and two of dragoons; whereof three are Colonel Scroop's,—and Captain Pennyfeather's troop, and the other two dragoons. I could not, by the judgment of the Colonels here, spare more, nor send them sooner, without manifest hazard to these parts. Here is, as I have formerly acquainted your Excellency, a very desperate Enemy; who, being put out of all hope of mercy, are resolved to endure to the uttermost extremity; being very many 'of them' gentlemen of quality, and men thoroughly resolved. They have made some notable sallies upon Lieutenant-Colonel Reade's quarter,[1] to his loss. We are forced to keep divers posts, or

[1] Reade had been entrusted with the Siege of Tenby: that had ended June 2d and Reade is now assisting at Pembroke.

else they would have relief, or their horse break away. Our foot about them are Four-and-twenty hundred; we always necessitated to have some in garrisons.

The Country, since we sat down before this place, have made two or three insurrections; and are ready to do it every day: so that,—what with looking to them, and disposing our horse to that end, and to get us in provisions, without which we should starve, this country being so miserably exhausted and so poor, and we no money to buy victuals,—indeed, whatever may be thought, it's a mercy we have been able to keep our men together in the midst of such necessity, the sustenance of the foot for most part being but bread and water. Our guns, through the unhappy accident at Berkley, not yet come to us;—and indeed it was a very unhappy thing they were brought thither; the wind having been always so cross, that since they were recovered from sinking, they could not 'come to us;' and this place not being to be had without fit instruments for battering, except by starving.[1] And truly I believe the Enemy's straits do increase upon them very fast, and that within a few days an end will be put to this business;—which surely might have been before, if we had received things wherewith to have done it. But it will be done in the best time.[2]

I rejoice much to hear of the blessing of God upon your Excellency's endeavours. I pray God that this Nation, and those that are over us, and your Excellency and all we that are under you, 'may discern' what the mind of God may be in all this, and what our duty is. Surely it is not that the poor Godly People of this Kingdom should still be made the object of wrath and anger; nor that our God would have our necks under a yoke of bondage. For these things that have lately come to pass have been the wonderful works of God; breaking the rod of the oppressor, as in the day of Midian,—not with garments much rolled in blood, but by the terror of the Lord; who will yet save His people and confound His enemies, as on that day. The Lord multiply His grace upon you, and bless you, and keep your heart upright; and then, though you be not conformable to the men of this world, nor to their wisdom, yet you shall be precious in the eyes of God, and He will be to you a horn and a shield.

---

[1] 'Without *either* fit instruments for battering *except* by starving.' Great haste, and considerable stumbling in the grammar of this last sentence! After 'starving,' a mere comma; and so on.

[2] God's time is the best.

My Lord, I do not know that I have had a Letter from any of your Army, of the glorious successes God has vouchsafed you. I pray pardon the complaint made. I long to 'be' with you. I take leave; and rest,

My Lord,
Your most humble and faithful servant,
OLIVER CROMWELL.

July 5th. Young Villiers Duke of Buckingham, son of the assassinated Duke; he with his Brother Francis, with the Earl of Holland, and others who will pay dear for it, started up about Kingston on Thames with another open Insurrectionary Armament; guided chiefly by Dutch Dalbier, once Cromwell's instructor, but now gone over to the other side. Fairfax and the Army being all about Colchester in busy Siege, there seemed a good opportunity here. They rode towards Reigate, these Kingston Insurgents, several hundreds strong: but a Parliament Party 'under Major Gibbons' drives them back; following close, comes to action with them between 'Nonsuch Park and Kingston,' where the poor Lord Francis, Brother of the Duke, fell mortally wounded;—drives them across the river 'into Hertfordshire;' into the lion's jaws. For Fairfax sent a Party out from Colchester; overtook them at St. Neot's; and captured, killed, or entirely dissipated them. Dutch Dalbier was hacked in pieces, 'so angry were the soldiers at him.' The Earl of Holland stood his trial afterwards; and lost his head. The Duke of Buckingham got off;—might almost as well have died with poor Brother Francis here, for any good he afterwards did. Two pretty youths, as their Vandyke Portraits in Hampton Court still testify; one of whom lived to become much uglier!

July 8th. Duke Hamilton, with the actual Scotch Army, is 'at Annan' on the Western Border, ready to step across to England. Not quite Forty-thousand; yet really about half that number, tolerably effective. Langdale, with a vanguard of Three-thousand Yorkshiremen, is to be guide; Monro, with a body of horse that had long served in Ulster, is to bring up the rear. The great Duke dates from Annan, 8th July 1648. Poor old Annan;—never saw such an Army gathered, since the Scotch James went to wreck in Solway Moss, above a hundred years ago![1] Scotland is in a disastrous, distracted condition; **overridden by a Hamilton majority in Parliament.** Poor

---

[1] James V. A.D. 1542.

Scotland will, with exertion, deliver its 'King from the power of Sectaries;' and is dreadfully uncertain what it will do with him when delivered! Perhaps Oliver will save it the trouble.

July 11th. Oliver at last is loose from Pembroke; as the following brief Letter will witness.

LETTER XXIII

To the Honourable William Lenthall, Esquire, Speaker of the House of Commons: These.

'Pembroke,' 11th July 1648.

SIR,

The Town and Castle of Pembroke were surrendered to me this day, being the Eleventh of July; upon the Propositions which I send you here enclosed. What Arms, Ammunition, Victual, Ordnance or other Necessaries of War are in 'the' Town, I have not to certify you,—the Commissioners I sent-in to receive the same not being yet returned, nor like suddenly to be; and I was unwilling to defer the giving you an account of this mercy for a day.

The Persons Excepted are such as have formerly served you in a very good Cause: but, being now apostatised, I did rather make election of them, than of those who had always been for the King;—judging their iniquity double; because they have sinned against so much light, and against so many evidences of Divine Providence going along with and prospering a just Cause, in the management of which they themselves had a share.

I rest,
Your humble servant
OLIVER CROMWELL.

Drunken Colonel Poyer, Major-General Laughern and certain others, 'persons excepted,' have had to surrender at mercy; a great many more on terms: Pembroke happily is down;—and the Welsh War is ended. Cromwell hurries northward: by Gloucester, Warwick; gets '3,000 pairs of shoes' at Leicester; leaves his prisoners at Nottingham (with Mrs. Hutchinson and her Colonel, in the Castle there); joins Lambert among the hills of Yorkshire,[1] where his presence is much needed now.

[1] At Barnard Castle, on the 27th July, 'his horse' joined (Rushworth, vii. 1211); he himself not till a fortnight after, at Wetherby farther south.

July 27th. In these tumultuous months the Fleet too, as we heard at Pembroke once, has partially revolted; 'set Colonel Admiral Rainsborough ashore,' in the end of May last. The Earl of Warwick, hastily sent thither, has brought part of it to order again; other part of it has fled to Holland, to the Young Prince of Wales. The Young Prince goes hopefully on board, steers for the coast of England; emits his summons and manifesto from Yarmouth roads, on the 27th of this month. Getting nothing at Yarmouth, he appears next week in the Downs: orders London to join him, or at least to lend him 20,000*l.*

It all depends on Hamilton and Cromwell now. His Majesty from Carisbrook Castle, the revolted Mariners, the London Presbyterians, the Besieged in Colchester, and all men, are waiting anxiously what they now will make of it when they meet.

LETTERS XXIV., ETC.

PRESTON BATTLE

THE Battle of Preston or Battle-and-Rout of Preston lasts three days; and extends over many miles of wet Lancashire country. —from 'Langridge Chapel a little on the east of Preston,' southward to Warrington Bridge, and northward also as far as you like to follow. A wide-spread, most confused transaction; the essence of which is, That Cromwell, descending the valley of the Ribble, with a much smaller but prompt and compact force, finds Hamilton flowing southward at Preston in very loose order; dashes in upon him, cuts him in two, drives him north *and* south, into as miserable ruin as his worst enemy could wish.

There are four accounts of this Affair by eye-witnesses, still accessible: Cromwell's account in these Two Letters; a Captain Hodgson's rough brief recollections written afterwards; and on the other side, Sir Marmaduke Langdale's Letter in vindication of his conduct there; and lastly the deliberate Narrative of Sir James Turner ('alias Dugald Dalgetty,' say some). As the Affair was so momentous, one of the most critical in all these Wars, and as the details of it are still so accessible, we will illustrate Cromwell's own account by some excerpts from the others. Combining all which, and considering well, some image of this rude old tragedy and triumph may rise upon the reader.

Captain Hodgson, an honest-hearted, pudding-headed Yorkshire Puritan, now with Lambert in the Hill Country, hovering on the left flank of Hamilton and his Scots, saw Cromwell's face at Ripon, much to the Captain's satisfaction. 'The Scots,' says he, 'marched towards Kendal ; we towards Ripon, where 'Oliver met us with horse and foot. We were then between 'Eight and Nine thousand : a fine smart Army, fit for action. 'We marched up to Skipton ; the Forlorn of the Enemy's 'horse,' Sir Marmaduke's, 'was come to Gargrave ; having made havoc of the country,—it seems, intending never to come 'there again.' 'Stout Henry Cromwell,' he gave them a check at Gargrave ;—and better still is coming.

Here, however, let us introduce Sir James Turner, a stout pedant and soldier-of-fortune, original *Dugald Dalgetty* of the Novels, who is now marching with the Scots, and happily has a turn for taking Notes. The reader will then have a certain ubiquity, and approach Preston on both sides. Of the Scotch Officers, we may remark, Middleton and the Earl of Calendar have already fought in England for the Parliament : Baillie, once beaten by Montrose, has been in many wars, foreign and domestic ; he is lefthand cousin to the Reverend Mr. Robert, who heard the Apprentices in Palaceyard bellowing " Justice on Strafford !" long since, in a loud and hideous manner. Neither of the Lesleys is here, on this occasion ; they abide at home with the oppressed minority. The Duke, it will be seen, marches in extremely loose order ; vanguard and rearguard very far apart,—and a Cromwell attending him on flank !

'At Hornby,' says the learned Sir James alias Dugald, 'a 'day's march beyond Kendal, it was advised, Whether we 'should march to Lancashire, Cheshire, and the Western 'Counties ; or if we should go into Yorkshire, and so put our-'selves in the straight road to London, with a resolution to 'fight all who would oppose us ? Calendar was indifferent ; 'Middleton was for Yorkshire ; Baillie for Lancashire. When 'my opinion was asked, I was for Yorkshire ; and for this 'reason only, That I understood Lancashire was a close country 'full of ditches and hedges ; which was a great advantage the 'English would have over our raw and undisciplined musketeers ; 'the Parliament's army consisting of disciplined and well-trained 'soldiers, and excellent firemen ; while on the other hand, 'Yorkshire was a more open country and full of heaths, where 'we might both make use of our horse, and come sooner to 'push of pike' with our foot. 'My Lord Duke was for

'Lancashire way; and it seems he had hopes that some forces
'would join with him in his march that way. I have indeed
'heard him say, that he thought Manchester his own if he
'came near it. Whatever the matter was, I never saw him
'tenacious in anything during the time of his command but in
'that. We chose to go that way, which led us to our ruin.

'Our march was much retarded by most rainy and tempestu-
'ous weather, the elements fighting against us; and by staying
'for country horses to carry our little ammunition. The
'vanguard is constantly given to Sir Marmaduke, upon con-
'dition that he should constantly furnish guides; pioneers for
'clearing the ways; and, which was more than both these, have
'good and certain intelligence of all the Enemy's motions. But
'whether it was by our fault or his neglect, want of intelligence
'helped to ruin us; for,'—in fact we were marching in extremely
loose order; left hand not aware what the right was doing;
van and rear some twenty or thirty miles apart;—far too loose
for men that had a Cromwell on their flank!

On the night of Wednesday 16th August 1648, my Lord
Duke has got to Preston with the main body of his foot; his
horse lying very wide,—ahead of him at Wigan, arear of him,
one knows not where, he himself hardly knows where. Sir
Marmaduke guards him on the left, 'on Preston Moor, about
Langridge Chapel,' some four miles up the Ribble,—and knows
not, in the least, what storm is coming. For Cromwell, this
same night, has got across the hills to Clitheroe and farther;
this same Wednesday night he lies 'at Stonyhurst,' where now
the College of Stonyhurst is,—'a Papist's house, one Sherburne's;' and tomorrow morning there will be news of
Cromwell.

'That night,' says Hodgson, 'we pitched our camp at
'*Stanyares* Hall, a Papist's house, one Sherburne's; and the next
'morning a Forlorn of horse and foot was drawn out. And at
'Langridge Chapel our horse ' came upon Sir Marmaduke;
'drawn up very formidably. One Major Poundall' (Pownel,
you pudding-head!) 'and myself commanded the Forlorn of
'foot. And here being drawn up by the Moorside (a mere
'scantling of us, as yet, not half the number we should have
'been), the General Cromwell comes to us, orders us To march.
'We not having half of our men come up, desired a little
'patience; he gives out the word, "March!"'—not having any
patience, he, at this moment! And so the Battle of Preston,
the first day of it, is begun. Here is the General's own Report

of the business at night. Poor Langdale did not know at first, and poor Hamilton did not know all day, that it was Cromwell who was now upon them. Sir Marmaduke complains bitterly that he was not supported; that they did not even send him powder,—marched away the body of their force as if this matter had been nothing; 'merely some flying party, Ashton and the Lancashire Presbyterians.' Cromwell writes in haste, late at night

LETTER XXIV

For the Honourable Committee of Lancashire sitting at Manchester. (I desire the Commander of the Forces there to open this Letter if it come not to their hands.)

'Preston,' 17th August 1648.

GENTLEMEN,

It hath pleased God, this day, to show His great power by making the Army successful against the common Enemy.

We lay last night at Mr. Sherburn's of Stonyhurst, nine miles from Preston, which was within three miles of the Scots quarters. We advanced betimes next morning towards Preston, with a desire to engage the Enemy; and by that time our Forlorn had engaged the Enemy, we were about four miles from Preston, and thereupon we advanced with the whole Army: and the Enemy being drawn out on a Moor betwixt us and the Town, the Armies on both sides engaged; and after a very sharp dispute, continuing for three or four hours, it pleased God to enable us to give them a defeat; which I hope we shall improve, by God's assistance, to their utter ruin; and in this service your countrymen have not the least[1] share.

We cannot be particular, having not time to take account of the slain and prisoners; but we can assure you we have many prisoners, and many of those of quality; and many slain; and the Army so dissipated 'as I say.' The principal part whereof, with Duke Hamilton, is on south side Ribble and Darwen Bridge, and we lying with the greatest part of the Army close to them; nothing hindering the ruin of that part of the Enemy's Army but the night. It shall be our care that they shall not pass over any ford beneath the Bridge, to go Northward, or to come betwixt us and Whalley.

We understand Colonel-General Ashton's are at Whalley; we have seven troops of horse or dragoons that we believe lie

[1] Meaning 'the not least.

at Clitheroe. This night I have sent order to them expressly to march to Whalley, to join to those companies ; that so we may endeavour the ruin of this Enemy. You perceive by this Letter how things stand. By this means the Enemy is broken : and most of their Horse having gone Northwards, and we having sent a considerable party at the very heel of them ; and the Enemy having lost almost all his ammunition, and near four-thousand arms, so that the greatest part of the Foot are naked ;—therefore, in order to perfecting this work, we desire you to raise your County ; and to improve your forces to the total ruin of that Enemy, which way soever they go ; and if[1] you shall accordingly do your part, doubt not of their total ruin.

We thought fit to speed this to you ; to the end you may not be troubled if they shall march towards you, but improve your interest as aforesaid, that you may give glory to God for this unspeakable mercy. This is all at present from,

Your very humble servant,
OLIVER CROMWELL.

LETTER XXV

CROMWELL, on this Thursday Night, does not yet know all the havoc he has made. Listen to stout Sir James from the other side ; and pity poor men embarked in a hollow Cause, with a Duke of Hamilton for General !

'Beside Preston in Lancashire,' says the stout Knight, 'Cromwell falls on Sir Marmaduke's flank. The English' of Sir Marmaduke 'imagined it was one Colonel Ashton, a 'powerful Presbyterian, who had got together 3,000 men to 'oppose us, because we came out of Scotland without the 'General Assembly's permission. Mark the quarrel. While 'Sir Marmaduke disputes the matter, Baillie, by the Duke's 'order, marches to Ribble Bridge, and passes it with all the 'foot except two brigades.' Never dreaming that Cromwell is upon us ! 'This was two miles from Preston. By my 'Lord Duke's command, I have sent some ammunition and 'commanded-men to Sir Marmaduke's assistance : but to no

---

[1] 'that' in the Original.—The punctuation and grammar of these sentences might have been improved ; but their breathless impetuosity, directness, sincere singleness of purpose, intent on the despatch of business only, would have been obscured in the process.

VICTORY AT PRESTON

'purpose; for Cromwell prevailed; so that our English first
'retired, and then fled. It must be remembered that, the night
'before this sad encounter, Earl Calendar and Middleton were
'gone to Wigan, eight miles from thence, with a considerable
'part of the cavalry. Calendar was come back, and was with
'the Duke,' while the action took place; 'and so was I: but
'upon the rout of Sir Marmaduke's people, Calendar got away
'to Ribble, where he arrived safely by a miracle, as I think;
'for the Enemy was between the Bridge and us, and had killed
'or taken most part of our two brigades of foot,' which was
all that Baillie had left here.

'The Duke with his guard of horse, Sir Marmaduke with
'many officers, among others myself, got into Preston Town;
'with intention to pass a ford below it, though at that time
'not rideable. At the entry of the Town, the enemy pursued
'us hard. The Duke faced about, and put two troops of them
'to a retreat; but so soon as we turned from them, they again
'turned upon us. The Duke facing the second time, charged
'them, which succeeded well. Being pursued the third time,
'my Lord Duke cried To charge once more for King Charles!
'One trooper refusing, he beat him with his sword. At that
'charge we put the enemy so far behind us, that he could not
'so soon overtake us again. Then Sir Marmaduke and I
'entreated the Duke to hasten to his Army:—and truly here
'he showed as much personal valour as any man could be capable
'of. We swam the Ribble River; and so got to the place where
'Lieutenant-General Baillie had advantageously lodged the foot,
'on the top of a Hill, among very fencible enclosures.

'After Calendar came to the infantry, he had sent 600 muske-
'teers to defend Ribble Bridge. Very unadvisedly; for the way
'Cromwell had to it was a descent from a hill that commanded
'all the champaign; which was about an English quarter of a
'mile in length between the Bridge and that Hill where *our* foot
'were lodged. So that our musketeers, having no shelter, were
'forced to receive all the musket-shot of Cromwell's infantry,
'which was secure within thick hedges; and after the loss of
'many men, were forced to run back to our foot. Here Claude
'Hamilton, the Duke's Lieutenant-Colonel, had his arm broke
'with a musket-bullet.

'The Bridge of Ribble being lost, the Duke called all the
'Colonels together on horseback to advise what was next to be
'done. We had no choice but one of two: Either stay, and
'maintain our ground till Middleton (who was sent for) came

'back with his cavalry; Or else march away that night, and
'find him out. Calendar would needs speak first; whereas by
'the custom of war he should have told his opinion last,—and it
'was, To march away that night so soon as it was dark. This
'was seconded by all the rest, except by Lieut.-General Baillie
'and myself. But all the arguments we used,—as the impos-
'sibility of a safe retreat, from an enemy so powerful of horse;
'in so very foul weather, and extremely deep ways; our soldiers
'exceedingly wet, weary and hungry; the inevitable loss of all
'our ammunition,—could not move my Lord Duke by his
'authority to contradict the shameful resolution taken by the
'major part of his officers.

'After that drumless march was resolved upon, and but few
'horse appointed to stay in rear of the foot, I inquired, What
'should become of our unfortunate Ammunition, since forward
'with us we could not get it? It was not thought fit to blow
'it up that night, lest thereby the Enemy should know of our
'retreat, or rather flight. I was of that opinion too; but for
'another reason: for we could not have blown it up then,
'without a visible mischief to ourselves, being so near it. It was
'ordered it should be done, three hours after our departure, by a
'train: but that being neglected, Cromwell got it all.

'Next morning we appeared at Wigan Moor; half our
'number less than we were;—most of the faint and weary
'soldiers having lagged behind; whom we never saw again.
'Lieutenant-General Middleton had missed us,' such excellent
'order was in this Army, for he came by *another* way to Ribble
'Bridge. It was to be wished he had still stayed with us! He,
'not finding us there, followed our track: but was himself hotly
'pursued by Cromwell's horse; with whom he skirmished the
'whole way till he came within a mile of us. He lost some
'men, and several were hurt, among others Colonel Urrey got
'a dangerous shot on the left side of his head; whereof, though
'he was afterwards taken prisoner, he recovered. In this retreat
'of Middleton's, which he managed well, Cromwell lost one of
'the gallantest officers he had, Major Thornhaugh; who was
'run into the breast with a lance, whereof he died.

'After Lieutenant-General Middleton's coming, we began to
'think of fighting in that Moor: but that was found impossible,
'—in regard it was nothing large, and was environed with
'enclosures which commanded it, and these we could not
'maintain long, for want of that ammunition we had left behind
'us. And therefore we marched forward with intention to gain

'Warrington, ten miles from the Moor we were in; and there
'we conceived we might face about, having the command of a
'Town, a River, and a Bridge. Yet I conceive there were but
'few of us could have foreseen we might be beaten, *before* we
'were masters of any of them.

'It was towards evening and in the latter end of August,'
Friday 18th of the month, 'when our horse began to march.
'Some regiments of them were left with the rear of the foot:
'Middleton stayed with these; my Lord Duke and Calendar
'were before.—As I marched with the last brigade of foot
'through the Town of Wigan, I was alarmed, That our horse
'behind me were beaten, and running several ways, and that
'the enemy was in my rear. I faced about with that brigade;
'and in the Market-place, serried the pikes together, shoulder
'to shoulder, to entertain any that might charge: and sent
'orders to the rest of the brigades before, To continue their
'march, and follow Lieutenant-General Baillie who was before
'them. It was then night, but the moon shone bright. A
'regiment of horse of our own appeared first, riding very dis-
'orderly. I got them to stop, till I commanded my pikes to
'open, and give way for them to ride or run away, since they
'would not stay. But now my pikemen, being demented (as I
'think we were all), would not hear me; and two of them ran
'full tilt at me,'—poor Dalgetty! 'One of their pikes, which
'was intended for my belly, I griped with my left hand; the
'other ran me nearly two inches into the inner side of my right
'thigh; all of them crying, of me and those horse, "They are
'Cromwell's men!" This was an unseasonable wound; for it
'made me, after that night, unserviceable. This made me forget
'all rules of modesty, prudence, and discretion,'—my choler being
up, and my blood flowing! 'I rode to the horse, and desired
'them to charge through these foot. They fearing the hazard
'of the pikes, stood: I then made a cry come from behind them,
'That the enemy was upon them. This encouraged them to
'charge my foot, so fiercely that the pikemen threw down their
'pikes, and got into houses. All the horse galloped away, and
'as I was told afterwards, rode not through but *over* our whole
'foot, treading them down;—and in this confusion Colonel
'Lockhart,'—let the reader note that Colonel,—'was trod down
'from his horse, with great danger of his life.

'Though the Enemy was near, yet I beat drums to gather my
'men together. Shortly after came Middleton with some horse.
'I told him what a disaster I had met with, and what a greater I

'expected. He told me he would ride before, and make the horse
'halt. I marched, however, all that night till it was fair day;
'and then Baillie, who had rested a little, entreated me to go
'into some house and repose on a chair; for I had slept none
'in two nights, and eaten as little. I alighted; but the constant
'alarms of the Enemy's approach made me resolve to ride
'forward to Warrington, which was but a mile; and indeed I
'may say I slept all that way, notwithstanding my wound.'

While the wounded Dalgetty rides forward, let us borrow
another glimpse from a different source; of bitter struggle still
going on a little to the rear of him. 'At a place called Red-
'bank,' near Winwick Church, two miles from Warrington,
'the Scots made a stand with a body of pikes, and lined the
'hedges with muskets; who so rudely entertained the pursuing
'Enemy, that they were compelled to stop until the coming up
'of Colonel Pride's regiment of foot, who, after a sharp dispute,
'put those same brave fellows to the run. They were com-
'manded by a little spark in a blue bonnet, who performed the
'part of an excellent commander, and was killed on the spot.'
Does any one know this little spark in the blue bonnet? No
one. His very mother has long ceased to weep for him now.
Let him have burial, and a passing sigh from us!—Dugald
Turner continues:

'I expected to have found either the Duke or Calendar, or
'both of them, at Warrington: but I did not; and indeed I
'have often been told that Calendar carried away the Duke with
'him, much against his mind. Here did the Lieutenant-General
'of the foot meet with an Order, whereby he is required "To
'make as good conditions for himself and those under him as he
'could; for the horse would not come back to him, being re-
'solved to preserve themselves for a better time." Baillie was
'surprised with this: and looking upon that action which he
'was ordered to do, as full of dishonour, he lost much of that
'patience of which naturally he was master; and beseeched any
'that would to shoot him through the head,'—poor Baillie!
'At length having something composed himself, and being much
'solicited by the officers that were by him, he wrote to Cromwell.
'—I then told him, That so long as there was a resolution to
'fight, I would not go a foot from him; but now that they
'were to deliver themselves prisoners, I would preserve my
'liberty as long as I could: and so took my leave of him,
'carrying my wounded thigh away with me. I met immediately
'with Middleton; who sadly condoled the irrecoverable losses of

'the last two days Within two hours after, Baillie and all the
'officers and soldiers that were left of the foot were Cromwell's
'prisoners. I got my wound dressed that morning by my own
'surgeon ; and took from him those things I thought necessary
'for me ; not knowing when I might see him again ; as indeed
'I never saw him after.'

This was now the Saturday morning when Turner rode away,
'carrying his wounded thigh with him ;' and got up to Hamilton
and the vanguard of horse ; who rode, aimless, or as good as
aimless henceforth, till he and they were captured at Uttoxeter,
or in the neighbourhood. Monro with the *rear*-guard of horse,
'always a day's march behind,' hearing now what had befallen,
instantly drew bridle ; paused uncertain ; then, in a marauding
manner, rode back towards their own country.

Of which disastrous doings let us now read Cromwell's victorious account, drawn up with more deliberation on the morrow
after. 'This Gentleman,' who brings up the Letter, is Major
Berry ; 'once a Clerk in the Shropshire Iron-works ;' now a
very rising man. 'He had lived with me,' says Richard Baxter,
'as guest in my own house ;' he has now high destinies before
him,—which at last sink lower than ever.

*To the Honourable William Lenthall, Esquire, Speaker of the
House of Commons: These.*

'Warrington,' 20th August 1648.

SIR,
    I have sent up this Gentleman to give you an account
of the great and good hand of God towards you, in the late
victory obtained against the Enemy in these parts.

After the conjunction of that Party which I brought with
me out of Wales with the Northern Forces about Knaresborough
and Wetherby,—hearing that the Enemy was advanced with
their Army into Lancashire, we marched the next day, being the
13th of this instant August, to Otley (having cast off our
Train, and sent it to Knaresborough, because of the difficulty
of marching therewith through Craven, and to the end we
might with more expedition attend the Enemy's motion) : and
on the 14th to Skipton ; the 15th to Gisburne ; the 16th
to Hodder Bridge over Ribble ;[1] where we held a council of

[1] Over Hodder rather, which is the chief tributary of the Ribble in
those upland parts, and little inferior to the main stream in size.
Ribble from the Northeast, Hodder from the North, then a few
miles farther, Calder from the South: after which Ribble pursues

war. At which we had in consideration, Whether we should march to Whalley that night, and so on, to interpose between the Enemy and his further progress into Lancashire and so southward,—which we had some advertisement the Enemy intended, and 'we are' since confirmed that they intended for London itself: Or whether to march immediately over the said Bridge, there being no other betwixt that and Preston, and there engage the Enemy,—who we did believe would stand his ground, because we had information that the Irish Forces under Monro lately come out of Ireland, which consisted of Twelve-hundred horse and Fifteen-hundred Foot, were on their march towards Lancashire to join them.

It was thought that to engage the Enemy to fight was our business; and the reason aforesaid giving us hopes that our marching on the North side of Ribble would effect it, it was resolved we should march over the Bridge; which accordingly we did; and that night quartered the whole Army in the field by Stonyhurst Hall, being Mr. Sherburn's house, a place nine miles distant from Preston. Very early the next morning we marched towards Preston: having intelligence that the Enemy was drawing together thereabouts from all his outquarters, we drew out a Forlorn of about two-hundred horse and four-hundred foot, the horse commanded by Major Smithson, the foot by Major Pownel. Our Forlorn of horse marched, within a mile 'to' where the Enemy was drawn up, —in the enclosed grounds by Preston, on that side next us; and there, upon a Moor, about half a mile distant from the Enemy's Army, met with their Scouts and Outguard; and did behave themselves with that valour and courage as made their Guards (which consisted both of horse and foot) to quit their ground; and took divers prisoners; holding this dispute with them until our Forlorn of foot came up for their justification; and by these we had opportunity to bring up our whole Army.

So soon as our foot and horse were come up, we resolved that night to engage them if we could; and therefore, advancing with our Forlorn, and putting the rest of our Army into as good a posture as the ground would bear (which was totally inconvenient for our horse, being all enclosure and miry ground),

its old direction; draining an extensive hill-tract by means of frequent inconsiderable brooks, and receiving no notable stream on either side till, far down, the Darwen from the East and South falls in near Preston, and the united waters, now a respectable River, rush swiftly into the Irish sea.

we pressed upon them. The regiments of foot were ordered as followeth. There being a Lane, very deep and ill, up to the Enemy's Army, and leading to the Town, we commanded two regiments of horse, the first whereof was Colonel Harrison's and next was my own, to charge up that Lane; and on either side of them advanced the 'Main'-battle,—which were Lieutenant-Colonel Reade's, Colonel Dean's and Colonel Pride's on the right; Colonel Bright's and my Lord General's on the left; and Colonel Ashton with the Lancashire regiments in reserve. We ordered Colonel Thornhaugh's and Colonel Twistleton's regiments of horse on the right; and one regiment in reserve for the Lane; and the remaining horse on the left:—so that, at last, we came to a Hedge-dispute; the greatest of the impression from the Enemy being upon our left wing, and upon the 'Main'-battle on both sides the Lane, and upon our horse in the Lane: in all which places the Enemy were forced from their ground, after four hours dispute;—until we came to the Town; into which four troops of my own regiment first entered; and, being well seconded by Colonel Harrison's regiment, charged the Enemy in the Town, and cleared the streets.

There came no band of your foot to fight that day but did it with incredible valour and resolution; among which Colonel Bright's, my Lord General's, Lieutenant-Colonel Reade's and Colonel Ashton's had the greatest work; they often coming to push of pike and to close firing, and always making the Enemy to recoil. And indeed I must needs say, God was as much seen in the valour of the officers and soldiers of these before-mentioned as in any action that hath been performed; the Enemy making, though he was still worsted, very stiff and sturdy resistance. Colonel Dean's and Colonel Pride's, outwinging the Enemy, could not come to so much share of the action; the Enemy shogging [1] down towards the Bridge; and keeping almost all in reserve, that so he might bring fresh hands often to fight. Which we not knowing, and lest we should be outwinged, 'we' placed those two regiments to enlarge our right wing; this was the cause they had not at that time so great a share in that action.

At the last the Enemy was put into disorder; many men

[1] *Shog* is from the same root as *shock;* 'shogging,' a word of Oliver's in such cases, signifies moving by pulses, intermittently. Ribble Bridge lay on the Scotch right; Dean and Pride, therefore, who fought on the English right, got gradually less and less to do.

slain, many prisoners taken; the Duke, with most of the Scots horse and foot, retreated over the Bridge; where,—after a very hot dispute betwixt the Lancashire regiments, part of my Lord General's, and them, being often at push of pike,—they were beaten from the Bridge; and our horse and foot, following them, killed many and took divers prisoners; and we possessed the Bridge over Darwen 'also,' and a few houses there; the Enemy being driven up within musket-shot of us where we lay that night,[1]—we not being able to attempt farther upon the Enemy, the night preventing us. In this posture did the Enemy and we lie most part of that night. Upon entering the Town, many of the Enemy's horse fled towards Lancaster; in the chase of whom went divers of our horse, who pursued them near ten miles, and had execution of them, and took about five-hundred horse and many prisoners. We possessed in this Fight very much of the Enemy's ammunition; I believe they lost four or five thousand arms. The number of slain we judge to be about a thousand; the prisoners we took were about four-thousand.

In the night the Duke was drawing off his Army towards Wigan; we were so wearied with the dispute that we did not so well attend the Enemy's going off as might have been; by means whereof the Enemy was gotten at least three miles with his rear, before ours got to them. I ordered Colonel Thornhaugh to command two or three regiments of horse to follow the Enemy, if it were possible to make him stand till we could bring up the Army. The Enemy marched away seven or eight thousand foot and about four-thousand horse; we followed him with about three-thousand foot and two-thousand five-hundred horse and dragoons; and, in this prosecution, that worthy gentleman, Colonel Thornhaugh, pressing too boldly, was slain, being run into the body and thigh and head by the Enemy's lancers And give me leave to say, he was a man as faithful and gallant in your service as any; and one who often heretofore lost blood in your quarrel, and now his last. He hath left some behind him to inherit a Father's honour; and a sad Widow;—both now the interest of the Commonwealth.

Our horse still prosecuted the Enemy; killing and taking divers all the way. At last the Enemy drew up within three miles of Wigan; and by that time our Army was come up, they drew off again, and recovered Wigan before we could attempt any thing upon them. We lay that night in the field

---

[1] The Darwen between us and them.

close by the Enemy; being very dirty and weary, and having marched twelve miles of such ground as I never rode in all my life, the day being very wet. We had some skirmishing, that night, with the Enemy, near the Town; where we took General Van Druske and a Colonel, and killed some principal Officers, and took about a hundred prisoners: where I also received a Letter from Duke Hamilton, for civil usage towards his kinsman Colonel Hamilton,[1] whom he left wounded there. We took also Colonel Hurry and Lieutenant-Colonel Innes, sometimes in your service. The next morning the Enemy marched towards Warrington, and we at the heels of them. The Town of Wigan, a great and poor Town, and very Malignant, were plundered almost to their skins by them.

We could not engage the Enemy until we came within three miles of Warrington; and there the Enemy made a stand, at a place near Winwick. We held them in some dispute till our Army came up; they maintaining the Pass with great resolution for many hours; ours and theirs coming to push of pike and very close charges,—which forced us to give ground; but our men, by the blessing of God, quickly recovered it, and charging very home upon them, beat them from their standing; where we killed about a thousand of them, and took, as we believe, about two-thousand prisoners; and prosecuted them home to Warrington Town; where they possessed the Bridge, which had a strong barricado and a work upon it, formerly made very defensive. As soon as we came thither, I received a message from General Baillie, desiring some capitulation. To which I yielded. Considering the strength of the Pass, and that I could not go over the River 'Mersey' within ten miles of Warrington with the Army, I gave him these terms: That he should surrender himself and all his officers and soldiers prisoners of war, with all his arms and ammunition and horses, to me; I giving quarter for life, and promising civil usage. Which accordingly is done: and the Commissioners deputed by me have received,

[1] Claud Hamilton; see Turner *supra*. Who 'Van Druske' is, none knows. 'Colonel Hurry' is the ever-changing Sir John Hurry, sometimes called Urry and Hurrey, who whisks like a most rapid actor of all work, ever on a new side, ever charging in the van, through this Civil-War Drama. The notablest feat he ever did was leading Prince Rupert on that marauding party, from Oxford to High Wycombe, on the return from which Hampden met his death (Clarendon, ii. 351). Hurry had been on the Parliament-side before. He was taken, at last, when Montrose was taken; and hanged out of the way. Of Innes ('Ennis') I know nothing at present.

and are receiving, all the arms and ammunition; which will be, as they tell me, about Four-thousand complete arms; and as many prisoners: and thus you have their Infantry totally ruined. What Colonels and Officers are with General Baillie, I have not yet received the list.

The Duke is marching with his remaining Horse, which are about three-thousand, towards Nantwich; where the Gentlemen of the County have taken about five-hundred of them: of which they sent me word this day. The country will scarce suffer any of my men to pass, except they have my hand-'writing;' telling them, They are Scots. They bring in and kill divers of them, as they light upon them. Most of the Nobility of Scotland are with the Duke. If I had a thousand horse that could but trot thirty miles, I should not doubt but to give a very good account of them: but truly we are so harassed and haggled out in this business, that we are not able to do more than walk 'at' an easy pace after them.—I have sent post to my Lord Grey, to Sir Henry Cholmely and Sir Edward Rhodes to gather all together, with speed, for their prosecution; as likewise to acquaint the Governor of Stafford therewith.

I hear Monro is about Cumberland with the horse that ran away,[1] and his 'own' Irish horse and foot, which are a considerable body. I have left Colonel Ashton's three regiments of foot, with seven troops of horse (six of Lancashire and one of Cumberland), at Preston; and ordered Colonel Scroop with five troops of horse and two troops of dragoons, 'and' with two regiments of foot (Colonel Lascelles's and Colonel Wastell's), to embody with them; and have ordered them to put their prisoners to the sword if the Scots shall presume to advance upon them, because they cannot bring them off with security.[2]

Thus you have a Narrative of the particulars of the success which God hath given yon: which I could hardly at this time have done, considering the multiplicity of business; but truly, when I was once engaged in it, I could hardly tell how to say less, there being so much of God in it; and I am not willing

---

[1] Northward from Preston on the evening of the 17th, the Battle-day.

[2] It is to be hoped the Scots under Monro will not presume to advance, for the prisoners here in Preston are about four-thousand! These are not Baillie's Warrington men 'who surrendered on quarter for life:' these are 'at discretion.'

to say more, lest there should seem to be any of man. Only
give me leave to add one word, showing the disparity of forces
on both sides ; that so you may see, and all the world acknowledge, the great hand of God in this business. The Scots
Army could not be less than twelve-thousand effective foot,
well armed, and five-thousand horse ; Langdale not less than
two-thousand five-hundred foot, and fifteen-hundred horse : in
all Twenty-one Thousand —and truly very few of their foot
but were as well armed if not better than yours, and at divers
disputes did fight two or three hours before they would quit
their ground. Yours were about two-thousand five-hundred
horse and dragoons of your old Army ; about four-thousand
foot of your old Army ; also about sixteen-hundred Lancashire
foot, and about five-hundred Lancashire horse : in all, about
Eight-thousand Six-hundred. You see by computation about
two-thousand of the Enemy slain ; betwixt eight and nine
thousand prisoners ; besides what are lurking in hedges and
private places, which the Country daily bring in or destroy.
Where Langdale and his broken forces are, I know not ; but
they are exceedingly shattered.

Surely, Sir, this is nothing but the hand of God ; and wherever
anything in this world is exalted, or exalts itself, God will pull it
down ; for this is the day wherein He alone will be exalted. It
is not fit for me to give advice, nor to say a word what use you
should make of this ;—more than to pray you, and all that
acknowledge God, That they would exalt Him,—and not hate
His people, who are as the apple of His eye, and for whom even
Kings shall be reproved ; and that you would take courage to do
the work of the Lord, in fulfilling the end of your Magistracy,
in seeking the peace and welfare of this Land,—that all that
will live peaceably may have countenance from you, and they
that are incapable and will not leave troubling the Land may
speedily be destroyed out of the Land. And if you take courage
in this, God will bless you ; and good men will stand by you ;
and God will have glory, and the Land will have happiness by
you in spite of all your enemies. Which shall be the prayer of,
    Your most humble and faithful servant,
        OLIVER CROMWELL.

Postscript. We have not, in all this, lost a considerable Officer
but Colonel Thornhaugh ; and not many soldiers, considering
the service : but many are wounded, and our horse much
wearied. I humbly crave that some course may be taken to

dispose of the Prisoners. The trouble, and extreme charge of the Country where they lie, is more than the danger of their escape. I think they would not go home if they might, without a convoy; they are so fearful of the Country, from whom they have deserved so ill. Ten men will keep a thousand from running away.

LETTER XXVI

LET the following hasty Letter, of the same date with that more deliberate one to Lenthall, followed by another as hasty, terminate the Preston Business. Letters of hot Haste, of Hue-and-Cry; two remaining out of many such, written 'to all the Countries,' in that posture of affairs;—the fruit of which we shall soon see. Colonels 'Cholmely, White, Hatcher, Rhodes,' Country Colonels of more or less celebrity, need not detain us at present.

For the Honourable the Committee at York: These.

Warrington, 20th August 1648.

'GENTLEMEN,'

We have quite tired our horses in pursuit of the Enemy: we have killed, taken and disabled all their Foot; and left them only some Horse, with whom the Duke is fled into Delamere Forest, having neither Foot nor Dragooners. They have taken Five-hundred of them,—I mean the Country Forces 'have,' as they send me word this day.

They are so tired, and in such confusion, that if my Horse could but trot after them, I could take them all. But we are so weary, we can scarce be able to do more than walk after them. I beseech you therefore, let Sir Henry Cholmely, Sir Edward Rhodes, Colonel Hatcher, and Colonel White, and all the Countries about you, be sent to, to rise with you and follow them. For they are the miserablest party that ever was: I durst engage myself, with Five-hundred fresh Horse, and Five-hundred nimble Foot, to destroy them all. My Horse are miserably beaten out; and I have Ten thousand of them Prisoners.

We have killed we know not what; but a very great number; having done execution upon them about thirty miles together, —besides what we killed in the Two great Fights, the one at Preston, the other at Warrington, or 'Winwick Pass.' The

Enemy was Twenty-four thousand horse and foot; whereof Eighteen-thousand foot and Six-thousand horse: and our number about Six-thousand foot and Three-thousand horse at the utmost.

This is a glorious Day:—God help England to answer His mercies!—I have no more; but beseech you in all your parts to gather into bodies, and pursue. I rest,

Your most humble servant,
OLIVER CROMWELL.

'P.S.' The greatest part, by far, of the Nobility of Scotland are with Duke Hamilton.

On Friday 25th, at Uttoxeter in Staffordshire, the poor Duke of Hamilton, begirt with enemies, distracted with mutinies and internal discords, surrenders and ceases; 'very ill, and unable to march.' 'My Lord Duke and Calendar,' says Dalgetty, 'fell out and were at very high words at supper, where I was,' the night before: 'each blaming the other for the misfortune and miscarriage of our affairs:' a sad employment! Dalgetty himself went prisoner to Hull; lay long with Colonel Robert Overton, an acquaintance of ours there. 'As we rode from Uttoxeter, we 'made a stand at the Duke's window; and he looking out with 'some kind words, we took our eternal farewell of him,'—never saw him more. He died on the scaffold for this business; being Earl of Cambridge, and an *English* Peer as well as Scotch:—the unhappiest of men; one of those 'singularly able men' who, with all their 'ability,' have never succeeded in any enterprise whatever!—

Colchester Siege, one of the most desperate defences, being now plainly without object, terminates, on Monday next. Surrender, 'on quarter' for the inferior parties, 'at discretion' for the superior. Two of the latter, Sir Charles Lucas and Sir George Lisle, gallant Officers both, are sentenced and shot on the place. 'By Ireton's instigation,' say some: yes, or without any special instigation; merely by the nature of the case! They who, contrary to Law and Treaty, have again involved this Nation in blood, do they deserve nothing? Two more, Goring and Lord Capel, stood trial at Westminster; of whom Lord Capel lost his head. He was 'the first man that rose to complain of Grievances' in November 1640; being then Mr. Capel, and Member for Hertfordshire.

In Scotland itself there is no farther resistance. The oppressed

Kirk Party rise rather, and almost thank the conquerors. 'Sir George Monro,' says Turner, 'following constantly a whole day's march to the rear of us,' finding himself, by this unhappy Battle, cut asunder from my Lord Duke, and brought into contact with Cromwell instead, 'marched straight back to Scotland and joined with Earl Lanark's forces,' my Lord Duke's brother. '*Straight* back,' as we shall find, is not the word for this march.

'But so soon as the news of our Defeat came to Scotland,' continues Turner, 'Argyle and the Kirk Party rose in arms; every mother's son; and this was called the "*Whiggamore* Raid:"' 1648,—first appearance of the Whig Party on the page of History, I think! 'David Lesley was at their head, and old Leven,' the Fieldmarshal of 1639, 'in the Castle of Edinburgh; who *cannonaded* the Royal' Hamilton 'troops whenever they came in view of him!'

Cromwell proceeds northward, goes at last to Edinburgh itself, to compose this strange state of matters.

At Norham on September 21st, he marches on and reaches Seaton, the Earl of Winton's House, which is the head-quarters of the horse, a few miles east of Edinburgh, on Tuesday evening. Next day, Wednesday 4th October 1648, come certain Dignitaries of the Argyle or Whiggamore Party, and escort him honourably into Edinburgh; 'to the Earl of Murrie's House in the Cannigate' (so, in good Edinburgh Scotch, do the old Pamphlets spell it); 'where a strong guard,' an English Guard, 'is appointed to keep constant watch at the Gate;' and all manner of Earls and persons of Whiggamore quality come to visit the Lieutenant-General; and even certain Clergy come, who have a leaning that way.—The Earl of Moray's House, Moray House, still stands in the Canon-gate of Edinburgh, well known to the inhabitants there. A solid spacious mansion, which, when all bright and new two-hundred years ago, must have been a very adequate lodging. There are remains of noble gardens; one of the noble state-rooms, when I last saw it, was an extensive Paper Warehouse. There is no doubt but the Lieutenant-General did lodge here; Guthry seeming to contradict this old Pamphlet, turns out to confirm it.

In London, matters are coming rapidly to a crisis. The resumed Debate, " Shall the Army Remonstrance be taken into consideration ?" does not come out affirmative; on the contrary,

THE ARMY IN LONDON

on Thursday the 30th, it comes out negative by a Majority of Ninety : "No, we will not take it into consideration."—"No?" The Army at Windsor, thereupon, spends again 'a Day in Prayer.' The Army at Windsor has decided on the morrow that it will march to London;—marches, arrives accordingly, on Saturday December 2d, quarters itself in Whitehall, in St. James's ; 'and other great vacant Houses in the skirts of the City and villages about, no offence being given anywhere.' In the drama of Modern History one knows not any graver, more noteworthy scene,—earnest as very Death and Judgment. They have decided to have Justice, these men ; to see God's Justice done, and His judgments executed on this Earth. The abysses where the thunders and the splendours are bred,—the reader sees them again laid bare ; and black Madness lying close to the Wisdom which is brightest and highest :—and owls and godless men who hate the lightning and the light, and love the mephitic dusk and darkness, are no judges of the actions of heroes ! 'Shedders of blood ?' Yes, blood is occasionally shed. The healing Surgeon, the sacrificial Priest, the august Judge pronouncer of God's oracles to men, these and the atrocious Murderer, are alike shedders of blood ; and it is an owl's eye that, except for the *dresses* they wear, discerns no difference in these !—Let us leave the owl to his hootings ; let us get on with our Chronology and swift course of events.

On *Monday 4th December*, the House, for the last time, takes 'into farther debate' the desperate question, Whether his Majesty's concessions in that Treaty of Newport are a ground of settlement ?—debates it all Monday, has debated it all Friday and Saturday before. Debates it all Monday, 'till five o'clock next morning ;' at five o'clock next morning, decides it, Yea. By a Majority of Forty-six, One-hundred-and-twenty-nine to Eighty-three, it is at five o'clock on Tuesday morning decided, Yea, they are a ground of settlement. The Army Chiefs and the Minority consult together, in deep and deepest deliberation, through that day and night ; not, I suppose, without Prayer ; and on the morrow morning this is what we see :

Wednesday 6th December 1648, 'Colonel Rich's regiment of 'horse and Colonel Pride's regiment of foot were a guard to the 'Parliament ; and the City Trainbands were discharged' from that employment. Yes, they were ! Colonel Rich's horse stand ranked in Palaceyard, Colonel Pride's foot in Westminster Hall and at all entrances to the Commons House, this day : and in Colonel Pride's hand is a written list of names, names of the chief among the Hundred-and-twenty-nine ; and at his side is my Lord Grey of Groby, who, as this Member after that comes up, whispers or beckons, "He is one of them : he cannot enter !" And Pride gives the word, "To the Queen's Court ;" and Member after Member is marched thither, Forty-one of them this day, and kept there in a state bordering on rabidity, asking, By what Law ? and ever again, By what Law ? Is there a colour or faintest shadow of Law, to be found in any of the Books, Yearbooks, Rolls of Parliament, Bractons, Fletas, Cokes upon Lyttleton, for this ? Hugh Peters visits them ; has little comfort, no light as to the Law ; confesses, "It is by the Law of Necessity ; truly, by the Power of the Sword."

It must be owned the Constable's baton is fairly down, this day ; overborne by the Power of the Sword, and a Law not to be found in any of the Books. At evening the distracted Forty-one are marched to Mr. Duke's Tavern hard-by, a 'Tavern called Hell ;' and very imperfectly accommodated for the night. Sir Symonds D'Ewes, who has ceased taking notes long since ; Mr. William Prynne, louder than any in the question of Law ; Waller, Massey, Harley, and other remnants of the old Eleven, are of this unlucky Forty-one ; among whom too we count little Clement Walker 'in his gray suit with his little stick,'—asking in the voice of the indomitablest terrier or Blenheim cocker, "By what Law ? I ask again, By what Law ?" Whom no mortal will ever be able to answer. Such is the far-famed Purging of the House by Colonel Pride.

This evening, while the Forty-one are getting lodged in Mr. Duke's, Lieutenant-General Cromwell came to Town. Pontefract Castle is not taken : he has left Lambert looking after that, and come up hither to look after more important things.

The Commons on Wednesday did send out to demand 'the Members of this House' from Colonel Pride ; but Pride made respectful evasive answer ;—could not, for the moment, comply with the desires of the Honourable House. On the Thursday Lieutenant-General Cromwell is thanked ; and *Pride's Purge* continues : new men of the Majority are seized ; others scared away need no seizing ;—above a Hundred in all ; who are sent into their countries, sent into the Tower ; sent out of our way, and trouble us no farther. The Minority has now become Majority ; there is now clear course for it, clear resolution there has for some time back been in it What its resolution was, and its action that it did in pursuance thereof, 'an action not done in a corner, but in sight of all the nations,' and of God who made the Nations, we know, and the whole world knows!—

DEATH-WARRANT

THE Trial of Charles Stuart falls not to be described in this place; the deep meanings that lie in it cannot be so much as glanced at here. Oliver Cromwell attends in the High Court of Justice at every session except one; Fairfax sits only in the first. Ludlow, Whalley, Walton, names known to us, are also constant attendants in that High Court, during that long-memorable Month of January 1649. The King is thrice brought to the Bar; refuses to plead, comports himself with royal dignity, with royal haughtiness, strong in his divine right: 'smiles' contemptuously, 'looks with an austere countenance,' —does not seem, till the very last, to have fairly believed that they would dare to sentence him. But they were men sufficiently provided with daring; men, we are bound to see, who sat there as in the Presence of the Maker of all men, as executing the judgments of Heaven above, and had not the fear of any man or thing on the Earth below. Bradshaw said to the King, "Sir, you are not permitted to issue out in these discoursings. "This Court is satisfied of its authority. No Court will bear "to hear its authority questioned in that manner."—"Clerk, "read the Sentence!"—

And so, under date, Monday 29th of January 1648-9, there is this stern Document to be introduced; not specifically of Oliver's composition; but expressing in every letter of it the conviction of Oliver's heart, in this, one of his most important appearances on the stage of earthly life.

To Colonel Francis Hacker, Colonel Huncks, and Lieutenant-Colonel Phayr, and to every of them.

At the High Court of Justice for the Trying and Judging of Charles Stuart, King of England, 29th January 1648.

WHEREAS Charles Stuart, King of England, is and standeth convicted, attainted and condemned of High Treason and other high Crimes; and Sentence upon Saturday last was pronounced against him by this Court, To be put to death by the severing of his head from his body; of which Sentence execution yet remaineth to be done:

These are therefore to will and require you to see the said Sentence executed, in the open Street before Whitehall, upon the morrow, being the Thirtieth day of this instant month of January, between the hours of Ten in the morning and Five in the afternoon, with full effect. And for so doing, this shall be your warrant.

And these are to require all Officers and Soldiers, and others the good People of this Nation of England, to be assisting unto you in this service.

                Given under our hands and seals,
                    JOHN BRADSHAW.
                    THOMAS GREY, 'LORD GROBY.'
                    OLIVER CROMWELL.
                        ('and Fifty-six others.')

Thus ends the Second Civil War. In Regicide, in a Commonwealth and Keepers of the Liberties of England. In punishment of Delinquents, in abolition of Cobwebs;—if it be possible, in a Government of Heroism and Veracity; at lowest, of Anti-Flunkeyism, Anti-Cant, and the *endeavour* after Heroism and Veracity.

PART V

CAMPAIGN IN IRELAND

1649

ON *Tuesday 30th January* 1648-9, it is ordered in the Commons House, 'That the Post be stayed until tomorrow morning, ten of the clock;' and the same afternoon, the King's Execution having now taken place, Edward Dendy, Sergeant-at-Arms, with due trumpeters, pursuivants and horse-troops, notifies, loud as he can blow, at Cheapside and elsewhere, openly to all men, That whosoever shall proclaim a new King, Charles Second or another, without authority of Parliament, in this Nation of England, shall be a Traitor and suffer death. For which service, on the morrow, each trumpeter receives 'ten shillings' of the public money, and Sergeant Dendy himself—shall see what he will receive. And all Sheriffs, Mayors of Towns and such like are to do the same in their respective localities, that the fact be known to every one.

After which follow, in Parliament and out of it, such debatings, committee-ings, consultings towards a Settlement of this Nation, as the reader can in a dim way sufficiently fancy for himself on considering the two following facts.

First, That on *February* 13*th*, Major Thomas Scott, an honourable Member whom we shall afterwards know better, brings in his Report or Ordinance for a COUNCIL OF STATE, to be henceforth the Executive among us; which Council, to the number of Forty-one Persons, is thereupon nominated by Parliament; and begins its Sessions at Derby House on the 17th. Bradshaw, Fairfax, Cromwell, Whitlocke, Harry Marten,

Ludlow, Vane the Younger, and others whom we know, are of this Council.

Second, That, after much adjustment and new-modelling, new Great Seals, new Judges, Sergeants-maces, there comes out, on *May* 19*th*, an emphatic Act, brief as Sparta, in these words: 'Be it declared and enacted by this present Parliament, and by 'the authority of the same: That the People of England, and 'of all the dominions and territories thereunto belonging, are 'and shall be, and are hereby constituted, made, established and 'confirmed to be, A COMMONWEALTH OR FREE-STATE; and 'shall from henceforth be governed as a Commonwealth and 'Free-State,—by the Supreme Authority of this Nation the 'Representatives of the People in Parliament, and by such as 'they shall appoint and constitute officers and ministers under 'them for the good of the People, and that without any King 'or House of Lords.'—What modelling and consulting has been needed in the interim, the reader shall conceive.

On March 9th, 1648, poor versatile Hamilton, poor versatile Holland, with the Lord Capel who the first of all in this Parliament rose to complain of Grievances, meet their death in Palace-yard. The High Court was still sitting in Westminster Hall as they passed through 'from Sir Robert Cotton's house.' Hamilton lingered a little, or seemed to linger, in the Hall; still hopeful of reprieve and fine of 100,000*l*.: but the Earl of Denbigh, his brother-in-law, a Member of the Council of State, stept up to him; whispered in his ear;—the poor Duke walked on. That is the end of all his diplomacies; his Scotch Army of Forty-thousand, his painful ridings to Uttoxeter, and to many other places, have all issued here. The Earl of Lanark will now be Duke of Hamilton in Scotland: may a better fate await him!

The once gay Earl of Holland has been 'converted' some days ago, as it were for the nonce,—poor Earl! With regard to my Lord Capel again, who followed last in order, he behaved, says Bulstrode, 'much after the manner of a stout Roman. He 'had no Minister with him, nor showed any sense of death 'approaching; but carried himself all the time he was upon 'the scaffold with that boldness and resolution as was to be 'admired. He wore a sad-coloured suit, his hat cocked up, and 'his cloak thrown under one arm; he looked towards the 'people at his first coming up, and put off his hat in manner of 'a salute; he had a little discourse with some gentlemen, and

MILTON AS SECRETARY

'passed up and down in a careless posture.' Thus died Lord Capel, the first who complained of Grievances: in seven years time there are such changes for a man; and the first acts of his Drama little know what the last will be!—

This new High Court of Justice is one of some Seven or Eight that sat in those years, and were greatly complained of by Constitutional persons. Nobody ever said that they decided contrary to evidence; but they were not the regular Judges. They took the Parliament's law as good, without consulting Fleta and Bracton about it. They consisted of learned Sergeants and other weighty persons nominated by the Parliament, usually in good numbers, for the occasion.

Some weeks hence, drunken Poyer of Pembroke and the confused Welsh Colonels are tried by Court Martial; Poyer, Powel, Laughern are found to merit death. Death however shall be executed only upon one of them; let the other two be pardoned: let them draw lots which two. 'In two of the lots was written, '*Life given by God*; the third lot was a blank. The Prisoners 'were not willing to draw their own destiny; but a child drew 'the lots, and gave them: and the lot fell to Colonel Poyer to 'die.' He was shot in Covent Garden; died like a soldier, poor confused Welshman; and so ended.

And with these executions, the chief Delinquents are now got punished. The Parliament lays up its axe again; willing to pardon the smaller multitude, if they will keep quiet henceforth.

On March 13th, 1648, furthermore, one discerns in a faint but an authentic manner, certain dim gentlemen of the highest authority, young Sir Harry Vane to appearance one of them, repairing to the lodging of one Mr. Milton, 'a small house in Holborn which opens backwards into Lincoln's Inn Fields;' to put an official question to him there! Not a doubt of it they saw Mr. John this evening. In the official Book this yet stands legible:

'*Die Martis*, 13° *Martii* 1648.' 'That it is referred to the 'same Committee,' Whitlocke, Vane, Lord Lisle, Earl of Denbigh, Harry Marten, Mr. Lisle, 'or any two of them, to 'speak with Mr. Milton, to know, Whether he will be employed 'as Secretary for the Foreign Languages? and to report to the 'Council.' I have authority to say that Mr. Milton, thus unexpectedly applied to, consents; is formally appointed on Thursday next; makes his proof-shot, 'to the Senate of Hamburg,' about a week hence;—and gives, and continues to give, great satisfaction to that Council, to me, and to the whole Nation now, and to all Nations! Such romance lies in the State-Paper Office.

LETTERS XXVII ETC.

Tuesday, 10*th July* 1649. 'This evening about five of the clock, 'the Lord Lieutenant of Ireland began his journey; by the way 'of Windsor, and so to Bristol. He went forth in that state and 'equipage as the like hath hardly been seen; himself in a coach 'with six gallant Flanders mares, whitish gray; divers coaches 'accompanying him; and very many great Officers of the 'Army; his Lifeguard consisting of eighty gallant men, the 'meanest whereof a Commander or Esquire, in stately habit;— 'with trumpets sounding, almost to the shaking of Charing 'Cross, had it been now standing. Of his Lifeguard many are 'Colonels; and believe me, it's such a guard as is hardly to be 'paralleled in the world. And now have at you, my Lord of 'Ormond! You will have men of gallantry to encounter; 'whom to overcome will be honour sufficient, and to be beaten 'by them will be no great blemish to your reputation. If you 'say, Cæsar or Nothing: they say, A Republic or Nothing. 'The Lord Lieutenant's colours are white.'

Thus has Lord-Lieutenant Cromwell gone to the Wars in Ireland. But before going, and while just on the eve of going, he has had a multiplicity of other businesses to attend to. [Here omitted.—EDITOR.]

Cromwell, leaving London as we saw on Tuesday evening July 10th, had arrived at Bristol on Saturday evening, which was the 14th. He had to continue here, making his preparations, gathering his forces, for several weeks. Mrs. Cromwell means seemingly to pass a little more time with him before he go. In the end of July, he quits Bristol; moving westward by Tenby and Pembroke, where certain forces were to be taken up,— towards Milford Haven; where he dates his next Letters, just in the act of sailing.

LETTER XXVII

THE new Lord Lieutenant had at first designed for Munster, where it seemed his best chance lay. Already he has sent some regiments over, to reinforce our old acquaintance Colonel, now

Lieutenant-General Michael Jones, at present besieged in Dublin, and enable him to resist the Ormond Army there But on the 2d of August an important Victory has turned up for Jones : surprisal, and striking into panic and total rout, of the said Ormond Army ; which fortunate event, warmly recognised in the following Letter, clears Dublin of siege, and opens new outlooks for the Lord Lientenant there. He sails thitherward ; from Milford Haven, Monday, August 13th. Ireton, who is Major-General, or third in command, Jones being second, follows with another division of the force, on Wednesday. Hugh Peters also went ; and 'Mr. Owen' also, for another chaplain.

The good ship John is still lying in Milford waters, we suppose, waiting for a wind, for a turn of the tide. 'My Son' Richard Cromwell, and perhaps Richard's Mother, we may dimly surmise, had attended the Lord Lieutenant thus far, to wish him speed on his perilous enterprise ?

'*For my loving Brother Richard Mayor, Esquire, at Hursley. These.*'

'Milford Haven,' From Aboard the John,
13th August 1649.

LOVING BROTHER,

I could not satisfy myself to omit this opportunity by my Son of writing to you ; especially there being so late and great an occasion of acquainting you with the happy news I received from Lieutenant-General Jones yesterday.

The Marquis of Ormond besieged Dublin with Nineteen-thousand men or thereabouts ; Seven-thousand Scots and Three thousand more were coming to 'join him in' that work. Jones issued out of Dublin with Four-thousand foot and Twelve-hundred horse ; hath routed this whole Army ; killed about Four-thousand upon the place ; taken 2,517 prisoners, above Three-hundred 'of them' officers, some of great quality.[1]

This is an astonishing mercy ; so great and seasonable that indeed we are like them that dreamed. What can we say! The Lord fill our souls with thankfulness, that our mouths may be full of His praise,—and our lives too ; and grant we may never forget His goodness to us. These things seem to strengthen our faith and love, against more difficult times. Sir, pray for me, That I may walk worthy of the Lord in all tha He hath called me unto !—

[1] The round numbers of this account have, as is usual, come over greatly exaggerated (Carte, *ubi supra*).

I have committed my Son to you; pray give him advice. I envy him not his contents; but I fear he should be swallowed up in them. I would have him mind and understand Business, read a little History, study the Mathematics and Cosmography: —these are good, with subordination to the things of God. Better than Idleness, or mere outward worldly contents. These fit for Public services, for which a man is born.

Pardon this trouble. I am thus bold because I know you love me; as indeed I do you, and yours. My love to my dear Sister, and my Cousin Ann your Daughter, and all Friends. I rest,

Sir,
Your loving brother,
OLIVER CROMWELL.

LETTER XXVIII

Same date, same conveyance

To my beloved Daughter Dorothy Cromwell, at Hursley: These.

From Aboard the John, 13th August 1649.

MY DEAR DAUGHTER,
Your Letter was very welcome to me. I like to see anything from your hand; because indeed I stick not to say I do entirely love you. And therefore I hope a word of advice will not be unwelcome nor unacceptable to thee.

I desire you both to make it above all things your business to seek the Lord; to be frequently calling upon Him, that He would manifest Himself to you in His Son; and be listening what returns He makes to you,—for He will be speaking in your ear and in your heart, if you attend thereunto. I desire you to provoke your Husband likewise thereunto. As for the pleasures of this Life, and outward Business, let that be upon the bye. Be above all these things, by Faith in Christ; and then you shall have the true use and comfort of them,—and not otherwise. I have much satisfaction in hope your spirit is this way set; and I desire you may grow in grace, and in the knowledge of our Lord and Saviour Jesus Christ; and that I may hear thereof. The Lord is very near: which we see by His wonderful works: and therefore He looks that we of this generation draw near to Him. This late great Mercy of Ireland is a great manifestation thereof. Your Husband

will acquaint you with it. We should be much stirred up in
our spirits to thankfulness. We much need the spirit of Christ,
to enable us to praise God for so admirable a mercy.

The Lord bless thee, my dear Daughter.

I rest,
Thy loving Father,
OLIVER CROMWELL.

'P.S.' I hear thou didst lately miscarry. Prithee take heed
of a coach by all means; borrow thy Father's nag when thou
intendest to go abroad.

Is the last phrase ironical; or had the 'coach,' in those
ancient roads, overset, and produced the disaster? Perhaps 'thy
Father's nag' is really safer? Oliver is not given to irony; nor
in a tone for it at this moment. These gentle domesticities and
pieties are strangely contrasted with the fiery savagery and iron
grimness, stern as Doom, which meets us in the next set of
Letters we have from him!

On the second day following, on the 15th of August, Cromwell with a prosperous wind arrived in Dublin; 'where,' say the
old Newspapers, ' he was received with all possible demonstrations
'of joy; the great guns echoing forth their welcome, and the
'acclamations of the people resounding in every street. The
'Lord Lieutenant being come into the City,—where the con-
'course of the people was very great, they all flocking to see him
'of whom before they had heard so much,—at a convenient place
'he made a stand,' rising in his carriage we suppose, 'and with
'his hat in his hand made a speech to them.' Speech unfortun-
ately lost: it is to this effect; "That as God had brought him
"thither in safety, so he doubted not but by Divine Providence
"to restore them all to their just liberties and properties,"
much trodden down by those unblessed Papist-Royalist combinations, and the injuries of war: "and that all persons whose
"hearts' affections were real for the carrying on of this great
"work against the barbarous and bloodthirsty Irish and their
"confederates and adherents, and for propagating of Christ's
"Gospel and establishing of Truth and Peace, and restoring
"of this bleeding Nation of Ireland to its former happiness and
"tranquillity,—should find favour and protection from the
"Parliament of England and him, and withal receive such
"rewards and gratuities as might be answerable to their merits."

'This Speech,' say the old Newspapers, 'was entertained with 'great applause by the people; who all cried out, "We will live 'and die with you!"'

IRISH WAR

THE history of the Irish War is, and for the present must continue, very dark and indecipherable to us. Ireland, ever since the Irish Rebellion broke out and changed itself into an Irish Massacre, in the end of 1641, has been a scene of distracted controversies, plunderings, excommunications, treacheries, conflagrations, of universal misery and blood and bluster, such as the world before or since has never seen. The History of it does not form itself into a picture; but remains only as a huge blot, an indiscriminate blackness; which the human memory cannot willingly charge itself with! There are Parties on the back of Parties; at war with the world and with each other. There are Catholics of the Pale, demanding freedom of religion; under my Lord This and my Lord That. There are Old-Irish Catholics, under Pope's Nuncios, under Abbas O'Teague of the excommunications, and Owen Roe O'Neil;—demanding not religious freedom only, but what we now call 'Repeal of the Union;' and unable to agree with the Catholics of the English Pale. Then there are Ormond Royalists, of the Episcopalian and mixed creeds, strong for King without Covenant: Ulster and other Presbyterians, strong for King *and* Covenant: lastly, Michael Jones and the Commonwealth of England, who want neither King nor Covenant. All these plunging and tumbling, in huge discord, for the last eight years, have made of Ireland and its affairs the black unutterable blot we speak of.

At the date of Oliver's arrival, all Irish Parties are united in a combination very unusual with them; very dangerous for the incipient Commonwealth. Ormond, who had returned thither with new Commission, in hopes to cooperate with Scotch Hamilton during the Second Civil War, arrived too late for that object; but has succeeded in rallying Ireland into one mass of declared opposition to the Powers that now rule. Catholics of the Pale, and Old-Irish Catholics of the Massacre, will at length act together; Protestant English Royalism, which has fled hither for shelter; nay, now at last Royalist Presbyterianism, and the very Scots in Ulster,—have all joined with Ormond 'against the Regicides.' They are eagerly inviting the young

Charles Second to come thither, and be crowned and made
victorious. He as yet hesitates between that and Scotland ;—
may probably give Scotland the preference. But in all Ireland,
when Cromwell sets foot on it, there remain only two Towns,
Dublin and Derry, that hold for the Commonwealth ; Dublin
lately besieged, Derry still besieged. A very formidable combination. All Ireland kneaded together, by favourable accident
and the incredible patience of Ormond, stands up in one great
combination, resolute to resist the Commonwealth. Combination great in bulk ; but made of iron and clay ;—in meaning
not so great. Oliver has taken survey and measure of it ; Oliver
descends on it like the hammer of Thor ; smites it, as at one
fell stroke, into dust and ruin, never to reunite against him more.

One could pity this poor Irish people ; their case is pitiable
enough ! The claim they started with, 1641, was for religious
freedom. Their claim, we can now all see, was just : essentially
just, though full of intricacy ; difficult to render clear and con-
cessible ;—nay, at that date of the World's History, it was hardly
recognisable to any Protestant man for just ; and these frightful
massacrings and sanguinary blusterings have rendered it, for the
present, entirely unrecognisable. A just, though very intricate
claim : but entered upon, and prosecuted, by such methods as
were never yet available for asserting any claim in this world !
Treachery and massacre : what could come of it ? Eight years
of cruel fighting, of desperate violence and misery, have left
matters worse a thousand-fold than they were at first. No want
of daring, or of patriotism so-called ; but a great want of other
things ! Numerous large masses of armed men have been on
foot ; full of fiery vehemence and audacity, but without worth
as Armies : savage hordes rather; full of hatred and mutual
hatred, of disobedience, falsity and noise. Undrilled, unpaid,—
driving herds of plundered cattle before them for subsistence ;
rushing down from hillsides, from ambuscadoes, passes in the
mountains ; taking shelter always 'in bogs whither the cavalry
cannot follow them.' Unveracious, violent, disobedient men.
False in speech ;—alas, false in thought, first of all ; who have
never let the Fact tell its own harsh story to them ; who have
said always to the harsh Fact, "Thou art not that way, thou
art this way !" The Fact, of course, asserts that it *is* that way :
the Irish Projects end in perpetual discomfiture ; have to take
shelter in bogs whither cavalry cannot follow ! There has been
no scene seen under the sun like Ireland for these eight years.
Murder, pillage, conflagration, excommunication ; wide-flowing

blood, and bluster high as Heaven and St. Peter;—as if wolves or rabid dogs were in fight here; as if demons from the Pit had mounted up, to deface this fair green piece of God's Creation with *their* talkings and workings! It is, and shall remain, very dark to us. Conceive Ireland wasted, torn in pieces; black Controversy as of demons and rabid wolves rushing over the face of it so long; incurable, and very dim to us: till here at last, as in the torrent of Heaven's lightning descending liquid on it, we have clear and terrible view of its affairs for a time!—

STORM OF TREDAH

The next letter here, a Summons to Dundalk, will be fully understood so soon as the Two following it are read. The Two following it, on Tredah, or Drogheda as we now name it, contain in themselves, especially the Second and more deliberate of the two contains, materials for a pretty complete account of the Transaction there. It requires only to be added, what Cromwell himself has forborne to do, that on the repulse of the first attack, it was he, in person, who, 'witnessing it from the batteries,' hastened forward and led on the new attack: My pretty men, we must positively not be repulsed; we must enter here, we cannot do at all without entering!—The rest of these Irish Letters may, I hope, tell their own tale.

LETTER XXIX

For the Chief Officer commanding in Dundalk: These.

'Tredah,' 12th September 1649.

Sir,

I offered mercy to the Garrison of Tredah, in sending the Governor a Summons before I attempted the taking of it. Which being refused brought their evil upon them.

If you, being warned thereby, shall surrender your Garrison to the use of the Parliament of England, which by this I summon you to do, you may thereby prevent effusion of blood. If, upon refusing this Offer, that which you like not befalls you, you will know whom to blame. I rest,

Your servant,
OLIVER CROMWELL.

The Chief Officer commanding in Dundalk never received this Letter, I believe! What, in the interim, had become of Dundalk and its Chief and other Officers, will shortly appear.

LETTER XXX

To the Honourable John Bradshaw, Esquire, President of the Council of State: These.'

'Dublin,' 16th September 1649.

SIR,

It hath pleased God to bless our endeavours at Tredah. After battery, we stormed it. The Enemy were about 3,000 strong in the Town. They made a stout resistance; and near 1,000 of our men being entered, the Enemy forced them out again. But God giving a new courage to our men, they attempted again, and entered; beating the Enemy from their defences.

The Enemy had made three retrenchments, both to the right and left 'of' where we entered; all which they were forced to quit. Being thus entered, we refused them quarter; having, the day before, summoned the Town. I believe we put to the sword the whole number of the defendants. I do not think Thirty of the whole number escaped with their lives. Those that did are in safe custody for the Barbadoes. Since that time, the Enemy quitted to us Trim and Dundalk. In Trim they were in such haste that they left their guns behind them.

This hath been a marvellous great mercy. The Enemy, being not willing to put an issue upon a field-battle, had put into this Garrison almost all their prime soldiers, being about 3,000 horse and foot, under the command of their best officers; Sir Arthur Ashton being made Governor. There were some seven or eight regiments, Ormond's being one, under the command of Sir Edmund Varney. I do not believe, neither do I hear, that any officer escaped with his life, save only one Lieutenant, who, I hear, going to the Enemy said, That he was the only man that escaped of all the Garrison. The Enemy upon this were filled with much terror. And truly I believe this bitterness will save much effusion of blood, through the goodness of God.

I wish that all honest hearts may give the glory of this to God alone, to whom indeed the praise of this mercy belongs. 'As' for instruments, they were very inconsiderable the work throughout.   *   *   *   *

Captain Brandly did with forty or fifty of his men very

gallantly storm the Tenalia ; for which he deserves the thanks of the State. 'I rest,

Your most humble servant,'
OLIVER CROMWELL.

'*Tenalia*,' I believe, is now called *Tenaille* by engineers ; a kind of advanced defensive-work, which takes its name from resemblance, real or imaginary, to the lip of a pair of *pincers*.

The 'Sir Edmund Varney' who perished here was the son of the Standard-bearer at Edgehill. For Sir Arthur Ashton see Clarendon. Poor Sir Arthur had a wooden leg which the soldiers were very eager for, understanding it to be full of gold coin ; but it proved to be mere timber : all his gold, 200 broad pieces, was sewed into his belt, and scrambled for when that came to light. There is in Wood's Life an old-soldier's account of the Storm of Tredah, sufficiently emphatic, by Tom Wood, Anthony's brother, who had been there.

LETTER XXXI

'*For the Honourable William Lenthall, Esquire, Speaker of the Parliament of England : These.*'

Dublin, 17th September 1649.

SIR,
Your Army being safely arrived at Dublin ; and the Enemy endeavouring to draw all his forces together about Trim and Tecroghan, as my intelligence gave me,—from whence endeavours were made by the Marquis of Ormond to draw Owen Roe O'Neil with his forces to his assistance, but with what success I cannot yet learn,—I resolved, after some refreshment taken for our weather-beaten men and horses, and accommodations for a march, to take the field. And accordingly, upon Friday the 30th of August[1] last, rendezvoused with eight regiments of foot, six of horse and some troops of dragoons, three miles on the north side of Dublin. The design was, To endeavour the regaining of Tredah ; or tempting the Enemy, upon his hazard of the loss of that place, to fight.

Your Army came before the Town upon Monday following.[2] Where having pitched, as speedy course was taken

[1] Friday is 31st ; this error as to the day of the month continues through the Letter.
[2] 3d September.

as could be to frame our batteries; which took up the more time because divers of the battering guns were on shipboard. Upon Monday the 9th[1] of this instant, the batteries began to play. Whereupon I sent Sir Arthur Ashton, the then Governor, a summons, To deliver the Town to the use of the Parliament of England. To the which receiving no satisfactory answer, I proceeded that day to beat down the Steeple of the Church on the south side of the Town, and to beat down a Tower not far from the same place, which you will discern by the Chart enclosed.

Our guns not being able to do much that day, it was resolved to endeavour to do our utmost the next day to make breaches assaultable, and by the help of God to storm them. The place pitched upon was that part of the Town-wall next a Church called St. Mary's; which was the rather chosen because we did hope that if we did enter and possess that Church, we should be the better able to keep it against their horse and foot until we could make way for the entrance of our horse; and we did not conceive that any part of the Town would afford the like advantage for that purpose with this. The batteries planted were two: one was for that part of the Wall against the east end of the said Church; the other against the Wall on the south side. Being somewhat long in battering, the Enemy made six retrenchments: three of them from the said Church to Duleek Gate; and three of them from the east end of the Church to the Town-wall and so backward. The guns, after some two or three hundred shot, beat down the corner Tower, and opened two reasonable good breaches in the east and south Wall.

Upon Tuesday the 10th of this instant, about five o'clock in the evening, we began the Storm: and after some hot dispute we entered, about seven or eight hundred men; the Enemy disputing it very stiffly with us. And indeed, through the advantages of the place, and the courage God was pleased to give the defenders, our men were forced to retreat quite out of the breach, not without some considerable loss; Colonel Castle being there shot in the head, whereof he presently died; and divers officers and soldiers doing their duty killed and wounded. There was a Tenalia to flanker the south Wall of the Town, between Duleek Gate and the corner Tower before mentioned;—which our men entered, wherein they found some forty or fifty of the Enemy, which they put to the sword. And this 'Tenalia' they

---

[1] 10th September.

held ; but it being without the Wall, and the sally-port through the Wall into that Tenalia being choked up with some of the Enemy which were killed in it, it proved of no use for an entrance into the Town that way.

Although our men that stormed the breaches were forced to recoil, as is before expressed ; yet, being encouraged to recover their loss, they made a second attempt : wherein God was pleased so to animate them that they got ground of the Enemy, and by the goodness of God, forced him to quit his entrenchments. And after a very hot dispute, the Enemy having both horse and foot, and we only foot, within the Wall,—they gave ground, and our men became masters both of their retrenchments and 'of' the Church ; which indeed, although they made our entrance the more difficult, yet they proved of excellent use to us ; so that the Enemy could not 'now' annoy us with their horse, but thereby we had advantage to make good the ground, that so we might let in our own horse ; which accordingly was done, though with much difficulty.

Divers of the Enemy retreated into the Mill-Mount : a place very strong and of difficult access ; being exceedingly high, having a good graft, and strongly palisadoed. The Governor, Sir Arthur Ashton, and divers considerable Officers being there, our men getting up to them, were ordered by me to put them all to the sword. And indeed, being in the heat of action, I forbade them to spare any that were in arms in the Town : and, I think, that night they put to the sword about 2,000 men ;— divers of the officers and soldiers being fled over the Bridge into the other part of the Town, where about 100 of them possessed St. Peter's Church-steeple, some the west Gate, and others a strong Round Tower next the Gate called St. Sunday's. These being summoned to yield to mercy, refused. Whereupon I ordered the steeple of St. Peter's Church to be fired, when one of them was heard to say in the midst of the flames : "God damn me, God confound me ; I burn, I burn."

The next day, the other two Towers were summoned ; in one of which was about six or seven score ; but they refused to yield themselves : and we knowing that hunger must compel them, set only good guards to secure them from running away until their stomachs were come down. From one of the said Towers, notwithstanding their condition, they killed and wounded some of our men. When they submitted, their officers were knocked on the head ; and every tenth man of the soldiers killed ; and the rest shipped for the Barbadoes. The soldiers in the other

Tower were all spared, as to their lives only ; and shipped likewise for the Barbadoes.

I am persuaded that this is a righteous judgment of God upon these barbarous wretches, who have imbrued their hands in so much innocent blood ; and that it will tend to prevent the effusion of blood for the future. Which are the satisfactory grounds to such actions, which otherwise cannot but work remorse and regret. The officers and soldiers of this Garrison were the flower of their army. And their great expectation was, that our attempting this place would put fair to ruin us ; they being confident of the resolution of their men, and the advantage of the place. If we had divided our force into two quarters to have besieged the North Town and the South Town, we could not have had such a correspondency between the two parts of our Army, but that they might have chosen to have brought their Army, and have fought with which part 'of ours' they pleased,—and at the same time have made a sally with 2,000 men upon us, and have left their walls manned ; they having in the Town the number hereafter specified, but some say near 4,000.

Since this great mercy vouchsafed to us, I sent a party of horse and dragoons to Dundalk ; which the Enemy quitted, and we are possessed of,—as also 'of' another Castle they deserted, between Trim and Tredah, upon the Boyne. I sent a party of horse and dragoons to a House within five miles of Trim, there being then in Trim some Scots Companies, which the Lord of Ardes brought to assist the Lord of Ormond. But upon the news of Tredah, they ran away ; leaving their great guns behind them, which also we have possessed.

And now give me leave to say how it comes to pass that this work is wrought. It was set upon some of our hearts, That a great thing should be done, not by power or might, but by the Spirit of God. And is it not so, clearly ? That which caused your men to storm so courageously, it was the Spirit of God ; who gave your men courage, and took it away again ; and gave the Enemy courage, and took it away again ; and gave your men courage again, and therewith this happy success. And therefore it is good that God alone have all the glory.

It is remarkable that these people, at the first, set up the Mass in some places of the Town that had been monasteries ; but afterwards grew so insolent that, the last Lord's day before the storm, the Protestants were thrust out of the great Church called St. Peter's, and they had public Mass there : and in this very place near 1,000 of them were put to the sword, fleeing thither for safety. I believe all their friars were knocked on the head promiscuously but two; the one of which was Father Peter Taaff, brother to the Lord Taaff, whom the soldiers took, the next day, and made an end of. The other was taken in the Round Tower, under the repute of a Lieutenant, and when he understood that the officers in that Tower had no quarter, he confessed he was a Friar; but that did not save him.

A great deal of loss in this business fell upon Colonel Hewson's, Colonel Castle's, and Colonel Ewer's regiments. Colonel Ewer having two Field-Officers in his regiment shot; Colonel Castle and a Captain of his regiment slain; Colonel Hewson's Captain-Lieutenant slain. I do not think we lost 100 men upon the place, though many be wounded.

I most humbly pray the Parliament may be pleased 'that' this Army may be maintained; and that a consideration may be had of them, and of the carrying on affairs here, 'such' as may give a speedy issue to this work. To which there seems to be a marvellous fair opportunity offered by God. And although it may seem very chargeable to the State of England to maintain so great a force; yet surely to stretch a little for the present, in following God's providence, in hope the charge will not be long—I trust it will not be thought by any (that have not irreconcilable or malicious principles) unfit for me to move, For a constant supply; which, in human probability as to outward things, is most likely to hasten and perfect this work. And indeed if God please to finish it here as He hath done in England, the War is like to pay itself.

We keep the field much; our tents sheltering us from the wet and cold. But yet the Country-sickness overtakes many: and therefore we desire recruits, and some fresh regiments of foot, may be sent us. For it's easily conceived by what the Garrisons already drink up, what our Field-Army will come to, if God shall give more Garrisons into our hands. Craving pardon for this great trouble, I rest,

Your most obedient servant,
OLIVER CROMWELL.

P.S. Since writing of my Letter, a Major who brought off forty-three horse from the Enemy told me that it's reported in their camp that Owen Roe and they are agreed.

The defendants in Tredah consisted of: The Lord of Ormond's regiment (Sir Edmund Varney Lieutenant-Colonel), of

400 ; Colonel Byrn's, Colonel Warren's, and Colonel Wall's, of 2,000 ; the Lord of Westmeath's, of 200 ; Sir James Dillon's, of 200 ; and 200 horse.

Such was the Storm of Tredah. A thing which, if one *wanted* good assurance as to the essential meaning of it, might well 'work remorse and regret :' for indisputably the outer body of it is emphatic enough ! Cromwell, not in a light or loose manner, but in a very solemn and deep one, takes charge for himself, at his own peril, That it *is* a Judgment of God : and that it did 'save much effusion of blood,' we and all spectators can very readily testify. ' The execrable policy 'of that Regicide,' says Jacobite Carte on the occasion, 'had the 'effect he proposed. It spread abroad the terror of his name ; 'it cut'—In fact, it cut through the heart of the Irish War. Wexford Storm followed (not by forethought, it would seem, but by chance of war) in the same stern fashion ; and there was no other storm or slaughter needed in that Country. Rose-water Surgeons might have tried it otherwise ; but that was not Oliver's execrable policy, not the Rose-water one. And so we leave it, standing on such basis as it has.

Ormond had sent orders to 'burn' Dundalk and Trim before quitting them ; but the Garrisons, looking at Tredah, were in too much haste to apply the coal. They marched away at double-quick time ; the Lord Lieutenant got possession of both Towns unburnt. He has put Garrisons there, we see, which 'drink up' some of his forces. He has also despatched Colonel Venables, of whom we shall hear again, with a regiment or two, to reduce Carlingford, Newry,—to raise what Siege there may be at Derry, and assist in settling distracted Ulster : of whose progress here are news.

LETTER XXXII

STORM OF WEXFORD

For the Honourable William Lenthall, Esquire, Speaker of the Parliament of England : These.

Wexford, 14th October 1649.

SIR,

The Army marched from Dublin, about the 23d of September, into the County of Wicklow, where the Enemy had a Garrison about fourteen miles from Dublin, called Killincarrick; which they quitting, a Company of the Army was put therein. From thence the Army marched through almost a desolated country, until it came to a passage over the River Doro,[1] about a mile above the Castle of Arklow, which was the first seat and honour of the Marquis of Ormond's family. Which he had strongly fortified; but it was, upon the approach of the Army, quitted; wherein we left another Company of Foot.

From thence the Army marched towards Wexford; where in the way was a strong and large Castle, at a town called Limbrick, the ancient seat of the Esmonds; where the Enemy had a strong Garrison; which they burnt and quitted, the day before our coming thither. From thence we marched towards Ferns, an episcopal seat, where was a Castle; to which I sent Colonel Reynolds with a party to summon it. Which accordingly he did, and it was surrendered to him; where we having put a company,—advanced the Army to a passage over the River Slaney, which runs down to Wexford; and that night we marched into the fields of a Village called Enniscorthy, belonging to Mr. Robert Wallop;[2] where was a strong Castle very well manned and provided for by the Enemy; and, close under it, a very fair House belonging to the same worthy person,—a Monastery of Franciscan Friars, the considerablest in all Ireland: they ran away the night before we came. We summoned the Castle; and they refused to yield at the first; but upon better consideration, they were willing to deliver the place to us: which accordingly they did; leaving their great guns, arms, ammunition and provisions behind them.

Upon Monday the First of October, we came before Wexford. Into which the Enemy had put a Garrison, consisting of 'part of' their Army; this Town having, until then, been so confident of their own strength as that they would not, at any time, suffer a Garrison to be imposed upon them. The Com-

[1] River Darragh;—a branch of what is now called the Avoca; well known to musical persons.

[2] Wallop is Member ('recruiter') for Andover; a King's-Judge; Member of the Council of State; now and afterwards a conspicuous rigorous republican man. He has advanced money, long since, we suppose, for the Public Service in Ireland, and obtained in payment this 'fair House,' and Superiority of Enniscorthy: properties the value or no-value of which will much depend on the Lord Lieutenant's success at present—Wallop's representative, a Peer of the Realm, is still owner here, as it has proved.

mander that brought in those forces was Colonel David Sinnott ; who took upon him the command of the place. To whom I sent a Summons, a Copy whereof is this enclosed ; between whom and me there passed Answers and Replies, Copies whereof these also are :

"*To the Commander-in-Chief of the Town of Wexford*
"Before Wexford, 3d October 1649.

"SIR,

"Having brought the Army belonging to the Parlia-"ment of England before this place, to reduce it to its "due obedience : to the end effusion of blood may be prevented, "and the Town and country about it preserved from ruin, I "thought fit to summon you to deliver the same to me, to the "use of the State of England.

"By this offer, I hope it will clearly appear where the guilt "will lie, if innocent persons should come to suffer with the "nocent. I expect your speedy answer ; and rest,
"SIR,
"Your servant,
"OLIVER CROMWELL."

"*For the Commander-in-Chief in the Town of Wexford.*
"'Before Wexford,' 11th October 1649.

"SIR,

"I have had the patience to peruse your Propositions ; "to which I might have returned an Answer with some disdain "But, to be short,—

"I shall give the Soldiers and Noncommissioned Officers "quarter for life, and leave to go to their several habitations, "with their wearing-clothes ;—they engaging themselves to live "quietly there, and to take up arms no more against the "Parliament of England. And the Commissioned Officers "quarter for their lives, but to render themselves Prisoners. "And as for the Inhabitants, I shall engage myself That no "violence shall be offered to their goods, and that I shall protect "the Town from plunder.

"I expect your positive Answer instantly ; and if you will "upon these terms surrender and quit, 'and' shall, in one hour, "send forth to me Four Officers of the quality of Field-Officers, "and Two Aldermen, for the performance thereof,—I shall "thereupon forbear all acts of hostility.
"Your servant,
"OLIVER CROMWELL."

Which 'Answer' indeed had no effect. For whilst I was preparing of it; studying to preserve the Town from plunder, that it might be of the more use to you and your Army,—the Captain, who was one of the Commissioners, being fairly treated, yielded up the Castle to us. Upon the top of which our men no sooner appeared, but the Enemy quitted the Walls of the Town; which our men perceiving, ran violently upon the Town with their ladders, and stormed it. And when they were come into the market-place, the Enemy making a stiff resistance, our forces brake them; and then put all to the sword that came in their way. Two boatfuls of the Enemy attempting to escape, being overprest with numbers, sank; whereby were drowned near three-hundred of them. I believe, in all, there was lost of the Enemy not many less than Two-thousand; and I believe not Twenty of yours from first to last of the Siege. And indeed it hath, not without cause, been deeply set upon our hearts, That, we intending better to this place than so great a ruin, hoping the Town might be of more use to you and your Army, yet God would not have it so; but, by an unexpected providence, in His righteous justice, brought a just judgment upon them; causing *them* to become a prey to the soldier who in their piracies had made preys of so many families, and now with their bloods to answer the cruelties which they had exercised upon the lives of divers poor Protestants: Two 'instances' of which I have been lately acquainted with. About seven or eight score poor Protestants were by them put into an old vessel; which being, as some say, bulged by them, the vessel sank, and they were all presently drowned in the Harbour. The other 'instance' was thus: They put divers poor Protestants into a Chapel (which, since, they have used for a Mass-house, and in which one or more of their priests were now killed), where they were famished to death.

The soldiers got a very good booty in this place: and had not they[1] had opportunity to carry their goods over the River, whilst we besieged it, it would have been much more:—I could have wished for their own good, and the good of the Garrison, they had been more moderate.[2] Some things which were not easily portable, we hope we shall make use of to your behoof. There are great quantities of iron, hides, tallow, salt, pipe- and barrel-staves; which are under commissioners' hands, to be

---

[1] The Townsfolk.   [2] Not forced us to storm them.

CAPTURE OF WEXFORD

secured. We believe there are near a hundred cannon in the Fort, and elsewhere in and about the Town. Here is likewise some very good shipping: here are three vessels, one of them of thirty-four guns, which a week's time would fit to sea; there is another of about twenty guns, very near ready likewise. And one other Frigate of twenty guns, upon the stocks; made for sailing: which is built up to the uppermost deck; for her handsomeness' sake, I have appointed the workmen to finish her, here being materials to do it, if you or the Council of State shall approve thereof. The Frigate, also, taken beside the Fort, is a most excellent vessel for sailing. Besides divers other ships and vessels in the Harbour.

This Town is now so in your power, that of the former inhabitants, I believe scarce one in twenty can challenge any property in their houses. Most of them are run away, and many of them killed in this service. And it were to be wished, that an honest people would come and plant here;—where are very good houses, and other accommodations fitted to their hands, which may by your favour be made of encouragement to them. As also a seat of good trade, both inward and outward;—and of marvellous great advantage in the point of the herring and other fishing. The Town is pleasantly seated and strong, having a rampart of earth within the wall, near fifteen feet thick.

Thus it hath pleased God to give into your hands this other mercy. For which, as for all, we pray God may have all the glory. Indeed your instruments are poor and weak, and can do nothing but through believing,—and that is the gift of God also.

I humbly take leave, and rest

Your most humble servant,

OLIVER CROMWELL.

'P.S.' A day or two before our Battery was planted, Ormond, the Earl of Castlehaven, the Lord of Ardes and Clanneboyes were on the other side of the Water, with about 1,800 horse 'and' 1,500 foot; and offered to put in four or five hundred foot more into the Town; which the Town refusing, he marched away in all haste. I sent the Lieutenant-General after him, with about 1,400 horse; but the Enemy made haste from him.

LETTER XXXIII

Here is Cromwell's official account of the Capture of Ross, in a Letter to Lenthall.

'For the Honourable William Lenthall, Esquire, Speaker of the Parliament of England: These.'

Ross, 25th October 1649.

Sir,
   Since my last from Wexford, we marched to Ross; a walled Town, situated upon the Barrow; a port-town, up to which a ship of seven or eight hundred tons may come.

We came before it upon Wednesday the 17th instant, with three pieces of cannon. That evening I sent a Summons; Major-General Taaff, being Governor, refused to admit my Trumpet into the Town; but took the Summons in, returning me no answer. I did hear that near 1,000 foot had been put into this place some few days before my coming to it. The next day was spent in making preparations for our battery; and in our view there were boated over from the other side of the river, of English, Scots, and Irish, 1,500 more, Ormond, Castlehaven, and the Lord of Ardes, being on the other side of the water to cause it to be done.

That night we planted our battery; which began to play very early the next morning. The Governor immediately sent forth an Answer to my Summons; copies of all which I make bold herewith to trouble you 'with;' the rather because you may see how God pulls down proud stomachs. The Governor desired commissioners might treat, and that in the mean time there might be a ceasing of acts of hostility on both sides. Which I refused; sending in word, That if he would march away with arms, bag and baggage, and give me hostages for performance, he should. Indeed he might have done it without my leave, by the advantage of the River. He insisted upon having the cannon with him; which I would not yield unto, but required the leaving the artillery and ammunition; which he was content to do, and marched away, leaving the great artillery and the ammunition in the stores to me.—When they marched away, at least 500 English, many of them of the Munster forces, came to us.

The rendition of this Garrison was a seasonable mercy, as

giving us an opportunity towards Munster; and is for the
present a very good refreshment for our men. We are able to
say nothing as to all this, but that the Lord is still pleased to
own a company of poor worthless creatures; for which we
desire His name to be magnified, and 'that' the hearts of all
concerned may be provoked to walk worthy of such continued
favours. This is the earnest desire of

Your most humble servant,
OLIVER CROMWELL.

LETTER XXXIV

THE 'General Blake' of this Letter, 'Colonel Blake' of the
last, is Admiral Blake; he, with Ayscough, Deane and vigilant
Sea-officers, cooperating with Oliver on land, now dominates
these waters. Prince Rupert, with the residue of the Revolted
Ships, is lying close, for shelter from him, under the guns of
Kinsale ;—verging, poor Prince, to a fugitive roaming sea-life,
very like Piracy in some of its features. He abandoned it as
desperate, before long. Poor Prince Maurice, sea-roving in
like fashion, went to the bottom ; sank, in the West Indies,
mouse and man ; and ended, none knows exactly where, when,
or how. Rupert invented, or helped to invent, 'pinchbeck' in
subsequent years, and did no other service to the public that I
know of.

The defection of Cork and Youghal, full of English influences and complex distractions, followed naturally on Cromwell's successes. In *Lady Fanshawe's Memoirs* is a vivid account
of the universal hurlyburly that took place at Cork, on the
verge of this occurrence there : tremulous instant decision what
you will do, which side you will join ; swift packing in the
dead of night; swift riding off, in any carriage, cart, or ass-cart
you can bargain with for love or money ! Poor Lady Fanshawe
got to Galway, there to try it yet a little longer.

For the Honourable William Lenthall, Esquire, Speaker of
the Parliament of England: These.

Ross, 14th November 1649.

SIR,

About a fortnight since, I had some good assurance that
Cork was returned to its obedience ; and had refused Inchiquin,
who did strongly endeavour to redintegrate himself there, but

without success. I did hear also that Colonel Townsend was coming to me with their submission and desires, but was interrupted by a Fort at the mouth of Cork Harbour. But having sufficient grounds upon the former information, and other confirmation out of the Enemy's camp that it was true, I desired General Blake, who was here with me, that he would repair thither in Captain Mildmay's Frigate, called the Nonsuch. Who, when they came thither, received such entertainment as these enclosed will let you see.

In the mean time the Garland, one of your third-rate Ships, coming happily into Waterford Bay, I ordered her, and a great Prize lately taken in that Bay, to transport Colonel Phayr[1] to Cork; whitherward he went, having along with him near Five-hundred foot, which I spared him out of this poor Army, and 1,500*l*. in money; giving him such instructions as were proper for the promoting of your interest there. As they went with an intention for Cork, it pleased God the wind coming cross, they were forced to ride off from Dungarvan. Where they met Captain Mildmay *returning* with the Nonsuch Frigate, with Colonel Townsend aboard, coming to me; who advertised them that Youghal had also declared for the Parliament of England. Whereupon they steered their course thither; and sent for Colonel Gifford, Colonel Warden, Major Purden (who with Colonel Townsend have been very active instruments for the return both of Cork and Youghal to their obedience, having some of them ventured their lives twice or thrice to effect it), and the Mayor of Youghal aboard them; who, accordingly, immediately came and made tender of some propositions to be offered to me. But my Lord Broghil being on board the Ship, assuring them it would be more for their honour and advantage to desire no conditions, they said they would submit. Whereupon my Lord Broghil, Sir William Fenton, and Colonel Phayr, went to the Town; and were received,—I shall give you my Lord Broghil's own words—" *with all the real demonstrations of gladness an overjoyed people were capable of*."

Not long after, Colonel Phayr landed his foot. And by the endeavours of the noble person[2] afore mentioned, and the rest

---

[1] He of the King's Death-Warrant.
[2] Lord Broghil. The somewhat romantic story of Cromwell's first visit to him, and chivalrous conquest of him, at his lodgings in London, ' in the dusk of the evening,' is in Collins's Peerage (London 1741), iv. 253; and in many other Books;—copied from Morrice's *Life of Orrery*.

of the gentlemen, the Garrison is put in good order ; and the
Munster officers and soldiers in that Garrison in a way of
settlement. Colonel Phayr intends, as I hear, to leave Two-
hundred men there, and to march with the rest overland to
Cork. I hear by Colonel Townsend, and the rest of the gentlemen that were employed to me, that Baltimore, Castlehaven,
Cappoquin, and some other places of hard names, are come in,—
I wish Foot come over seasonably to man them ; as also that
there are hopes of other places.

From Sir Charles Coote, Lord President of Connaught, I had
a Letter, about three or four days since, That he is come over
the Bann, and hath taken Coleraine by storm ; and that he is
in conjunction with Colonel Venables,—who I hear hath besieged
Carrickfergus ; which if through the mercy of God it be taken,
I know nothing considerable in the North of Ireland, but Charle-
mont, that is not in your hands.

We lie with the Army at Ross ; where we have been making
a bridge over the Barrow, and 'have' hardly yet accomplished
'it' as we could wish. The Enemy lies upon the Nore, on the
land between the Barrow and it ; having gathered together all
the force they can get. Owen Roe's men, as they report them,
are Six-thousand foot, and about Four-thousand horse, beside
their own Army 'in this quarter ;' and they give out they will
have a day for it :—which we hope the Lord of His mercy will
enable us to give them, in His own good time. In whom we
desire our only trust and confidence may be.

Whilst we have lain here, we have not been without some
sweet taste of the goodness of God. Your ships have taken
some good prizes. The last was thus : There came-in a Dunkirk man-of-war with 32 guns ; who brought-in a Turkish man-
of-war whom she had taken, and another ship of 10 guns laden
with poor-john and oil. These two your ships took. But the
man-of-war whose prizes these two were, put herself under the
Fort of Duncannon, so that your ships could not come near her.
It pleased God we had two demi-cannon with the foot, on the
shore ; which being planted, raked her through, killing and
wounding her men ; so that after ten shot she weighed anchor,
and ran into your Fleet, with a flag of submission, surrendering
herself. She was well manned, the prisoners taken being Two-
hundred-and-thirty.—I doubt the taking prisoners of this sort
will cause the wicked trade of Piracy to be endless. They were
landed here before I was aware : and a hundred of them, as I

hear, are gotten into Duncannon, and have taken up arms there; and I doubt the rest, that are gone to Waterford, will do us no good. The seamen, being so full of prizes and unprovided of victual, knew not how otherwise to dispose of them.

Sir, having given you this account, I shall not trouble you much with particular desires. Those I shall humbly present to the Council of State. Only, in the general, give me leave humbly to offer what in my judgment I conceive to be for your service, with a full submission to you. We desire recruits may be speeded to us. It is not fit to tell you how your Garrisons will be unsupplied, and no Field marching Army considerable, if but three Garrisons more were in our hands. It is not well not to follow providences. Your recruits, and the forces desired will not raise your charge, if your assignments already for the forces here do come to our hands in time. I should not doubt 'but' by the addition of assessments here, to have your charge in some reasonable measure borne; and the soldier upheld, without too much neglect or discouragement,—which sickness, in this country so ill agreeing with their bodies, puts upon them; and 'which' this Winter's-action, I believe not heretofore known by English in this country, subjects them to. To the praise of God I speak it, I scarce know one officer of forty amongst us that hath not been sick. And how many considerable ones we have lost, is no little thought of heart to us.

Wherefore I humbly beg, that the moneys desired may be seasonably sent over; and those other necessaries, clothes, shoes and stockings, formerly desired; that so poor creatures may be encouraged: and, through the same blessed Presence that has gone along with us, I hope, before it be long, to see Ireland no burden to England, but a profitable part of its Commonwealth. And certainly the extending your help in this way, at this time, is the most profitable means speedily to effect it. And if I did not think it your best thrift, I would not trouble you at all with it.

Craving pardon for this trouble, I rest,
Your most humble and faithful servant,
OLIVER CROMWELL.

LETTER XXXV

OFFICIAL Despatch, briefly recapitulating that affair of Kilkenny and some others;—points also towards return to England.

For the Honourable William Lenthall, Esquire, Speaker of the Parliament of England: These.

Carrick, 2d April 1650.

MR. SPEAKER,

I think the last Letter I troubled you with, was about the taking of Cahir, since which time there were taken, by beating-up their quarters, two Colonels, a Lieutenant-Colonel, Major, and divers Captains, all of horse: Colonel Johnson, Lieutenant-Colonel Laughern, and Major Simes, were shot to death, as having served under the Parliament, but now taken up arms with the Enemy.

Hearing that Castlehaven and Lieutenant-General Ferral were about Kilkenny, with their Army lying there quartered, and about Carlow and Leighlin Bridge; and hearing also that Colonel Hewson, with a good Party from Dublin, was come as far as Ballysonan, and had taken it,—we thought fit to send an express to him, To march up towards us for a conjunction. And because we doubted the sufficiency of his Party to march with that security that were to be wished, Colonel Shilbourn was ordered to go with some troops of horse out of the County of Wexford, which was his station, to meet him. And because the Enemy was possessed of the fittest places upon the Barrow for our conjunction, we sent a Party of seven or eight hundred horse and dragoons, and about five-hundred foot, to attempt upon Castlehaven in the rear, if he should have endeavoured to defend the place against Colonel Hewson.

Our Party, being a light nimble Party, was at the Barrow-side before Colonel Hewson could be heard of; and possessed a House, by the Graigue: they marched towards Leighlin, and faced Castlehaven at a pretty distance; but he showed no forwardness to engage. Our Party not being able to hear of Colonel Hewson, came back as far as Thomastown, a small walled Town, and a pass upon the Nore, between Kilkenny and Ross. Which our men attempting to take, the Enemy made no great resistance; but, by the advantage of the bridge, quitted the Town, and fled to a Castle about half a mile distant off, which they had formerly possessed. That night the President of Munster and myself came up to the Party. We summoned the Castle; and, after two days, it was surrendered to us; the Enemy leaving their arms, drums, colours and ammunition behind them, and engaging never to bear arms more against the Parliament of England.

We lay still after this about two or three days. The President went back to Fethard, to bring up some great guns, with a purpose to attempt upon the Granny, and some Castles thereabouts, for the better blocking-up of Waterford ; and to cause to advance up to us some more of our foot. In the end we had advertisement that Colonel Hewson was come to Leighlin ; where was a very strong Castle and pass over the Barrow. I sent him word that he should attempt it ; which he did ; and, after some dispute, reduced it. By which means we have a good pass over the Barrow, and intercourse between Munster and Leinster. I sent Colonel Hewson word that he should march up to me ; and we advancing likewise with our Party, met 'him,'— near by Gowran ; a populous Town, where the Enemy had a very strong Castle, under the command of Colonel Hammond ; a Kentishman, who was a principal actor in the Kentish Insurrection, and did manage the Lord Capel's business at his Trial. I sent him a civil invitation to deliver up the Castle unto me ; to which he returned me a very resolute answer, and full of height. We planted our artillery ; and before we had made a breach considerable, the Enemy beat a parley for a treaty ; which I, having offered so fairly to him, refused ; but sent him in positive conditions, That the soldiers should have their lives, and the Commission Officers to be disposed of as should be thought fit ; which in the end was submitted to. The next day, the Colonel, the Major, and the rest of the Commission Officers were shot to death ; all but one, who, being a very earnest instrument to have the Castle delivered, was pardoned. In the same Castle also we took a Popish Priest, who was chaplain to the Catholics in this regiment ; who was caused to be hanged. I trouble you with this the rather, because this regiment was the Lord of Ormond's own regiment. In this Castle was good store of provisions for the Army.

After the taking of this Castle, it was agreed amongst us to march to the City of Kilkenny. Which we did upon Friday the 22d of March : and coming with our body within a mile of the Town, we advanced with some horse very near unto it ; and that evening I sent Sir Walter Butler and the Corporation a Letter. We took the best view we could where to plant our batteries ; and upon Monday the 25th, our batteries, consisting of three guns, began to play. After near a hundred shot, we made a breach, as we hoped stormable. Our men were drawn out ready for the attempt ; and Colonel Ewer 'was' ordered,

CAPTURE OF KILKENNY

with about one thousand foot, to endeavour to possess the Irish Town, much about the time of our storming;—which he accordingly did, with the loss of not above three or four men. Our men upon the signal fell on upon the breach: which indeed was not performed with usual courage nor success; for they were beaten off, with the loss of one Captain, and about twenty or thirty men killed and wounded. The Enemy had made two retrenchments or counterworks, which they had strongly palisadoed: and both of them did so command our breach, that indeed it was a mercy to us we did not farther contend for an entrance there; it being probable that, if we had, it would have cost us very dear.

Having possessed the Irish Town; and there being another Walled Town on the other side of the River, eight companies of foot were sent over the River to possess that. Which accordingly was effected, and not above the like number lost that were in possessing the Irish Town. The Officer that commanded this party in chief attempted to pass over the Bridge into the City, and to fire the Gate; which indeed was done with good resolution;—but, lying too open to the Enemy's shot, he had forty or fifty men killed and wounded; which was a sore blow to us. We made our preparations for a second battery; which was well near perfected: 'but' the Enemy, seeing himself thus begirt, sent for a Treaty; and had it; and, in some hours, agreed to deliver up the Castle upon the Articles enclosed. Which, 'accordingly,' we received upon Thursday the 28th of March.— We find the Castle exceeding well fortified by the industry of the Enemy; being also very capacious: so that if we had taken the Town, we must have had a new work for the Castle, which might have cost much blood and time. So that, we hope, the Lord hath provided better for us; and we look at it as a gracious mercy that we have the place for you upon these terms.

Whilst these affairs were transacting, a Lieutenant-Colonel, three Majors, eight Captains, being English, Welsh and Scotch, with others, possessed of Cantwell Castle,[1]—a very strong Castle, situated in a bog, well furnished with provisions of corn,—were ordered by Sir Walter Butler to come to strengthen the Garrison of Kilkenny. But they sent two Officers to me, to offer me the place, and their service,—that they might have passes to go

[1] 'Cantwell,' still known among the peasantry by that name, is now called Sandford's Court; close upon Kilkenny: 'Donkill' seems to be Donhill, a ruined Strength not far from Waterford. Of Pulkerry and Ballopoin, in this paragraph, I can hear no tidings.

beyond sea to serve foreign states, with some money to bear their charges : the last whereof 'likewise' I consented to ; they promising to do nothing to the prejudice of the Parliament of England. Colonel Abbot also attempted Ennisnag : where were gotten a company of rogues which 'had' revolted from Colonel Jones. The Soldiers capitulated for life, and their two Officers were hanged for revolting. Adjutant-General Sadler was commanded with two guns to attempt some Castles in the County of Tipperary and Kilkenny ; which being reduced 'would' exceedingly tend to the blocking-up of two considerable Towns. He summoned Pulkerry, a Garrison under Clonmel ; battered it ; they refusing to come out, stormed it ; put thirty or forty of them to the sword, and the rest remaining obstinate were fired in the Castle. He took Ballopoin : the Enemy marching away, leaving their arms behind them. He took also the Granny and Donkill, two very considerable places to Waterford, upon the same terms.—We have advanced our quarters towards the Enemy, a considerable way above Kilkenny ; where we hope, by the gaining of ground, to get subsistence ; and still to grow upon the Enemy, as the Lord shall bless us.

Sir,
Your most humble servant,
OLIVER CROMWELL.

In the end of this month, 'the President Frigate,' President Bradshaw Frigate, sails from Milford Haven, 'to attend his Excellency's pleasure,' and bring him home if he see good to come. He has still one storm to do there first ; that of Clonmel, where 'Two-thousand foot, all Ulster men,' are gathered for a last struggle ;—the death-agony of this War, after which it will fairly die, and be buried. A very fierce storm, and fire-whirlwind of last agony ; whereof take this solid account by an eye-witness and hand-actor ; and so leave this part of our subject. The date is 10th May 1650 ; 'a Letter from Clonmel in Ireland :'

"Worthy Sir,—Yesterday," Thursday 9th May, "we stormed "Clonmel : in which work both officers and soldiers did as "much and more than could be expected. We had, with our "guns, made a breach in their works ;—where, after an hot "fight, we gave back a while ; but presently charged up to "the same ground again. But the Enemy had made themselves "exceeding strong, by double-works and traverse, which were

"worse to enter than the breach; when we came up to it, they
"had cross-works, and were strongly flanked from the houses
"within their works. The Enemy defended themselves against
"us that day, until towards the evening, our men all the while
"keeping up close to their breach; and many on both sides
"were slain." The fierce death-wrestle, in the breaches here,
lasted four hours: so many hours of hot storm and continuous
tug of war, "and many men were slain." "At night, the
"Enemy drew out, on the other side, and marched away
"undiscovered to us; and the inhabitants of Clonmel sent
"out for a parley. Upon which, Articles were agreed on,
"before we knew the Enemy was gone. After signing of the
"Conditions, we discovered the Enemy to be gone; and, very
"early this morning, pursued them; and fell upon their rear
"of stragglers, and killed above 200,—besides those we slew in
"the storm. We entered Clonmel this morning, and have kept
"our Conditions with them. The place is considerable; and
"very advantageous to the reducing of these parts wholly to
"the Parliament of England." Whitlocke has heard by other
Letters, 'That they found in Clonmel the stoutest Enemy this
'Army had ever met in Ireland; and that there was never seen
'so hot a storm of so long continuance, and so gallantly de-
'fended, either in England or Ireland.'

The Irish Commander here was Hugh O'Neil, a kinsman of
Owen Roe's: vain he too, this new brave O'Neil! It is a lost
Cause. It is a Cause he has not yet seen into the secret of, and
cannot prosper in. Fiery fighting cannot prosper in it; no,
there needs something other first, which has never yet been
done! Let the O'Neil go elsewhither, with his fighting talent;
here it avails nothing, and less. To the surrendered Irish
Officers the Lord Lieutenant granted numerous permissions to
embody regiments, and go abroad with them into any country
not at war with England. Some 'Five-and-Forty' Thousand
Kurisees, or whatever name they had, went in this way to France,
to Spain, and fought there far off; and their own land had peace.

The Lord Lieutenant would fain have seen Waterford surrender before he went: but new Letters arrive from the Parliament; affairs in Scotland threaten to become pressing. He
appoints Ireton his Deputy, to finish the business here; rapidly
makes what survey of Munster, what adjustment of Ireland,
military and civil, is possible;—steps on board the President
Frigate, in the last days of May, and spreads sail for England.

He has been some nine months in Ireland ; leaves a very handsome spell of work done there.

At Bristol, after a rough passage, the Lord Lieutenant is received with all the honours and acclamations, 'the great guns firing thrice ;' hastens up to London, where on Friday 31st May, all the world is out to welcome him. Fairfax, the chief Officers, and Members of Parliament, with solemn salutation, on Hounslow Heath : from Hounslow Heath to Hyde Park, where are Trainbands and Lord Mayors ; on to Whitehall and the Cockpit, where are better than these,—it is one wide tumult of salutation, congratulation, artillery-volleying, human shouting ;—Hero-worship after a sort, not the best sort. It was on this occasion that Oliver said, or is reported to have said, when some sycophantic person observed, "What a crowd come out to see your Lordship's triumph !"—"Yes, but if it were to see me hanged, how many more would there be !"—

Such is what the Irish common people still call the "Curse of Cromwell ;" this is the summary of his work in that country. The remains of the War were finished out by Ireton, by Ludlow ; Ireton died of fever, at Limerick, in the end of the second year ; and solid Ludlow, who had been with him for some ten months, succeeded. The ulterior arrangements for Ireland were those of the Commonwealth Parliament and the proper Official Persons ; not specially Oliver's arrangements, though of course he remained a chief authority in that matter, and nothing could well be done which he with any emphasis deliberately condemned.

PART VI

WAR WITH SCOTLAND

1650—1651

WAR WITH SCOTLAND

THE Scotch People, the first beginners of this grand Puritan Revolt, which we may define as an attempt to bring the Divine Law of the Bible into actual practice in men's affairs on the Earth, are still one and all resolute for that object; but they are getting into sad difficulties as to realising it. Not easy to realise such a thing: besides true will, there need heroic gifts, the highest that Heaven gives, for realising it! Gifts which have not been vouchsafed the Scotch People at present. The letter of their Covenant presses heavy on these men; traditions, formulas, dead letters of many things press heavy on them. On the whole, they too are but what we call Pedants in conduct, not Poets: the sheepskin record failing them, and old use-and-wont ending, they cannot farther; they look into a sea of troubles, shoreless, starless, on which there seems no navigation possible.

The faults or misfortunes of the Scotch People, in their Puritan business, are many: but properly their grand fault is this, That they have produced for it no sufficiently heroic man among them. No man that has an eye to see beyond the letter and the rubric; to discern, across many consecrated rubrics of the Past, the inarticulate divineness too of the Present and the Future, and dare all perils in the faith of that! With Oliver Cromwell born a Scotchman; with a Hero King and a unanimous Hero Nation at his back, it might have been far otherwise. With Oliver born Scotch, one sees not but the whole world might have become Puritan ; might have struggled, yet a long while, to fashion itself according to that divine Hebrew Gospel,—to the exclusion of other Gospels not Hebrew, which also are divine, and will have their share of fulfilment here !— But of such issue there is no danger. Instead of inspired Olivers, glowing with direct insight and noble daring, we have Argyles, Loudons, and narrow, more or less opaque persons of the Pedant species. Committees of Estates, Committees of Kirks, much tied up in formulas, both of them : a bigoted Theocracy *without* the Inspiration ; which is a very hopeless phenomenon indeed ! The Scotch People are all willing, eager of heart ; asking, Whitherward ? But the Leaders stand aghast at the new forms of danger ; and in a vehement discrepant manner some calling, Halt ! others calling, Backward ! others, Forward !—huge confusion ensues. Confusion which will need an Oliver to repress it, to bind it up in tight manacles, if not otherwise ; and say, "There, sit there and consider thyself a little ! "—

The meaning of the Scotch Covenant was, That God's divine Law of the Bible should be put in practice in these Nations ; verily *it*, and not the Four Surplices at Allhallowtide, or any Formula or cloth or sheepskin here or elsewhere which merely pretended to be it. But then the Covenant says expressly, there is to be a Stuart King in the business ; we cannot do without our Stuart King ! Given a divine Law of the Bible on one hand, and a Stuart King, Charles First or Charles Second, on the other : alas, did History ever present a more irreducible case of equations in this world ? I pity the poor Scotch Pedant Governors ; still more the poor Scotch People, who had no other to follow ! Nay, as for that, the People did get through, in the end ; such was their indomitable pious constancy, and other worth and fortune : and Presbytery became a Fact among them, to the whole length possible for it : not without endless results. But for the poor Governors this irreducible case proved, as it were, fatal ! They have never since, if we will look narrowly at it, governed Scotland, or even well known that they were there to attempt governing it. Once they lay on Dunse Hill, 'each Earl with his Regiment of Tenants round him,' *For Christ's Crown and Covenant*; and never since had they any noble National act which it was given them to do. Growing desperate of Christ's Crown and Covenant, they, in the next generation when our *Annus Mirabilis* arrived, hurried up to Court, looking out for other Crowns and Covenants ; deserted Scotland and her Cause, somewhat basely ; took to *booing* and *booing* for Causes of their own, unhappy mortals ;—and Scotland and all Causes that were Scotland's have had to go on very much without *them* ever since! Which is a very fatal issue indeed, as I reckon ;—and the time for settlement of accounts about it, which could not fail always, and seems now fast drawing nigh, looks very ominous to me. For in fact there is no creature more fatal than your Pedant ; safe as he esteems himself, the terriblest issues spring from him. Human crimes are many : but the crime of being deaf to the God's Voice, of being blind to all but parchments and antiquarian rubrics when the Divine Handwriting is abroad on the sky,—certainly there is no crime which the Supreme Powers do more terribly avenge !

But leaving all that,—the poor Scotch Governors, we remark, in that old crisis of theirs, have come upon the desperate expedient of getting Charles Second to adopt the Covenant the best he can. Whereby our parchment formula is indeed saved ; but the divine fact has gone terribly to the wall ! The Scotch Governors hope otherwise. By treaties at Jersey, treaties at Breda, they and the hard Law of Want together have constrained this poor young Stuart to their detested Covenant ; as the Frenchman said, they have 'compelled him to adopt it voluntarily.' A fearful crime, thinks Oliver, and think we. How dare you enact such mummery under High Heaven ! exclaims he. You will prosecute Malignants ; and, with the aid of some poor varnish, transparent even to yourselves, you adopt into your bosom the Chief Malignant ? My soul come not into your secret ; mine honour be not united unto you !—

In fact, his new Sacred Majesty is actually under way for the Scotch court ; will become a Covenanted King there. Of himself a likely enough young man ;—very unfortunate he too. Satisfactorily descended from the Steward of Scotland and Elizabeth Muir of Caldwell (whom some have called an improper female) ; satisfactory in this respect, but in others most unsatisfactory. A somewhat loose young man ; has Buckingham, Wilmot and Company, at one hand of him, and painful Mr. Livingston and Presbyterian ruling-elders at the other ; is hastening now, as a Covenanted King, towards such a Theocracy as we described. Perhaps the most anomalous phenomenon ever produced by Nature and Art working together in this World !—He had sent Montrose before him, poor young man, to try if war and force could effect nothing ; whom instantly the Scotch Nation took, and tragically hanged. They now, winking hard at that transaction, proffer the poor young man their Covenant; compel him to sign it voluntarily, and be Covenanted King over them.

The result of all which for the English Commonwealth cannot be doubtful. What Declarations, Papers, Protocols, passed on the occasion,—numerous, flying thick between Edinburgh and London in late months,—shall remain unknown to us. The Commonwealth has brought Cromwell home from Ireland; and got forces ready for him: that is the practical outcome of it. The Scotch also have got forces ready: will either invade us, or (which we decide to be preferable) be invaded by us. Cromwell must now take up the Scotch coil of troubles, as he did the Irish, and deal with that too. Fairfax, as we heard, was unwilling to go; Cromwell, urging the Council of State to second him, would fain persuade Fairfax; gets him still nominated Commander-in-Chief; but cannot persuade him;—will himself have to be Commander-in-Chief and go.

On *Wednesday 26th June* 1650, the Act appointing 'That 'Oliver Cromwell, Esquire, be constituted Captain-General and 'Commander-in-Chief of all the Forces raised or to be raised by 'authority of Parliament within the Commonwealth of England,' was passed. 'Whereupon,' says Whitlocke, 'great ceremonies 'and congratulations of the new General were made to him 'from all sorts of people; and he went on roundly with his 'business.' Roundly, rapidly; for in three days more, on Saturday the 29th, 'the Lord General Cromwell went out of 'London towards the North: and the news of him marching 'northward much startled the Scots.'

He has Lambert for Major-General, Cousin Whalley for Commissary-General; and among his Colonels are Overton, whom we knew at Hull; Pride, whom we have seen in Westminster Hall, and a taciturn man, much given to chewing tobacco, whom we have transiently seen in various places, Colonel George Monk by name. An excellent officer; listens to what you say, answers often by a splash of brown juice merely, but punctually does what is doable of it. Puddingheaded Hodgson the Yorkshire Captain is also there; from whom perhaps we may glean a rough lucent-point or two. The Army, as my Lord General attracts it gradually from the right and left on his march northward, amounts at Tweedside to some Sixteen-thousand horse and foot. Rushworth goes with

him as Secretary; historical John; having now done with
Fairfax :—but, alas, his Papers for this Period are all lost to us :
it was not safe to print them with the others; and they are
lost! The *Historical Collections*, with their infinite rubbish and
their modicum of jewels, cease at the Trial of the King; leaving
us, fallen into far worse hands, to repent of our impatience, and
regret the useful John!

[Here are omitted letters passing between Cromwell and
Lesley, and Cromwell and the Scottish General Assembly.
—Ed.]

LETTER XXXVI

DOROTHY CROMWELL, we are happy to find, has a 'little brat;'—
but the poor little thing must have died soon: in Noble's
inexact lists there is no trace of its ever having lived. The Lord
General has got into Northumberland. He has a good excuse
for being 'silent this way,'—the way of Letters.

*For my very loving Brother Richard Mayor, Esquire, at his
House at Hursley: These.*

Alnwick, 17th July 1650.

DEAR BROTHER,
   The exceeding crowd of business I had at London is the
best excuse I can make for my silence this way. Indeed, Sir,
my heart beareth me witness I want no affection to you or
yours; you are all often in my poor prayers.

I should be glad to hear how the little Brat doth. I could
chide both Father and Mother for their neglects of me: I know
my Son is idle, but I had better thoughts of Doll. I doubt
now her Husband hath spoiled her; pray tell her so from me.
If I had as good leisure as they, I should write sometimes. If
my Daughter be breeding, I will excuse her; but not for her
nursery! The Lord bless them. I hope you give my Son
good counsel; I believe he needs it. He is in the dangerous
time of his age; and it's a very vain world. O, how good it is
to close with Christ betimes!—there is nothing else worth the
looking after. I beseech you call upon him,—I hope you will
discharge my duty and your own love: you see how I am
employed. I need pity, I know what I feel. Great place and
business in the world is not worth the looking after; I should

have no comfort in mine but that my hope is in the Lord's presence. I have not sought these things ; truly I have been called unto them by the Lord, and therefore am not without some assurance that He will enable His poor worm and weak servant to do His will, and to fulfil my generation In this I desire your prayers. Desiring to be lovingly remembered to my dear Sister, to our Son and Daughter, to my Cousin Ann and the good Family, I rest,

Your very affectionate brother,
OLIVER CROMWELL.

LETTER XXXVII

'COPPERSPATH,' of which the General here speaks, is the country pronunciation of Cockburnspath ; name of a wild rock-and-river chasm, through which the great road goes, some miles to the eastward of Dunbar. Of which we shall hear again. A very wild road at that time, as may still be seen. The ravine is now spanned by a beautiful Bridge, called *Pease Bridge*, or Path's Bridge, which pleasure-parties go to visit.—The date of this Letter, in all the old Newspapers, is ' 30th July ; ' and doubtless in the Original too ; ' but the real day, as appears by the context, is Wednesday 31st.

To the Right Honourable the Lord President of the Council of State :
These.

Musselburgh, 30th July 1650.

MY LORD,

We marched from Berwick upon Monday, being the 22d of July ; and lay at my Lord Mordington's house, Monday night, Tuesday, and Wednesday. On Thursday we marched to Copperspath ; on Friday to Dunbar, where we got some small pittance from our ships ; from whence we marched to Haddington.

On the Lord's day, hearing that the Scottish Army meant to meet us at Gladsmoor, we laboured to possess the Moor before them ; and beat our drums very early in the morning. But when we came there, no considerable body of the Army appeared. Whereupon Fourteen-hundred horse, under the command of Major-General Lambert and Colonel Whalley, were sent as a vanguard to Musselburgh, to see likewise if they could find out

and attempt any thing upon the Enemy; I marching in the
heel of them with the residue of the Army. Our party encountered with some of their horse; but they could not abide
us. We lay at Musselburgh, encamped close, that night; the
Enemy's Army lying between Edinburgh and Leith, about four
miles from us, entrenched by a Line flankered from Edinburgh
to Leith; the guns also from Leith scouring most part of the
Line, so that they lay very strong.

Upon Monday 29th instant, we were resolved to draw up to
them, to see if they would fight with us. And when we came
upon the place, we resolved to get our cannons as near them as
we could; hoping thereby to annoy them. We likewise perceived that they had some force upon a Hill that overlooks
Edinburgh, from whence we might be annoyed; 'and' did
resolve to send up a party to possess the said Hill;—which
prevailed: but, upon the whole, we did find that their Army
were not easily to be attempted. Whereupon we lay still all
the said day; which proved to be so sore a day and night of
rain as I have seldom seen, and greatly to our disadvantage;
the Enemy having enough to cover them, and we nothing at
all considerable.[1] Our soldiers did abide this difficulty with
great courage and resolution, hoping they should speedily come
to fight. In the morning, the ground being very wet, 'and'
our provisions scarce, we resolved to draw back to our quarters
at Musselburgh, there to refresh and revictual.

The Enemy, when we drew off, fell upon our rear; and put
them into some little disorder; but our bodies of horse being in
some readiness, came to a grabble with them; where indeed
there was a gallant and hot dispute; the Major-General[2] and
Colonel Whalley being in the rear; and the Enemy drawing
out great bodies to second their first affront. Our men charged
them up to the very trenches, and beat them in. The Major-
General's horse was shot in the neck and head; himself run
through the arm with a lance, and run into another place of his
body,—was taken prisoner by the Enemy, but rescued immediately by Lieutenant Empson of my regiment. Colonel
Whalley, who was then nearest to the Major-General, did charge
very resolutely; and repulsed the Enemy, and killed divers of

[1] 'Near a little village named, I think, Lichnagarie,'—means, Lang
Niddery (Hodgson, p. 132); the *Niddery* near Duddingston, still
deservedly called *Lang* by the people, though map-makers append the
epithet elsewhere.

[2] Lambert.

them upon the place, and took some prisoners, without any considerable loss. Which indeed did so amaze and quiet them, that we marched off to Musselburgh, but they dared not send out a man to trouble us. We hear their young King looked on upon all this, but was very ill satisfied to see their men do no better.

We came to Musselburgh that night ; so tired and wearied for want of sleep, and so dirty by reason of the wetness of the weather, that we expected the Enemy would make an infall upon us. Which accordingly they did, between three and four of the clock this morning ; with fifteen of their most select troops, under the command of Major-General Montgomery and Strahan, two champions of the Church :—upon which business there was great hope and expectation laid. The Enemy came on with a great deal of resolution ; beat in our guards, and put a regiment of horse in some disorder : but our men, speedily taking the alarm, charged the Enemy ; routed them, took many prisoners, killed a great many of them ; did execution 'to' within a quarter of a mile of Edinburgh ; and, I am informed, Strahan [1] was killed there, besides divers other Officers of quality. We took the Major to Strahan's regiment, Major Hamilton ; a Lieutenant-Colonel, and divers other Officers, and persons of quality, whom yet we know not. Indeed this is a sweet beginning of your business, or rather the Lord's ; and I believe is not very satisfactory to the Enemy, especially to the Kirk party. We did not lose any in this business, so far as I hear, but a Cornet ; I do not hear of four men more. The Major-General will, I believe, within few days be well to take the field. And I trust this work, which is the Lord's, will prosper in the hands of His servants.

I did not think advisable to attempt upon the Enemy, lying as he doth : but surely this would sufficiently provoke him to fight if he had a mind to it. I do not think he is less than Six or Seven thousand horse, and Fourteen or Fifteen thousand foot. The reason, I hear, that they give out to their people why they do not fight us, is, Because they expect many bodies of men more out of the North of Scotland ; which when they come, they give out they will then engage. But I believe they would rather tempt us to attempt them in their fastness, within which they

---

[1] We shall hear of Strahan again, not 'killed.' This Montgomery is the Earl of Eglinton's son Robert, neither is he 'slain,' as will be seen by and by.

are entrenched ; or else hoping we shall famish for want of provisions ; which is very likely to be, if we be not timely and fully supplied. I remain,
My Lord,
Your most humble servant,
OLIVER CROMWELL.

'P.S.' I understand since writing of this Letter, that Major General Montgomery is slain.

Cautious David Lesley lies thus within his Line 'flankered' from Leith shore to the Calton Hill, with guns to 'scour' it : with outposts or flying parties, as we see, stationed on the back slope of Salisbury Crags or Arthur's Seat ; with all Edinburgh safe behind him, and indeed all Scotland safe behind him for supplies : and nothing can tempt him to come out. The factions and distractions of Scotland, and its Kirk Committees and State Committees, and poor Covenanted King and Courtiers, are many : but Lesley, standing steadily to his guns, persists here. His Army, it appears, is no great things of an Army : 'altogether governed by the Committee of Estates and Kirk,' snarls an angry *Un*covenanted Courtier, whom the said Committee has just ordered to take himself away again ; 'altogether 'governed by the Committee of Estates and Kirk,' snarls he, 'and 'they took especial care in their levies not to admit any '*Malignants* or *Engagers*' (who had been in Hamilton's Engagement) ; 'placing in command, for most part, Ministers' Sons, 'Clerks and other sanctified creatures, who hardly ever saw or 'heard of any sword but that of the spirit !'[1] The more reason for Lesley to lie steadily within his Line here. Lodged in 'Bruchton Village,' which means Broughton, now a part of Edinburgh New Town ; there in a cautious solid manner lies Lesley ; and lets Cromwell attempt upon him. It is his history, the military history of these two, for a month to come.

Meanwhile the General Assembly have not been backward with their Answer to the Cromwell Manifesto, or 'Declaration of the English Army to all the Saints in Scotland,' spoken of above. Nay, already while he lay at Berwick, they had drawn up an eloquent Counter-Declaration, and sent it to him ; which he, again, has got 'some godly Ministers' of his to declare against and reply to : the whole of which Declarations, Replies and Re-replies shall, like the primary Document itself, remain

[1] Sir Edward Walker : Historical Discourses (London, 1705), p 162.

suppressed on the present occasion.¹ But along with this 'Reply by some godly Ministers,' the Lord General sends a Letter of his own.

David Lesley, however, continues within his Line ; stands steadily to his guns ; and the weather is wet ; Oliver's provision is failing. His Letter to the Kirk was written on Saturday : on the Monday following, 'about the 6th of August,' as Major Hodgson dates it, the tempestuous state of the weather not permitting ship-stores to be landed at Musselburgh, Cromwell has to march his Army back to Dunbar, and there provision it. Great joy in the Kirk-and-Estates Committee thereupon : Lesley steadily continues in his place.

The famine among the Scots themselves, at Dunbar, is great ; picking our horses' beans, eating our soldiers' leavings : 'they are much enslaved to their Lords,' poor creatures ; almost destitute of private capital, and ignorant of soap to a terrible extent ! Cromwell distributes among them 'pease and wheat to the value of 240*l*.' On the 12th he returns to Musselburgh ; finds, as heavy Bulstrode spells it in good Scotch, with a friskiness we hardly looked for in him, That Lesley has commanded 'The gude women should awe come away with their 'gear, and not stay to brew or bake, any of them, for the 'English :'—which makes it a place more forlorn than before. Oliver decides to encamp on the Pentland Hills, which lie on the other side of Edinburgh, overlooking the Fife and Stirling roads ; and to try whether he cannot force Lesley to fight, by cutting off his supplies.

The encampment on Pentland Hills, 'some of our tents within sight of Edinburgh Castle and City,' threatens to cut off Lesley's supplies ; but will not induce him to fight. 'The gude wives fly with their bairns and gear' in great terror of us, poor gude wives ; and 'when we set fire to furze-bushes, report that we are burning their houses.' Great terror of us ; but no other result. Lesley brings over his guns to the western side of Edinburgh and awaits, steady within his fastnesses there

Hopes have arisen that the Godly Party in Scotland, seeing now by these Letters and Papers what our real meaning is, may perhaps quit a Malignant King's Interest, and made bloodless peace with us, 'which were the best of all.' The king boggles

---

[1] Titles of them, copies of several of them, in Parliamentary History, xix.

about signing that open Testimony, that Declaration against his Father's sins which was expected of him. 'A great Commander of the Enemy's, Colonel Gibby Carre' (Colonel Gilbert Ker, of whom we shall hear farther), solicits an interview with some of ours, and has it; and other interviews and free communings take place, upon the Burrow-Moor and open fields that lie between us. Gibby Ker, and also Colonel Strahan who was thought to be slain: these and some minority of others are clear against Malignancy in every form; and if the Covenanted Stuart King will not sign this Declaration—!— Whereupon the Covenanted Stuart King does sign it; signs this too,[1]—what will he not sign?—and these hopes of accommodation vanish.

Neither still will they risk a Battle; though in their interviews upon the Burrow-Moor, they said they longed to do it. Vain that we draw out in battalia; they lie within their fastnesses. We march, with defiant circumstance of war, round all accessible sides of Edinburgh; encamp on the Pentlands, return to Musselburgh for provisions; go to the Pentlands again,— enjoy one of the beautifullest prospects, over deep-blue seas, over yellow corn-fields, dusky Highland mountains, from Ben Lomond round to the Bass again; but can get no Battle. And the weather is broken, and the season is advancing,—equinox within ten days, by the modern Almanac. Our men fall sick; the service is harassing!—and it depends on wind and tide whether even biscuit can be landed for us nearer than Dunbar.

Here is an Excerpt which, in spite of imperfections, may be worth transcribing. 'The English Army lay' at first 'near 'Musselburgh, about Stony Hill. But shortly after, they 'marched up to Braid House,' to Braid Hills, to Pentland Hills, Colinton and various other Hills and Houses in succession; 'and the Scots Army, being put in some readiness, marched 'up to Corstorphine Hill. But because the English feared it 'was too near the Castle of Edinburgh, they would not hazard 'battle there. Wherefore both Armies marched to Gogar, 'Tuesday August 27th; and played each upon other with 'their great guns: but because of Gogar Burn (*Brook*) and other 'ditches betwixt the Armies, they could not join battle. Next 'day, about midday,' more precisely Wednesday about ten or eleven o'clock, 'the English began to retire; and went first to 'their Leaguer at Braid Hills,' within a mile of Edinburgh as

[1] At our Court at Dunfermline this 16th day of August 1650.

their General says. 'The English removing, the Scots followed by Corstorphine the long gate' (*roundabout road*),—which is hard ground, and out of shot-range. 'The English,' some of them, 'marched near to Musselburgh; and, in the mid night, 'planted some guns in Niddry: the Scots having marched about 'the Hill of Arthur's Seat, towards Craigmillar, there planted 'some guns against those in Niddry;'—and in fact, as we have seen, were drawn up on Arthur's Seat on the morrow morning, looking on amid the rain, and not attempting to do anything.

The Lord General writes this Letter at Musselburgh on Friday the 30th, the morrow after his return: and directly on the heel of it there is a Council of War held, and an important resolution taken. With sickness, and the wild weather coming on us, rendering even victual uncertain, and no Battle to be had, we clearly cannot continue here. Dunbar, which has a harbour, we might fortify for a kind of citadel and winter-quarter; let us retire at least to Dunbar, to be near our sole friends in this country, our Ships. On the morrow evening, Saturday the 31st, the Lord General fired his huts, and marched towards Dunbar. At sight whereof Lesley rushes out upon him; has his vanguard in Prestonpans before our rear got away. Saturday night throught Haddington, and all Sunday to Dunbar, Lesley hangs, close and heavy, on Cromwell's rear; on Sunday night bends southward to the hills that overlook Dunbar, and hems him in there. As will be more especially related in the next fascicle of Letters.

LETTERS XXXVIII. ETC.

BATTLE OF DUNBAR

THE small Town of Dunbar stands, high and windy, looking down over its herring-boats, over its grim old Castle now much honeycombed,—on one of those projecting rock-promontories with which that shore of the Frith of Forth is niched and vandyked, as far as the eye can reach. A beautiful sea; good land too, now that the plougher understands his trade; a grim niched barrier of whinstone sheltering it from the chafings and tumblings of the big blue German Ocean. Seaward St. Abb's Head, of whinstone, bounds your horizon to the east, not very far off; west, close by, is the deep bay, and fishy little village of Belhaven: the gloomy Bass and other rock-islets, and farther the Hills of Fife, and fore-shadows of the Highlands, are visible as you look seaward. From the bottom of Belhaven bay to that of the next seabight St. Abb's-ward, the Town and its environs form a peninsula. Along the base of which peninsula, 'not much above a mile and a half from sea to sea,' Oliver Cromwell's Army, on Monday 2d of September 1650, stands ranked, with its tents and Town behind it,—in very forlorn circumstances. This now is all the ground that Oliver is lord of in Scotland. His Ships lie in the offing, with biscuit and transport for him; but visible elsewhere in the Earth no help.

Landward as you look from the Town of Dunbar there rises, some short mile off, a dusky continent of barren heath Hills; the Lammermoor, where only mountain-sheep can be at home. The crossing of *which*, by any of its boggy passes, and brawling stream-courses, no Army, hardly a solitary Scotch Packman could attempt, in such weather. To the edge of these Lammermoor Heights, David Lesley has betaken himself; lies now along the outmost spur of them,—a long hill of considerable height, which the Dunbar people call the Dun, Doon, or sometimes for fashion's sake the Down, adding to it the Teutonic *Hill* likewise, though *Dun* itself in old Celtic signifies Hill. On this Doon Hill lies David Lesley with the victorious Scotch Army, upwards of Twenty-thousand strong; with the Committees of Kirk and Estates, the chief Dignitaries of the Country, and in fact the flower of what the pure Covenant in this the Twelfth year of its existence can still bring forth. There lies he since Sunday night, on the top and slope of this Doon Hill, with the impassable heath-continents behind him; embraces, as within outspread tiger-claws, the base-line of Oliver's Dunbar peninsula; waiting what Oliver will do. Cockburnspath with its ravines has been seized on Oliver's left, and made impassable; behind Oliver is the sea; in front of him Lesley, Doon Hill, and the heath-continent of Lammermoor. Lesley's force is of Three-and-twenty-thousand, in spirits as of men chasing, Oliver's about half as many, in spirits as of men chased. What is to become of Oliver?

LETTER XXXVIII

HASELRIG, as we know, is Governor of Newcastle. Oliver on Monday writes this Note; means to send it off, I suppose, by

sea. Making no complaint for himself, the remarkable Oliver;
doing, with grave brevity, in the hour the business of the hour.
'He was a strong man,' so intimates Charles Harvey, who knew
him; 'in the dark perils of war, in the high places of the
'field, hope shone in him like a pillar of fire, when it had gone
'out in all the others.' A genuine King among men, Mr.
Harvey. The divinest sight this world sees,—when it is
privileged to see such, and not be sickened with the unholy
apery of such! He is just now upon an 'engagement,' or
complicated concern, 'very difficult.'

*To the Honourable Sir Arthur Haselrig at Newcastle or elsewhere:
These. Haste, Haste.*

'Dunbar,' 2d September 1650.

DEAR SIR,

We are upon an Engagement very difficult. The
Enemy hath blocked up our way at the Pass at Copperspath,
through which we cannot get without almost a miracle. He
lieth so upon the Hills that we know not how to come that
way without great difficulty; and our lying here daily con-
sumeth our men, who fall sick beyond imagination.

I perceive, your forces are not in a capacity for present re-
lease. Wherefore, whatever becomes of us, it will be well for
you to get what forces you can together; and the South to help
what they can. The business nearly concerneth all Good
People. If your forces had been in a readiness to have fallen
upon the back of Copperspath, it might have occasioned supplies
to have come to us. But the only wise God knows what is
best. All shall work for Good. Our spirits are comfortable,
praised be the Lord,—though our present condition be as it
is. And indeed we have much hope in the Lord; of whose
mercy we have had large experience.

Indeed do you get together what forces you can against
them. Send to friends in the South to help with more. Let
H. Vane know what I write. I would not make it public, lest
danger should accrue thereby. You know what use to make
hereof. Let me hear from you. I rest,

Your servant,
OLIVER CROMWELL.

'P.S.' It's difficult for me to send to you. Let me hear
from 'you' after 'you receive this.'

The base of Oliver's 'Dunbar Peninsula,' as we have called it

THE POSITION AT DUNBAR

(or Dunbar Pinfold where he is now hemmed in, upon 'an entanglement very difficult'), extends from Belhaven Bay on his right, to Brocksmouth House on his left; 'about a mile and a half from sea to sea.' Brocksmouth House, the Earl (now Duke) of Roxburgh's mansion, which still stands there, his soldiers now occupy as their extreme post on the left. As its name indicates, it is the *mouth* or issue of a small Rivulet, or *Burn*, called *Brock*, *Brocksburn*; which, springing from the Lammermoor, and skirting David Lesley's Doon Hill, finds its egress here into the sea. The reader who would form an image to himself of the great Tuesday 3d of September 1650, at Dunbar, must note well this little *Burn*. It runs in a deep grassy glen, which the South-country Officers in those old Pamphlets describe as a 'deep *ditch*, forty feet in depth, and about as many in width,'—ditch dug out by the little Brook itself, and carpeted with greensward, in the course of long thousands of years. It runs pretty close by the foot of Doon Hill : forms, from this point to the sea, the boundary of Oliver's position : his force is arranged in battle-order along the left bank of this Brocksburn, and its grassy glen; he is busied all Monday, he and his Officers, in ranking them there. 'Before sunrise on Monday' Lesley sent down his horse from the Hill-top, to occupy the other side of this Brook; 'about four in the afternoon' his train came down, his whole Army gradually came down; and they now are ranking themselves on the opposite side of Brocksburn,—on rather narrow ground; cornfields, but swiftly sloping upwards to the steep of Doon Hill. This goes on, in the wild showers and winds of Monday 2d September 1650, on both sides of the Rivulet of Brock. Whoever will begin the attack, must get across this Brook and its glen first; a thing of much disadvantage.

Behind Oliver's ranks, between him and Dunbar, stand his tents; sprinkled up and down, by battalions, over the face of this 'Peninsula;' which is a low though very uneven tract of ground; now in our time all yellow with wheat and barley in the autumn season, but at that date only partially tilled,— describable by Yorkshire Hodgson as a place of plashes and rough bent-grass; terribly beaten by showery winds that day, so that your tent will hardly stand. There was then but one Farm-house on this tract, where now are not a few : thither were Oliver's Cannon sent this morning; they had at first been lodged 'in the Church,' an edifice standing then as now somewhat apart, 'at the south end of Dunbar.' We have notice of only one other 'small house,' belike some poor shepherd's homestead, in Oliver's tract of ground : it stands close by the Brock Rivulet itself, and in the bottom of the little glen ; at a place where the banks of it flatten themselves out into a slope passable for carts: this of course, as the one 'pass' in that quarter, it is highly important to seize. Pride and Lambert lodged 'six horse and fifteen foot' in this poor hut early in the morning : Lesley's horse came across, and drove them out ; killing some and 'taking three prisoners ;'—and so got possession of this pass and hut ; but did not keep it. Among the three prisoners was one musketeer, 'a very stout man, though he has but a wooden arm,' and some iron hook at the end of it, poor fellow. He 'fired thrice,' not without effect, with his wooden arm ; and was not taken without difficulty ; a handfast stubborn man ; they carried him across to General Lesley to give some account of himself. In several of the old Pamphlets, which agree in all the details of it, this is what we read :

'General *David* Lesley (old Leven,' the other Lesley, 'being 'in the Castle of Edinburgh, as they relate), asked this man, 'If the Enemy did intend to fight ? He replied, "What do you 'think we come here for ? We come for nothing else !"— '"Soldier," says Lesley, "how will you fight, when you have 'shipped half of your men, and all your great guns ?" The 'Soldier replied, "Sir, if you please to draw down your men, 'you shall find both men and great guns too !"'—A most dogged handfast man, this with the wooden arm, and iron hook on it ! 'One of the Officers asked, How he durst answer the 'General so saucily ? He said, "I only answer the question put 'to me !"' Lesley sent him across, free again, by a trumpet : he made his way to Cromwell ; reported what had passed, and added doggedly, He for one had lost twenty shillings by the business,—plundered from him in this action. 'The Lord General gave him thereupon two pieces,' which I think are forty shillings ; and sent him away rejoicing.—This is the adventure at the 'pass' by the shepherd's hut in the bottom of the glen, close by the Brocksburn itself.

And now farther, on the great scale, we are to remark very specially that there is just one other 'pass' across the Brocksburn ; and this is precisely where the London road now crosses it ; about a mile east from the former pass, and perhaps two gunshots west from Brocksmouth House. There the great road

then as now crosses the Burn of Brock ; the steep grassy glen,
or 'broad ditch forty feet deep,' flattening itself out here once
more into a passable slope: passable, but still steep on the
southern or Lesley side, still mounting up there, with considerable acclivity, into a high table-ground, out of which the Doon
Hill, as outskirt of the Lammermoor, a short mile to your right,
gradually gathers itself. There, at this 'pass,' on and about the
present London road, as you discover after long dreary dim
examining, took place the brunt or essential agony of the Battle
of Dunbar long ago. Read in the extinct old Pamphlets, and
ever again obstinately read, till some light rise in them, look
even with unmilitary eyes at the ground as it now is, you do at
last obtain small glimmerings of distinct features here and there,
—which gradually coalesce into a kind of image for you ; and
some spectrum of the Fact becomes visible ; rises veritable, face
to face, on you, grim and sad in the depths of the old dead
Time. Yes, my travelling friends, vehiculating in gigs or
otherwise over that piece of London road, you may say to yourselves, Here without monument is the grave of a valiant thing
which was done under the Sun ; the footprint of a Hero, not
yet quite undistinguishable, is here !—

'The Lord General about four o'clock,' say the old Pamphlets,
went into the Town to take some refreshment,' a hasty late
dinner, or early supper, whichever we may call it ; 'and very
soon returned back,'—having written Sir Arthur's Letter, I
think, in the interim. Coursing about the field, with enough of
things to order ; walking at last with Lambert in the Park or
Garden of Brocksmouth House, he discerns that Lesley is astir
on the Hill-side ; altering his position somewhat. That Lesley
in fact is coming wholly down to the basis of the Hill, where
his horse had been since sunrise : coming wholly down to the
edge of the Brook and glen, among the sloping harvest-fields
there ; and also is bringing up his left wing of horse, most part
of it, towards his right ; edging himself, 'shogging,' as Oliver
calls in, his whole line more and more to the right ! His meaning
is, to get hold of Brocksmouth House and the pass of the Brook
there ; after which it will be free to him to attack us when he
will !—Lesley in fact considers, or at least the Committee of
Estates and Kirk consider, that Oliver is lost ; that, on the
whole, he must not be left to retreat, but must be attacked and
annihilated here. A vague story, due to Bishop Burnet, the
watery source of many such, still circulates about the world,
That it was the Kirk Committee who forced Lesley down

against his will; that Oliver, at sight of it, exclaimed, "The Lord hath delivered" &c.: which nobody is in the least bound to believe. It appears, from other quarters, that Lesley *was* advised or sanctioned in this attempt by the Committee of Estates and Kirk, but also that he was by no means hard to advise; that, in fact, lying on the top of Doon Hill, shelterless in such weather, was no operation to spin out beyond necessity; —and that if anybody pressed too much upon him with advice to come down and fight, it was likeliest to be Royalist Civil Dignitaries, who had plagued him with their cavillings at his cunctations, at his 'secret fellow-feeling for the Sectarians and Regicides,' ever since this War began. The poor Scotch Clergy have enough of their own to answer for in this business; let every back bear the burden that belongs to it. In a word, Lesley descends, has been descending all day, and 'shogs' himself to the right,—urged, I believe, by manifold counsel, and by the nature of the case; and, what is equally important for us, Oliver sees him, and sees through him, in this movement of his.

At sight of this movement, Oliver suggests to Lambert standing by him, Does it not give *us* an advantage, if we, instead of him, like to begin the attack? Here is the Enemy's right wing coming out to the open space, free to be attacked on any side; and the main-battle hampered in narrow sloping ground between Doon Hill and the Brook, has no room to manœuvre or assist:[1] beat this right wing where it now stands; take it in flank and front with an overpowering force,—it is driven upon its own main-battle, the whole Army is beaten? Lambert eagerly assents, "had meant to say the same thing." Monk, who comes up at the moment, likewise assents; as the other Officers do, when the case is set before them. It is the plan resolved upon for battle. The attack shall begin tomorrow before dawn.

And so the soldiers stand to their arms, or lie within instant reach of their arms, all night; being upon an engagement very difficult indeed. The night is wild and wet;—2d of September means 12th by our calendar: the Harvest Moon wades deep among clouds of sleet and hail. Whoever has a heart for prayer, let him pray now, for the wrestle of death is at hand. Pray,—and withal keep his powder dry! And be ready for extremities, and quit himself like a man!—Thus they pass the

---

[1] Hodgson.

night ; making that Dunbar Peninsula and Brock Rivulet long memorable to me. We English have some tents ; the Scots have none. The hoarse sea moans bodeful, swinging low and heavy against these whinstone bays ; the sea and the tempests are abroad, all else asleep but we,—and there is One that rides on the wings of the wind.

Towards three in the morning the Scotch foot, by order of a Major-General say some, extinguish their matches, all but two in a company ; cower under the corn-shocks, seeking some imperfect shelter and sleep. Be wakeful, ye English ; watch, and pray, and keep your powder dry. About four o'clock comes order to my puddingheaded Yorkshire friend, that his regiment must mount and march straightway ; his and various other regiments march, pouring swiftly to the left to Brocksmouth House, to the Pass over the Brock. With overpowering force let us storm the Scots right wing there ; beat that, and all is beaten. Major Hodgson riding along, heard, he says, 'a Cornet praying in the night :' a company of poor men, I think, making worship there, under the void Heaven, before battle joined : Major Hodgson, giving his charge to a brother Officer, turned aside to listen for a minute, and worship and pray along with them ; haply his last prayer on this Earth, as it might prove to be. But no : his Cornet prayed with such effusion as was wonderful ; and imparted strength to my Yorkshire friend, who strengthened his men by telling them of it. And the Heavens, in their mercy, I think, have opened us a way of deliverance !—The Moon gleams out, hard and blue, riding among hail-clouds ; and over St. Abb's Head, a streak of dawn is rising.

And now is the hour when the attack should be, and no Lambert is yet here, he is ordering the line far to the right yet ; and Oliver occasionally, in Hodgson's hearing, is impatient for him. The Scots too, on this wing, are awake ; thinking to surprise us ; there is their trumpet sounding, we heard it once ; and Lambert, who was to lead the attack, is not here. The Lord General is impatient ;—behold Lambert at last ! The trumpets peal, shattering with fierce clangour Night's silence ; the cannons awaken along all the Line : "The Lord of Hosts ! The Lord of Hosts !" On, my brave ones, on !—

The dispute 'on this right wing was hot and stiff, for three quarters of an hour.' Plenty of fire, from fieldpieces, snaphances, matchlocks, entertains the Scotch main-battle across the Brock ; —poor stiffened men, roused from the corn-shocks with their matches all out! But here on the right, their horse, 'with lancers in the front rank,' charge desperately; drive us back across the hollow of the Rivulet;—back a little; but the Lord gives us courage, and we storm home again, horse and foot, upon them, with a shock like tornado tempests; break them, beat them, drive them all adrift. 'Some fled towards Copperspath, but most across their own foot.' Their own poor foot, whose matches were hardly well alight yet! Poor men, it was a terrible awakening for them: field-pieces and charge of foot across the Brocksburn; and now here is their own horse in mad panic trampling them to death. Above Three-thousand killed upon the place: 'I never saw such a charge of foot and horse,' says one; nor did I. Oliver was still near to Yorkshire Hodgson when the shock succeeded; Hodgson heard him say, "They run! I profess they run!" And over St. Abb's Head and the German Ocean, just then, bursts the first gleam of the level Sun upon us, 'and I heard Nol say, 'in the words of the Psalmist, "Let God arise, let His enemies be scattered,"'—or in Rous's metre,

> Let God arise, and scattered
> Let all His enemies be;
> And let all those that do Him hate
> Before His presence flee!

Even so. The Scotch Army is shivered to utter ruin; rushes in tumultuous wreck, hither, thither; to Belhaven, or, in their distraction, even to Dunbar; the chase goes as far as Haddington; led by Hacker. 'The Lord General made a halt,' says Hodgson, 'and sang the Hundred-and seventeenth Psalm,' till our horse could gather for the chase. Hundred-and-seventeenth Psalm, at the foot of the Doon Hill; there we uplift it, to the tune of Bangor, or some still higher score, and roll it strong and great against the sky:

> O give ye praise unto the Lord,
> All nations that be;
> Likewise ye people all, accord
> His name to magnify!
>
> For great to-us-ward ever are
> His lovingkindnesses;
> His truth endures forevermore:
> The Lord O do ye bless!

And now, to the chase again.

The Prisoners are Ten-thousand,—all the foot in a mass.

Many Dignitaries are taken; not a few are slain; of whom see Printed Lists,—full of blunders. Provost Jaffray of Aberdeen, Member of the Scots Parliament, one of the Committee of Estates, was very nearly slain: a trooper's sword was in the air to sever him, but one cried, He is a man of consequence; he can ransom himself!—and the trooper kept him prisoner. The first of the Scots Quakers, by and by; and an official person much reconciled to Oliver. Ministers also of the Kirk Committee were slain; two Ministers I find taken, poor Carstairs of Glasgow, poor Waugh of some other place,—of whom we shall transiently hear again.

General David Lesley, vigorous for flight as for other things, got to Edinburgh by nine o'clock; poor old Leven, not so light of movement, did not get till two. Tragical enough. What a change since January 1644, when we marched out of this same Dunbar up to the knees in snow! It was to help and save these very men that we then marched; with the Covenant in all our hearts. We have stood by the letter of the Covenant; fought for our Covenanted Stuart King as we could;—they again, they stand by the substance of it, and have trampled us and the letter of it into this ruinous state!—Yes, my poor friends;—and now be wise, be taught! The letter of your Covenant, in fact, will never rally again in this world. The spirit and substance of it, please God, will never die in this or in any world!

Such is Dunbar Battle; which might also be called Dunbar Drove, for it was a frightful rout. Brought on by miscalculation; misunderstanding of the difference between substances and semblances;—by mismanagement, and the chance of war. My Lord General's next Letters, all written on the morrow, will now be intelligible to the reader. First, however, take the following

PROCLAMATION

FORASMUCH as I understand there are several Soldiers of the Enemy's Army yet abiding in the Field, who by reason of their wounds could not march from thence:

These are therefore to give notice to the Inhabitants of this Nation That they may and hereby have free liberty to repair to the Field aforesaid, and, with their carts or 'in' any other peaceable way, to carry away the said Soldiers to such places as they shall think fit :—provided they meddle not with, or take away, any the Arms there. And all Officers and Soldiers are to take notice that the same is permitted.

Given under my hand, at Dunbar, 4th September 1650.

OLIVER CROMWELL.

To be proclaimed by beat of drum.

LETTER XXXIX

For the Honourable William Lenthall, Esquire, Speaker of the Parliament of England: These.

Dunbar, 4th September 1650.

SIR,

I hope it's not ill taken, that I make no more frequent addresses to the Parliament. Things that are in trouble, in point of provision for your Army, and of ordinary direction, I have, as I could, often presented to the Council of State, together with such occurrences as have happened;—who, I am sure, as they have not been wanting in their extraordinary care and provision for us, so neither in what they judge fit and necessary to represent the same to you. And this I thought to be a sufficient discharge of my duty on that behalf.

It hath now pleased God to bestow a mercy upon you, worthy of your knowledge, and of the utmost praise and thanks of all that fear and love His name; yea, the mercy is far above all praise. Which that you may the better perceive, I shall take the boldness to tender unto you some circumstances accompanying this great business, which will manifest the greatness and seasonableness of this mercy.

We having tried what we could to engage the Enemy, three or four miles West of Edinburgh; that proving ineffectual, and our victual failing,—we marched towards our ships for a recruit of our want. The Enemy did not at all trouble us in our rear; but marched the direct way towards Edinburgh, and partly in the night and morning slips-through his whole Army; and quarters himself in a posture easy to interpose between us and our victual. But the Lord made him to lose the opportunity. And the morning proving exceeding wet and dark, we recovered, by that time it was light, a ground where they could not hinder us from our victual: which was an high act of the Lord's

Providence to us. We being come into the said ground, the
Enemy marched into the ground we were last upon; having
no mind either to strive to interpose between us and our victuals,
or to fight; being indeed upon this 'aim of reducing us to a'
lock,—hoping that the sickness of your Army would render
their work more easy by the gaining of time. Whereupon
we marched to Musselburgh, to victual, and to ship away our
sick men; where we sent aboard near five-hundred sick and
wounded soldiers.

And upon serious consideration, finding our weakness so to
increase, and the Enemy lying upon his advantage,—at a general
council it was thought fit to march to Dunbar, and there to
fortify the Town. Which (we thought), if anything, would
provoke them to engage. As also, That the having of a
Garrison there would furnish us with accommodation for our
sick men 'and' would be a good Magazine,—which we exceedingly wanted; being put to depend upon the uncertainty of
weather for landing provisions, which many times cannot be
done though the being of the whole Army lay upon it, all the
coasts from Berwick to Leith having not one good harbour.
As also, To lie more conveniently to receive our recruits of
horse and foot from Berwick.

Having these considerations,—upon Saturday the 30th[1] of
August we marched from Musselburgh to Haddington. Where,
by that time we had got the van-brigade of our horse, and our
foot and train, into their quarters, the Enemy had marched with
that exceeding expedition that they fell upon the rear-forlorn of
our horse, and put it in some disorder; and indeed had like to
have engaged our rear-brigade of horse with their whole Army,
—had not the Lord by His Providence put a cloud over the
Moon, thereby giving us opportunity to draw off those horse
to the rest of our Army. Which accordingly was done without
any loss, save of three or four of our aforementioned forlorn;
wherein the Enemy, as we believe, received more loss.

The Army being put into a reasonable secure posture,—
towards midnight the Enemy attempted our quarters, on the
west end of Haddington: but through the goodness of God we
repulsed them. The next morning we drew into an open field,
on the south side of Haddington; we not judging it safe for us
to draw to the Enemy upon his own ground, he being prepos-
sessed thereof;—but rather drew back, to give him way to come

---

[1] *sic:* but Saturday is 31st.

to us, if he had so thought fit. And having waited about the space of four or five hours, to see if he would come to us; and not finding any inclination in the Enemy so to do,—we resolved to go, according to our first intendment, to Dunbar.

By that time we had marched three or four miles, we saw some bodies of the Enemy's horse draw out of their quarters; and by that time our carriages were gotten near Dunbar, their whole Army was upon their march after us. And indeed, our drawing back in this manner, with the addition of three new regiments added to them, did much heighten their confidence, if not presumption and arrogancy.—The Enemy, that night, we perceived, gathered towards the Hills; labouring to make a perfect interposition between us and Berwick. And having in this posture a great advantage,—through his better knowledge of the country, he effected it: by sending a considerable party to the strait Pass at Copperspath; where ten men to hinder are better than forty to make their way. And truly this was an exigent to us,[1] wherewith the Enemy reproached us;—'as' with that condition the Parliament's Army was in when it made its hard conditions with the King in Cornwall[2] By some reports that have come to us, they had disposed of us, and of their business, in sufficient revenge and wrath towards our persons; and had swallowed up the poor Interest of England; believing that their Army and their King would have marched to London without any interruption;—it being told us (we know not how truly) by a prisoner we took the night before the fight, That their King was very suddenly to come amongst them, with those English they allowed to be about him. But in what they were thus lifted up, the Lord was above them.

The Enemy lying in the posture before mentioned, having those advantages; we lay very near him, being sensible of our disadvantages, having some weakness of flesh, but yet consolation and support from the Lord himself to our poor weak faith, wherein I believe not a few amongst us stand: That because of their numbers, because of their advantages, because of their confidence, because of our weakness, because of our strait, we were

[1] A disgraceful summons of caption to us: 'exigent' is a law-writ issued against a fugitive,—such as we knew long since, in our young days, about Lincoln's Inn!

[2] Essex's Army six years ago, in Autumn 1644, when the King had impounded it among the Hills there.

in the Mount, and in the Mount the Lord would be seen ; and that He would find out a way of deliverance and salvation for us :—and indeed we had our consolations and our hopes.

Upon Monday evening,—the Enemy's whole numbers were very great ; about Six-thousand horse, as we heard, and Sixteen-thousand foot at least ; ours drawn down, as to sound men, to about Seven-thousand five-hundred foot, and Three-thousand five-hundred horse,—'upon Monday evening,' the Enemy drew down to the right wing about two-thirds of their left wing of horse. To the right wing ; shogging also their foot and train much to the right ; causing their right wing of horse to edge down towards the sea. We could not well imagine but that the Enemy intended to attempt upon us, or to place themselves in a more exact condition of interposition. The Major-General and myself coming to the Earl Roxburgh's House, and observing this posture, I told him I thought it did give us an opportunity and advantage to attempt upon the Enemy. To which he immediately replied, That he had thought to have said the same thing to me. So that it pleased the Lord to set this apprehension upon both of our hearts, at the same instant. We called for Colonel Monk, and showed him the thing : and coming to our quarters at night, and demonstrating our apprehensions to some of the Colonels, they also cheerfully concurred.

We resolved therefore to put our business into this posture : That six regiments of horse, and three regiments and a half of foot should march in the van ; and that the Major-General, the Lieutenant-General of the horse, and the Commissary-General,[1] and Colonel Monk to command the brigade of foot, should lead on the business ; and that Colonel Pride's brigade, Colonel Overton's brigade, and the remaining two regiments of horse should bring up the cannon and rear. The time of falling-on to be by break of day :—but through some delays it proved not to be so ; 'not' till six o'clock in the morning.

The Enemy's word was, *The Covenant*; which it had been for divers days. Ours, *The Lord of Hosts*. The Major-General, Lieutenant-General Fleetwood, and Commissary-General Whalley, and Colonel Twistleton, gave the onset ; the Enemy being in a very good posture to receive them, having the advantage of their cannon and foot against our horse. Before our foot could come up, the Enemy made a gallant resistance, and there

---

[1] Lambert, Fleetwood, Whalley.

was a very hot dispute at sword's point between our horse and
theirs. Our first foot, after they had discharged their duty
(being overpowered with the Enemy), received some repulse,
which they soon recovered. For my own regiment, under the
command of Lieutenant-Colonel Goffe and my Major, White,
did come seasonably in ; and, at the push of pike, did repel the
stoutest regiment the Enemy had there, merely with the courage
the Lord was pleased to give. Which proved a great amazement to the residue of their foot ; this being the first action
between the foot. The horse in the mean time did, with a
great deal of courage and spirit, beat back all oppositions ;
charging through the bodies of the Enemy's horse, and of their
foot ; who were, after the first repulse given, made by the
Lord of Hosts as stubble to their swords.—Indeed, I believe I
may speak it without partiality : both your chief Commanders
and others in their several places, and soldiers also, were acted[1]
with as much courage as ever hath been seen in any action
since this War. I know they look not to be named ; and
therefore I forbear particulars.

The best of the Enemy's horse being broken through and
through in less than an hour's dispute, their whole Army being
put into confusion, it became a total rout ; our men having the
chase and execution of them near eight miles. We believe that
upon the place and near about it were about Three-thousand
slain. Prisoners taken : of their officers, you have this enclosed
List ; of private soldiers, near Ten-thousand. The whole
baggage and train, taken, wherein was good store of match,
powder and bullet ; all their artillery, great and small,—thirty
guns. We are confident they have left behind them not less
than Fifteen-thousand arms. I have already brought-in to me
near Two-hundred colours, which I herewith send you.[2] What
officers of theirs of quality are killed, we yet cannot learn ; but
yet surely divers are : and many men of quality are mortally
wounded, as Colonel Lumsden, the Lord Libberton and others.
And, that which is no small addition, I do not believe we have

---

[1] 'actuated,' as we now write it.

[2] They hung long in Westminster Hall ; beside the Preston ones,
and still others that came. Colonel Pride has been heard to wish,
and almost to hope, that the Lawyers' gowns might all be hung
up beside the Scots colours yet,—and the Lawyers' selves, except
some very small and most select needful remnant, be ordered
peremptorily to disappear from those localities, and seek an honest
trade elsewhere ! (Walker's *History of Independency.*)

lost twenty men. Not one Commission Officer slain as I hear of, save one Cornet; and Major Rooksby, since dead of his wounds; and not many mortally wounded :—Colonel Whalley only cut in the handwrist, and his horse (twice shot) killed under him; but he well recovered another horse, and went on in the chase.

Thus you have the prospect of one of the most signal mercies God hath done for England and His people, this War :—and now may it please you to give me the leave of a few words. It is easy to say, The Lord hath done this. It would do you good to see and hear our poor foot to go up and down making their boast of God. But, Sir, it's in your hands, and by these eminent mercies God puts it more into your hands, To give glory to Him; to improve your power, and His blessings, to His praise. We that serve you beg of you not to own us,—but God alone. We pray you own His people more and more; for they are the chariots and horsemen of Israel. Disown yourselves;—but own your Authority; and improve it to curb the proud and the insolent, such as would disturb the tranquillity of England, though under what specious pretences soever. Relieve the oppressed, hear the groans of poor prisoners in England. Be pleased to reform the abuses of all professions: —and if there be any one that makes many poor to make a few rich, that suits not a Commonwealth. If He that strengthens your servants to fight, please to give you hearts to set upon these things, in order to His glory, and the glory of your Commonwealth,—'then' besides the benefit England shall feel thereby, you shall shine forth to other Nations, who shall emulate the glory of such a pattern, and through the power of God turn-in to the like!

These are our desires. And that you may have liberty and opportunity to do these things, and not be hindered, we have been and shall be (by God's assistance) willing to venture our lives;—and 'will' not desire you should be precipitated by importunities, from your care of safety and preservation; but that the doing of these good things may have their place amongst those which concern wellbeing, and so be wrought in their time and order.

Since we came in Scotland, it hath been our desire and longing to have avoided blood in this business; by reason that God hath a people here fearing His name, though deceived. And to that end have we offered much love unto such, in the bowels of

Christ; and concerning the truth of our hearts therein, have we appealed unto the Lord. The Ministers of Scotland have hindered the passage of these things to the hearts of those to whom we intended them. And now we hear, that not only the deceived people, but some of the Ministers are also fallen in this Battle. This is the great hand of the Lord, and worthy of the consideration of all those who take into their hands the instruments of a foolish shepherd,—to wit, meddling with worldly policies, and mixtures of earthly power, to set up that which they call the Kingdom of Christ, which is neither it, nor, if it were it, would such means be found effectual to that end,—and neglect, or trust not to, the Word of God, the sword of the Spirit; which is alone powerful and able for the setting up of that Kingdom; and, when trusted to, will be found effectually able to that end, and will also do it! This is humbly offered for their sakes who have lately too much turned aside: that they might return again to preach Jesus Christ, according to the simplicity of the Gospel;—and then no doubt they will discern and find your protection and encouragement.

Beseeching you to pardon this length, I humbly take leave; and rest,

Sir,
Your most obedient servant,
OLIVER CROMWELL.

LETTER XL

For my beloved Wife Elizabeth Cromwell, at the Cockpit: These.

Dunbar, 4th September 1650.

MY DEAREST,

I have not leisure to write much. But I could chide thee that in many of thy Letters thou writest to me, That I should not be unmindful of thee and thy little ones. Truly, if I love you not too well, I think I err not on the other hand much. Thou art dearer to me than any creature; let that suffice.

The Lord hath showed us an exceeding mercy:—who can tell how great it is! My weak faith hath been upheld. I have been in my inward man marvellously supported;—though I assure thee, I grow an old man, and feel infirmities of age marvellously stealing upon me. Would my corruptions did as fast decrease! Pray on my behalf in the latter respect. The

particulars of our late success Harry Vane or Gilbert Pickering will impart to thee. My love to all dear friends. I rest thine,
OLIVER CROMWELL.

LETTER XLI

'*To the Right Honourable the Lord President of the Council of State: These.*'

Edinburgh, 25th September 1650.

* * * On Saturday the 14th instant, we marched six miles towards Stirling; and, by reason of the badness of the ways, were forced to send back two pieces of our greatest artillery. The day following, we marched to Linlithgow, not being able to go farther by reason of much rain that fell that day. On the 16th, we marched to Falkirk; and the next day following, within cannon-shot of Stirling;—where, upon Wednesday the 18th, our Army was drawn forth, and all things in readiness to storm the Town.

But finding the work very difficult; they having in the Town Two-thousand horse and more foot; and the place standing upon a river not navigable for shipping to relieve the same, 'so that' we could not, with safety, make it a Garrison, if God should have given it into our hands:—upon this, and other considerations, it was not thought a fit time to storm. But such was the unanimous resolution and courage both of our Officers and Soldiers, that greater could not be (as to outward appearance) in men.

On Thursday the 19th, we returned from thence to Linlithgow; and at night we were informed that, at Stirling, they shot off their great guns for joy their King was come thither. On Friday the 20th, three Irish soldiers came from them to us; to whom we gave entertainment in the Army; they say, Great fears possessed the soldiers when they expected us to storm. That they know not whether old Leven be their General or not. the report being various; but that Sir John Browne, a Colonel of their Army, was laid aside. That they are endeavouring to raise all the Forces they can, in the North; that many of the soldiers, since our victory, are offended at their Ministers; that Colonel Gilbert Ker and Colonel Strahan are gone with shattered forces to Glasgow, to levy soldiers there. As yet we hear not of any of the old Cavaliers being entertained as Officers among them; 'the expectation of' which occasions differences betwixt their Ministers and the Officers of the Army.

The same day, we came to Edinburgh 'again.' Where we abide without disturbance; saving that about ten at night, and before day in the morning, they sometimes fire three or four great guns at us; and if any of our men come within musket-shot, they fire at them from the Castle. But, blessed be God, they have done us no harm, except one soldier shot (but not to the danger of his life), that I can be informed of. There are some few of the inhabitants of Edinburgh returned home; who, perceiving our civility, and 'our' paying for what we receive of them, repent their departure; open their shops, and bring provisions to the market. It's reported they have in the Castle provisions for fifteen months; some say, for a longer time. Generally the poor acknowledge that our carriage to them is better than that of their own Army; and 'that' had they who are gone away known so much, they would have stayed at home. They say, one chief reason wherefore so many are gone was, They feared we would have imposed upon them some oath wherewith they could not have dispensed.

I am in great hopes, through God's mercy, we shall be able this Winter to give the People such an understanding of the justness of our Cause, and our desires for the just liberties of the People, that the better sort of them will be satisfied therewith; although, I must confess, hitherto they continue obstinate. I thought I should have found in Scotland a conscientious People, and a barren country: about Edinburgh, it is as fertile for corn as any part of England; but the People generally 'are so' given to the most impudent lying, and frequent swearing, as is incredible to be believed.

I rest,
'Your Lordship's most humble servant,'
OLIVER CROMWELL.

What to do with Scotland, in these mixed circumstances, is a question. We have friends among them, a distinct coincidence with them in the great heart of their National Purpose, could they understand us aright; and we have all degrees of enemies among them, up to the bitterest figure of Malignancy itself. What to do? For one thing, Edinburgh Castle ought to be reduced. 'We have put forces into Linlithgow, and 'our Train is lodged in Leith,' Lesley's old citadel there; 'the

'wet being so great that we cannot march with our Train.'
Do we try Edinburgh Castle with a few responsive shots from
the Calton Hill ; or from what point ? My Scotch Antiquarian
friends have not informed me. We decide on reducing it by
mines.

'*Sunday 29th September* 1650. Resolution being taken for the
'springing of mines in order to the reducing of Edinburgh Castle,
'and our men beginning their galleries last night, the Enemy
'fired five pieces of ordnance, with several volleys of shot, from
'the Castle ; but did no execution. We hope this work will
'take effect ; notwithstanding the height, rockiness and strength
'of the place.—His Excellency with his Officers met this day
'in the High Church of Edinburgh, forenoon and afternoon ;
'where was a great concourse of people.' Mr. Stapylton, who
did the Hursley Marriage-treaty, and is otherwise transiently
known to mankind,—he, as was above intimated, occupies
the pulpit there ; the Scots Clergy still sitting sulky in their
Castle, with Derby miners now operating on them. 'Many
'Scots expressed much affection at the doctrine preached by Mr.
'Stapylton, in their usual way of groans,'—Hum-m—mrrh !—
'and it's hoped a good work is wrought in some of their
'hearts.' I am sure I hope so. But to think of brother worshippers, partakers in a Gospel of this kind, cutting one another's
throats for a Covenanted Charles Stuart,—Hum-m-mrrh !

While Ker and Strahan are busy 'at Dumfries,' says Baillie,
'Cromwell with the whole body of his Army and cannon comes
'peaceably by way of Kilsyth to Glasgow.' It is Friday
evening, 18th October 1650. 'The Ministers and Magistrates
'flee all away. I got to the Isle of Cumbrae with my Lady
'Montgomery ; but left all my family and goods to Cromwell's
'courtesy,—which indeed was great ; for he took such a course
'with his soldiers that they did less displeasure at Glasgow
'than if they had been in London ; though Mr. Zachary Boyd,'
a fantastic old gentleman still known in Glasgow and Scotland,
'railed on them all, to their very face, in the High Church ;'[1]
calling them Sectaries and Blasphemers, the fantastic old gentleman ! 'Glasgow, though not so big or rich as Edinburgh,
'is a much sweeter place ; the completest town we have yet
'seen here, and one of their choicest Universities.' The people
were much afraid of us till they saw how we treated them.
'Captain Covel of the Lord General's regiment of horse was

[1] Baillie, iii. 119 : Whitlocke, p. 459.

'cashiered here, for holding some blasphemous opinions.'—This is Cromwell's first visit to Glasgow : he made two others, of which on occasion notice shall be taken. In *Pinkerton's Correspondence* are certain 'anecdotes of Cromwell at Glasgow;' which, like many others on Cromwell, need not be repeated anywhere except in the nursery.

The next affair is that of Edinburgh Castle. Our Derbyshire miners found the rock very hard, and made small way in it : but now the Lord General has got his batteries ready ; and, on Thursday 12th December, after three months blockade, salutes the place with his 'guns and mortars,' and a set of Summonses ; which prove effectual.

LETTER XLII

For the Honourable William Lenthall, Esquire, Speaker of the Parliament of England : These.

Edinburgh, 24th Dec. 1650.

RIGHT HONOURABLE,

It hath pleased God to cause this Castle of Edinburgh to be surrendered into our hands, this day about eleven o'clock. I thought fit to give you such account thereof as I could, and 'as' the shortness of time would permit.

I sent a Summons to the Castle upon the 12th instant ; which occasioned several Exchanges and Replies, which for their unusualness, I also thought fit humbly to present to you. Indeed the mercy is very great, and seasonable. I think, I need to say little of the strength of the place ; which, if it had not come in as it did, would have cost very much blood to have attained, if at all to be attained; and did tie up your Army to that inconvenience, That little or nothing could have been attempted whilst this was in design ; or little fruit had of anything brought into your power by your Army hitherto, without it. I must needs say, not any skill or wisdom of ours, but the good hand of God hath given you this place.

I believe all Scotland hath not in it so much brass ordnance as this place. I send you here enclosed a List thereof,[1] and of

---

[1] Drakes, minions, murderers, monkeys, of brass and iron,—not interesting to us, except it be 'the great iron murderer called *Muckle-Meg*,' already in existence, and still held in some confused remembrance in those Northern parts.

the arms and ammunition, so well as they could be taken on a
sudden. Not having more at present to trouble you with, I
take leave, and rest,

       Sir,
     Your most humble servant,
       OLIVER CROMWELL.

LETTER XLIII

LET us now read a Letter which is unique of its kind: A
Letter from the Lord General's Wife.

'My Lord Chief Justice' is Oliver St. John, known to us this
long while; 'President' is Bradshaw; 'Speaker' is Lenthall:
high official persons; to whom it were better if the Lord
General took his Wife's advice, and wrote occasionally.

*"The Lady Elizabeth Cromwell to her Husband the Lord
     General at Edinburgh.*

     '"'Cockpit, London,' 27th December 1650.

"MY DEAREST,—I wonder you should blame me for writing
"no oftener, when I have sent three for one: I cannot but
"think they are miscarried. Truly if I know my own heart,
"I should as soon neglect myself as to 'omit' the least thought
"towards you, who in doing it, I must do it to myself. But
"when I do write, my Dear, I seldom have any satisfactory
"answer; which makes me think my writing is slighted; as
"well it may: but I cannot but think your love covers my
"weakness and infirmities.

"I should rejoice to hear your desire in seeing me; but I
"desire to submit to the Providence of God; hoping the Lord,
"who hath separated us, and hath often brought us together
"again, will in His good time bring us again, to the praise
"of His name. Truly my life is but half a life in your absence,
"did not the Lord make it up in Himself, which I must
"acknowledge to the praise of His grace.

'I would you would think to write sometimes to your dear
"friend, my Lord Chief Justice, of whom I have often put you
"in mind. And truly, my Dear, if you would think of what
"I put you in mind of some, it might be to as much purpose
"as others; writing sometimes a Letter to the President, and

"sometimes to the Speaker. Indeed, my Dear, you cannot think
"the wrong you do yourself in the want of a Letter, though
"it were but seldom. I pray think on ; and so rest,—yours in
"all faithfulness,

"ELIZABETH CROMWELL."

This Letter, in the original, is frightfully spelt ; but otherwise exactly as here : the only Letter extant of this Heroine ; and not unworthy of a glance from us. It is given in *Harris* too and in *Noble* very incorrectly.

On Tuesday, 4th February 1650-1, the Lord General's Army issuing from its Leith Citadel and other Winter-quarters, has marched westward towards Stirling ; he himself follows on the morrow. His Army on Tuesday got to Linlithgow ; the Lord General overtook them at Falkirk on Wednesday. Two such days of wind, hail, snow and rain as made our soldiers very uncomfortable indeed. On Friday, the morning proving fair, we set out again ; got to Kilsyth ;—but the hail-reservoirs also opened on us again : we found it impossible to get along ; and so returned, by the road we came ; back to Edinburgh on Saturday,—coated with white sleet, but endeavouring not to be discouraged. We hope we much terrified the Scots at Stirling ; but the hail-reservoirs proved friendly to them.

LETTER XLIV

BY that tempestuous sleety expedition in the beginning of February, my Lord General caught a dangerous illness, which hung about him, reappearing in three successive relapses, till June next ; and greatly alarmed the Commonwealth and the Authorities. As this to Bradshaw, and various other Letters still indicate.

*To the Right Honourable the Lord President of the Council
of State : These.*

Edinburgh, 24th March 1650.

MY LORD,
I do with all humble thankfulness acknowledge your high favour, and tender respect of me, expressed in your Letter,

and the Express sent therewith to inquire after one so unworthy as myself.

Indeed, my Lord, your service needs not me: I am a poor creature; and have been a dry bone; and am still an unprofitable servant to my Master and you. I thought I should have died of this fit of sickness; but the Lord seemeth to dispose otherwise. But truly, my Lord, I desire not to live, unless I may obtain mercy from the Lord to approve my heart and life to Him in more faithfulness and thankfulness, and 'to' those I serve in more profitableness and diligence. And I pray God, your Lordship, and all in public trust, may improve all those unparalleled experiences of the Lord's wonderful Workings in your sight, with singleness of heart to His glory, and the refreshment of His People; who are to Him as the apple of His eye; and upon whom your enemies, both former and latter, who have fallen before you, did split themselves.

This shall be the unfeigned prayer of,
My Lord, your most humble servant,
OLIVER CROMWELL.

From Edinburgh, of date 18th March, by special Express we have this comfortable intelligence: 'The Lord General 'is now well recovered: he was in his dining-room today with 'his Officers, and was very cheerful and pleasant.' And the symptoms, we see, continue good and better on the 24th. 'So 'that there is not any fear, by the blessing of God, but our 'General will be enabled to take the field when the Provisions 'arrive.' 'Dr. Goddard' is attending him. Before the end of the month he is on foot again; sieging Blackness, sieging the Island of Inchgarvie, or giving Colonel Monk directions to that end.

LETTER XLV

The following Letter brings its own commentary:

For my beloved Wife Elizabeth Cromwell, at the Cockpit: These.

'Edinburgh,' 12th April 1651.

MY DEAREST,

I praise the Lord I am increased in strength in my outward man: But that will not satisfy me except I get a heart to love and serve my heavenly Father better; and get more of the light of His countenance, which is better than life, and more power over my corruptions :—in these hopes I wait, and am not without expectation of a gracious return. Pray for me; truly I do daily for thee, and the dear Family; and God Almighty bless you all with His spiritual blessings.

Mind poor Betty of the Lord's great mercy. Oh, I desire her not only to seek the Lord in her necessity, but in deed and in truth to turn to the Lord; and to keep close to Him; and to take heed of a departing heart, and of being cozened with worldly vanities and worldly company, which I doubt she is too subject to. I earnestly and frequently pray for her and for him. Truly they are dear to me, very dear; and I am in fear lest Satan should deceive them,—knowing how weak our hearts are, and how subtle the Adversary is, and what way the deceitfulness of our hearts and the vain world make for his temptations The Lord give them truth of heart to Him. Let them seek Him in truth, and they shall find Him.

My love to the dear little ones; I pray for grace for them. I thank them for their Letters; let me have them often.

Beware of my Lord Herbert's resort to your house. If he do so, it may occasion scandal, as if I were bargaining with him. Indeed, be wise,—you know my meaning. Mind Sir Henry Vane of the business of my Estate. Mr. Floyd knows my whole mind in that matter.

If Dick Cromwell and his Wife be with you, my dear love to them. I pray for them : they shall, God willing, hear from me. I love them very dearly.—Truly I am not able as yet to write much. I am weary; and rest,

Thine,
OLIVER CROMWELL.

'Betty' and 'he' are Elizabeth Claypole and her Husband; of whom, for the curious, there is a longwinded intricate account by Noble, but very little discoverable in it. They lived at Norborough, which is near Market Deeping, but in Northamptonshire; where, as already intimated, the Lady Protectress, Widow Elizabeth Cromwell, after the Restoration, found a retreat. 'They had at least three sons and daughters.' Claypole became 'Master of the Horse' to Oliver; sat in Parliament; made an elegant appearance in the world :—but dwindled sadly after his widowerhood; his second marriage ending in 'separation,' in a third *quasi-marriage*, and other

confusions, poor man! But as yet the Lady Claypole lives;
bright and brave. 'Truly they are dear to me, very dear.'

'Dick Cromwell and his Wife' seem to be up in Town on a
visit;—living much at their ease in the Cockpit, they. Brother
Henry, in these same days, is out 'in the King's County' in
Ireland; doing hard duty at 'Ballybawn,' and elsewhere,—the
distinguished Colonel Cromwell. And Deputy Ireton, with his
labours, is wearing himself to death. In the same house, one
works, another goes idle.

'The Lord Herbert' is Henry Somerset, eldest son of the now
Marquis of Worcester,—of the Lord Glamorgan whom we knew
slightly at Ragland, in underhand 'Irish Treaties' and such
like; whose *Century of Inventions* is still slightly known to here
and there a reader of Old Books. 'This Lord Herbert,' it
seems, 'became Duke of Beaufort after the Restoration.' For
obvious reasons, you are to 'beware of his resort to your house
at present.' A kind of professed Protestant he, but come of
rank Papists and Malignants; which may give rise to commentaries. One stupid Annotator on a certain Copy of this
Letter says, 'his Lordship had an intrigue with Mrs. Claypole;'
—which is evidently downright stupor and falsehood, like so
much else.

LETTER XLVI

'*For my beloved Wife Elizabeth Cromwell, at the Cockpit:
These.*'

Edinburgh, 3d May 1651.

MY DEAREST,

I could not satisfy myself to omit this post, although
I have not much to write; yet indeed I love to write to my
Dear, who is very much in my heart. It joys me to hear thy
soul prospereth: the Lord increase His favours to thee more and
more. The great good thy soul can wish is, That the Lord
lift upon thee the light of His countenance, which is better
than life. The Lord bless all thy good counsel and example to
all those about thee, and hear all thy prayers, and accept thee
always.

I am glad to hear thy Son and Daughter are with thee. I
hope thou wilt have some good opportunity of good advice to

him. Present my duty to my Mother, my love to all the Family. Still pray for

      Thine,
       Oliver Cromwell.

'Thy Son and Daughter' are, to all appearance, Richard and his Wife, who prolong their visit at the Cockpit. The good old 'Mother' is still spared with us, to have 'my duty' presented to her. A pale venerable Figure; who has lived to see strange things in this world;—can piously, in her good old tremulous heart, rejoice in such a Son.

Precisely in these days, a small ship driven by stress of weather into Ayr Harbour, and seized and searched by Cromwell's Garrison there, discloses a matter highly interesting to the Commonwealth. A Plot, namely, on the part of the English Presbyterian-Royalists, English Royalists Proper, and all manner of Malignant Interests in England, to unite with the Scots and their King: in which certain of the London Presbyterian Clergy, Christopher Love among others, are deeply involved. The little ship was bound for the Isle of Man, with tidings to the Earl of Derby concerning the affair; and now we have caught her within the Bars of Ayr; and the whole matter is made manifest! Reverend Christopher Love is laid hold of, 7th May; he and others: and the Council of State is busy. It is the same Christopher who preached at Uxbridge Treaty long since, That 'Heaven might as well think of uniting with Hell.' Were a new High Court of Justice once constituted, it will go hard with Christopher.

As for the Lord General, a march to Glasgow has thrown him into a new relapse, which his Doctor counts as the third since March last. The disease is now ague; comes and goes till, in the end of this month, the Council of State, as ordered by Parliament, requests him to return, in the mean while, to England for milder air; and despatches two London Doctors to him; whom the Lord Fairfax is kind enough to 'send in his own coach;' who arrive in Edinburgh on the 30th of May, 'and are affectionately entertained by my Lord.' The two Doctors are Bates and Wright. Bates, in his loose-tongued *History of the Troubles*, redacted in aftertimes, observes strict silence as to this Visit. Here is the Lord General's Answer; indicating with much thankfulness that he will not now need to return.

LETTER XLVII

'To the Lord President of the Council of State: These.'

Edinburgh, 3d June 1651.

MY LORD,

I have received yours of the 27th of May; with an Order from the Parliament for my Liberty to return into England for change of air, that thereby I might the better recover my health. All which came unto me whilst Dr. Wright and Dr. Bates, whom your Lordship sent down, were with me.

I shall not need to recite the extremity of my last sickness: it was so violent that indeed my nature was not able to bear the weight thereof. But the Lord was pleased to deliver me, beyond expectation; and to give me cause to say once more, "He hath plucked me out of the grave!"[1]—My Lord, the indulgence of the Parliament expressed by their Order is a very high and undeserved favour: of which although it be fit I keep a thankful remembrance, yet I judge it would be too much presumption in me to return a particular acknowledgment. I beseech you give me the boldness to return my humble thankfulness to the Council for sending two such worthy Persons, so great a journey, to visit me. From whom I have received much encouragement, and good directions for recovery of health and strength,—which I find 'now,' by the goodness of God, growing to such a state as may yet, if it be His good will, render me useful according to my poor ability, in the station wherein He hath set me.

I wish more steadiness in your Affairs here than to depend, in the least degree, upon so frail a thing as I am. Indeed they do not,—nor own any instrument. This Cause is of God, and it must prosper. Oh, that all that have any hand therein, being *so* persuaded, would gird up the loins of their mind, and endeavour in all things to walk worthy of the Lord! So prays,

My Lord,

Your most humble servant,

OLIVER CROMWELL.

The Lord General's case was somewhat grave; at one time, it seemed hopeless for this summer. 'My Lord is not sensible that he is grown an old man.' The Officers were to proceed without him; directed by him from the distance. Here, how-

---

[1] Psalm xxx. 3, 'hast brought up my soul from the grave;' or, lxxxvi. 3, 'delivered my soul from:' but 'plucked' is not in any of the texts.

ever, is an improvement; and two days after, on the 5th of June, the Lord General is seen abroad in his coach again; shakes his ailments and infirmities of age away, and takes the field in person once more. The Campaign is now vigorously begun; though as yet no great result follows from it.

On the 25th of June, the Army from all quarters reassembled 'in its old Camp on the Pentland Hills;' marched westward; left Linlithgow July 2d, ever westward, with a view to force the Enemy from his strong ground about Stirling. Much pickeering, vapouring, and transient skirmishing ensues; but the Enemy, strongly entrenched at Torwood, secured by bogs and brooks, cannot be forced out. We take Calendar House, and do other insults, before their eyes; they will not come out. Cannonadings there are 'from opposite Hills;' but not till it please the Enemy can there be any battle. David Lesley, second in rank, but real leader of the operations, is at his old trade again. The Problem is becoming difficult. We decide to get across into Fife; to take them in flank, and at least cut off an important part of their supplies.

Here is the Lord General's Letter on the result of that enterprise. Farther details of the Battle, which is briefly spoken of here,—still remembered in those parts as the *Battle of Inverkeithing*,—may be found in Lambert's own Letter concerning it.[1] 'Sir John Browne, their Major-General,' was once a zealous Parliamenteer; 'Governor of Abingdon' and much else; but the King gained him, growls Ludlow, 'by the gift of a pair of silk stockings,'—poor wretch! Besides Browne, there are Massey, and various Englishmen of mark with this Malignant Army. Massey's Brother, a subaltern person in London, is one of the conspirators with Christopher Love.—The Lord General has in the interim made his Third Visit to Glasgow; concerning which there are no details worth giving here. Christopher Love, on the 5th of this month, was condemned to die.

LETTER XLVIII

For the Honourable William Lenthall, Esquire, Speaker of the Parliament of England: These.

Linlithgow, 21st July 1651.

SIR,

After our waiting upon the Lord, and not knowing what

[1] North Ferry, 22d July 1651: the Battle was on Sunday the 20th.

course to take, for indeed we know nothing but what God pleaseth to teach us of His great mercy,—we were directed to send a Party to get us a landing 'on the Fife coast' by our boats, whilst we marched towards Glasgow.

On Thursday morning last, Colonel Overton, with about One-thousand four-hundred foot and some horse and dragoons, landed at the North Ferry in Fife; we with the Army lying near the Enemy (a small river parted us and them), and having consultations to attempt the Enemy within his fortifications: but the Lord was not pleased to give way to that counsel, proposing a better way for us. The Major-General 'Lambert' marched, on Thursday night, with two regiments of horse and two regiments of foot, for better securing the place; and to attempt upon the Enemy as occasion should serve. He getting over, and finding a considerable body of the Enemy there (who would probably have beaten our men from the place if he had not come), drew out and fought them; he being about two regiments of horse, with about four-hundred of horse and dragoons more, and three regiments of foot; the Enemy five regiments of foot, and about four or five of horse. They came to a close charge, and in the end totally routed the Enemy; having taken about forty or fifty colours, killed near Two-thousand, some say more; have taken Sir John Browne their Major-General, who commanded in chief,—and other Colonels and considerable Officers killed and taken, and about Five or Six Hundred prisoners. The Enemy is removed from their ground with their whole Army; but whither we do not certainly know.

This is an unspeakable mercy. I trust the Lord will follow it until He hath perfected peace and truth. We can truly say, we were gone as far as we could in our counsel and action; and we did say one to another, we knew not what to do Wherefore it's sealed upon our hearts, that this, as all the rest, is from the Lord's goodness, and not from man. I hope it becometh me to pray, That we may walk humbly and self-denyingly before the Lord, and believingly also. That you whom we serve, as the Authority over us, may do the work committed to you, with uprightness and faithfulness,—and thoroughly, as to the Lord. That you may not suffer anything to remain that offends the eyes of His jealousy. That common weal may more and more be sought, and justice done impartially. For the eyes of the Lord run to and fro; and as He finds out His enemies here, to be avenged on them, so will He not spare them for whom He doth good, if by His lovingkindness they become not good. I shall take the humble boldness to represent this Engagement of David's, in the Hundred-and-nineteenth Psalm, verse Hundred-and-thirty-fourth, *Deliver me from the oppression of man so will I keep Thy precepts*.

I take leave, and rest,

Sir, your most humble servant,

OLIVER CROMWELL.

P.S. The carriage of the Major-General, as in all other things so in this, is worthy of your taking notice of; as also the Colonels Okey, Overton, Daniel, West, Lydcot, Syler, and the rest of the Officers.

Matters now speedily take another turn. At the Castle of 'Dundas' we are still on the South side of the Frith; in front of the Scotch lines, though distant: but Inchgarvie, often tried with gunboats, now surrenders; Burntisland, by force of gunboats and dispiritment, surrenders: the Lord General himself goes across into Fife.

LETTER XLIX

To the Honourable William Lenthall, Esquire, Speaker of the Parliament of England: These.

Burntisland, 29th July 1651.

Sir,

The greatest part of the Army is in Fife; waiting what way God will farther lead us. It hath pleased God to give us in Burntisland; which is indeed very conducing to the carrying-on of our affairs. The Town is well seated; pretty strong; but marvellous capable of further improvement in that respect, without great charge. The Harbour, at a high spring, is near a fathom deeper than at Leith; and doth not lie commanded by any ground without the Town. We took three or four small men-of-war in it, and I believe thirty or forty guns.

Commissary-General Whalley marched along the sea-side in Fife, having some ships to go along the coast; and hath taken great store of great artillery, and divers ships. The Enemy's affairs are in some discomposure, as we hear. Surely the Lord will blow upon them.

'I rest,'
Your most humble servant,
OLIVER CROMWELL.

LETTER L

IN effect, the crisis has now arrived. The Scotch King and Army, finding their supplies cut off, and their defences rendered unavailing, by this flank-movement,—break up suddenly from Stirling; march direct towards England,—for a stroke at the heart of the Commonwealth itself. Their game now is, All or nothing. A desperate kind of play. Royalists, Presbyterian-Royalists and the large miscellany of Discontented Interests may perhaps join them there;—perhaps also not! They march by Biggar; enter England by Carlisle, on Wednesday 6th of August 1651. 'At Girthhead, in the Parish of Wamphray, in Annandale,' human Tradition, very faintly indeed, indicates some Roman Stones or Mile-stones, by the wayside, as the place where his Sacred Majesty passed the Tuesday night;— which are not quite so venerable now as formerly.

To the Honourable William Lenthall, Esquire, Speaker of the Parliament of England; These.

Leith, 4th August 1651.

Sir,

In pursuance of the Providence of God, and that blessing lately given to your forces in Fife; and finding that the Enemy, being masters of the Pass at Stirling, could not be gotten out there except by hindering his provisions at St. Johnston,—we, by general advice, thought fit to attempt St. Johnston; knowing that that would necessitate him to quit his Pass. Wherefore, leaving with Major-General Harrison about three-thousand horse and dragoons, besides those which are with Colonel Rich, Colonel Saunders, and Colonel Barton, upon the Borders, we marched to St. Johnston;[1] and lying one day before it, we had it surrendered to us.

[1] 2d August 1651: 'St. Johnston,' as we know, is *Perth.*

During which time we had some intelligence of the Enemy's marching southward; though with some contradictions, as if it had not been so. But doubting it might be true, we (leaving a Garrison in St. Johnston, and sending Lieutenant-General Monk with about Five or Six thousand to Stirling to reduce that place, and by it to put your affairs into a good posture in Scotland) marched, with all possible expedition, back again; and have passed our foot and many of our horse over the Frith this day; resolving to make what speed we can up to the Enemy,—who, in his desperation and fear, and out of inevitable necessity, is run to try what he can do this way.

I do apprehend that if he goes for England, being some few days march before us, it will trouble some men's thoughts; and may occasion some inconveniences;—which I hope we are as deeply sensible of, and have been, and I trust shall be, as diligent to prevent, as any. And indeed this is our comfort, That in simplicity of heart as towards God, we have done to the best of our judgments; knowing that if some issue were not put to this Business, it would occasion another Winter's war: to the ruin of your soldiery, for whom the Scots are too hard in respect of enduring the Winter difficulties of this country; and to the endless expense of the treasure of England in prosecuting this War. It may be supposed we might have kept the Enemy from this, by interposing between him and England. Which truly I believe we might: but how to remove him out of this place, without doing what we have done, unless we had had a commanding Army on both sides of the River of Forth, is not clear to us; or how to answer the inconveniences aforementioned, we understand not.

We pray therefore that (seeing there is a possibility for the Enemy to put you to some trouble) you would, with the same courage, grounded upon a confidence in God, wherein you have been supported to the great things God hath used you in hitherto,—improve, the best you can, such forces as you have in readiness, or 'as' may on the sudden be gathered together, To give the Enemy some check, until we shall be able to reach up to him; which we trust in the Lord we shall do our utmost endeavour in. And indeed we have this comfortable experience from the Lord, That this Enemy is heart-smitten by God; and whenever the Lord shall bring us up to them, we believe the Lord will make the desperateness of this council of theirs to appear, and the folly of it also. When England was much more unsteady than now; and when a much more considerable

Army of theirs, unfoiled, invaded you; and we had but a weak force to make resistance at Preston,—upon deliberate advice, we chose rather to put ourselves between their Army and Scotland: and how God succeeded that, is not well to be forgotten! This 'present movement' is not out of choice on our part, but by some kind of necessity; and, it is to be hoped, will have the like issue. Together with a hopeful end of your work;—in which it's good to wait upon the Lord, upon the earnest of former experiences, and hope of His presence, which only is the life of your Cause.

Major-General Harrison, with the horse and dragoons under him, and Colonel Rich and the rest in those parts, shall attend the motions of the Enemy; and endeavour the keeping of them together, as also to impede his march. And will be ready to be in conjunction with what forces shall gather together for this service:—to whom orders have been speeded to that purpose; as this enclosed to Major-General Harrison will show. Major-General Lambert, this day, marched with a very considerable body of horse, up towards the Enemy's rear. With the rest of the horse, and nine regiments of foot, most of them of your old foot and horse, I am hasting up; and shall, by the Lord's help, use utmost diligence. I hope I have left a commanding force under Lieutenant-General Monk in Scotland.

This account I thought my duty to speed to you; and rest,

Your most humble servant,
OLIVER CROMWELL.

The Scots found no Presbyterian-Royalists, no Royalists Proper to speak of, nor any Discontented Interest in England disposed to join them in present circumstances. They marched, under rigorous discipline, weary and uncheered, south through Lancashire; had to dispute their old friend the Bridge of Warrington with Lambert and Harrison, who attended them with horse-troops on the left; Cromwell with the main Army steadily advancing behind. They carried the Bridge at Warrington; they summoned various Towns, but none yielded; proclaimed their King with all force of lungs and heraldry, but none cried, God bless him. Summoning Shrewsbury, with the usual negative response, they quitted the London road; bent southward towards Worcester, a City of slight Garrison and Loyal Mayor; there to entrench themselves, and repose a little.

Poor Earl Derby, a distinguished Royalist Proper, had hastened over from the Isle of Man, to kiss his Majesty's hand in passing. He then raised some force in Lancashire, and was in hopes to kindle that country again, and go to Worcester in triumph :— but Lilburn, Colonel Robert, whom we have known here before, fell upon him at Wigan ; cut his force in pieces ; the poor Earl had to go to Worcester in a wounded and wrecked condition. To Worcester,—and, alas, to the scaffold by and by, for that business. The Scots at Worcester have a loyal Mayor, some very few adventurous loyal Gentry in the neighbourhood ; and excitable Wales, perhaps again excitable, lying in the rear : but for the present, except in their own poor Fourteen-thousand right-hands, no outlook. And Cromwell is advancing steadily ; by York, by Nottingham, by Coventry and Stratford ; 'raising all the County Militias,' who muster with singular alacrity ;— flowing towards Worcester like the Ocean-tide : begirdling it with 'upwards of Thirty-thousand men.' His Majesty's royal summons to the Corporation of London is burnt there by the hands of the common hangman ; Speaker Lenthall and the Mayor have a copy of it burnt by that functionary at the head of every regiment, at a review of the Trainbands in Moorfields. London, England generally, seems to have made up its mind.

At London on the 22d of August, a rigorous thing was done. Reverend Christopher Love, eloquent zealous Minister of St. Lawrence in the Jewry, was, after repeated respites and negotiations, beheaded on Tower Hill. To the unspeakable emotion of men. Nay the very Heavens seemed to testify a feeling of it, —by a thunderclap, by two thunderclaps. When the Parliament passed their vote on the 4th of July, That he should die according to the sentence of the Court, there was then a terrible thunderclap, and darkening of daylight. And now when he actually dies, 'directly after his beheading,' arises thunderstorm that threatens the dissolution of Nature ! Nature, as we see, survived it.

The old Newspaper says, It was on the 22d August 1642, that Charles late King erected his Standard at Nottingham : and now on this same day, 22d August 1651, Charles Pretender erects his at Worcester ; and the Reverend Christopher dies. Men may make their reflections.

Charles's Standard, it would seem then, was erected at Worcester on Friday the 22d, the day of poor Christopher's death. On which same Friday, about sunrise, 'our Messenger' (the Parliament's) 'left the Lord General at Mr. Pierpoint's House,'

—William Pierpoint, of the Kingston Family, much his friend,
—the House called Thoresby, 'near Mansfield'; just starting
for Nottingham, to arrive there at night. From Nottingham,
by Coventry, by Stratford and Evesham, to 'the southeast side
of Worcester,' rallying Country forces as we go, will take till
Thursday next.

Charles's Standard has been floating over Worcester some six
days; and now on Thursday 28th of August, comes in sight
Cromwell's also; from the Evesham side; with upwards of
Thirty-thousand men now near him; and some say, upwards
of Eighty-thousand rising in the distance to join him if need
were.

LETTERS LI., LII

BATTLE OF WORCESTER

THE Battle of Worcester was fought on the evening of Wednesday 3d September 1651; anniversary of that at Dunbar last
year. It could well have but one issue; defeat for the Scots and
their Cause;—either swift and complete; or else incomplete,
ending in slow sieges, partial revolts, and much new misery and
blood. The swift issue was the one appointed; and complete
enough; severing the neck of the Controversy now at last, as
with one effectual stroke, no need to strike a second time.

The Battle was fought on both sides of the Severn; part of
Cromwell's forces having crossed to the Western bank, by
Upton Bridge, some miles below Worcester, the night before.
About a week ago, Massey understood himself to have ruined
this Bridge at Upton; but Lambert's men 'straddled across by
the parapet,'—a dangerous kind of *saddle* for such riding,
I think!—and hastily repaired it; hastily got hold of Upton
Church, and maintained themselves there; driving Massey
back with a bad wound in the hand. This was on Thursday
night last, the very night of the Lord General's arrival in those
parts; and they have held this post ever since. Fleetwood
crosses here with a good part of Cromwell's Army, on the
evening of Tuesday September 2d; shall, on the morrow, attack
the Scotch posts on the Southwest, about the Suburb of St.
John's, across the River; while Cromwell, in person, on this

side, plies them from the Southeast. St. John's Suburb lies at some distance from Worcester; west, or southwest as we say, on the Herefordshire Road! and connects itself with the City by Severn Bridge. Southeast of the City, again, near the then and present London Road, is 'Fort Royal,' an entrenchment of the Scots: on this side Cromwell is to attempt the Enemy, and second Fleetwood, as occasion may serve. Worcester City itself is on Cromwell's side of the River; stands high, surmounted by its high Cathedral; close on the left or eastern margin of the Severn; surrounded by fruitful fields, and hedges unfit for cavalry-fighting. This is the posture of affairs on the eve of Wednesday 3d September 1651.

But now, for Wednesday itself, we are to remark that between Fleetwood at Upton, and the Enemy's outposts at St. John's on the west side of Severn, there runs still a River Teme; a western tributary of the Severn, into which it falls about a mile below the City. This River Teme Fleetwood hopes to cross, if not by the Bridge at Powick which the Enemy possesses, then by a Bridge of Boats which he is himself to prepare lower down, close by the mouth of Teme. At this point also, or 'within pistol-shot of it,' there is to be a Bridge of Boats laid across the Severn itself, that so both ends of the Army may communicate. Boats, boatmen, carpenters, aquatic and terrestrial artificers and implements, in great abundance, contributed by the neighbouring Towns, lie ready on the River, about Upton, for this service. Does the reader now understand the ground a little?

Fleetwood, at Upton, was astir with the dawn September 3d. But it was towards 'three in the afternoon' before the boatmen were got up; must have been towards five before those Bridges were got built, and Fleetwood set fairly across the Teme to begin business. The King of Scots and his Council of War, 'on the top of the Cathedral,' have been anxiously viewing him all afternoon; have seen him build his Bridges of Boats; see him now in great force got across Teme River, attacking the Scotch on the South, fighting them from hedge to hedge towards the Suburb of St. John's. In great force: for new regiments, horse and foot, now stream across the Severn Bridge of Boats to assist Fleetwood: nay, if the Scots knew it, my Lord General himself is come across, 'did lead the van in person, and was the first that set foot on the Enemy's ground.'—The Scots, obstinately struggling, are gradually beaten there; driven from hedge to hedge. But the King of Scots and his War-Council decide that most part of Cromwell's Army must now be over in that quarter, on the West side of the River, engaged among the hedges ;—decide that they, for their part, will storm out, and offer him battle on their own East side, now while he is weak there. The Council of War comes down from the top of the Cathedral ; their trumpets sound : Cromwell also is soon back, across the Severn Bridge of Boats again ; and the deadliest tug of war begins.

Fort Royal is still known at Worcester, and Sudbury Gate at the southeast end of the City is known, and those other localities here specified ; after much study of which and of the old dead Pamphlets, this Battle will at last become conceivable. Besides Cromwell's Two Letters, there are plentiful details, questionable and unquestionable, in *Bates* and elsewhere. The fighting of the Scots was fierce and desperate. 'My Lord General did 'exceedingly hazard himself, riding up and down in the midst 'of the fire ; riding, himself in person, to the Enemy's foot 'to offer them quarter, whereto they returned no answer but 'shot.' The small Scotch Army, begirdled with overpowering force, and cut off from help or reasonable hope, storms forth in fiery pulses, horse and foot ; charges now on this side of the River, now on that ;—can on no side prevail. Cromwell recoils a little ; but only to rally, and return irresistible. The small Scotch Army is, on every side, driven in again. Its fiery pulsings are but the struggles of death : agonies as of a lion coiled in the folds of a boa !

' As stiff a contest, for four or five hours, as ever I have seen.' But it avails not. Through Sudbury Gate, on Cromwell's side, through St. John's Suburb, and over Severn Bridge on Fleetwood's, the Scots are driven-in again to Worcester Streets ; desperately struggling and recoiling, are driven through Worcester Streets, to the North end of the City,—and terminate there. A distracted mass of ruin : the foot all killed or taken ; the horse all scattered on flight, and their place of refuge very far ! His sacred Majesty escaped, by royal oaks and other miraculous appliances well known to mankind : but Fourteen-thousand other men, sacred too after a sort though not majesties, did not escape. One could weep at such a death for brave men in such a Cause ! But let us now read Cromwell's Letters.

LETTER LI

For the Honourable William Lenthall, Esquire, Speaker of the Parliament of England: These.

Near Worcester, 3d September 1651.
(10 at night).

SIR,

Being so weary, and scarce able to write, yet I thought it my duty to let you know thus much. That upon this day, being the 3d of September (remarkable for a mercy vouchsafed to your Forces on this day twelvemonth in Scotland), we built a Bridge of Boats over Severn, between it and Teme, about half a mile from Worcester; and another over Teme, within pistol-shot of our other Bridge. Lieutenant-General Fleetwood and Major-General Dean marched from Upton on the southwest side of Severn up to Powick, a Town which was a Pass the Enemy kept. We, 'from our side of Severn,' passed over some horse and foot, and were in conjunction with the Lieutenant-General's Forces. We beat the Enemy from hedge to hedge till we beat him into Worcester.

The Enemy then drew all his Forces on the other side the Town, all but what he had lost; and made a very considerable fight with us, for three hours space: but in the end we beat him totally, and pursued him to his Royal Fort, which we took, —and indeed have beaten his whole Army. When we took this Fort, we turned his own guns upon him. The Enemy hath had great loss: and certainly is scattered, and run several ways. We are in pursuit of him, and have laid forces in several places, that we hope will gather him up.

Indeed this hath been a very glorious mercy;—and as stiff a contest, for four or five hours, as ever I have seen. Both your old Forces and those new-raised have behaved themselves with very great courage; and He that made them come out, made them willing to fight for you. The Lord God Almighty frame our hearts to real thankfulness for this, which is alone His doing. I hope I shall within a day or two give you a more perfect account.

In the mean time I hope you will pardon, Sir,
Your most humble servant,
OLIVER CROMWELL

On Saturday the 6th comes a farther Letter from my Lord General: 'the effect whereof speaketh thus:'

LETTER LII

For the Honourable William Lenthall, Esquire, Speaker of the Parliament of England: These.

Worcester, 4th September 1651.

SIR,
I am not able yet to give you an exact account of the great things the Lord hath wrought for this Commonwealth and for His People: and yet I am unwilling to be silent; but, according to my duty, shall represent it to you as it comes to hand.

This Battle was fought with various success for some hours, but still hopeful on your part; and in the end became an absolute victory,—and so full an one as proved a total defeat and ruin of the Enemy's Army; and a possession of the Town, our men entering at the Enemy's heels, and fighting with them in the streets with very great courage. We took all their baggage and artillery. What the slain are, I can give you no account, because we have not taken an exact view; but they are very many:—and must needs be so; because the dispute was long and very near at hand; and often at push of pike, and from one defence to another. There are about Six or Seven thousand prisoners taken here; and many Officers and Noblemen of very great quality: Duke Hamilton, the Earl of Rothes, and divers other Noblemen,—I hear, the Earl of Lauderdale; many Officers of great quality; and some that will be fit subjects for your justice.

We have sent very considerable parties after the flying Enemy; I hear they have taken considerable numbers of prisoners, and are very close in the pursuit. Indeed, I hear the Country riseth upon them everywhere; and I believe the forces that lay, through Providence, at Bewdley, and in Shropshire and Staffordshire, and those with Colonel Lilburn, were in a condition, as if this had been foreseen, to intercept what should return.

A more particular account than this will be prepared for you as we are able. I hear they had not many more than a Thousand horse in their body that fled: and I believe you have near Four-thousand forces following, and interposing between them and home;—what fish they will catch, Time will declare. Their

Army was about Sixteen-thousand strong; and fought ours on the Worcester side of Severn almost with their whole, whilst we had engaged about half our Army on the other side but with parties of theirs. Indeed it was a stiff business; yet I do not think we have lost Two-hundred men. Your new-raised forces did perform singular good service; for which they deserve a very high estimation and acknowledgment; as also for their willingness thereunto,—forasmuch as the same hath added so much to the reputation of your affairs. They are all despatched home again; which I hope will be much for the ease and satisfaction of the Country; which is a great fruit of these successes.

The dimensions of this mercy are above my thoughts. It is, for aught I know, a crowning mercy. Surely, if it be not, such a one we shall have, if this provoke those that are concerned in it to thankfulness; and the Parliament to do the will of Him who hath done His will for it, and for the Nation;—whose good pleasure it is to establish the Nation and the Change of the Government, by making the People so willing to the defence thereof, and so signally blessing the endeavours of your servants in this late great work. I am bold humbly to beg, That all thoughts may tend to the promoting of His honour who hath wrought so great salvation; and that the fatness of these continued mercies may not occasion pride and wantonness, as formerly the like hath done to a chosen Nation;[1] but that the fear of the Lord, even for His mercies, may keep an Authority and a People so prospered, and blessed, and witnessed unto, humble and faithful; and that justice and righteousness, mercy and truth may flow from you, as a thankful return to our gracious God. This shall be the prayer of,

Sir,
Your most humble and obedient servant,
OLIVER CROMWELL.

Your Officers behaved themselves with much honour in this service; and the Person[2] who is the Bearer hereof was equal, in the performance of his duty, to most that served you that day.

[1] 'But Jeshurun waxed fat and kicked:—(and thou art waxen fat, thou art grown thick, thou art covered with fatness:) then he forsook God which made him, and lightly esteemed the rock of his salvation' (*Deuteronomy*, xxxii. 15).

[2] Major Cobbet, 'who makes a relation,' and gets 100*l.*

CAPTURE OF DUNDEE

This is the last of my Lord General's Battles and Victories, technically so called. Of course his Life, to the very end of it, continues, as from the beginning it had always been, a *battle*, and a dangerous and strenuous one, with due modicum of victory assigned now and then; but it will be with other than the steel weapons henceforth. He here sheaths his warsword; with that, it is not his Order from the Great Captain that he fight any more.

The distracted Scheme of the Scotch Governors to accomplish their Covenant by this Charles-Stuart method has here ended. By and by they shall have their Charles Stuart back, as a general Nell-Gwynn Defender of the Faith to us all;—and shall see how they will like him! But as Covenanted King he is off upon his travels, and will never return more. Worcester Battle has cut the heart of that affair in two: and Monk, an assiduous Lieutenant to the Lord General in his Scotch affairs, is busy suppressing the details.

On Monday the 1st of September, two days before the Battle of Worcester, Lieutenant-General Monk had stormed *Dundee*, the last stronghold of Scotland; where much wealth, as in a place of safety, had been laid up. Governor Lumsden would not yield on summons: Lieutenant-General Monk stormed him; the Town took fire in the business; there was once more a grim scene, of flame and blood, and rage and despair, transacted in this Earth; and taciturn General Monk, his choler all up, was become surly as the Russian bear; nothing but negatory growls to be got out of him: nay, to one clerical dignitary of the place he not only gave his "No!" but audibly threatened a slap with the fist to back it,—'ordered him, 'Not to speak one word, or he would scobe his mouth for 'him!'

Scotland therefore, like Ireland, has fallen to Cromwell to be administered. 'Scotland,' thus testifies a competent eye-witness, 'was kept in great order. Some Castles in the Highlands had 'Garrisons put into them, which were so careful of their 'discipline, and so exact to their rules,' the wild Highlanders were wonderfully tamed thereby. Cromwell built three Citadels, Leith, Ayr and Inverness, besides many little Forts, over Scotland. Seven or Eight thousand men, well paid, and paying well; of the strictest habits, military, spiritual and moral: these it was everywhere a kind of Practical Sermon to take

note of! 'There was good justice done; and vice was sup-
'pressed and punished. So that we always reckon those Eight
'years of Usurpation a time of great peace and prosperity,'—
though we needed to be twice beaten, and to have our foolish
Governors flung into the Tower, before we would accept the
same. We, and mankind generally, are an extremely wise set
of creatures.

PART VII

THE LITTLE PARLIAMENT

1651-1653

THE LITTLE PARLIAMENT

BETWEEN Worcester Battle on the 3d of September 1651, and the Dismissal of the Long Parliament on the 20th of April 1653, are Nineteen very important months in the History of Oliver, which, in all our Books and Historical rubbish-records, lie as nearly as possible dark and vacant for us.

Concerning the Residue, Fag-end, or 'Rump' as it had now got nicknamed, of the Long Parliament, into whose hands the Government of England had been put, we have hitherto, ever since the King's Death-Warrant, said almost nothing : and in fact there was not much to be said. 'Statesmen of the Commonwealth' so-called : there wanted not among them men of real mark ; brave men, of much talent, of true resolution, and nobleness of aim : but though their title was chief in this Commonwealth, all men may see their real function in it had been subaltern all along. Not in St. Stephen's and its votings and debatings, but in the battle-field, in Oliver Cromwell's fightings, has the destiny of this Commonwealth decided itself. One unsuccessful Battle, at Preston or at any time since, had probably wrecked it ;—one stray bullet hitting the life of a certain man had soon ended this Commonwealth. Parliament, Council of State, they sat like dilgent Committees of Ways and Means, in a very wise and provident manner : but the soul of the Commonwealth was at Dunbar, at Worcester, at Tredah :

Destiny, there questioned, "Life or Death for this Commonwealth?" has answered, "Life yet for a time!"—That is a fact which the candid imagination will have to keep steadily in view.

And now if we practically ask ourselves, What is to become of this small junto of men, somewhat above a Hundred in all, hardly above Half-a-hundred the active part of them, who now sit in the chair of authority? the shaping-out of any answer will give rise to considerations. These men have been raised thither by miraculous interpositions of Providence; they may be said to sit there only by a continuance of the like. They cannot sit there forever. They are not Kings by birth, these men; nor in any of them have I discovered qualities as of a very indisputable King by attainment. Of dull Bulstrode, with his lumbering law-pedantries, and stagnant official self-satisfactions, I do not speak; nor of dusky tough St. John, whose abstruse fanaticisms, crabbed logics, and dark ambitions, issue all, as was very natural, in 'decided avarice' at last :—not of these. Harry Marten is a tight little fellow, though of somewhat loose life: his witty words pierce yet, as light arrows, through the thick oblivious torpor of the generations; testifying to us very clearly, Here was a right hard-headed, stout-hearted little man, full of sharp fire and cheerful light; sworn foe of Cant in all its figures; an indomitable little Roman Pagan if no better: but Harry is not quite one's King either; it would have been difficult to be altogether loyal to Harry! Doubtful too, I think, whether without great effort you could have worshipped even the Younger Vane. A man of endless virtues, says Dryasdust, who is much taken with him, and of endless intellect ;—but you must not very specially ask, How or Where; Vane was the Friend of Milton: that is almost the only answer that can now be given. A man, one rather finds, of light fibre, this Sir Harry Vane. Grant all manner of purity and elevation; subtle high discourse; much intellectual and practical dexterity; there is an amiable, devoutly zealous, very pretty man ;—but not a royal man; alas, no; On the whole rather a thin man. Whom it is even important to keep strictly subaltern. Whose tendency towards the Abstract, or Temporary-Theoretic, is irresistible; whose hold of the Concrete, in which lies always the Perennial, is by no means that of a giant, or born Practical King ;—whose 'astonishing subtlety of intellect' conducts him not to new clearness, but to ever new abstruseness, wheel within wheel, depth under depth: marvellous temporary empire of the air,—

wholly vanished now, and without meaning to any mortal.
My erudite friend, the astonishing intellect that occupies itself
in splitting hairs, and not in twisting some kind of cordage
and effectual draught-tackle to take the road with, is not to me
the most astonishing of intellects ! And if, as is probable, it
get into narrow fanaticisms ; become irrecognisant of the Perennial because not dressed in the fashionable Temporary ; become
self-secluded, atrabiliar, and perhaps shrill-voiced and spasmodic,
—what can you do but get away from it, with a prayer, " The
Lord deliver me from thee ! " I cannot do with *thee*. I want
twisted cordage, steady pulling, and a peaceable bass tone of
voice : not split hairs, hysterical spasmodics, and treble ! Thou
amiable, subtle, elevated individual, the Lord deliver me from
thee !

These men cannot continue Kings forever ; nor in fact did
they in the least design such a thing, only they find a terrible
difficulty in getting abdicated. Difficulty very conceivable to us.
Some weeks after Pride's Purge, which may be called the constituting of this remnant of members into a Parliament and
Authority, there had been presented to it, by Fairfax and the
Army, what we should now call a Bentham-Sieyes Constitution,
what was then called an 'Agreement of the People,'—which
might well be imperative on honourable members sitting there ;
whereby it was stipulated for one thing, That this present
Parliament should dissolve itself, and give place to another
'equal Representative of the People,'—in some three months
hence ; on the 30th of April, namely. The last day of April,
1649 : this Parliament was then to have its work finished,
and go its ways, giving place to another. Such was our
hope.

They did accordingly pass a vote to that effect ; fully
intending to fulfil the same : but, alas, it was found impossible.
How summon a new Parliament, while the Commonwealth is
still fighting for its existence ? All we can do is to resolve
ourselves into Grand Committee, and consider about it. After
much consideration, all we can decide is, That we shall go
weekly into Grand Committee, and consider farther. Duly
every Wednesday we consider, for the space of eleven months
and odd ; find, more and more, that it is a thing of some
considerableness ! In brief, when my Lord General returns to
us from Worcester, on the 16th of September 1651, no advance
whatever towards a dissolution of ourselves has yet been made.
The Wednesday Grand Committees had become a thing like

the meeting of Roman augurs, difficult to go through with complete gravity ; and so, after the eleventh month, have silently fallen into desuetude We sit here very immovable. We are scornfully called the Rump of a Parliament by certain people, but we have an invincible Oliver to fight for us : we can afford to wait here, and consider to all lengths ; and by one name we shall smell as sweet as by another.

I have only to add at present, that on the morrow of my Lord General's reappearance in Parliament, this sleeping question was resuscitated ; new activity infused into it ; some show of progress made ; nay, at the end of three months, after much labour and struggle, it was got decided, by a neck-and-neck division, That the present *is* a fit time for fixing a limit beyond which this Parliament shall not sit. Fix a limit therefore ; give us the *non-plus-ultra* of you. Next Parliament-day we do fix a limit, Three years hence, 3d November 1654 ; three years of rope still left us : a somewhat wide limit ; which, under conceivable contingencies, may perhaps be tightened a little. My honourable friends, you ought really to get on with despatch of this business ; and know of a surety that not being, any of you, Kings by birth, nor very indubitably by attainment, you will actually have to go, and even in case of extremity to be shoved and sent !

July 9th, 1652. A great external fact which, no doubt, has its effect on all internal movements, is the War with the Dutch. The Dutch, ever since our Death-Warrant to Charles First, have looked askance at this New Commonwealth, which wished to stand well with them ; and have accumulated offence on offence against it. Ambassador Dorislaus was assassinated in their country ; Charles Second was entertained there ; evasive slow answers were given to tough St. John, who went over as new Ambassador : to which St. John responding with great directness, in a proud, brief and very emphatic manner, took his leave, and came home again ; and passed the celebrated Navigation Act,[1] forbidding that any goods should be imported into England except either in English ships or in ships of the country where the goods were produced. Thereby terribly maiming the 'Carrying Trade of the Dutch ;' and indeed, as the issue proved, depressing the Dutch Maritime Interest not a little,

[1] Introduced, 5th August 1651 ; passed, 9th October 1651 : given in Scobell, ii. 176.

and proportionally elevating that of England. Embassies in consequence, from their irritated High Mightinesses; sea-fightings in consequence; and much negotiating, apologising, and bickering mounting ever higher;—which at length, at the date above given, issues in declared War. Dutch War: cannonadings and fierce sea-fights in the narrow seas; land-soldiers drafted to fight on shipboard; and land-officers, Blake, Dean, Monk, who became very famous sea-officers; Blake a thrice-famous one;—poor Dean lost his life in this business. They doggedly beat the Dutch, and again beat them: their best Van Tromps and De Ruyters could not stand these terrible Puritan Sailors and Gunners. The Dutch gradually grew tame.

Wednesday, 20th April 1653. My Lord General is in his reception-room this morning, 'in plain black clothes and gray worsted stockings;' he, with many Officers: but few Members have yet come, though punctual Bulstrode and certain others are there. Some waiting there is; some impatience that the Members would come. The Members do not come: instead of Members, comes a notice that they are busy getting on with their Bill in the House, hurrying it double-quick through all the stages. Possible? New message that it will be Law in a little while, if no interposition take place! Bulstrode hastens off to the House: my Lord General, at first incredulous, does now also hasten off,—nay orders that a Company of Musketeers of his own regiment attend him. Hastens off, with a very high expression of countenance, I think;—saying or feeling: Who would have believed it of them? "It is not honest; yea, it is contrary to common honesty!"—My Lord General, the big hour is come!

Young Colonel Sidney, the celebrated Algernon, sat in the House this morning; a House of some Fifty-three. Algernon has left distinct note of the affair; less distinct we have from Bulstrode, who was also there, who seems in some points to be even wilfully wrong. Solid Ludlow was far off in Ireland, but gathered many details in after-years; and faithfully wrote them down, in the unappeasable indignation of his heart. Combining these three originals, we have, after various perusals and collations and considerations, obtained the following authentic, moderately conceivable account.

'The Parliament sitting as usual, and being in debate upon
'the Bill with the amendments, which it was thought would have
'been passed that day, the Lord General Cromwell came into

'the House, clad in plain black clothes and gray worsted
'stockings, and sat down as he used to do, in an ordinary place.'
For some time he listens to this interesting debate on the Bill;
beckoning once to Harrison, who came over to him, and
answered dubitatingly. Whereupon the Lord General sat still,
for about a quarter of an hour longer. But now the question
being to be put, That this Bill do now pass, he beckons again
to Harrison, says, "'This is the time; I must do it!'"—and so
'rose up, put off his hat, and spake. At the first, and for a good
'while, he spake to the commendation of the Parliament for
'their pains and care of the public good; but afterwards he
'changed his style, told them of their injustice, delays of justice,
'self-interest, and other faults,'—rising higher and higher into
a very aggravated style indeed. An honourable Member, Sir
Peter Wentworth by name, not known to my readers, and by
me better known than trusted, rises to order, as we phrase it;
says, "It is a strange language this; unusual within the walls of
Parliament this! And from a trusted servant too; and one
whom we have so highly honoured; and one,"—"'Come,
come!'" exclaims my Lord General in a very high key, "we
have had enough of this,"—and in fact my Lord General now
blazing all up into clear conflagration, exclaims, "'I will put an
end to your prating,'" and steps forth into the floor of the
House, and 'clapping on his hat,' and occasionally 'stamping
the floor with his feet,' begins a discourse which no man can
report! He says—Heavens! he is heard saying: "'It is not
"fit that you should sit here any longer!' You have sat too
"long here for any good you have been doing lately. 'You shall
"now give place to better men!—Call them in!'" adds he briefly,
to Harrison, in word of command: and 'some twenty or thirty'
grim musketeers enter, with bullets in their snaphances; grimly
prompt for orders; and stand in some attitude of Carry-arms
there. Veteran men: men of might and men of war, their
faces are as the faces of lions, and their feet are swift as the roes
upon the mountains;—not beautiful to honourable gentlemen at
this moment!

"You call yourselves a Parliament," continues my Lord General
in clear blaze of conflagration: "'You are no Parliament;
I say you are no Parliament! Some of you are drunkards,'"
and his eye flashes on poor Mr. Chaloner, an official man of
some value, addicted to the bottle; "'some of you are———'"
and he glares into Harry Marten, and the poor Sir Peter who
rose to order, lewd livers both; "living in open contempt of

"God's Commandments. Following your own greedy appetites,
"and the Devil's Commandments. 'Corrupt unjust persons,'"
and here I think he glanced 'at Sir Bulstrode Whitlocke, one
'of the Commissioners of the Great Seal, giving him and others
'very sharp language, though he named them not:' "'Corrupt
"unjust persons; scandalous to the profession of the Gospel:'
"how can you be a Parliament for God's People? Depart,
"I say; and let us have done with you. In the name of God,—
"go!"

The House is of course all on its feet,—uncertain almost
whether not on its head: such a scene as was never seen before
in any House of Commons. History reports with a shudder that
my Lord General, lifting the sacred Mace itself, said, "'What
shall we do with this bauble? Take it away!'"—and gave it
to a musketeer. And now,—"Fetch him down!" says he to
Harrison, flashing on the Speaker. Speaker Lenthall, more an
ancient Roman than anything else, declares, He will not come
till forced. "Sir," said Harrison, "I will lend you a hand;" on
which Speaker Lenthall came down, and gloomily vanished.
They all vanished; flooding gloomily clamorously out, to their
ulterior businesses, and respective places of abode: the Long
Parliament is dissolved! "'It's you that have forced me to
"this,'" exclaims my Lord General: "'I have sought the Lord
"night and day, that He would rather slay me than put me upon
"the doing of this work.'" 'At their going out, some say the
'Lord General said to young Sir Harry Vane, calling him by
'his name, That *he* might have prevented this; but that he
'was a juggler, and had not common honesty.' "'O Sir Harry
"Vane,' thou with thy subtle casuistries and abstruse hair-
"splittings, thou art other than a good one, I think! 'The
"Lord deliver me from thee, Sir Harry Vane!'" 'All being
'gone out, the door of the House was locked, and the Key
'with the Mace, as I heard, was carried away by Colonel
'Otley;'—and it is all over, and the unspeakable catastrophe
has come, and remains.

Such was the destructive wrath of my Lord General Cromwell
against the Nominal Rump Parliament of England. Wrath
which innumerable mortals since have accounted extremely
diabolic; which some now begin to account partly divine.
Divine or diabolic, it is an indisputable fact; left for the
commentaries of men. The Rump Parliament has gone its
way;—and truly, except it be in their own, I know not in what

eyes are tears at their departure. They went very softly, softly as a Dream, say all witnesses. "We did not hear a dog bark at their going!" asserts my Lord General elsewhere.

It is said, my Lord General did not, on his entrance into the House, contemplate quite as a certainty this strong measure; but it came upon him like an irresistible impulse, or inspiration, as he heard their Parliamentary eloquence proceed. "Perceiving "the spirit of God so strong upon me, I would no longer consult "flesh and blood." He has done it, at all events; and is responsible for the results it may have. A responsibility which he, as well as most of us, knows to be awful: but he fancies it was in answer to the English Nation, and to the Maker of the English Nation and of him; and he will do the best he may with it.

The *Declaration of the Lord General and his Council of Officers*, which came out on the Friday following the grand Catastrophe, does not seem to be of Oliver's composition: it is a Narrative of calm pious tone, of considerable length; promises, as a second Declaration still more explicitly does, a Real Assembly of the Puritan Notables;—and on the whole can be imagined by the reader; nay we shall hear the entire substance of it from Oliver's own mouth, before long. These Declarations and other details we omit. Conceive that all manner of Authorities, with or without some little preambling, agree to go on as heretofore; that adherences arrive from Land-Generals and Sea-Generals by return of post; that the old Council of State having vanished with its Mother, a new Interim Council of State, with 'Oliver Cromwell Captain General' at the head of it, answers equally well; in a word, that all people are looking eagerly forward to those same 'Known Persons, Men fearing God, and of approved Integrity,' who are now to be got together from all quarters of England, to say what *shall* be done with this Commonwealth,—whom there is now no Fag-end of a corrupt Parliament to prevent just men from choosing with their best ability. Conceive all this; and read the following

SUMMONS
To ——— ———

FORASMUCH as, upon the dissolution of the late Parliament, it became necessary, that the peace, safety and good government of this Commonwealth should be provided for: And in order

thereunto, divers Persons fearing God, and of approved Fidelity
and Honesty, are, by myself with the advice of my Council
of Officers, nominated ; to whom the great charge and trust
of so weighty affairs is to be committed : And having good
assurance of your love to, and courage for, God and the interest of
His Cause, and 'that' of the good People of this Commonwealth:

I, Oliver Cromwell, Captain General and Commander-in-
Chief of all the Armies and Forces raised and to be raised
within this Commonwealth, do hereby summon and require
You, —— ——, being one of the Persons nominated,—Person-
ally to be and appear at the Council-Chamber, commonly
known or called by the name of the Council-Chamber at
Whitehall, within the City of Westminster, upon the Fourth
day of July next ensuing the date hereof ; Then and there
to take upon you the said Trust ; unto which you are hereby
called, and appointed to serve as a Member for the County
of——. And hereof you are not to fail.

Given under my hand and seal the 6th day of June 1653.

OLIVER CROMWELL.

SPEECH

SUCH is the Assembly called the Little Parliament, and wittily
Barebones's Parliament; which meets on the 4th of July. Their
witty name survives ; but their history is gone all dark ; and no
man, for the present, has in his head or in his heart the faintest
intimation of what they did, or what they aimed to do. They
are very dark to us ; and will never be illuminated much !
Here is one glance of them face to face ; here in this Speech of
Oliver's,—if we can read it, and listen along with them to it.
There is this one glance ; and for six generations, we may say,
in the English mind there has not been another.

Listening from a distance of two Centuries, across the Death-
chasms, and howling kingdoms of Decay, it is not easy to catch
everything ! But let us faithfully do the best we can.

Read this first, from the old Newspapers ; and then the Speech
tself, which a laborious Editor has, with all industry, copied and
corrected from Two Contemporaneous Reports by different
hands, and various editions of these. Note, however : The
Italic sentences in brackets, most part of which, and yet perhaps
not enough of which I have suppressed, are evidently by an
altogether modern hand !

'*July 4th*, 1653. This being the day appointed by the
'Letters of Summons from his Excellency the Lord General, for
'the meeting of the Persons called to the Supreme Authority,
'there came about a Hundred-and-twenty of them to the
'Council Chamber in Whitehall. After each person had given-
'in a Ticket of his Name, they all entered the room, and sat
'down in chairs appointed for them, round about the table.
'Then his Excellency the Lord General, standing by the
'window opposite to the middle of the table, and as many of the
'Officers of the Army as the room could well contain, some on
'his right hand and others on his left, and about him,—made
'the following Speech to the Assembly:'

GENTLEMEN,
I suppose the Summons that hath been instrumental to bring you hither gives you well to understand the occasion of your being here. Howbeit, I have something farther to impart to you, which is an Instrument drawn up by the consent and advice of the principal Officers of the Army; which is a little (as we conceive) more significant than the Letter of the Summons We have that here to tender you; and somewhat likewise to say farther for our own exoneration;[1] which we hope may be somewhat farther for your satisfaction. And withal seeing you sit here somewhat uneasily by reason of the scantness of the room, and heat of the weather, I shall contract myself with respect thereunto.

We have not thought it amiss a little to remind you of that Series of Providences wherein the Lord hath appeared, dispensing wonderful things to these Nations from the beginning of our Troubles to this very day.

If I should look much backward, we might remind you of the state of affairs as they were before the Short, that is the last, Parliament,—in what posture the things of this Nation then stood: but they do so well, I presume, occur to all your memories and knowledge, that I shall not need to look so far backward. Nor yet to those hostile occasions which arose between the King that was and the Parliament[2] that then followed. And indeed should I begin much later, the things that would fall very necessarily before you, would rather be for a History than for a verbal Discourse at this present.

[1] 'exoneration' does not here mean 'excuse' or 'shifting-away of blame, but mere laying down of office with due form.'
[2] The Long Parliament.

HIS FIRST SPEECH TO PARLIAMENT

But thus far we may look back. You very well know, it pleased God, much about the midst of this War, to winnow (if I may so say) the Forces of this nation;[1] and to put them into the hands of other men of other principles than those that did engage at the first. By what ways and means that was brought about, would ask more time than is allotted me to mind you of it. Indeed there are Stories that do recite those Transactions, and give you narratives of matters of fact: but those things wherein the life and power of them lay; those strange windings and turnings of Providence; those very great appearances of God, in crossing and thwarting the purposes of men, that He might raise up a poor and contemptible company of men,[2] neither versed in military affairs, nor having much natural propensity to them, 'into wonderful success—'! Simply by their owning a Principle of Godliness and Religion; which so soon as *it* came to be owned, and the state of affairs put *upon the foot of that account*,[3] how God blessed them, furthering all undertakings, yet using the most improbable and the most contemptible and despicable means (for that we shall ever own): is very well known to you.

What the several Successes and Issues have been, is not fit to mention at this time neither;—though I confess I thought to have enlarged myself upon that subject; forasmuch as Considering the works of God, and the operations of His hands, is a principal part of our duty; and a great encouragement to the strengthening of our hands and of our faith, for that which is behind. And among other ends which those marvellous Dispensations have been given us for, that's a principal end, which ought to be minded by us.

'Certainly' in this revolution of affairs, as the issue of those Successes which God was pleased to give to the Army, and 'to' the Authority that then stood, there were very great things brought about;— besides those dints that came upon the Nations and places where the War itself was, very great things in Civil matters too. 'As first,' the bringing of Offenders to justice,— and the Greatest of them. Bringing of the State of this Government to the name (at least) of a Commonwealth. Searching and sifting of all persons and places. The King removed, and brought to justice; and many great ones with him. The house

---

[1] Self-denying Ordinance; beginning of 1645.
[2] Fairfax's Army.
[3] upon that footing.

of Peers laid aside. The House of Commons itself, the representative of the People of England, winnowed, sifted, and brought to a handful; as you very well remember.

I shall now begin a little to remind you of the passages that have been transacted since Worcester. Coming from whence, with the rest of my fellow Officers and Soldiers, we did expect, and had some reasonable confidence our expectations would not be frustrated, That, having such an history to look back unto, such a God, so eminently visible, even our enemies confessing that "God Himself was certainly engaged against them, else "they should never have been disappointed in *every* engage-"ment,"—and that may be used by the way, That if we had but miscarried in the least, all our former mercies were in danger to be lost :—I say, coming up then, we had some confidence That the mercies God had shown, and the expectations which were upon our hearts, and upon the hearts of all good men, would have prompted those who were in Authority to do those good things which might, by honest men, have been judged fit for such a God, and worthy of such mercies; and indeed been a discharge of duty from those to whom all these mercies had been shown, for the true interest of this Nation !—If I should now labour to be particular in enumerating how businesses have been transacted from that time to the Dissolution of the late Parliament, indeed I should be upon a theme which would be troublesome to myself. For I think I may say for myself and my fellow Officers, That we have rather desired and studied Healing and Looking-forward than to rake into sores and to look backward,—to give things forth in those colours that would not be very pleasing to any good eye to look upon. Only this we shall say for our own vindication, as pointing out the ground for that unavoidable necessity, nay even that duty that was incumbent upon us, to make this last great Change—I think it will not be amiss to offer a word or two to that. As I said before, we are loath to rake into businesses, were there not a necessity so o do.

Indeed we may say that, ever since the coming-up of myself and those Gentlemen who have been engaged in the military part, it hath been full in our hearts and thoughts, To desire and use all the fair and lawful means we could to have the Nation reap the fruit of all the blood and treasure that had been spent in this Cause : and we have had many desires, and thirstings in our spirits, to find out ways and means wherein we might be anywise instrumental to help it forward. We were very tender, for a long time, so much as to petition. For some of the Officers being Members ; and others having very good acquaintance with, and some relations to, divers Members of Parliament,—we did, from time to time, solicit such ; thinking if there had been nobody to prompt them, nor call upon them, these things might have been attended to, from ingenuity[1] and integrity in those that had it in their power to answer such expectations.

Truly when we saw nothing would be done, we did, as we thought according to our duty, a little, to remind them by a Petition ; which I suppose you have seen : it was delivered, as I remember, in August last. What effect that had, is likewise very well known. The truth is, we had no return at all for our satisfaction,—a few words given us ; the things presented by us, or the most of them, we were told, "were under consideration :" and those not presented by us had very little or no consideration at all. Finding the People dissatisfied in every corner of the Nation, and 'all men' laying at our doors the non-performance of these things, which had been promised, and were of duty to be performed,—truly we did then think ourselves concerned, if we would (as becomes honest men) keep up the reputation of honest men in the world. And therefore we, divers times, endeavoured to obtain meetings with divers Members of Parliament ;—and we did not begin those till about October last. And in these meetings we did, with all faithfulness and sincerity, beseech them that they would be mindful of their duty to God and men, in the discharge of the trust reposed in them. I believe (as there are many gentlemen here know), we had at least ten or twelve meetings ; most humbly begging and beseeching of them, That by their own means they would bring forth those good things which had been promised and expected ; that so it might appear they did not do them by any suggestion from the Army, but from their own ingenuity : so tender were we to preserve them in the reputation of the People. Having had very many of those meetings ; and declaring plainly that the issue would be the displeasure and judgment of God, the dissatisfaction of the People, the putting of 'all' things into a confusion : yet how little we prevailed, we very well know, and we believe it's not unknown to you.

At last, when indeed we saw that things would not be laid to heart, we had a very serious consideration among ourselves what

[1] ingenuousness.

other ways to have recourse unto; and when we grew to more
closer considerations, then they 'the Parliament men' began to
take the Act for a Representative[1] to heart, and seemed exceeding
willing to put it on. And had it been done with integrity, there
could nothing have happened more welcome to our judgments
than that. But plainly the intention was, Not to give the
People a right of choice; it would have been but a seeming
right: that 'semblance' of giving them a choice was only to
recruit the House, the better to perpetuate *themselves*. And
truly, having been, divers of us, spoken unto to give way here-
unto, to which we made perpetual aversions, indeed abominating
the thoughts of it,—we declared our judgments against it, and
our dissatisfaction with it. And yet they that would not hear
of a Representative formerly, when it lay three years before
them, without proceeding one line, or making any considerable
progress,—I say, those that would not hear of this Bill formerly,
did now, when they saw us falling into more closer considerations,
make, instead of protracting their Bill, as much preposterous haste
with it on the other side, and run into that 'opposite' extremity.

Finding that this spirit was not according to God; and that
the whole weight of this Cause,—which must needs be very dear
unto us who had so often adventured our lives for it, and we believe it was so to you,—did hang upon the business now in hand;
and seeing plainly that there was not here any consideration to
assert this Cause, or provide security for *it*, but only to cross the
troublesome people of the Army, who by this time were high
enough in their displeasures: Truly, I say, when we saw all this,
having power in our hands, 'we could not resolve' to let such
monstrous proceedings go on, and so to throw away all our
liberties into the hands of those whom we had fought against
[*Presbyterian-Royalists; at Preston and elsewhere,—"fought
against," yea and beaten to ruin, your Excellency might add*[1]]; we
came, first, to this conclusion among ourselves, That if we had
been *fought* out of our liberties and rights, Necessity would have
taught us patience; but that to deliver them 'sluggishly' up
would render us the basest persons in the world, and worthy to
be accounted haters of God and of His People. When it pleased
God to lay this close to our hearts; and indeed to show us that
the interest of His People was grown cheap, 'that *it* was' not at
all laid to heart, but that if things came to real competition, His
Cause, even among themselves, would also in every point go to

[1] For a New Parliament and Method of Election.

the ground : indeed this did add more considerations to us, That there was a duty incumbent upon us, 'even upon us.' And,—I speak here, in the presence of some that were at the closure of our consultations, and as before the Lord,—the thinking of an act of violence was to us worse than any battle that ever we were in, or that could be, to the utmost hazard of our lives [*Hear him!*] : so willing were we, even very tender and desirous if possible that these men might quit their places with honour.

It remains now for me to acquaint you 'a little' farther with what relates to your taking upon you this great Business. 'But indeed' that is contained in the Paper[1] here in my hand, which will be offered presently to you to read. But having done that we have done [*Dissolving of the Parliament; which cannot be repented of, and need not be boasted of!*] upon such ground of necessity as we have 'now' declared, which was not a feigned necessity but a real,—'it did behove us,' to the end we might manifest to the world the singleness of our hearts and our integrity who did these things, Not to grasp at the power ourselves or keep it in military hands, no not for a day ; but, as far as God enabled us with strength and ability, to put it into the hands of Proper Persons that might be called from the several parts of the Nation. This necessity ; and I hope we may say for ourselves, this integrity of concluding to divest the Sword of all power in the Civil Administration,—hath been that that hath moved us to put You to this trouble 'of coming hither :' and having done that, truly we think we cannot, with the discharge of our own consciences, but offer somewhat to you on the devolving of the burden on your shoulders. It hath been the practice of others who have, voluntarily and out of a sense of duty, divested themselves, and devolved the Government into new hands; I say, it hath been the practice of those that have done so ; it hath been practised, and is very consonant to reason, To lay 'down,' together with their Authority, some charge 'how to employ it'[2] (as we hope we have done), and to press the duty ,'of employing it well' : concerning which we have a word or two to offer you.

[1] An Indenture or Instrument of Government.
[2] He seems embarrassed lest he be thought to have some authority over this new Little Parliament, and to treat them as if he were their King The dissolving of the old Parliament has also its embarrassment, though not so prominent here ; and both together make an intricate paragraph.

Truly God hath called you to this Work by, I think, as wonderful providences as ever passed upon the sons of men in so short a time. And truly I think, taking the argument of necessity, for the Government must not *fall*; taking the appearance of the hand of God in this thing,—'I think' you would have been loath it should have been resigned into the hands of wicked men and enemies! I am sure, God would not have it so. It's come, therefore, to you by the way of necessity; by the way of the wise Providence of God,—through weak hands. And therefore, I think, coming through our hands, though such as we are, it may not be ill taken if we do offer somewhat (as I said before) as to the discharge of the Trust which is now incumbent upon you. [*Certainly not!*] And although I seem to speak of that which may have the face and interpretation of a Charge, it's a very humble one : and if he that means to be a Servant to you, who hath now called you to the exercise of the Supreme Authority, discharge what he conceives to be a duty to you, we hope you will take it in good part.

I am sorry I have troubled you, in such a place of heat as this is, so long. All I have to say, in my own name, and that of my fellow Officers who have joined with me in this work, is : That we shall commend you to the grace of God, to the guidance of His Spirit : 'That' having thus far served you, or rather our Lord Jesus Christ 'in regard to you,' we shall be ready in our stations, according as the Providence of God shall lead us, to be subservient to the 'farther' work of God, and to that Authority which we shall reckon God hath set over us. And though we have no formal thing to present you with, to which the hands, or visible expressions, of the Officers and Soldiers of the three Nations of England, Scotland and Ireland, 'are set'; yet we may say of them, and we may say also with confidence for our brethren at Sea,—with whom neither in Scotland, Ireland nor at Sea, hath there been any artifice used to persuade their consents to this work,—that nevertheless their consents have flowed in to us from all parts, beyond our expectations : and we may with all confidence say, that as we have their approbation and full consent to the other work, so you have their hearts and affections unto this.[1] And not only theirs : we have very many Papers

---

[1] 'other work' delicately means *dissolving the old Parliament*; 'this' is *assembling of you*, 'this very thing.'

from the Churches of Christ throughout the Nation ; wonderfully both approving what hath been done in removing of obstacles, and approving what we have done in this very thing. And having said this, we shall trouble you no more. But if you will be pleased that this Instrument be read to you, which I have signed by the advice of the Council of Officers,—we shall then leave you to your own thoughts and the guidance of God ; to dispose of yourselves for a farther meeting, as you shall see cause.

I have only this to add. The affairs of the Nation lying on our hands to be taken care of; and we knowing that both the Affairs at Sea, the Armies in Ireland and Scotland, and the providing of things for the preventing of inconveniences, and the answering of emergencies, did require that there should be no Interruption, but that care ought to be taken for these things ; and foreseeing likewise that before you could digest yourselves into such a method, both for place, time and other circumstances, as you shall please to proceed in, some time would be required, —which the Commonwealth could not bear in respect to the managing of things : I have, within a week 'past,' set up a Council of State, to whom the managing of affairs is committed. Who, I may say, very voluntarily and freely, before they see how the issue of things will be, have engaged themselves in business ; eight or nine of them being Members of the House that late was.—I say I did exercise that power which, I thought, was devolved upon me at that time ; to the end affairs might not have any interval 'or interruption.' And now when you are met, it will ask some time for the settling of your affairs and your way. And, 'on the other hand,' a day cannot be lost, 'or left vacant,' but they must be in continual Council till you take farther order. So that the whole matter of their consideration also which regards them, is at your disposal, as you shall see cause. And therefore I thought it my duty to acquaint you with thus much, to prevent distractions in your way : That things have been thus ordered ; that your affairs will 'not stop, but' go on, 'in the meanwhile,'—till you see cause to alter this Council ; they having no authority or continuance of sitting, except simply until you take farther order.

Concerning this Puritan Convention of the Notables, which in English History is called the *Little Parliament*, and derisively *Barebones's Parliament*, we have not much more to say. They are, if by no means the remarkablest Assembly, yet the Assembly for the remarkablest purpose who have ever met in the Modern World. The business is, No less than introducing of the Christian Religion into real practice in the Social Affairs of this Nation. Christian Religion, Scriptures of the Old and New Testament: such, for many hundred years, has been the universal solemnly recognised Theory of all men's Affairs; Theory sent down out of Heaven itself: but the question is now that of reducing it to Practice in said Affairs;—a most noble, surely, and most necessary attempt; which should not have been put off so long in this Nation! We have conquered the Enemies of Christ; let us now, in real practical earnest, set about doing the Commandments of Christ, now that there is free room for us! Such was the purpose of this Puritan Assembly of the Notables, which History calls the *Little Parliament*, or derisively *Barebones's Parliament*.

It is well known they failed: to us, alas, it is too evident they could not but fail. Fearful impediments lay against that effort of theirs: the sluggishness, the slavish half-and-halfness, the greediness, the cowardice, and general opacity and falsity of some ten million men against it;—alas, the whole world, and what we call the Devil and all his angels, against it! Considerable angels, human and other: most extensive arrangements, investments, to be sold off at a tremendous sacrifice;—in general the entire set of luggage-traps and very extensive stock of merchant-goods and real and floating property, amassed by that assidious Entity above-mentioned, for a thousand years or more! For these, and also for other obstructions, it could not take effect at that time;—and the *Little Parliament* became a *Barebones's Parliament*, and had to go its ways again.

On the whole, we have to say of this Little Parliament, that it sat for five months and odd days, very earnestly striving; earnestly, nobly,—and by no means unwisely, as the ignorant Histories teach. But the farther it advanced towards real Christianism in human affairs, the louder grew the shrieks of Sham-Christianism everywhere profitably lodged there;—and prudent persons, responsible for the issue, discovered that of a truth, for one reason or another, for reasons evident and for reasons not evident, there could be no success according to that method. We said, the History of this Little Parliament lay all buried very deep in the torpors of Human Stupidity, and was not likely ever to be brought into daylight in this world. In

THE LITTLE PARLIAMENT

their five months time they passed various good Acts; chose, with good insight, a new Council of State; took wise charge of the needful Supplies; did all the routine business of a Parliament in a quite unexceptionable, or even in a superior manner. Concerning their Council of State, I find this Note; which, though the Council had soon to alter itself, and take new figures, may be worth appending here.[1]

Routine business done altogether well by this Little Parliament. But, alas, they had decided on abolishing Tithes, on supporting a Christian Ministry by some other method than Tithes,—nay far worse, they had decided on abolishing the Court of Chancery; Finding grievances greater than could be borne; finding, for one thing, 'Twenty-three thousand Causes of from five to thirty years continuance' lying undetermined in Chancery, it seemed to the Little Parliament that some Court ought to be contrived which would actually determine these and the like Causes; and that, on the whole, Chancery would be better for abolition. Vote to that effect stands registered in the Commons Journals; but still, for near two-hundred years now, only expects fulfilment. —So far as one can discover in the huge twilight of Dryasdust, it was mainly by this attack on the Lawyers, and attempt to abolish Chancery, that the Little Parliament perished. Tithes helped, no doubt; and the clamours of a safely-settled Ministry, Presbyterian-Royalist many of them. But the Lawyers exclaimed : " Chancery ? Law of the Bible ? Do you mean to " bring-in the *Mosaic Dispensation*, then ; and deprive men of their " properties ? Deprive men of their properties ; and us of our " learned wigs, and lucrative longwindednesses,—with your search " for ' Simple Justice,' and ' God's Law,' instead of Learned-

---

[1] Council of State elected,—Tuesday 1st November 1653 (Commons Journals, vii. 344). The Election is by ballot, 113 Members present; 'Colonel Montague' (Sandwich), 'Colonel Cromwell' (Henry), and 'Sir Anthony Ashley Cooper,' are three of the Four Scrutineers. Among the Names reported as chosen, here are some, with the Numbers voting for them: Lord General Cromwell (113, one and all); Sir Gilbert Pickering (Poet Dryden's Cousin and Patron,—110); Desborow (74); Harrison (58); Mayor (of Hursley,—57); Colonel Montague (59); Ashley Cooper (60); Lord Viscount Lisle (Algernon Sidney's Brother, —58); Colonel Norton (idle Dick, recovered from the Pride's Purge again, but liable to relapse again,—57). The Council is of Thirty-one; Sixteen of the Old or Interim Council (above referred to in Cromwell's Speech) are to continue; Fifteen new; these mentioned here are all among the Old, whom the Lord General and his Officers had already nominated.

"Sergeant's Law?" There was immense 'carousing in the Temple' when this Parliament ended; as great tremors had been in the like quarters while it continued.

But in brief, on Friday the 2d of December 1653, there came a 'Report from the Tithes-Committee,' recommending that Ministers of an incompetent, simoniacal, loose, or otherwise scandalous nature, plainly unfit to preach any Gospel to immortal creatures, should have a Travelling Commission of chosen Puritan Persons appointed, to travel into all Counties, and straightway inspect them, and eject them, and clear Christ's Church of them:—whereupon there ensued high debatings: Accept the Report, or Not accept it? High debatings, for the space of ten days; with Parliamentary manœuverings, not necessary to specify here. Which rose ever higher; and on Saturday the 10th, had got so high that, as I am credibly informed, certain leading persons went about colleaguing and consulting, instead of attending Public Worship on the Lord's Day:—and so, on Monday morning early, while the extreme Gospel Party had not yet assembled in the House, it was surreptitiously moved and carried, old Speaker Rouse somewhat treacherously assenting to it, 'That the sitting of this Parliament any longer, as now constituted, will not be for the good of the Commonwealth; and that therefore it is requisite to 'deliver up unto the Lord General Cromwell the Powers which 'we received from him!' Whereupon, adds the same Rhadamantine Record, 'the House rose; and the Speaker, with many 'of the Members of the House, departed out of the House to 'Whitehall: where they, being the greater number of the 'Members sitting in Parliament, did, by a Writing,' hastily redacted in the waiting-room there, and signed on separate bits of paper hastily wafered together, 'resign unto his Excellency 'their said Powers. And Mr. Speaker, attended by the 'Members, did present the same unto his Excellency accordingly,' —and retired into private life again.

The Lord General Cromwell testified much emotion and surprise at this result;—emotion and surprise which Dryasdust knows well how to interpret. In fact the Lord General is responsible to England and Heaven for this result; and it is one of some moment! He and the established Council of State, 'Council of Officers and' non-established 'Persons of Interest in the Nation,' must consider what they will now do!

Clearly enough to them, and to us, there can only one thing

be done: search be made, Whether there is any King, *Konning*, Canning, or Supremely Able-Man that you can fall-in with, to take charge of these conflicting and colliding elements, drifting towards swift wreck otherwise;—any 'Parish Constable,' as Oliver himself defines it, to bid good men keep the peace to one another. To your unspeakable good-luck, such Supremely Able-Man, King, Constable, or by whatever name you will call him, is already found,—known to all persons for years past: your Puritan Interest is not yet necessarily a wreck; but may still float, and do what farther is in it, while he can float!

From Monday onwards, the excitement of the public mind in old London and whithersoever the news went, in those winter days, must have been great. The 'Lord General called a Council of Officers and other persons of Interest in the Nation,' as we said; and there was 'much seeking of God by prayer,' and abstruse advising of this matter,—the matter being really great, and to some of us even awful! The dialogues, conferences, and abstruse advisings are all lost; the result we know for certain. Monday was 12th of December; on Friday 16th, the result became manifest to all the world: That the ablest of Englishmen, Oliver Cromwell, was henceforth to be recognised for Supremely Able; and that the Title of him was to be LORD PROTECTOR OF THE COMMONWEALTH OF ENGLAND, SCOTLAND AND IRELAND, with 'Instrument of Government,' 'Council of Fifteen or of Twenty-one,' and other necessary less important circumstances, of the like conceivable nature.

The Instrument of Government, a carefully constitutional piece in Forty-two Articles; the Ceremony of Installation, transacted with due simplicity and much modest dignity, 'in the Chancery Court in Westminster Hall,' that Friday afternoon; —the chair of state, the Judges in their robes, Lord Mayors with caps of maintenance; the state-coaches, outriders, outrunners, and 'great shoutings of the people;' the procession from and to Whitehall, and 'Mr. Lockier the Chaplain's Exhortation' to us there: these, with the inevitable adjuncts of the case, shall be conceived by ingenious readers, or read in innumerable Pamphlets and Books, and omitted here. 'His 'Highness was in a rich but plain suit; black velvet, with 'cloak of the same: about his hat a broad band of gold.' Does the reader see him? A rather likely figure, I think. Stands some five feet ten or more; a man of strong solid stature, and dignified, now partly military carriage: the expression of him valour and devout intelligence,—energy and delicacy on a basis of simplicity. Fifty-four years old, gone April last; ruddy-fair complexion, bronzed by toil and age; light-brown hair and moustache are getting streaked with gray. A figure of sufficient impressiveness;—not lovely to the man-milliner species, nor pretending to be so. Massive stature; big massive head, of somewhat leonine aspect, 'evident workshop and storehouse of a vast treasury of natural parts.' Wart above the right eyebrow; nose of considerable blunt-aquiline proportions; strict yet copious lips, full of all tremulous sensibilities, and also if need were, of all fiercenesses and rigours; deep loving eyes, call them grave, call them stern, looking from under those craggy brows, as if in lifelong sorrow, and yet not thinking it sorrow, thinking it only labour and endeavour:—on the whole, a right noble lion-face and hero-face; and to me royal enough. The reader, in his mind, shall conceive this event and its figures.

PART VIII

FIRST PROTECTORATE PARLIAMENT

1654

THE 3d of September ever since Worcester Battle has been kept as a day of Thanksgiving ; commemorative of the mercy at Dunbar in 1650, and of the crowning-mercy which followed next year ;—a memorable day for the Commonwealth of England. By Article Seventh of the Instrument of Government, it is now farther provided that a Parliament shall meet on that auspicious Anniversary when it next comes round. September 3d, 1654, then shall the First Protectorate Parliament meet ; successive Parliaments, one at least every Three years, are to follow, but this shall be the First. Not to be dissolved, or prorogued for at least Five months. Free Parliament of Four-hundred ; for England Three-hundred-and-forty, for Scotland Thirty, for Ireland Thirty ; fairly chosen by election of the People, according to rules anxiously constitutional, laid down in that same Instrument,—which we do not dwell upon here Smaller Boroughs are excluded ; among Counties and larger Boroughs is a more equable division of representatives according to their population : nobody to vote that has not some clearly visible property to the value of Two-hundred Pounds ; but all that have can vote, and can be voted for,— except, of course, all such as have appeared against the Parliament in any of these Wars 'since the First of January 1642,' and 'not since given signal testimony ' of their repenting that step. To appearance a very reasonable Reform Bill ;—understood to be substantially the same with that invaluable measure once nearly completed by the Rump: only with this essential difference, That the Rump Members are not now to sit by nature and without election; not now to decide, they, in case of extremity, Thou shalt sit, Thou shalt not sit;—others than they will now decide that, in cases of extremity. How this Parliament, in its Five-months Session, will welcome the new Protector and Protectorate is naturally the grand question during those Nine or Ten Months that intervene.

A question for all Englishmen; and most of all for Oliver Protector;—who however, as we can perceive, does not allow it to overawe him very much; but diligently doing this day the day's duties, hopes he may find, as God has often favoured him to do, some good solution for the morrow, whatsoever the morrow please to be. A man much apt to be overawed by any question that is smaller than Eternity, or by any danger that is lower than God's Displeasure, would not suit well in Oliver's place at present! Perhaps no more perilous place, that I know clearly of, was ever deliberately accepted by a man. 'The post of honour,'—the post of terror and of danger and forlorn-hope: this man has all along been used to occupy such.

Secretary Thurloe, once St. John's Secretary in Holland, has come now, ever since the Little-Parliament time, into decided action as Oliver's Secretary, or the State Secretary; one of the expertest Secretaries, in the real meaning of the word Secretary, any State or working King could have. He deals with all these Plots; it is part of his function, supervised by his Chief. Mr John Milton, we all lament to know, has fallen blind in the Public Service; lives now in Bird-cage Walk, still doing a little when called upon; bating no jot of heart or hope. Mr. Milton's notion is, That this Protectorate of his Highness Oliver was a thing called for by the Necessities and the Everlasting Laws; and that his Highness ought now to quit himself like a Christian Hero in it, as in other smaller things he has been used to do.[1]

March 20th, 1653-4. By the Instrument of the Government, the Lord Protector with his Council,[2] till once the First

---

[1] *Defensio Secunda.*

[2] Fifteen in number, which he may enlarge to Twenty-one, if he see good. Not removable any of them, except by himself with advice of the rest. A very remarkable Majesty's Ministry;—of which, for its own sake and the Majesty's, take this List, as it stood in 1654:

Philip Viscount Lisle (Algernon Sidney's Brother); Fleetwood; Lambert; Montague (of Hinchinbrook); Desborow (Protector's Brother-

'ORDINANCE' ON RELIGION

Parliament were got together, was empowered not only to raise moneys for the needful supplies, but also 'to make Laws and Ordinances for the peace and welfare of these Nations;' which latter faculty he is by no means slack to exercise. Of his 'Sixty Ordinances' passed in this manner before the Parliament met, which are well approved of by good judges, we cannot here afford to say much : but there is one bearing date as above, which must not be omitted. First Ordinance relating to the Settlement of a Gospel Ministry in this Nation ; Ordinance of immense interest to Puritan England at that time. An object which has long been on the anvil, this same 'Settlement;' much laboured at, and striven for, ever since the Long Parliament began ; and still, as all confess, no tolerable result has been attained. Yet is it not the greatest object ; properly the soul of all these struggles and confused wrestlings and battlings, since we first met here ? For the thing men are taught, or get to *believe*, that is the thing they will infallibly *do*; the kind of 'Gospel' you settle, kind of 'Ministry' you settle, or do not settle, the root of all is there ! Let us see what the Lord Protector can accomplish in this business.

Episcopacy being put down, and Presbytery not set up, and Church-Government for years past being all a Church-Anarchy, the business is somewhat difficult to deal with. The Lord Protector, as we find, takes it up in simplicity and integrity, intent upon the real heart or practical outcome of it ; and makes a rather satisfactory arrangement. Thirty-eight chosen Men, the acknowledged Flower of English Puritanism, are nominated by this Ordinance of the 20th of March, nominated a Supreme Commission for the Trial of Public Preachers. Any person pretending to hold a Church-living, or levy tithes or clergy-dues in England, has first to be tried and approved by these men. Thirty-eight, as Scobell teaches us ; nine are Laymen, our

in-law; Ashley Cooper (Earl of Shaftesbury afterwards) ; Walter Strickland (Member for Minehead in the Long Parliament, once Ambassador in Holland); Colonel Henry Lawrence (for Westmoreland in the Long Parliament, of whom we have transiently heard,— became *President* of the Council); Mayor (of Hursley), Francis Rouse (our old friend) ; pious old Major-General Skippon ; Colonels Philip Jones and Sydenham, Sirs Gilbert Pickering and Charles Wolseley, of whom my readers do not know much. Fifteen Councillors in all. To whom Nathaniel Fiennes (son of Lord Say and Sele) was afterwards added; with the Earl of Mulgrave; and another, Colonel Mackworth, who soon died (*Thurloe*, iii. 581). Thurloe is Secretary; and blind Milton, now with assistants, is Latin Secretary.

friend old Francis Rouse at the head of them ; twenty-nine are Clergy. His Highness, we find, has not much inquired of what Sect they are; has known them to be Independents, to be Presbyterians, one or two of them to be even Anabaptists ;—has been careful only of one characteristic, That they were men of wisdom, and had the root of the matter in them. Owen, Goodwin, Sterry, Marshall, Manton, and others not yet quite unknown to men, were among these Clerical *Triers* : the acknowledged Flower of Spiritual England at that time ; and intent, as Oliver himself was, with an awful earnestness, on actually having the Gospel taught to England.

This is the First branch or limb of Oliver's scheme for Church-Government, this Ordinance of the 20th March 1653-4. A second, which completes what little he could do in the matter at present, developed itself in August following. By this August Ordinance, a Body of Commissioners, distinguished Puritan Gentry, distinguished Puritan Clergy, are nominated in all Counties of England, from Fifteen to Thirty in each County ; who are to inquire into 'scandalous, ignorant, insufficient,' and otherwise deleterious alarming Ministers of the Gospel ; to be a tribunal for judging, for detecting, ejecting them (only in case of ejection, if they have wives, let some small modicum of living be allowed them) : and to sit there, judging and sifting, till gradually all is sifted clean, and can be kept clean. This is the Second branch of Oliver's form of Church-Government ; this, with the other Ordinance, makes at last a kind of practicable Ecclesiastical Arrangement for England.

April 14th, 1654. This day, let it be noted for the sake of poor Editors concerned with undated Letters, and others, his Highness removed from his old Lodging in the Cockpit, into new properly Royal Apartments in Whitehall, now ready for him, and lived there henceforth, usually going out to Hampton Court on the Saturday afternoon. He has 'assumed somewhat of the state of a King;' due ceremonial, decent observance beseeming the Protector of the Commonwealth of England ; life-guards, ushers, state-coaches,—in which my erudite friend knows well what delight this Lord Protector had ! Better still, the Lord Protector has concluded good Treaties ; received congratulatory Embassies,—France, Spain itself have sent Embassies. Treaty with the Dutch, with Denmark, Sweden, Portugal : all much to our satisfaction.

SPEECH II

But now the New Parliament has got itself elected ; not without much interest : the first Election there has been in England for fourteen years past. Parliament of Four-hundred, thirty Scotch, thirty Irish; freely chosen according to the Instrument, according to the Bill that was in progress when the Rump disappeared.

We recognise old faces, in fair proportion, among those Four-hundred ;—many new withal, who never become known to us. Learned Bulstrode, now safe home from perils in Hyperborean countries, is here ; elected for several places, the truly valuable man. Old-Speaker Lenthall sits, old Major-General Skippon, old Sir William Masham, old Sir Francis Rouse. My Lord Herbert (Earl of Worcester's son) is here ; Owen, Doctor of Divinity, for Oxford University ;—a certain not entirely useless Guibon Goddard, for the Town of Lynn, to whom we owe some Notes of the procedure. Leading Officers and high Official persons have been extensively elected ; several of them twice and thrice : Fleetwood, Lambert, the Claypoles, Dunches, both the young Cromwells ; Montague for his County, Ashley Cooper for his. On the other hand, my Lord Fairfax is here ; nay Bradshaw, Haselrig, Robert Wallop, Wildman, and Republicans are here. Old Sir Harry Vane ; not young Sir Harry, who sits meditative in the North. Of Scotch Members we mention only Laird Swinton, and the Earl of Hartfell ; of the Irish, Lord Broghil and Commissary-General Reynolds, whom we once saw fighting well in that country.—And now hear the authentic Bulstrode ; and then the Protector himself.

'*September* 3*d*, 1654.—The Lord's day, yet the day of the 'Parliament's meeting. The Members met in the afternoon at 'sermon, in the Abbey Church at Westminster : after sermon 'they attended the Protector in the Painted Chamber ; who 'made a Speech to them of the cause of their summons,' Speech unreported ; 'after which, they went to the House, and adjourned 'to the next morning.

'*Monday, September* 4*th*.—The Protector rode in state from 'Whitehall to the Abbey Church in Westminster. Some 'hundreds of Gentlemen and Officers went before him bare ; 'with the Life-guard ; and next before the coach, his pages and 'laqueys richly clothed. On the one side of his coach went 'Strickland, one of his Council, and Captain of his Guard, with the 'Master of the Ceremonies ; both on foot. On the other side

'went Howard,[1] Captain of the Life-guard. In the coach with
'him were his son Henry, and Lambert; both sat bare. After
'him came Claypole, Master of the Horse; with a gallant led
'horse richly trapped. Next came the Commissioners of the
'Great Seal,' Lisle, Widdrington, and I; 'Commissioners of
'the Treasury, and divers of the Council in coaches; last the
'ordinary Guards.

'He alighting at the Abbey Church door,' and entering, 'the
'Officers of the Army and the Gentlemen went first; next them
'four maces; then the Commissioners of the Seal, Whitlocke
'carrying the Purse; after, Lambert carrying the Sword bare:
'the rest followed. His Highness was seated over against the
'Pulpit; the Members of the Parliament on both sides.

'After the sermon, which was preached by Mr. Thomas
'Goodwin, his Highness went, in the same equipage, to the
'Painted Chamber. Where he took seat in a chair of state set
'upon steps,' raised chair with a canopy over it, under which his
Highness sat covered, 'and the Members upon benches round
'about sat all bare All being silent, his Highness,' rising, 'put
'off his hat, and made a large and subtle speech to them.'

Here is a Report of the Speech, 'taken by one who stood very
near,' and 'published to prevent mistakes.' As we, again, stand
at some distance,—two centuries with their chasms and ruins,—
our hearing is nothing like so good! To help a little, I have,
with reluctance, admitted from the latest of the Commentators a
few annotations; and intercalated them the best I could;
suppressing very many. Let us listen well; and again we shall
understand somewhat.

GENTLEMEN,

You are met here on the greatest occasion that, I believe,
England ever saw; having upon your shoulders the Interests of
Three great Nations with the territories belonging to them;—
and truly, I believe I may say it without any hyperbole, you
have upon your shoulders the Interest of all the Christian
People in the world. And the expectation is, that I should let
you know, as far as I have cognisance of it, the occasion of your
assembling together at this time.

It hath been very well hinted to you this day, that you come
hither to settle the Interests above mentioned: for your work
here, in the issue and consequences of it, *will* extend so far,
'even to all Christian people.' In the way and manner of my

[1] Colonel Charles, ancestor of the Earl of Carlisle.

SPEECH TO PARLIAMENT

speaking to you, I shall study plainness ; and to speak to you
what is truth, and what is upon my heart, and what will in
some measure reach to these great concernments.

After so many changings and turnings, which this Nation
hath laboured under,—to have such a day of hope as this is,
and such a door of hope opened by God to us, truly I believe,
some months since, would have been beyond all our thoughts !—
I confess it would have been worthy of such a meeting as this
is, To have remembered that which was the rise 'of,' and gave
the first beginning to, all these Troubles which have been upon
this Nation : and to have given you a series of the Transactions,
—not of men, but of the Providence of God, all along unto
our late changes : as also the ground of our first undertaking to
oppose that usurpation and tyranny which was upon us, both
in civils and spirituals ; and the several grounds particularly
applicable to the several changes that have been. But I have
two or three reasons which divert me from such a way of
proceeding at this time.

What was our condition ! Every man's hand almost was
against his brother ;—at least his heart 'was' ; little regarding
anything that should cement, and might have a tendency in
it to cause us to grow into one. All the dispensations of God ;
His terrible ones, when He met us in the way of His judgment
in a Ten-years Civil War ; and His merciful ones : they did
not, they did not work upon us ! 'No.' But we had our
humours and interests ;—and indeed I fear our humours went
for more with us than even our interests. Certainly, as it falls
out in such cases, our passions were more than our judgments.—
Was not everything almost grown arbitrary ? Who of us knew
where or how to have right 'done him,' without some obstruc-
tion or other intervening ? Indeed we were almost grown
arbitrary in everything.

What was the face that was upon our affairs as to the Interest
of the Nation ? As to the Authority in the Nation ; to the
Magistracy ; to the Ranks and Orders of men,—whereby
England hath been known for hundreds of years ? [*The
Levellers !*] A nobleman, a gentleman, a yeoman ; ' the
distinction of these : ' that is a good interest of the Nation, and
a great one ! The 'natural' Magistracy of the Nation, was
it not almost trampled under foot, under despite and contempt,
by men of Levelling principles ? I beseech you, For the orders
of men and ranks of men, did not that Levelling principle tend

to the reducing of all to an equality ? Did it 'consciously' think to do so ; or did it 'only unconsciously' practise towards that for property and interest ? 'At all events,' what was the purport of it but to make the Tenant as liberal a fortune as the Landlord ? Which, I think, if obtained, would not have lasted long ! The men of that principle, after they had served their own turns, would *then* have cried up property and interest fast enough !—This instance is instead of many. And that the thing did 'and might well' extend far, is manifest ; because it was a pleasing voice to all Poor Men, and truly not unwelcome to all Bad Men. [*Far-extended classes, these two both!*] To my thinking, this is a consideration which, in your endeavours after settlement, you will be so well minded of, that I might have spared it here : but let that pass.—

We may reckon among our many Spiritual evils, an evil that hath more refinedness in it, more colour for it, and hath deceived more people of integrity than the rest have done ;—for few have been catched by the former mistakes except such as have apostatised from their holy profession, such as being corrupt in their consciences have been forsaken by God, and left to such noisome opinions. But, I say, there is another error of more refined sort ; 'which' many honest people whose hearts are sincere, many of them belonging to God, 'have fallen into :' and that is the mistaken notion of the Fifth Monarchy—

[Yes, your Highness !—But will his Highness and the old Parliament be pleased here to pause a little, till a faithful Editor take the great liberty of explaining somewhat to the modern part of the audience ? Here is a Note saved from destruction ; not without difficulty. To his Highness and the old Parliament it will be inaudible ; to them, standing very impassive,—serene, immovable in the fixedness of the old Eternities,—it will be no hardship to wait a little ! And to us who still live and listen, it may have its uses.

'The common mode of treating Universal History,' says our latest impatient Commentator, 'not yet entirely fallen obsolete in 'this country, though it has been abandoned with much ridicule 'everywhere else for half a century now, was to group the Aggre- 'gate Transactions of the Human Species into Four Monarchies : 'the Assyrian Monarchy of Nebuchadnezzar and Company ; the 'Persian of Cyrus and ditto, the Greek of Alexander ; and lastly 'the Roman. These I think were they, but am no great

'authority on the subject. Under the dregs of this last, or
'Roman Empire, which is maintained yet by express name in
'Germany, *Das heilige Römische Reich*, we poor moderns still live.
'But now say Major-General Harrison and a number of men,
'founding on Bible Prophecies, Now shall be a Fifth Monarchy,
'by far the blessedest and the only real one,—the Monarchy of
'Jesus Christ, his Saints reigning for Him here on Earth,—if
'not He himself, which is probable or possible,—for a thousand
'years, &c. &c.— — O Heavens, there are tears for human
'destiny; and immortal Hope itself is beautiful because it is
'steeped in Sorrow, and foolish Desire lies vanquished under its
'feet! They who merely laugh at Harrison take but a small
'portion of his meaning with them. Thou, with some tear for
'the valiant Harrison, if with any thought of him at all, tend
'thou also valiantly, in thy day and generation, whither he was
'tending; and know that, in far wider and diviner figure than
'that of Harrison, the Prophecy is very sure,—that it *shall* be
'sure while one brave man survives among the dim bewildered
'populations of this world. Good shall reign on this Earth:
'has *not* the Most High said it? To approve Harrison, to
justify Harrison, will avail little for thee; go and *do likewise.*
'Go and do better, thou that disapprovest him. Spend thou
'thy life for the Eternal: we will call thee also brave, and
'remember thee for a while!'

So much for 'that mistaken notion of the Fifth Monarchy:'
and now his Highness, tragically audible across the Centuries,
continues again:]

—Fifth Monarchy. A thing pretending more spirituality than
anything else. A notion I hope we all honour, and wait, and
hope for 'the fulfilment of:' That Jesus Christ *will* have a
time to set up His Reign in our hearts; by subduing those corruptions and lusts and evils that are there; which now reign
more in the world than, I hope, in due time they shall do. And
when more fulness of the Spirit is poured forth to subdue
iniquity, and bring-in everlasting righteousness, then will the
approach of that glory be. [*Most true;—and not till then!*
The carnal divisions and contentions among Christians, so common, are not the symptoms of that Kingdom!—But for men, on
this principle, to betitle themselves, that they are the only men
to rule kingdoms, govern nations, and give laws to people, and
determine of property and liberty and everything else,—upon
such a pretension as this is:—truly they had need to give clear

manifestations of God's presence with them, before wise men will receive or submit to their conclusions ! Nevertheless, as many of these men have good meanings, which I hope in my soul they have, it will be the wisdom of all knowing and experienced Christians to do as Jude saith. 'Jude,' when he reckoned up those horrible things, done upon pretences, and haply by some upon mistakes: "Of some," says he, "have compassion, making "a difference; others save with fear, pulling them out of the "fire." I fear they will give too often opportunity for this exercise ! But I hope the same will be for their good. If men do but 'so much as' pretend for justice and righteousness, and be of peaceable spirits, and will manifest this, let them be the subjects of the Magistrate's encouragement. And if the Magistrate, by punishing visible miscarriages, save them by that discipline, God having ordained him for that end,—I hope it will evidence *love* and not hatred, 'so' to punish where there is cause.

Indeed this is that which doth most declare the danger of that spirit. For if these were but notions,—I mean these instances I have given you of dangerous doctrines both in Civil things and Spiritual ; if, I say, they were but notions, they were best let alone. Notions will hurt none but those that have them. But when they come to such practices as telling us, 'for instance,' That Liberty and Property are not the badges of the Kingdom of Christ ; when they tell us, not that we are to regulate Law, but that Law is to be abrogated, indeed subverted ; and perhaps wish to bring in the Judaical Law—instead of our known laws settled among us : this is worthy of every Magistrate's consideration. Especially where every stone is turned to bring in confusion. I think, I say, this will be worthy of the Magistrate's consideration.

Whilst these things were in the midst of us ; and whilst the Nation was rent and torn in spirit and principle from one end to the other, after this sort and manner I have now told you ; family against family, husband against wife, parents against children ; and nothing in the hearts and minds of men but "Overturn, overturn, overturn !" (a Scripture phrase very much abused, and applied to justify unpeaceable practices by all men of discontented spirits),—the common Enemy sleeps not : our adversaries in civil and religious respects did take advantage of these distractions and divisions, and did practise accordingly in the three Nations of England, Scotland and Ireland. We know

very well that Emissaries of the Jesuits never came in such
swarms as they have done since those things were set on foot.'
And I tell you that divers Gentlemen here can bear witness with
me How that they, 'the Jesuits,' have had a Consistory abroad
which rules all the affairs of things ["*Affairs of things:*" *rough
and ready !*] in England, from an Archbishop down to the other
dependents upon him. And they had fixed in England,—of
which we are able to produce the particular Instruments in most
of the limits of their Cathedrals 'or pretended Dioceses,'—an
Episcopal Power [*Regular Episcopacy of their own !*], with Arch-
deacons, &c. And had persons authorised to exercise and
distribute those things [*I begin to love that rough-and-ready
method, in comparison with some others !*]; who pervert and
deceive the people. And all this, while we were in that sad,
and as I said deplorable condition.

And in the mean time all endeavours possible were used to
hinder the work 'of God' in Ireland, and the progress of the
work of God in Scotland ; by continual intelligences and correspondences, both at home and abroad, from hence into Ireland,
and from hence into Scotland. Persons were stirred up, from
our divisions and discomposure of affairs, to do all they could
to ferment the War in both these places. To add yet to our
misery, whilst we were in this condition, we were in a 'foreign'
War. Deeply engaged in War with the Portuguese ;[1] whereby
our Trade ceased: the evil consequences by that War were
manifest and very considerable. And not only this, but we
had a War with Holland ; consuming our treasure ; occasioning
a vast burden upon the people. A War that cost this Nation
full as much as the 'whole' Taxes came unto ; the Navy
being a Hundred-and-sixty Ships, which cost this Nation above
100,000*l.* a-month ; besides the contingencies, which would
make it 120,000*l.* That very one War (*sic*) did engage us to
so great a charge.—At the same time also we were in a War
with France. The advantages that were taken of the discontents
and divisions among ourselves did also ferment that War, and
at least hinder us of an honourable peace ; every man being
confident we could not hold out long. And surely they did
not calculate amiss, if the Lord had not been exceedingly
gracious to us ! I say, at the same time we had a War with
France. And besides the sufferings in respect to the Trade of
the Nation, it's most evident that the Purse of the Nation could

[1] Who protected Rupert in his quasi-piracies, and did require
chastisement from us.

not have been able much longer to bear it,—by reason of the advantages taken by other States to improve their own, and spoil our Manufactuie of Cloth, and hinder the vent thereof; which is the great staple commodity of this Nation. Such was our condition : spoiled in our Trade, and we at this vast expense ; thus dissettled at home, and having these engagements abroad.

Things being so,—and I am persuaded it is not hard to convince every person here they were so,—what a heap of confusions were upon these poor Nations ! And either things must have been left to sink into the miseries these premises would suppose, or else a remedy must be applied. A remedy hath been applied : that hath been this Government ;[1] a thing I shall say little unto. The thing is open and visible to be seen and read by all men ; and therefore let it speak for itself. Only let me say this,— because I can speak it with comfort and confidence before a Greater than you all : That in the intention of it, as to the approving of our hearts to God, let men judge as they please, it was calculated 'with our best wisdom' for the interest of the People. For the interest of the People alone, and for their good, without respect had to any other interest. And if that be not true, I shall be bold to say again, Let it speak for itself. Truly I may,—I hope, humbly before God, and modestly before you,—say somewhat on the behalf of the Government. Not that I would discourse of the particular heads of it, but acquaint you a little with the effects it has had : and this not for ostentation's sake, but to the end I may at this time deal faithfully with you ; and acquaint you with the state of things, and what proceedings have been entered-into by this Government, and what the state of our affairs is. This is the main end of my putting you to this trouble.

The Government hath had some things in desire; and it hath done some things actually. It hath desired to reform the Laws. I say to reform them :—and for that end it hath called together Persons, without offence be it spoken, of as great ability and as great interest as are in these Nations, to consider how the Laws might be made plain and short, and less chargeable to the People; how to lessen expense, for the good of the Nation. And those things are in preparation, and Bills pre-

---

[1] He means, and his hearers understand him to mean, '*Form* of Government' mainly; but he diverges now and then into our modern acceptation of the word 'Government,'—Administration or Supreme Authority.

pared ; which in due time, I make no question, will be tendered
to you. 'In the mean while' there hath been care taken to put
the administration of the Laws into the hands of just men ; men
of the most known integrity and ability. The Chancery hath been
reformed—I hope, to the satisfaction of all good men : and as for
the things, 'or causes,' depending there, which made the burden
and work of the honourable Persons intrusted in those services
too heavy for their ability, it[1] hath referred many of them to
those places where Englishmen love to have their rights tried,
the Courts of Law at Westminster.

This Government hath, 'further,' endeavoured to put a stop
to that heady way (likewise touched of 'in our Sermon,' this
day) of every man making himself a Minister and Preacher.
[*Commission of Triers*; *Yea!*] It hath endeavoured to settle a
method for the approving and sanctioning of men of piety and
ability to discharge that work. And I think I may say it hath
committed the business to the trust of Persons, both of the
Presbyterian and Independent judgments, of as known ability,
piety and integrity, as any, I believe, this Nation hath. And I
believe also that, in that care they have taken, they have
laboured to approve themselves to Christ, to the Nation and
to their own consciences. And indeed I think, if there be
anything of quarrel against them, though I am not here to
justify the proceedings of any,—it is that they, 'in fact,' go
upon such a character as the Scripture warrants : To put men
into that great Employment, and to approve men for it, who
are men that have "received gifts from Him that ascended up
on high, and gave gifts" for the work of the Ministry, and for
the edifying of the Body of Christ. The Government hath
also taken care, we hope, for the expulsion [*Commission of
Expurgation too,*] of all those who may be judged any way unfit
for this work ; who are scandalous, and the common scorn and
contempt of that function.

One thing more this Government hath done : it hath been
instrumental to call a free Parliament ;—which, blessed be
God, we see here this day ! I say, a free Parliament. [*Mark
the iteration !*] And that it may continue so, I hope is in the
heart and spirit of every good man in England,—save such
discontented persons as I have formerly mentioned. It's that
which as I have desired above my life, so I shall desire to keep
it above my life. [*Verily ?*]—

[1] The Government.

I did before mention to you the plunges we were in with respect to Foreign States ; by the War with Portugal, France, the Dutch, the Danes, and the little assurance we had from any of our neighbours round about. I perhaps forgot, but indeed it was a caution upon my mind, and I desire now it may be so understood, That if any good hath been done, it was the Lord, not we His poor instruments.—I did instance the Wars ; which did exhaust your treasure ; and put you into such a condition that you must have sunk therein, if it had continued but a few months longer : this I can affirm, if strong probability may be a fit ground. And now you have, though it be not the first in time,—Peace with Swedeland ; an honourable peace ; through the endeavours of an honourable Person here present as the instrument. I say you have an honourable peace with a Kingdom which, not many years since, was much a friend to France, and lately perhaps inclinable enough to the Spaniard. And I believe you expect not much good from any of your Catholic neighbours ; nor yet that they would be very willing you should have a good understanding with your Protestant friends. Yet, thanks be to God, that Peace is concluded ; and as I said before, it is an honourable Peace.

You have a Peace with the Danes,—a State that lay contiguous to that part of this Island which hath given us the most trouble. And certainly if your enemies abroad be able to annoy you, it is likely they will take their advantage (where it best lies) to give you trouble from that country. But you have a Peace there, and an honourable one. Satisfaction to your Merchants' ships ; not only to their content, but to their rejoicing.[1] I believe you will easily know it is so,—'an honourable peace.' You have the Sound open ; which used to be obstructed. That which was and is the strength of this Nation, the Shipping, will now be supplied thence. And, whereas you were glad to have anything of that kind[2] at secondhand, you have now all manner of commerce there, and at as much freedom as the Dutch themselves, 'who used to be the carriers

---

[1] 'Danish claims settled,' as was already said somewhere, 'on the 31st of July :' Dutch and English Commissioners did it, in Goldsmiths' Hall ; met on the 27th of June ; if the business were not done when August began, they were then to be ' shut-up without fire, candle, meat or drink,'—and to do it out very speedily ! They allowed our Merchants 98,000*l.* for damages against the Danes.

[2] Baltic Produce, namely.

and venders of it to us;' and at the same rates and tolls;—
and I think, by that Peace, the said rates now fixed-upon cannot
be raised to you 'in future.'

You have a Peace with the Dutch: a Peace unto which I
shall say little, seeing it is so well known in the benefit and consequences thereof. And I think it was as desirable, and as
acceptable to the spirit of this Nation, as any one thing that lay
before us. And, as I believe nothing so much gratified our
enemies as to see us at odds 'with that Commonwealth;' so I
persuade myself nothing is of more terror or trouble to them
than to see us thus reconciled. 'Truly' as a Peace with the
Protestant States hath much security in it, so it hath as much
of honour and of assurance to the Protestant Interest abroad;
without which no assistance can be given thereunto. I wish it
may be written upon our hearts to be zealous for that Interest!
For if ever it were like to come under a condition of suffering,
it is now. In all the Emperor's Patrimonial Territories, the
endeavour is to drive the Protestant part of the people out, as
fast as is possible; and they are necessitated to run to Protestant
States to seek their bread. And by this conjunction of Interests,
I hope you will be in a more fit capacity to help them. And
it begets some reviving of their spirits, that you will help them
as opportunity shall serve. [*We will!*]

You have a Peace likewise with the Crown of Portugal;
which Peace, though it hung long in hand, yet is lately
concluded. It is a Peace which, your Merchants make us
believe, is of good concernment to their trade; the rate of
insurance to that Country having been higher, and so the profit
which could bear such rate, than to other places. And one
thing hath been obtained in this treaty, which never 'before'
was, since the Inquisition was set up there: That our people
which trade thither have Liberty of Conscience,—'liberty to
worship in Chapels of their own.'

Indeed Peace is, as you were well told today, desirable with
all men, as far as it may be had with conscience and honour!
We are upon a Treaty with France. And we may say this,
That if God give us honour in the eyes of the Nations about us,
we have reason to bless Him for it, and so to own it. And I
dare say that there is not a Nation in Europe but is very willing
to ask a good understanding with you.

I am sorry I am thus tedious: but I did judge that it was
somewhat necessary to acquaint you with these things. And
things being so,—I hope you will not be unwilling to hear a

little again of the Sharp as well as of the Sweet ! And I should not be faithful to you, nor to the interest of these Nations which you and I serve, if I did not let you know *all*.

As I said before, when this Government was undertaken, we were in the midst of those 'domestic' divisions and animosities and scatterings; engaged also with those 'foreign' enemies round about us, at such a vast charge,—120,000*l*. a-month for the very Fleet. Which sum was the very utmost penny of your Assessments. Ay; and then all your treasure was exhausted and spent when this Government was undertaken: all *accidental* ways of bringing in treasure 'were,' to a very inconsiderable sum, consumed;—the 'forfeited' Lands sold, the sums on hand spent; Rents, Fee-farms, Delinquents' Lands, King's, Queen's, Bishops', Dean-and-Chapters' Lands, sold. These were *spent* when this Government was undertaken. I think it's my duty to let you know so much. And that's the reason why the Taxes do yet lie so heavy upon the People;—of which we have abated 30,000*l*. a-month for the next three months. Truly I thought it my duty to let you know, That though God hath dealt thus 'bountifully' with you,[1] yet these are but entrances and doors of hope. Whereby, through the blessing of God, you *may* enter into rest and peace. But you are not yet entered !

You were told, to-day, of a People brought out of Egypt towards the Land of Canaan ; but through unbelief, murmuring, repining, and other temptations and sins wherewith God was provoked, they were fain to come back again, and linger many years in the Wilderness before they came to the Place of Rest. *We* are thus far, through the mercy of God. We have cause to take notice of it, That we are not brought into misery, 'not totally wrecked;' but 'have,' as I said before, a door of hope open. And I may say this to you : If the Lord's blessing and His presence go along with the management of affairs at this Meeting, you will be enabled to put the topstone to the work, and make the Nation happy. But this must be by knowing the true state of affairs ! Your Peaces are but newly made. And it's a maxim not to be despised, "Though peace be made, yet it's interest that keeps peace ;"—and I hope you will not trust such peace except so far as you see interest upon it. 'But all settlement grows stronger by mere continuance.' And therefore I wish that you may go forward, and not backward ; and 'in brief' that you may have the blessing of God upon your

[1] In regard to our Successes and Treaties, &c. enumerated above.

endeavours! It's one of the great ends of calling this Parliament, that the Ship of the Commonwealth may be brought into a safe harbour; which, I assure you, it will not be, without your counsel and advice.

You have great works upon your hands. You have Ireland to look unto. There is not much done to the Planting thereof, though some things leading and preparing for it are. It is a great business to settle the Government of that Nation upon fit terms, such as will bear that work[1] through.—You have had laid before you some considerations, intimating your peace with several foreign States. But yet you have not made peace with *all*. And if they should see we do not manage our affairs with that wisdom which becomes us,—truly we may sink under disadvantages, for all that's done. And our enemies will have their eyes open, and be revived, if they see animosities amongst us; which indeed will be their great advantage.

I do therefore persuade you to a sweet, gracious and holy understanding of one another, and of your business. [*Alas!*] Concerning which you had so good counsel this day; which as it rejoiced my heart to hear, so I hope the Lord will imprint it upon your spirits,—wherein you shall have my Prayers.

Having said this, and perhaps omitted many other material things through the frailty of my memory, I shall exercise plainness and freeness with you; and say, That I have not spoken these things as one who assumes to himself dominion over you; but as one who doth resolve to be a fellow-servant with you to the interest of these great affairs, and of the People of these Nations. I shall trouble you no longer; but desire you to repair to your House, and to exercise your own liberty in the choice of a Speaker, that so you may lose no time in carrying on your work.

At this Speech, say the old Newspapers, 'all generally seemed 'abundantly to rejoice, by extraordinary expressions and hums 'at the conclusion,'—Hum-m-m! 'His Highness withdrew 'into the old House of Lords, and the Members of Parliament 'into the Parliament House. His Highness, so soon as the 'Parliament were gone to their House, went back to Whitehall, 'privately in his barge, by water.'

[1] Of planting Ireland with persons that will plough and pray, instead of quarrel and blarney!

SPEECH III

THIS First Protectorate Parliament was not successful. It chose, judiciously enough, old Lenthall for Speaker; appointed, judiciously enough, a Day of general Fasting:—but took, directly after that, into constitutional debate about Sanctioning the Form of Government (which nobody was specially asking it to 'sanction'); about Parliament and Single Person; powers of Single Person and of Parliamant; Coördination, Subordination; and other bottomless subjects; in which getting always the deeper the more it puddled in them, inquiry or intimation of inquiry rose not obscurely in the distance, Whether this Government should *be* by a Parliament and Single Person? These things the honourable gentlemen, with true industry, debated in Grand Committee, 'from eight in the morning till eight at night, with an hour for refreshment about noon,' debates waxing ever hotter, question ever more abstruse,— through Friday, Saturday, Monday; ready, if Heaven spared them, to debate it further for unlimited days. Constitutional Presbyterian persons, Use-and-wont Neuters; not without a spicing of sour Republicans, as Bradshaw, Haselrig, Scott, to keep the batch in leaven.

His Highness naturally perceived that this would never do, not this;—sent therefore to the Lord Mayor, late on Monday night I think, to look after the peace of the City; to Speaker Lenthall, that he must bring his people to the Painted Chamber before going farther; and early on Tuesday morning, poor Mr. Guibon Goddard, Member for Lynn, just about to proceed again, from the Eastern parts, towards his sublime constitutional day's-work, is overwhelmed by rumours, 'That the Parliament 'is dissolved; that, for certain, the Council of State, and a 'Council of War, had sat together all the Sabbath-day before, 'and had then contrived this Dissolution!'

'Notwithstanding,' continues Guibon, 'I was resolved to go 'to Westminster, to satisfy myself of the truth; and to take 'my share of what I should see or learn there. Going by 'water to Westminster, I was told that the Parliament-doors 'were locked up, and guarded with soldiers, and that the Barges 'were to attend the Protector to the Painted Chamber. As I 'went, I saw two Barges at the Privy Stairs. River and City in considerable emotion. 'Being come to the Hall, I was 'confirmed in what I had heard. Nevertheless I did purpose 'not to take things merely upon trust; but would receive

'an actual repulse, to confirm my faith. Accordingly, I at-
'tempted up the Parliament stairs; but a guard of Soldiers
'was there, who told me, "There was no passage that way;
'the House was locked up, and command given to give no
'admittance to any;—if I were a Member, I might go into
'the Painted Chamber, where the Protector would presently be."
'The Mace had been taken away by Commissary-General
'Whalley. The Speaker and all the Members were walking
'up and down the Hall, the Court of Requests, and the Painted
'Chamber; expecting the Protector's coming. The passages
'there likewise were guarded with soldiers.'

No doubt about it, therefore, my honourable friend! Dissolution, or something, is not far. Between nine and ten, the Protector arrived, with due escort of Officers, halberts, Lifeguards; took his place, covered, under 'the state' as before, we all sitting bareheaded on our benches as before; and with fit salutation spake to us;—as follows. 'Speech of an hour and a half long;' taken in characters by the former individual who 'stood near'; audible still to modern men. Tuesday morning, 12th September 1654; a week and a day since the last Speech here.

GENTLEMEN,
You have been called hither to save a Nation,—Nations. You had the best People, indeed, of the Christian world put into your trust, when you came hither. You had the affairs of these Nations delivered over to you in peace and quiet; you were, and we all are, put into an undisturbed possession, nobody making title to us. Through the blessing of God, our enemies were hopeless and scattered. We had peace at home; peace with almost all our Neighbours round about,—apt 'otherwise' to take advantages where God did administer them. 'These 'things we had, few days ago, when you came hither. And 'now?'—To have our peace and interest, whereof those were our hopes the other day, thus shaken, and put under such a confusion; and ourselves rendered hereby almost the scorn and contempt of those strangers who are amongst us to negotiate their masters' affairs! To give *them* opportunity to see our nakedness as they do: "A people that have been unhinged this twelve-years day,[1] and are unhinged still,"—as if scattering, division and confusion came upon us like things we desired: '*these*,' which are the greatest plagues that God ordinarily lays upon Nations for sin!

[1] An old phrase; 'day' emphatic.

I would be loath to say these are matters of our desire. But if not, then why not matters of our *care*,—as wisely as by our utmost endeavours we might, to *avoid* them! Nay if, by such actings as these 'now' are, these poor Nations shall be thrown into heaps and confusion, through blood, and ruin, and trouble [1]—And upon the saddest account that ever was, if breaking 'and confusion' should come upon us;—all because we would not settle when we could, when God put it into our hands! Your affairs now almost settled everywhere: and to have all recoil upon us; and ourselves 'to be' shaken in our affections, loosened from all known and public interests:— as I said before, who shall answer for these things to God?

Who can answer for these things to God, or to men? 'To men'—to the People who sent you hither; who looked for refreshment from you; who looked for nothing but peace and quietness, and rest and settlement? When we come to give an account to them, we shall have it to say, "Oh, we quarrelled "for the *Liberty of England*; we contested, and 'went to 'confusion,' for that!"—'Now,' Wherein, I pray you, for the Liberty of England?" I appeal to the Lord, that the desires and endeavours we have had — — Nay the things will speak for themselves. The "Liberty of England," the Liberty of the People; the avoiding of tyrannous impositions either upon men as men, or Christians as Christians;—is made so safe by this Act of Settlement, that it will speak for itself. And when it shall appear to the world what 'really' hath been said and done by all of us, and what our real transactions were— For God can discover; no Privilege will hinder the Lord from discovering! No Privilege, or condition of man can hide from the Lord; He can and will make all manifest, if He sees it for His glory! [2]—And when these 'things, as I say,' shall be manifested; and the People will come and ask, "Gentlemen, "what condition is this we are in? We hoped for light; and "behold darkness, obscure darkness! We hoped for rest after "ten-years Civil War, but are plunged into deep confusion "again!"—Ay; we know these consequences will come upon us, if God Almighty shall not find out some way to prevent them.

I had a thought within myself, That it would not have been

---

[1] 'What shall we then say?' his Highness means, but does not complete the sentence,—as is sometimes his habit.

[2] 'Privilege' of Parliament, in those days, strenuously forbids *reporting*; but it will not serve in the case referred to!

dishonest nor dishonourable, nor against true Liberty, no not
'the Liberty' of Parliaments, 'if,' when a Parliament was so
chosen 'as you have been,' in pursuance of this Instrument of
Government, and in conformity to it, and with such an approbation and consent to it,—some Owning of your Call and of
the Authority which brought you hither, had been required
before your entrance into the House. This was declined, and
hath not been done, because I am persuaded scarce any man
could doubt you came with contrary minds. And I have
reason to believe the people that sent you least of all doubted
thereof. Seeing the Authority which called you is so little
valued, and so much slighted,—till some such Assurance be
given and made known, that the Fundamental Interest shall
be settled and approved according to the proviso in the 'Writ
of' Return, and such a consent testified as will make it appear
that the same is accepted, I HAVE CAUSED A STOP TO BE PUT
TO YOUR ENTRANCE INTO THE PARLIAMENT HOUSE.

I am sorry, I am sorry, and I could be sorry to the death,
that there is cause for this! But there is cause: and if things
be not satisfied which are reasonably demanded, I, for my part,
will do that which becomes *me*, seeking my counsel from God.
—There is therefore Somewhat to be offered to you; which,
I hope, will answer, being understood with the qualifications
I have told you,—'namely, of' reforming as to Circumstantials,
and agreeing in the Substance and Fundamentals, 'that is to
say,' in the Form of Government now settled, which is expressly
stipulated in your Indentures "not to be altered." The
making of your minds know in that by giving your assent
and subscription to it, is the means that will let you in, to
act those things as a Parliament which are for the good of
the People. And this thing [*The Parchment!*], 'when once
it is' shown to you and signed as aforesaid, doth determine
the controversy; and may give a happy progress and issue
to this Parliament.

The place where you may come thus and sign, as many as
God shall make free thereunto, is in the Lobby without the
Parliament Door.

The 'Instrument of' Government doth declare that you have
a legislative power without a negative from me. As the
Instrument doth express it, you may make any Laws; and if
I give not my consent, within twenty days, to the passing of
your Laws, they are *ipso facto* Laws, whether I consent or no,—if
not contrary to the 'Frame of' Government. You have an

absolute Legislative Power in all things that can possibly concern the good and interest of the public ; and I think you may make these Nations happy by this Settlement. And I, for my part, shall be willing to be bound more than I am, in anything concerning which I can become convinced that it may be for the good of the People, or tend to the preservation of the Cause and Interest so long contended for.

Go your ways, my honourable friends, and sign, so many of you as God hath made free thereunto ! The place, I tell you, is in the Lobby without the Parliament Door. The 'Thing,' as you will find there, is a bit of Parchment with these words engrossed on it : '*I do hereby freely promise, and engage myself, to be true and faithful to the Lord Protector and the Commonwealth of England, Scotland and Ireland; and shall not (according to the tenor of the Indenture whereby I am returned to serve in this present Parliament) propose, or give my consent, to alter the Government as it is settled in a Single Person and a Parliament.*' Sign that, or go home again to your countries.

Let honourable gentlemen therefore consider what they will do !—'About a Hundred signed directly, within an hour.' Guibon Goddard and all the Norfolk Members (except one, who was among the direct Hundred) went and 'had dinner together,' to talk the matter over ;—mostly thought it would be better to sign ; and did sign, all but some two. The number who have signed this first day, we hear, is a Hundred and-twenty, a Hundred-and-thirty, nay a Hundred-and-forty. Blank faces of honourable gentlemen begin to take meaning again,—some mild, some grim. Tomorrow being Fastday, there is an adjournment. The recusants are treated 'with all tenderness ;' most of them come in by degrees : 'Three-hundred before the month ends.'

Deep Republicans, Bradshaw, Haselrig, Thomas Scott and the like, would not come in ; still less would shallow noisy ones, as Major Wildman ;—went home to their countries again, their blank faces settling into permanent grim. My Lord Protector molested no man for his recusancy ; did indeed take that absence as a comparative favour from the parties. Harrison and other suspect persons are a little looked after : the Parliament resumes its function as if little had happened. With a singular acquiescence on the part of the Public, write our correspondents, Dutch, and other. The Public, which I have known rebel against crowned Kings for twitching the tippet of a Parliament, permits this Lord Protector to smite it on the cheek, and say, "Have a care, wilt thou!" Perhaps this Lord Protector is believed to mean better than the King did? There is a difference in the objects of men, as the Public understands;—a difference in the men too for rebelling against! At any rate, here is singular submission everywhere; and my Lord Protector getting ready a powerful Sea-Armament, neither his Parliament nor any other creature can yet guess for what.

Friday, 29th September 1654. His Highness, say the old Lumber-Books, went into Hyde Park; made a small picnic dinner under the trees, with Secretary Thurloe, attended by a few servants;—was, in fact, making a small pleasure excursion, having in mind to try a fine new team of horses, which the Earl or Duke of Oldenburg had lately sent him. Dinner done, his Highness himself determined to drive,—two in hand I think, with a postilion driving other two. The horses, beautiful animals, tasting of the whip, became unruly; galloped, would not be checked, but took to plunging; plunged the postilion down; plunged or shook his Highness down, 'dragging him by the foot for some time,' so that 'a pistol went off in his pocket,' to the amazement of men. Whereupon? Whereupon—his Highness got up again, little the worse; was let blood; and went about his affairs much as usual! Small anecdote, that figures, larger than life, in all the Books and Biographies. I have known men thrown from their horses on occasion, and less noise made about it, my erudite friend! But the essential point was, his Highness wore a pistol.—Yes, his Highness is prepared to defend himself; has men, and has also truculent-flunkeys, and devils and devil's-servants of various kinds, to defend himself against;—and wears pistols, and what other furniture outward and inward may be necessary for the object. Such of you as have an eye that way can take notice of it!—

Thursday, 16th November 1654. On the other hand, what a glimpse into the interior domesticities of the Protector Household have we in the following brief Note! Amid the darkness and buzzard dimness, one light-beam, clear, radiant, mournfully beautiful, like the gleam of a sudden star, disclosing for a moment many things to us! On Friday, Secretary Thurloe writes incidentally: 'My Lord Protector's Mother, of Ninety- 'four years old, died last night. A little before her death she 'gave my Lord her blessing, in these words: "The Lord cause 'His face to shine upon you; and comfort you in all your 'adversities; and enable you to do great things for the glory

'ot your Most High God, and to be a relief unto His People.
'My dear Son, I leave my heart with thee. A good night!"'
—and therewith sank into her long sleep. Even so. Words of
ours are but idle. Thou brave one, Mother of a Hero, farewell!—Ninety-four years old: the royalties of Whitehall, says
Ludlow very credibly, were of small moment to her: 'at the
'sound of a musket she would often be afraid her Son was shot;
'and could not be satisfied unless she saw him once a day at
'least.' She, old, weak, wearied one, she cannot help him with
his refractory Pedant Parliaments, with his Anabaptist plotters,
Royalist assassins, and world-wide confusions; but she bids him,
Be strong, be comforted in God. And so Good night! And
in the still Eternities and divine Silences—Well, *are* they not
divine?—

December 26th, 1654. The refractory Parliament and other
dim confusions still going on, we mark as a public event of some
significance, the sailing of his Highness's Sea-Armament. It has
long been getting ready on the Southern Coast; sea-forces, land-forces; sails from Portsmouth on Christmas morrow, as above
marked. None yet able to divine whither bound; not even the
Generals, Venables and Penn, till they reach a certain latitude.
Many are much interested to divine! Our Brussels Correspondent writes long since, 'The Lord Protector's Government
'makes England more formidable and considerable to all Nations
'than ever it has been in my days.'

Finding this Parliament was equal to nothing in the Spiritual
way but tormenting of poor Heretics, receiving Petitions for
a small advance towards coal and candle; and nothing in the
Temporal, but constitutional air-fabrics and vigilant checkings
and balancings,—under which operations such precious fruits
at home and abroad were ripening,—Oliver's esteem for this
Parliament gradually sank to a marked degree. Check, check,
—like maladroit ship-carpenters hammering, adzing, sawing at
the Ship of the State, instead of diligently caulking and paying
it; idly gauging and computing, nay, recklessly tearing up and
remodelling;—when the poor Ship could hardly keep the water
as yet, and the Pirates and Sea-Krakens were gathering round!
All which most dangerous, not to say half-frantic operations,
the Lord Protector discerning well, and swallowing in silence as
his hest was,—had for a good while kept his eye upon the
Almanac, with more and more impatience for the arrival of the
Third of February. That will be the first delivesance of the

THE PARLIAMENT DISSOLVED

poor labouring Commonwealth, when at the end of Five Mouths we send these Parliament philosophers home to their countries again. Five Months by the Instrument they have to sit; O fly, lazy Time; it is yet but Four Months and— — Somebody suggested, Is not the Soldier-month counted by Four Weeks? Eight-and-twenty days are a soldier's Month : they have, in a sense, already sat five months, these vigilant Honourable Gentlemen !

Oliver Protector, on Monday morning, 22d of January 1654-5, surprises the Constitutioning Parliament with a message to attend him in the Painted Chamber, and leave 'Settling of the Government' for a while. They have yet voted no Supplies ; nor meant to vote any. They thought themselves very safe till February 3d, at soonest. But my Lord Protector, from his high place, speaks, and dissolves.

So ends the First Protectorate Parliament ; suddenly, very unsuccessfully. A most poor hidebound Pedant Parliament ; which reckoned itself careful of the Liberties of England ; and was careful only of the Sheepskin Formulas of these ; very blind to the Realities of these ! Regardless of the facts and clamorous necessities of the Present, this Parliament considered that its one duty was to tie up the hands of the Lord Protector well ; to give him no supplies, no power ; to make him and keep him the bound vassal and errand-man of this and succeeding Parliaments. This once well done, they thought all was done :— Oliver thought far otherwise. Their painful new-modelling and rebuilding of the Instrument of Government, with an eye to this sublime object, was pointing towards completion, little now but the key-stones to be let in—when Oliver suddenly withdrew the centres ! Constitutional arch and ashlar-stones, scaffolding, workmen, mortar-troughs and scaffold-poles sink in swift confusion : and disappear, regretted or remembered by no person,—not by this Editor[1] for one.

By the arithmetical account of heads in England, the Lord Protector may surmise that he has lost his Enterprise. But by the real divine and human worth of thinking-souls in England, he still believes that he has it ; by this, and by a higher mission too ;—and " will take a little pleasure to lose his life " before he loses it ! He is not here altogether to count heads, or to count costs, this Lord Protector ; he is in the breach of battle ; placed

[1] i.e. Thomas Carlyle.

there, as he understands, by his Great Commander: whatsoever his difficulties be, he must fight them, cannot quit them; must fight there till he die. This is the law of his position, in the eye of God, and also of men. There is no return for him out of this Protectorship he has got into! Called to this post as I have been, placed in it as I am, "To quit it, is what I will be "willing to be rolled into my grave, and buried with infamy "before I will consent unto!"—

PART IX

THE MAJOR-GENERALS

1655—1656

CHRONOLOGICAL

THE Plots and perils to the Commonwealth which my Lord Protector spoke of to his honourable Members, were not an imagination, but a very tragic reality. Under the shadow of this Constitutioning Parliament strange things had been ripening: without some other eye than the Parliament's, Constitution and Commonwealth in general had been, by this time, in a bad way! A universal rising of Royalists combined with Anabaptists is in a real state of progress. Dim meetings there have been of Royalist Gentlemen, on nocturnal moors, in this quarter and in that, 'with cart-loads of arms,'—terrified at their own jingle, and rapidly dispersing again till the grand hour come. Anabaptist Levellers have had dim meetings, dim communications; will prefer Charles Stuart himself to the traitor Oliver, who has dared to attempt actual 'governing' of men. Charles Stuart has come down to Middleburg, on the Dutch coast, to be in readiness; 'Hyde is cock-sure.' A Protector left without supplies, obliged to cut his Parliament adrift, and front the matter alone; England, from end to end of it, ripe for an explosion; for a universal blazing-up of all the heterogeneous combustibilities it had; the Sacred Majesty waiting at Middleburg, and Hyde cock-sure!

Nevertheless it came all to nothing;—there being a Protector in it. The Protector, in defect of Parliaments, issued his own Ordinance, the best he could, for payment of old rates and taxes which, as the necessity was evident, and the sum fixed upon was low, rather lower than had been expected, the Country quietly complied with. Indispensable supply was obtained : and as for the Plots, the Protector had long had his eye on them, had long had his nooses round them ;—the Protector strangled them everywhere at the moment suitablest for him, and lodged the ringleaders of them in the Tower.

May 28th, 1655. Desborow, who commands the Regular Troops in that insurrectionary Southwest region, is, by Commission bearing date this day, appointed *Major-General* of the Militia-forces likewise, and of all manner of civic and military forces at the disposal of the Commonwealth in those parts. Major-General over six counties specified in this Document ; with power somewhat enlarged, and not easy to specify,—power in fact to look after the peace of the Commonwealth there, and do what the Council of State shall order him. He coerces Royalists ; questions, commits to custody suspected persons ; keeps down disturbance by such methods as, on the spot, he finds wisest. A scheme found to answer well. The beginning of a universal Scheme of MAJOR-GENERALS, which develops itself into full maturity in the autumn of this year ; the Lord Protector and his Council of State having well considered it in the interim, and found it the feasiblest ; if not *good*, yet best.

By this Scheme, which we may as well describe here as afterwards, All England is divided into Districts ; Ten Districts, a Major-General for each ; let him be a man most carefully chosen, a man of real wisdom, valour and veracity, a man fearing God and hating covetousness; for his powers are great. He looks after the Good of the Commonwealth, spiritual and temporal, as he finds wisest. Ejects, or aids in ejecting, scandalous ministers ; summons disaffected, suspected persons before him ; demands an account of them ; sends them to prison, failing an account that satisfies him ;—and there is no appeal except to the Protector in Council. His force is the Militia of his Counties ; horse and foot, levied and kept in readiness for the occasion ; especially troops of horse. Involving, of course, new expense ;—which we decide that the Plotting Royalists, who occasion it, shall pay. On all Royalist disaffected Persons the Major-General therefore, as his first duty, is to lay an *Income-tax of Ten per-cent*; let them pay it quietly, or it may be worse for them. They pay it very quietly. Strange as it may seem, the Country submits very quietly to this arrangement ;—the Major-Generals being men carefully chosen. "It is an arbitrary

Government!" murmur many. Yes; arbitrary, but beneficial. These are powers unknown to the English Constitution, I believe; but they are very necessary for the Puritan English Nation at this time. With men of real wisdom, who do fear God and hate covetousness, when you can find such men, you may to some purpose entrust considerable powers!

It is in this way that Oliver Protector coerces the unruly elements of England; says to them: "Peace, ye! With the aid "of Parliament and venerable Parchment, if so may be; without "it, if so may not be,—I, called hither by a very good Authority, "will hold you down. Quiet shall you, for your part, keep your-"selves; or be 'barbadoesed,' and worse. Mark it; not while I "live shall you have dominion, you nor the Master of you!"— Cock-matches, Horse-races and other loose assemblages are, for limited times, forbidden; over England generally, or in Districts where it may be thought somewhat is a-brewing. Without cock-fighting we can do; but not without Peace, and the absence of Charles Stuart and his Copartneries. It is a Government of some arbitrariness.

And yet singular, observes my learned friend, how popular it seems to grow. These considerable infringements of the constitutional fabric, prohibition of cockfights, amercings of Royalists, taxing without consent in Parliament, seem not to awaken the indignation of England; rather almost the gratitude and confidence of England. Next year, we have 'Letters of great 'appearances of the Country at the Assizes; and how the 'Gentlemen of the greatest quality served on Grand Juries; 'which is fit to be observed.'

June 3d, 1655. This day come sad news out of Piedmont; confirmation of bad rumours there had been, which deeply affects all pious English hearts, and the Protector's most of all. It appears the Duke of Savoy had, not long since, decided on having certain poor Protestant subjects of his converted at last to the Catholic Religion. Poor Protestant people, who dwell in the obscure Valleys 'of Lucerna, of Perosa and St. Martin,' among the feeders of the Po, in the Savoy Alps: they are thought to be descendants of the old Waldenses; a pious inoffensive people; dear to the hearts and imaginations of all Protestant men. These, it would appear, the Duke of Savoy, in the past year, undertook to himself to get converted; for which object he sent friars to preach among them. The friars could convert nobody; one of the friars, on the contrary, was found assassinated,—signal to the rest that they had better take themselves away. The Duke thereupon sent other missionaries: six regiments of Catholic soldiers; and an order to the People of the Valleys either to be converted straightway, or quit the country at once. They could not be converted all at once: neither could they quit the country well; the month was December; among the Alps; and it was their home for immemorial years! Six regiments, however, say they must; six Catholic regiments;—and three of them are Irish, made of the banished *Kursees* we knew long since; whose humour, on such an occasion, we can guess at! It is admitted they behaved 'with little ceremony'; it is not to be denied they behaved with much bluster and violence: ferocities, atrocities, to the conceivable amount, still stand in authentic black-on-white against them. The Protestants of the Valleys were violently driven out of house and home, not without slaughters and tortures by the road;—had to seek shelter in French Dauphiné or where they could; and, in mute or spoken supplication, appeal to all generous hearts of men. The saddest confirmation of the actual banishment, the actual violences done, arrives at Whitehall this day, 3d June 1655.

Pity is perennial: "Ye have *compassion* on one another,"—is it not notable, beautiful? In our days too, there are Polish Balls and such like: but the pity of the Lord Protector and Puritan England for these poor Protestants among the Alps is not to be measured by ours. The Lord Protector is melted into tears, and roused into sacred fire. This day the French Treaty, not unimportant to him, was to be signed: this day he refuses to sign it till the King and Cardinal undertake to assist him in getting right done in those poor Valleys. He sends the poor exiles 2,000*l*. from his own purse; appoints a Day of Humiliation and a general Collection over England for that object;—has, in short, decided that he will bring help to these poor men; that England and he will see them helped and righted. How Envoys were sent; how blind Milton wrote Letters to all Protestant States, calling on them for coöperation; how the French Cardinal was shy to meddle, and yet had to meddle, and compel the Duke of Savoy, much astonished at the business, to do justice and *not* what he liked with his own: all this, recorded in the unreadablest stagnant deluges of old Official Correspondence, is very certain, and ought to be fished therefrom and made more apparent.

In all which, as we can well believe, it was felt that the Lord Protector had been the Captain of England, and had truly expressed the heart and done the will of England;—in this, as

in some other things. Milton's Sonnet and Six Latin Letters
are still readable ; the Protector's Act otherwise remains mute
hitherto. Small damage to the Protector, if no other suffer
thereby! Let it stand here as a symbol to us of his Foreign
Policy in general ; which had this one object, testified in all
manner of negotiations and endeavours, noticed by us and
not noticed, To make England Queen of the Protestant world ;
her, if there were no worthier Queen. To unite the Protestant
world of struggling Light against the Papist world of potent
Darkness. To stand upon God's Gospel, as the actual intrinsic
Fact of this Practical Earth ; and defy all potency of Devil's
Gospels on the strength of that. Wherein, again, Puritan
England felt gradually that this Oliver *was* her Captain ; and
in heart could not but say, Long life to him ; as we do now.

LETTER LIII

BESIDES the great Sea-Armament that sailed from Portsmouth
last December, and went Westward, with sealed orders, which
men begin to guess were for the Spanish West Indies,—the
Protector had another Fleet fitted out under Blake, already
famous as a Sea-General ; which has been in the Mediterranean,
during these late months ; exacting reparation for damages, old
or recent, done to the English Nation or to individuals of it,
by the Duke of Florence or by others ; keeping an eye on Spain
too, and its Plate Fleets, apparently with still ulterior objects.

The Duke of Florence has handsomely done justice ; the Dey
of Tunis was not so well advised, and has repented of it. There
are Letters, dated March last, though they do not come till
June : 'Letters that General Blake demanding at Tunis reparation for the losses of the English from Turkish Pirates, the
'Dey answered him with scorn, and bade him behold his Castles.'
Blake did behold them ; 'sailed into the Harbour within musket-
'shot of them ; and though the shore was planted with great
'guns, he set upon the Turkish ships, fired nine of them,' and
brought the Dey to reason, we apprehend.

To General Blake, '*at Sea.*'

Whitehall, 13th June 1655.

SIR,
I have received yours of the 25th of March, which gives
account of the late Transactions between yourself and the

Governors of Tunis, concerning the losses which the English have sustained by the piracies of that place; and 'of' the success it pleased God to give in the attempt you made upon their shipping, after their positive refusal to give you satisfaction upon your just demands. And as we have great cause to acknowledge the good hand of God towards us in this Action, who, in all the circumstances thereof, as they have been represented by you, was pleased to appear very signally with you; so I think myself obliged to take notice of your courage and good conduct therein; and do esteem that you have done therein a very considerable service to this Commonwealth.

I hope you have received the former Despatches which were sent unto you by the way of Legorne, for your coming into Cadiz Bay with the Fleet; as also those which were sent by a Ketch immediately from hence; whereby you had also notice of three-months provisions then preparing to be sent,—which have since been sent away, under convoy of the Frigates the *Centurion* and *Dragon*, and 'I' hope they are safely arrived with you, they sailing from hence about the 28th of April.

With this come further Instructions concerning your disposing of the Fleet for the future; whereunto we do refer you. Besides which, we, having taken into consideration the present Design we have in the West Indies, have judged it necessary, That not only the King of Spain's Fleets coming from thence be intercepted (which as well your former Instructions as those now sent unto you require and authorise you to do), but that we endeavour also, as much as in us lies, to hinder him from sending any relief or assistance thither. You are therefore, during your abode with the Fleet in those seas, to inform yourself, by the best means you can, concerning the going of the King of Spain's Fleet for the West Indies; and shall, according to such information as you can gain, use your best endeavours to intercept at sea, and fight with and take them, or otherwise to fire and sink them; as also any other of his ships which you shall understand to be bound for the West Indies with provisions of War, for the aid and assistance of his subjects there; carrying yourself towards other of his ships and people as you are directed by your general Instructions.

'I rest,
'Your loving friend,
'OLIVER P.'

The Sea-Armament *was* for the West Indies, then : good news of it were welcome !

Here is a short Letter of Blake's to the Protector, dated just the day before ; in cipher ;—which the reader, having never perhaps seen another Letter of Blake's, will not be displeased with. Unimportant ; but bringing the old Seas, with their Puritan Sea-kings, with their 'Plate Fleets,' and vanished populations and traffics, bodily before us for moments.

"George, 12th June 1655.

"MAY IT PLEASE YOUR HIGHNESS.—The secret Instructions
"sent by your Highness, referring me to a former Instruction,
"touching the Silver Fleet of Spain coming from America, I
"have received ; and shall carefully observe the same. We
"had information at Cadiz that the Fleet was expected about a
"month or five weeks hence. We are now off Cape Mary's ;
"intending to spread with our Fleet what we can, and to range
"this sea, according to the wind and the information we can
"get ; plying likewise over towards Cape Sprat, it being their
"most likely and usual course. They of Cadiz are very
"distrustful of us ; and there being four Galeons designed for
"the Mediterranean, and six for New Spain, it is doubtful how
"they may be employed.

" We shall use our best endeavours to put the Instructions in
"execution, as God shall afford an opportunity ; desiring your
"Highness to rest assured of our diligence, and of the integrity
"of,—your most humble and faithful servant,

"ROBERT BLAKE."

June 13th is Wednesday. On the morrow is universal Fast-Day, Humiliation and Prayer, and public Collection of Money for the Protestants of Piedmont. A day of much pious emotion in England ; and of liberal contribution, which continued on the following days. 'Clerks come to every man's house,' says a disaffected witness ; 'come with their papers, and you are forced to contribute.' The exact amount realised I never could very authentically learn. The Dutch Ambassador says 100,000*l.* The disaffected witness says, 'London City itself gave half-a-million,'—or seemed as it would give. 'The Ministers played their part to the full,'—the Ministers and the People and their Ruler. No French Treaty signed or signable till this thing be managed. At length the French were obliged to manage it ; 9th September of this same year the thing was got managed ;

—and by and by was got improved and still better managed, the Protector continuing all his days to watch over it, and over other similar things as they occurred, and to insist on seeing justice done respecting them.

LETTER LIV

WE fear there is little chance of the Plate Fleet this year; bad rumours come from the West Indies too, of our grand Armament and Expedition thither. The Puritan Sea-king meanwhile keeps the waters; watches the coasts of Spain;—which, however, are growing formidable at present.

The 'Person bound for Lisbon' is Mr. Meadows, one of Secretary Thurloe's Under-secretaries; concerning whom and whose business there will be farther speech by and by. Of the 'Commissioners of the Admiralty' we name only Colonel Montague of Hinchinbrook, who is getting very deep in these matters, and may himself be Admiral one day.

To the General of the Fleet, 'General Blake, at Sea.'

'Whitehall,' 30th July 1655.

SIR,

We have received yours of the 4th, as also that of the 6th instant, both at once; the latter signifying the great preparations which are making against you.

Some intelligence of that nature is also come to us from another hand. Which hath occasioned us to send away this Despatch unto you, immediately upon the receipt of yours, to let you know That we do not judge it safe for you, whilst things are in this condition, to send away any part of the Fleet, as you were directed by our Instructions of the 13th of June; and therefore, notwithstanding those Orders, you are to keep the whole Fleet with you, until you have executed the Secret Instructions, or find the opportunity is over for the doing thereof.

We think it likewise requisite that you keep with you the two Frigates which conveyed the victuals to you; as also the *Nantwich*, which was sent to you with a Person bound for Lisbon with our instructions to that King. And for the defects of the Fleet, the Commissioners of the Admiralty will take care thereof; and be you confident that nothing shall be omitted which can be done here for your supply and encouragement.

I beseech the Lord to be present with you. I rest,

Your very loving friend,

OLIVER P.

Copied 'in Secretary Thurloe's hand'; who has added the following Note: 'With this Letter was sent the intelligence of 'the twenty ships coming across the Straits, and of the thirty- 'one ships and eight fire-ships—[*word lost*]—in Cadiz;'— dangerous ships and fire-ships, which belong all now to the vanished generations: and have sailed, one knows not whence, one knows not whither!

COMPLIMENT

PRECISELY in those same summer days there has come a brilliant Swedish gentleman, as Extraordinary Ambassador to this Country from the King of Swedeland. A hot, high-tempered, clear-shining man; something fierce, metallic, in the lustre of him. Whose negotiations, festivities, impatiences, and sudden heats of temper, occupy our friend Bulstrode almost exclusively for a twelvemonth. We will say only, He has come hither to negotiate a still stricter league of amity between the two Countries; in which welcome enterprise the Lord Protector seems rather to complicate him by endeavouring to include the Dutch in it, the Prussians and Danes in it,—to make it in fact a general league, or basis for a League, of Protestants against the Power of Rome, and Antichristian Babylon at large; which in these days, under certain Austrian Kaisers, Spanish Kings, Italian Popes, whose names it may be interesting not to remember, is waxing very formidable. It was an object the Protector never ceased endeavouring after; though in this, as in other instances, with only partial, never with entire success.

Observe however, as all Old London observes, on the night of Saturday, July 28th, 1655, the far-shining Procession by torchlight. Procession 'from Tower-wharf to the late Sir Abraham Williams's in Westminster;' this brilliant Swedish Gentleman with numerous gilt coaches and innumerable outriders and onlookers, making his advent then and thus; Whitlocke, Montague, Strickland (for we love to be particular) officially escorting him. Observe next how he was nobly entertained

three days in that Williams House, at the Protector's charges;
and on the third day had his audience of the Protector; in a
style of dignity worth noting by Bulstrode. Sir Oliver Fleming;
'galleries full of ladies,' 'Lifeguards in their gray frock-coats
with velvet welts;' lanes of gentlemen, seas of general public:
conceive it all; truly dignified, decorous; scene 'the Banqueting
House of Whitehall, hung with arras:' and how at the upper
end of the room the Lord Protector was seen standing 'on a
footpace and carpet, with a chair of state behind him;' and
how the Ambassador saluted thrice as he advanced, thrice lifting
his noble hat and feathers, as the Protector thrice lifted his; and
then—Bulstrode shall give the rest:

'After a little pause, the Ambassador put off his hat, and
'began to speak, and then put it on again: and whensoever, in
'his speech, he named the King his master, or Sweden, or the
'Protector, or England, he moved his hat: especially if he
'mentioned anything of God, or the good of Christendom, he
'put off his hat very low; and the Protector still answered him
'in the like postures of civility. The Ambassador spake in the
'Swedish language; and after he had done, being but short, his
'Secretary Berkman did interpret it in Latin to this effect'— —
Conceivable, without repetition, to ingenious readers. A stately,
far-shining speech, done into Latin; 'being but short.'

And now 'after his Interpreter had done, the Protector stood
'still a pretty while; and, putting off his hat to the Ambassador,
'with a carriage full of gravity and state, he answered him in
'English to this effect:'

My Lord Ambassador, I have great reason to acknowledge,
with thankfulness, the respects and good affection of the King
your master towards this Commonwealth, and towards myself in
particular. Whereof I shall always retain a very grateful
memory; and shall be ready upon all occasions to manifest the
high sense and value I have of his Majesty's friendship and
alliance.

My Lord, you are welcome into England; and during your
abode here, you shall find all due regard and respect to be given
to your person, and to the business about which you come. I
am very willing to enter into a "nearer and more strict alliance
and friendship with the King of Swedeland," as that which, in
my judgment, will tend much to the honour and commodity of
both Nations, and to the general advantage of the Protestant
Interest. I shall nominate some Persons to meet and treat with

your Lordship, upon such particulars as you shall communicate to them.

After which, Letters were presented, *etceteras* were transacted, and then with a carriage full of gravity and state, they all withdrew to their ulterior employments, and the scene vanishes.

LETTER LV

It is too sad a truth, the Expedition to the West Indies has failed! Sea-General Penn, Land-General Venables have themselves come home, one after the other, with the disgraceful news; and are lodged in the Tower, a fortnight ago, for quitting their post without orders. Of all which we shall have some word to say anon. But take first these glimpses into other matters, foreign and domestic, on sea and land,—as the Oblivions have chanced to leave them visible for us. 'Cascais Bay' is at the mouth of the Tagus; General Blake seems still king of the waters in those parts.

'*To General Blake, at Sea.*'
Whitehall, 13th September 1655.

Sir,
We have received yours from Cascais Bay, of the 30th of August; and were very sensible of the wants of the Fleet as they were represented by your last before; and had given directions for three-months provisions,—which were all prepared, and sent from Portsmouth, some time since, under the convoy of the *Bristol* Frigate. But the Commissioners of the Admiralty have had Letters yesterday that they were forced back, by contrary winds, into Plymouth, and are there now attending for the first slack of wind, to go to sea again. And the Commissioners of the Admiralty are instructed to quicken them by an express; although it is become very doubtful whether those provisions can 'now' come in time for supplying of your wants.

And for what concerns the fighting of the Fleet of Spain, whereof your said Letter makes mention, we judge it of great consequence, and much for the service of the Commonwealth, that this Fleet were fought; as well in order to the executing your former Instructions, as for the preservation of our ships and interest in the West Indies: and our meaning was, by our former Order, and still is, That the Fleet which shall come for the guarding of the Plate Fleet, as we conceive this doth, should be attempted. But in respect we have not certain knowledge of the strength of the Spanish Fleet, nor of the condition of your Fleet, which may alter every day,—we think it reasonable, at this distance, not to oblige you by any positive order to engage; but must, as we do hereby, leave it to you, who are upon the place, and know the state of things, to handle the rein as you shall find your opportunity and the ability of the Fleet to be:—as we also do for your coming home, either for want of provisions or in respect of the season of the year, at such time as you shall judge it to be for the safety of the Fleet. And we trust the Lord will guide and be with you in the management of this thing.

Your very loving friend,
OLIVER P.

'P.S.' In case your return should be so soon as that you should not make use of the Provisions now sent you, or but little thereof, we desire you to cause them to be preserved; they may be applied to other uses.

The Major-Generals are now all on foot, openly since the middle of August last; and an Official Declaration published on the subject. Ten military Major-Generals, Ten or finally Twelve, with militia-forces, horse and foot, at their beck; coercing Royalist Revolt, and other Anarchy; 'decimating' it, that is, levying Ten per-cent upon the Income of it; summoning it, cross-questioning it,—peremptorily signifying to it that it will not be allowed here, that it had better cease in this Country. They have to deal with Quakers also, with Anabaptists, Scandalous Ministers, and other forms of Anarchy. The powers of these men are great: much need that they be just men and wise, men fearing God and hating covetousness;—all turns on that! they will be supportable, nay welcome and beneficial, if so. Insupportable enough, if not so:—as indeed what official person, or man under any form, except the form of a slave well-collared and driven by whips, is or ought to be supportable 'if *not* so'? We subjoin a list of their names, as historically worthy, known or unknown to the reader, here.[1]

---

[1] *General Desborow* has the Counties: Gloucester, Wilts, Dorset, Somerset, Devon, Cornwall.
Colonel Kelsey: Kent and Surrey.
Colonel Goffe: Sussex, Hants, Berks.

LETTERS LVI ETC.

JAMAICA

WE said already the grand Sea-Armament, which sailed from Portsmouth at Christmas 1654, had proved unsuccessful. It went westward; opened its Sealed Instructions at a certain latitude; found that they were instructions to attack Hispaniola, to attack the Spanish Power in the West Indies: it did attack Hispaniola, and lamentably failed; attacked the Spanish Power in the West Indies, and has hitherto realised almost nothing,—a mere waste Island of Jamaica, to all appearance little worth the keeping at such cost. It is hitherto the unsuccessfulest enterprise Oliver Cromwell ever had concern with. Desborow fitted it out at Portsmouth, while the Lord Protector was busy with his First refractory Pedant Parliament; there are faults imputed to Desborow: but the grand fault the Lord Protector imputes to himself, That he chose, or sanctioned the choice of, Generals improper to command it. Sea-General Penn, Land-General Venables, they were unfortunate, they were incompetent; fell into disagreements, into distempers of the bowels; had critical Civil Commissioners with them, too, who did not mend the matter. Venables lay 'six weeks in bed,' very ill of sad West-India maladies; for the rest, a covetous lazy dog, who cared nothing for the business, but wanted to be home at his Irish Government again. Penn is Father of Penn the Pennsylvanian Quaker; a man somewhat quick of temper, 'like to break his heart' when affairs went wrong; unfit to right them again. As we said, the two Generals came voluntarily home, in the end

Major-General Skippon: London.
Colonel Barkstead (Governor of the Tower): Middlesex and Westminster.
Lord Deputy Fleetwood (who never returns to Ireland): Oxford, Bucks, Herts; Cambridge, Essex, Norfolk, Suffolk,—for these last four he can appoint a substitute (*Colonel Haynes*)
General Whalley: Lincoln, Notts, Derby, Warwick, Leicester.
Major Butler: Northampton, Bedford, Rutland, Huntingdon.
Colonel Berry (Richard Baxter's friend, once a Clerk in the Ironworks): Hereford, Salop, North Wales.
General (Sea-General) *Dawkins*: Monmouth and South Wales.
Colonel Worseley: Cheshire, Lancashire Staffordshire,.
The Lord Lambert: York, Durham, Cumberland, Westmoreland, Northumberland,—can appoint substitutes (*Colonel Robert Lilburn, Colonel Charles Howard*).

of last August, leaving the wreck of their forces in Jamaica; and were straightway lodged in the Tower for quitting their post.

A great Armament of Thirty, nay of Sixty Ships; of Four-thousand soldiers, two regiments of whom were veterans, the rest a somewhat sad miscellany of broken Royalists, unruly Levellers, and the like, who would volunteer,—whom Venables augmented at Barbadoes, with a still more unruly set, to Nine-thousand: this great Armament the Lord Protector has strenuously hurled, as a sudden fiery bolt, into the dark Domdaniel of Spanish Iniquity in the far West; and it has exploded there, almost without effect. The Armament saw Hispaniola, and Hispaniola with fear and wonder saw it, on the 14th of April 1655: but the Armament, a sad miscellany of distempered unruly persons, durst not land 'where Drake had landed,' and at once take the Town and Island; the Armament hovered hither and thither; and at last agreed to land some sixty miles off; marched therefrom through thick-tangled woods, under tropical heats, till it was nearly dead with mere marching; was then set upon by ambuscadoes; fought miserably ill, the unruly persons of it, or would not fight at all; fled back to its ships a mass of miserable disorganic ruin; 'and dying there at the rate of two-hundred a day,' made for Jamaica.

Jamaica, a poor unpopulous Island, was quickly taken, as rich Hispaniola might have been, and the Spaniards were driven away: but to men in biliary humour it seemed hardly worth the taking or the keeping. 'Immense droves of wild cattle, cows and horses, run about Jamaica;' dusky Spaniards dwell in *hatos*, in unswept shealings; '80,000 hogs are killed every 'year for the sake of their lard, which is sold under the name of '*hog's-butter* at Carthagena:' but what can we do with all that! The poor Armament continuing to die as if by murrain, and all things looking worse and worse to poor biliary Generals, Sea-General Penn set sail for home, whom Land-General Venables swiftly followed; leaving 'Vice-Admiral Goodson,' 'Major-General Fortescue,' or almost whosoever liked, to manage in their absence, and their ruined moribund forces to die as they could;—and are now lodged in the Tower, as they deserved to be. The Lord Protector, and virtually England with him, had hoped to see the dark empire of bloody Antichristian Spain a little shaken in the West; some reparation got for its inhuman massacrings and long-continued tyrannies, —massacrings, exterminations of us, 'at St. Kitts in 1629, at

Tortuga in 1637, at Santa Cruz in 1650;' so, in the name of England, had this Lord Protector hoped; and he has now to take his disappointment.

The ulterior history of these Western Affairs, of this new Jamaica under Cromwell, lies far dislocated, drowned deep, in the Slumber-Lakes of *Thurloe* and Company; in a most dark, stupefied, and altogether dismal condition. A history, indeed, which, as you painfully fish it up and by degrees reawaken it to life, is in itself sufficiently dismal. Not much to be intermeddled with here. The English left in Jamaica, the English successively sent thither, prosper as ill as need be; still die, soldiers and settlers of them, at a frightful rate per day; languish, for most part, astonished in their strange new sultry element; and cannot be brought to front with right manhood the deadly inextricable jungle of tropical confusions, outer and inner, in which they find themselves. Brave Governors, Fortescue, Sedgwick, Brayne, one after the other, die rapidly, of the climate and of broken heart; their life-fire all spent there, in that dark chaos, and as yet no result visible. It is painful to read what misbehaviour there is, what difficulties there are.

Almost the one steady light-point in the business is the Protector's own spirit of determination. If England have now a 'West-India Interest,' and Jamaica be an Island worth something, it is to this Protector mainly that we owe it. Here too, as in former darkness, 'Hope shines in him, like a pillar of fire, when it has gone out in all the others.' Having put his hand to this work, he will not for any discouragement turn back. Jamaica shall yet be a colony; Spain and its dark Domdaniel shall yet be smitten to the heart,—the enemies of God and His Gospel, by the soldiers and servants of God. It must, and it shall. We have failed in the West, but not wholly; in the West and in the East, by sea and by land, as occasion shall be ministered, we will try it again and again.

'On the 28th of November 1655, the Treaty with France is proclaimed by heralds and trumpets,' say the Old Newspapers. Alliance with France, and *Declaration* against Spain,—within the tropics where there is never Peace, and without the tropics where Peace yet is, there shall now be War with Spain. Penn and Venables, cross questioned till no light farther could be had from them, are dismissed; in Penn's stead, Montague is made Admiral. We will maintain Jamaica, send reinforcement after reinforcement to it; we will try yet for the Spanish Plate Fleets; we will hurl yet bolt after bolt into the dark Domdaniel, and have no Peace with Spain. In all which, as I understand, the spirit of England, mindful of Armadas, and wedded once for all to blessed Gospel Light and Progress, and not to accursed Papal Jesuitry and Stagnancy, coöperates well with this Protector of the Commonwealth of England. Land-fighting too we shall by and by come upon; in all ways, a resolute prosecution of hostilities against Spain.

The Lady Mary Cromwell to Henry Cromwell, Major-General of the Army in Ireland.

"'Hampton-Court,' 7th December 1655.

"DEAR BROTHER,—I cannot be any longer without begging "an excuse for my so long silence. You cannot but hear of "my Sister's illness; which indeed has been the only cause of "it. You might justly take it ill otherwise, and think there "were want of that affection I owe unto you.

"Indeed, dear Brother, it was a great deal of trouble to me "to think I should give you any occasion to think amiss of "me: for I can truly say it, you are very dear to me; and "it is a great trouble to me to think of the distance we are "from one another; and would be more, if I did not think "you are doing the Lord's service;—and truly that ought to "satisfy us, for while we are here, we cannot expect but that "we must be separated. Dear Brother, the Lord direct you in "His ways, and keep your heart close unto Himself. And "I am sure, therein you will have true comfort; and that will "last when all this world shall pass away.

"I cannot but give you some item of One that is with you, "who, 'it' is so much feared by your friends that love you, "is some dishonour to you and my dear Sister, if you have not "a great care. For it is reported here, that she rules much "in your Family: and truly it is feared that she is a dis-"countenancer of the Godly People. Therefore, dear Brother, "take it not ill, that I give you an item of her: for, truly, if "I did not love both you and your honour, I would not give "you notice of her. Therefore I hope you will not take it ill, "that I have dealt thus plainly with you. I suppose you know "who it is I mean, therefore I desire to be excused for not "naming her. I desire not to be seen in it, and therefore desire "you that you would not take the least notice of my writing "to you about it: because I was desired not to speak of it;—

"nor should I, but that I know you will not take it amiss from "your poor Sister who loves you.

"Dear Brother, I take leave to rest—your sister and servant,
"MARY CROMWELL.

"Her Highness[1] desires to have her love to you and my "Sister; and my Sister Franke her respects to you both.'

'My Sister Franke' and the Lady Mary, these are my 'two little wenches,' grown now to be women; with dress-caps, fresh blossoming hearts, musical glib tongues,—not uninteresting to men! Anthony Ashley Cooper, I am told, is looking towards this Lady Mary; now turned of Eighteen, and a desirable match for any youth of ambition,—but not attainable I doubt by Ashley.

New Sea-Armaments, and ever new, are fitted out against the Spaniards and their Papist Domdaniel. Penn being dismissed, Councillor Colonel Montague, already in the Admiralty, was made Sea-General last January in his stead; and now Blake and he have their flags flying somewhere off Cadiz Bay it would appear.

LETTER LVI

A SMALL vestige, it is presumable, of this Protector's solicitude for the encouragement of Learning and Learned Men. Which is a feature of his character very conceivable to us, and well-demonstrated otherwise by testimony of facts and persons. Such we shall presume the purport of this small Civic Message to be:

For Our worthy Friends the Committee of the City of London for Gresham College: These

Whitehall, 9th May 1656.

GENTLEMEN,
We understanding that you have appointed an election this afternoon of a Geometry Professor in Gresham College,— We desire you to suspend the same for some time, till We shall

---

[1] 'our Mother.'

have an opportunity to speak with some of you in order to that business.

I rest,
Your loving friend,
OLIVER P.

Historical Neal says zealously, 'If there was a man in England 'who excelled in any faculty or science, the Protector would find 'him out, and reward him according to his merit.' The renowned Dr. Cudworth in Cambridge, I have likewise expressly read, had commission to mark among the ingenuous youth of that University such as he deemed apt for Public Employment, and to make the Protector aware of them. Which high and indeed sacred function we find the Doctor, as occasion offers, intent to discharge. The choice this Protector made of men,— 'in nothing was his good understanding better discovered;' 'which gave a general satisfaction to the Public,' say the Histories. As we can very well believe! He who is himself a true man, has a chance to know the truth of men when he sees them; he who is not, has none: and as for the poor Public and its satisfactions,—alas, is not the kind of 'man' you set upon it the liveliest symbol of its, and your, veracity and victory and blessedness, or unveracity and misery and cursedness; the general summation, and practical outcome, of all else whatsoever in the Public, and in you?

LETTER LVII

IT was last Spring Assizes, as we saw, that the 'great appearances of country gentlemen and persons of the highest quality' took place; leading to the inference generally that this Protectorate Government is found worth acknowledging by England. Certainly a somewhat successful Government hitherto; in spite of difficulties great and many. It carries eternal Gospel in the one hand, temporal drawn Sword in the other. Actually it has compressed the turbulent humours of this Country, and encouraged the better tendencies thereof, hitherto; it has set its foot resolutely on the neck of English Anarchy, and points with its armed hand to noble onward and upward paths. All which, England, thankful at lowest for peace and order, by degrees recognises; with acquiescence, not without some slow satisfactory feeling. England is in peace at home; stands as the Queen of

Protestantism abroad; defies Spain and Antichrist, protects poor Piedmont Protestants and servants of Christ; has taken, all men admit, a nobler attitude than it ever had before.

Nor has the task been easy hitherto; nor is it like to be. No holiday work, governing such an England as this of Oliver Protector's; with strong Papistry abroad, and a Hydra of Anarchies at home! The domestic Hydra is not slain; cannot, by the nature of it, be *slain*; can only be scotched and mowed down, head after head, as it successively protrudes itself;—till, by the aid of Time, it slowly *die*. As yet, on any hint of foreign encouragement it revives again, requires to be scotched and mowed down again. His exiled Majesty Charles Stuart has got a new lever in hand, by means of this War with Spain.

Seven years ago his exiled Majesty's 'Embassy to Spain,' embassy managed by Chancellor Hyde and another, proved rather a hungry affair; and ended, I think, in little,—except the murder of poor Ascham, the then Parliament's Envoy at Madrid; whom, like Dutch Dorislaus, as 'an accursed regicide or abettor of regicides,' certain cut-throat servants of the said hungry Embassy broke-in upon, one afternoon, and slew. For which violent deed no full satisfaction could be got from Spain,—the murderers having taken 'sanctuary,' as was pleaded. With that rather sorry result, and no other noticeable, Chancellor Hyde's Embassy took itself away again; Spain ordering it to go. But now, this fierce Protestant Protector breathing nothing but war, Spain finds that the English domestic Hydra, if well operated upon by Charles Stuart, might be a useful thing; and grants Charles Stuart some encouragements for that. His poor Majesty is coming to the seashore again; is to have 'Seven-thousand Spaniards' to invade England,—if the domestic Hydra will stir with effect. The domestic Hydra, I think, had better lie quiet for a while! This Letter to Henry Cromwell is to bid him too, for his part, be awake in Ireland to these things.

For the Hydra is not dead; and its heads are legion. Major Wildman, for example, sits safe in Chepstow: but Sexby, the Anabaptist Colonel, whom we could not take on that occasion, is still busy; has been 'trying to seduce the Fleet,' trying to do this and that; is now fairly gone to Spain, to treat with Antichrist himself for the purpose of bringing-in a Reign of Christ, —the truly desperate Anabaptist Colonel! It is a Hydra like few. Spiritual and Practical: Muggletonians, mad Quakers riding into Bristol, Fifth-Monarchists, Hungry Flunkeys: ever scheming, plotting with or without hope, to 'seduce the Protector's Guard,' 'to blow up the Protector in his bed-room,' and do "other little fiddling things," as the Protector calls them,—which one cannot waste time in specifying! Only the slow course of nature can kill that Hydra: till a Colonel Sexby *die*, how can you keep him quiet?—

But what doubtless gives new vitality to plotting, in these weeks, is the fact that a General Election to Parliament is going on. There is to be a new Parliament;—in which may lie who knows what contentions. The Protector lost it last time, by the arithmetical account of heads; will he gain it this time? Account of heads is not exactly the Protector's basis; but he hopes he may now gain it even so. At all events, this wide foreign and domestic Spanish War cannot be carried on without supplies; he will first try it so,—then otherwise if not so.

'To Henry Cromwell, Major-General of the Army in Ireland.'

'Whitehall,' 26th August 1656.

SON HARRY,

We are informed, from several hands, that the old Enemy are forming designs to invade Ireland, as well as other parts of the Commonwealth; and that he and Spain have very great correspondence with some chief men in that Nation, for raising a sudden rebellion there.

Therefore we judge it very necessary that you take all possible care to put the Forces into such a condition as may answer anything that may fall out in this kind. And to that end, that you contract the Garrisons in Ireland, as many as may be; and get a considerable marching Army into the field, in two or three bodies, to be left in the most proper and advantageous places for service, as occasion shall require. Taking also, in all other things, your best care you can to break and prevent the designs and combinations of the Enemy;—and a very particular regard is to be had to the North, where, without question, busy and discontented persons are working towards new disturbances. I do not doubt but you will communicate this thing to Colonel Cowper, to the end he may be more watchful and diligent in looking to this danger. I rest, your loving father.

OLIVER CROMWELL.

LETTER LVIII

THE Portugal has done justice; reluctantly aware at last that jesuitries would not serve him. The Spaniards cower close within their harbours; patient of every insult; no ship will venture out, and no Plate Fleet will come in: and as for attempting Cadiz or Gibraltar,' the Sea-Generals, after mature survey, decide that without other force it cannot prudently be done. This is what Montague, with his clear eyes, has had to report to Secretary Thurloe on the latter enterprise: "I perceive "much desire that Gibraltar should be taken. My thoughts as "to that are, in short, these: That the likeliest way to get it is, "By landing on the sand, and quickly cutting it off between sea "and sea, or so securing our men there as that they may hinder "the intercourse of the Town with the Main; frigates lying "near, too, to assist them;—and it is well known that Spain "never victualleth any place for one month. This will want "Four or Five thousand men, well formed and officered.—This "is my own only thought which I submit, at present."

Whereupon the Lord Protector sends the following Orders; one other Sea Letter of his which we happen to have left. Mainly of Thurloe's composition, I perceive; but worth preserving on various accounts.

To Generals Blake and Montague, at Sea.

Whitehall, 28th August 1656.

GENTLEMEN,

We have received your Letters of the 19th of June brought to us by Captain Lloyd, who arrived here the 11th of July.

By those Letters, and by what Captain Lloyd related by word of mouth,—which is not contradicted by yours of the 1st and 3d of July, 'since' received by the Squadron of Ten Ships (which are all safely arrived in the Channel), nor by any other intelligence received by other hands,—we find That the Spaniard keeps 'within' his Ports, and doth not yet prepare any considerable Fleet to come to Sea; and that, in the condition you and they were then in, they were not to be attempted in their Harbours. And as for any design upon Gibraltar, we see by General Montague's Letter to the Secretary, that nothing therein was feasible without a good Body of Landsmen.—So that, upon the whole, there remains nothing to be done, in those seas for the present, which should require the whole Fleet now with you to remain there. Besides that the Great Ships cannot, without great danger, be kept out, the winter-time, upon that coast.

Upon these grounds we are of opinion, with you, That a good Squadron of Frigates will, in this season, be sufficient to answer any opportunity of service which may present itself. And therefore we have resolved That about the number of Twenty Ships, such as you shall judge proper and fit for that purpose, be kept in those seas ; and the rest be sent home, with the first opportunity of wind and weather :—and desire that you will give order therein accordingly. And in respect it will be necessary that we advise with one of you at least, upon this whole affair ; and it being also very inconvenient that you should be *both* from the head of the Fleet which remains behind, the management thereof being of so great concernment to the Commonwealth,— we would have General Blake to stay with the Fleet, and General Montague to come with the Squadron which comes home.

For the service which these Ships 'that stay' should be applied to,—we need say nothing therein ; but refer you to the former Instructions. That which we believe the Enemy will most intend will be the carrying-on his Trade to the West Indies ; which if he can effectually do, he will not much care for what else is done upon him. And our intelligence is, That at this time he is fitting out some Ships of war, and others, to send from Cadiz into those parts ;—the certainty whereof we suppose you may know. And therefore that which is most to be endeavoured is, The spoiling him in that Trade, by intercepting his Fleets either going to or coming from those parts,—and as much as may be To destroy his correspondencies thither. It will be of great use also to prevent the coming of any Materials for Shipping, or other contraband goods into Cadiz or any of his Ports : which you can have an eye to ; and, as much as may be, prejudice his correspondency with Flanders.

Besides these things, and what other damage you may have an opportunity to do the Enemy, we, in our keeping the said Fleet in those Seas, had an eye to the Preservation of the Trade of this Commonwealth in the Straits and to Portugal : which we suppose could not be driven on without a very good countenance and strength,—in respect the Enemy would otherwise be able with a few ships to obstruct this Trade wholly, and to take all that passed either to or from the one place or the other. But our intention is not To reckon up every particular wherein this

Fleet may be useful, but only To let you know our general scope; and to leave the management and improvement thereof to the prudence and direction of him who is to abide upon the place. Whom we beseech the Lord to be present with; and to guide him to that which may be for the good of this Commonwealth, and according to His own will.

These have been our thoughts, and the considerations we have had upon this Affair. If anything else doth occur to you different from what is here expressed, either as to the number of Ships to remain in those seas, or the way and manner of weakening the Enemy and managing the War against him,—we desire to understand your sense and advice hereupon, with all possible speed; sooner, if it may be, than the return of the aforesaid Squadron. And in the mean time we are not willing to tie you up positively to the number of Twenty Ships to remain on that Coast; but give you a latitude to keep a lesser or greater number there, for answering the ends aforesaid, and 'so' as you shall find the occasion to require, which possibly may be very much varied since the last we had from you.—For what concerns the Provisions of victuals and other things which the Fleet will stand in need of, the Commissioners of the Admiralty have direction to write at large to you. Unto whose Letters we refer you;—and desire you and the whole Fleet to rest assured that nothing shall be omitted to be done, here, for your supply and encouragement upon all occasions.

Your loving friend,
'OLIVER P.'

SPEECH IV

BUT the new Parliament is now about assembling; wherein we shall see what conclusions will be tried! A momentous question for his Highness and the Council of State; who have been, with interest enough, perusing and pondering the List of Names returned. On the whole, a hopeful Parliament, as Thurloe had expected: Official persons, these and others known as friends to this Government, are copiously elected: the great body of the Parliament seems to consist of men well-affected to his Highness, and even loyal to him; who, witnessing the course he follows, wish him heartily God-speed thereon. Certain others there are, and in considerable number, of stiff Republican ways, or given to turbulence in general,—a Haselrig, a Thomas Scott, an Ashley Cooper: these, as a mass of leaven which might leaven the whole lump, and produce one knows not what in the way of fermentation, are clearly very dangerous. But for these also his Highness and the Council of State, in the present anomalous condition of the Nation, have silently provided an expedient. Which we hope may be of service. On the whole, we trust this Parliament may prove a better than the last.

At all events, on Wednesday 17th September 1656, Parliament, Protector, all in due state, do assemble at the Abbey Church; and, with reverence and credence, hear Doctor Owen, Vice-Chancellor of Oxford, very pertinently preach to them from these old words of Isaiah,—old and yet always new and true: *What shall one then answer to the Messengers of the Nation? That the Lord hath founded Zion, and the Poor of His People shall trust in it.* After which, all having removed, still in due state, to the Painted Chamber, and there adjusted themselves, the Protector, rising in his elevated place and taking off his hat, now speaks.

GENTLEMEN,

When I came hither, I did think that a duty was incumbent upon me a little to pity myself; because, this being a very extraordinary occasion, I thought I had very many things to say unto you, 'and was somewhat burdened and straitened thereby.' But truly now, seeing *you* in such a condition as you are,[1] I think I must turn off 'my pity' in this, as I hope I shall in everything else;—and consider *you* as certainly not being able long to bear that condition and heat that you are now in.—'So far as possible, on this large subject, let us be brief; not studying the Art of Rhetoricians.' Rhetoricians, whom I do not pretend to 'much concern with;' neither with them, nor with what they use to deal in: Words!

Truly *our* business is to speak Things! The Dispensations of God that are upon us do require it; and that subject upon which we shall make our discourse is somewhat of very great interest and concernment, both for the glory of God, and with reference to His Interest in the world. I mean His peculiar, His most peculiar Interest, 'His Church, the Communion of the faithful Followers of Christ;'—and that will not leave any of us

[1] Place crowded. weather hot.

to exclude His general Interest, which is the concernment of the
Living People, 'not as Christians but as human creatures,' within
these three Nations, and all the Dependencies thereupon. I
have told you I should speak to *things*; things that concern
these Interests: The Glory of God, and His Peculiar Interest
in the world,—which 'latter' is more extensive, I say more
extensive, than the People of all these three Nations with the
appurtenances, or the countries and places, belonging unto
them.[1]

The first thing, therefore, that I shall speak to is *That* that
is the first lesson of Nature: Being and Preservation. As
to that of Being, I do think I do not ill style it the *first*
consideration which Nature teacheth the Sons of Adam :—
and then I think we shall enter into a field large enough when
we come to consider that of Well-being. But if Being itself be
not first well laid, I think the other will hardly follow !

Now in order to this, to the Being and Subsistence of these
Nations with all their Dependencies: The conservation of that,
'namely of our National Being,' is first to be viewed with
respect to those who seek to undo it, and so make it *not to be*;
and then very naturally we shall come to the consideration of
what will make it *be*, of what will *keep* its being and subsistence.

Truly, your great Enemy is the Spaniard. He is a natural
enemy. He is naturally so ; he is naturally so throughout,—
by reason of that emnity that is in him against whatsoever is of
God. 'Whatsoever is of God' which is in *you*, or which may
be in you ; contrary to that which *his* blindness and darkness,
led on by superstition, and the implicitness of his faith in sub-
mitting to the See of Rome, actuate him unto ! With this
King and State, I say, you are at present in hostility. We put
you into this hostility. You will give us leave to tell you how.
For we are ready to excuse 'this and' most of our actions,—and
to justify them too, as well as to excuse them,—upon the ground
of Necessity. 'And' the ground of Necessity, for justifying of
men's actions, is above all considerations of instituted Law ; and
if this or any other State should go about,—as I know they

[1] 'more extensive:' *more important* would have better suited what
went before; yet 'extensive' is in all likelihood the word, for his
Highness is here branching out into a second idea, which he goes on
to blend with the primary one, of 'the concernment of the general
mass of the People.'

never will,—to make Laws against Events, against what *may* happen, 'then' I think it is obvious to any man, they will be making Laws against Providence; events, and issues of things, being from God alone, to whom all issues belong.

The Spaniard is your enemy; and your enemy, as I tell you, naturally, by that antipathy which is in him,— 'and also' providentially,[1] and this in divers respects. You could not get an honest or honourable Peace from him : it was sought by the Long Parliament ; it was not attained. It could not be attained with honour and honesty. I say, it could not be attained with honour and honesty. And truly when I say that, 'I do but say,' He is naturally throughout *an enemy*; an enmity is put into him by God. "I will put an enmity between thy seed and her seed ;"—which goes but for little among statesmen, but is more considerable than all things ! And he that considers not such natural enmity, the *providential* enmity, as well as the *accidental*, I think he is not well acquainted with Scripture and the things of God. And the Spaniard is not only our enemy accidentally, but he is providentially so ; God having in His wisdom disposed it so to be, when we made a breach with the Spanish Nation 'long ago.'

No sooner did this Nation form what is called (unworthily) the Reformed Religion after the death of Queen Mary, by the Queen Elizabeth of famous memory,—we need not be ashamed to call her so !—but the Spaniard's design became, By all unworthy, unnatural means, to destroy that Person, and to seek the ruin and destruction of these Kingdoms. For me to instance in particulars upon that account, were to trouble you at a very unseasonable time : there is a Declaration extant, which very fully hath in it the origin of the Spaniard venting himself upon this Nation ; and a series of it[2] from those very beginnings to this present day. But his enmity was partly upon that general account which all are agreed 'about.' The French, all the Protestants in Germany, all have agreed, That his design was the empire of the whole Christian World, if not more ;—and upon *that* ground he looks, 'and hath looked,' at this Nation as his greatest obstacle. And as to what his attempts have been for that end,—I refer you to that Declaration, and to the observations of men who read History. It would not be difficult to

---

[1] Means, not 'luckily' as now, but simply 'by special ordering of Providence.'

[2] Of 'his ventings,' namely.

call to mind the several Assassinations designed upon that Lady, that great Queen : the attempts upon Ireland, the Spaniards' invading of it ; their designs of the same nature upon *this* Nation,—public designs, private designs, all manner of designs, to accomplish this great and general end. Truly King James made a Peace ; but whether this Nation, and the interest of all Protestant Christians, suffered not more by that Peace, than ever by Spain's hostility, I refer to your consideration !

Thus a State which you can neither have peace with nor reason from,—that is the State with which you have enmity at this time, and against which you are engaged. And give me leave to say this unto you, because it is truth, and most men know it, That the Long Parliament did endeavour, but could not obtain satisfaction 'from the Spaniard' all the time they sat : for their Messenger was murdered : and when they asked satisfaction for the blood of your poor people unjustly shed in the West Indies, and for the wrongs done elsewhere ; when they asked liberty of conscience for your people who traded thither,—satisfaction in none of these things would be given, but was denied. I say, they denied satisfaction either for your Messenger that was murdered, or for the blood that was shed, or the damages that were done in the West Indies. No satisfaction at all ; nor any reason offered *why* there should not be liberty 'of conscience' given to your people that traded thither. Whose trade was very considerable there, and drew many of your people thither ; and begot an apprehension in *us* 'as to their treatment there,—whether in *you* or no, let God judge between you and Himself. I judge not : but all of us know that the people who went thither to manage the trade there were imprisoned. We desired 'but' such a liberty as 'that they might keep their Bibles in their pockets, to exercise their liberty of religion for themselves, and not be under restraint. But there is not liberty of conscience to be had 'from the Spaniard ;' neither is there satisfaction for injuries, nor for blood. When these two things were desired, the Ambassador told us, " It was to ask his Master's two eyes ;" to ask both his eyes, asking these things of him !—

Now if this be so, why truly then here is some little foundation laid to justify the War that has been entered-upon with the Spaniard ! And not only so : but the plain truth of it is, Make any peace with any State that is Popish and subjected to the determination of Rome and 'of' the Pope himself,—you are bound, and they are loose. It is the pleasure of the Pope at any time to tell you, That though the man is murdered [*Poor Ascham, for example!*], yet his murderer has got into the sanctuary! And equally true is it, and hath been found by common and constant experience, That Peace is but to be kept so long as the Pope saith Amen to it. [*What is to be done with such a set of people?*]—We have not 'now' to do with any Popish State except France: and it is certain that *they* do not think themselves under such a tie to the Pope; but think themselves at liberty to perform honesties with nations in agreement with them, and protest against the obligation of such a thing as that,—'of breaking your word at the Pope's bidding.' *They* are able to give us an explicit answer to anything reasonably demanded of them: and there is no other Popish State we can speak of, save this only, but will break their promise or keep it as they please upon these grounds,—being under the lash of the Pope, to be by him determined, 'and made to decide."

In the time when Philip Second was married to Queen Mary, and since that time, through Spanish power and instigation, Twenty-thousand Protestants were murdered in Ireland. We thought, being denied just things,—we thought it our duty to get that by the sword which was not to be had otherwise! And this hath been the spirit of Englishmen; and if so, certainly it is, and ought to be, the spirit of men that have *higher* spirits! With that State you are engaged. And it is a great and powerful State:—though I may say also, that with all other Christian States you are at peace. All these 'your other' engagements were upon you before this Government was undertaken: War with France, Denmark,—nay, upon the matter, War, 'or as good as War,' with Spain 'itself.' I could instance how it was said 'in the Long-Parliament time,' "We will have a war in the Indies, though we fight them not at home." I say, we are at peace with all other Nations, and have only a war with Spain. I shall say somewhat 'farther' to you, which will let you see our clearness 'as' to that, by and by.

Having thus 'said, we are' engaged with Spain,—'that is the root of the matter;' that is the party that brings *all* your enemies before you. It doth: for so it is now, that Spain hath espoused that Interest which you have all along hitherto been conflicting with,—Charles Stuart's Interest.

All the honest interests; yea, all interests of the Protestants, in Germany, Denmark, Helvetia and the Cantons, and all the interests in Christendom, are the same as yours. If you succeed, if you succeed well and act well, and be convinced what is God's

SPAIN THE ENEMY

Interest, and prosecute it, you will find that you act for a very great many who are God's own. Therefore I say that your danger is from the Common Enemy abroad; who is the head of the Papal Interest, the head of the Antichristian Interest,—who is so described in Scripture, so forespoken of, and so fully, under that charactcral name 'of Antichrist' given him by the Apostle in the *Epistle to the Thessalonians*, and likewise so expressed in the *Revelations*; which are sure and plain things! Except you will deny the truth of the Scriptures, you must needs see that that State is so described in Scripture to be Papal and Antichristian. I say, with this Enemy, and upon this account, you have the quarrel,—with the Spaniard.

And truly he hath an interest in your bowels;[1] he hath so. The Papists in England,—they have been accounted, ever since I was born, Spaniolised. There is not a man among us can hold up his face against that. They never regarded France; they never regarded any other Papist State where a 'hostile Interest was, 'but Spain only.' Spain was their patron. Their patron all along, in England, in Ireland and Scotland: no man can doubt of it. Therefore I must needs say, this 'Spanish' Interest is also, in regard to your home-affairs, a great source of your danger. It is, and it evidently is; and will be more so,—upon that account that I told you of: He hath espoused Charles Stuart! With whom he is fully in agreement; for whom he hath raised Seven or Eight Thousand men, and has them now quartered at Bruges; to which number Don John of Austria has promised that, as soon as the campaign is ended, which it is conceived will be in about five or six weeks, he shall have Four or Five Thousand added. And the Duke of Neuburg, who is a Popish prince, hath promised good assistance according to his power; and other Popish States the like. In this condition you are with that State 'of Spain:' and in this condition through unavoidable necessity; because your enemy was *naturally* an enemy, and is providentially too become so.

I would not have you be discouraged if you think the State is exceeding poor. Give me leave to tell you, we have managed the Treasury not unthriftily, nor to private uses; but for the use of the Nation and Government;—and shall give you this short account. When the Long Parliament sat,[2] this

[1] Old phrase for 'the interior of your own country.'
[2] Polite for 'ceased to sit.'

Nation owed 700,000*l*. We examined it ; it was brought unto that,—in that short Meeting 'of the Little Parliament,' within half a year after the Government came into our hands. I believe there was *more* rather than less. They 'the Long-Parliament people' had 120,000*l*. a-month ; they had the King's, Queen's, Prince's, Bishops' Lands ; all Delinquents' Estates, and the Dean-and-Chapter Lands ; which was a very rich Treasure. As soon as ever we came to the Government, we abated 30,000*l*. the first half-year, and 60,000*l*. after. We had no benefits of those Estates, at all considerable [*Only the merest fractions of them remaining now unsold*] ; I do not think, the fiftieth part of what they had :—and give me leave to tell you, *You are not so much in debt as we found you*. We know it hath been maliciously dispersed, as if we had set the Nation into 2,500,000*l*. of debt : but I tell you, you are not so much in debt, by some thousands, —I think I may say, by some hundreds of thousands ! This is true that I tell you. We have honestly,—it may be not so wisely as some others would have done,—but with honest and plain hearts, laboured and endeavoured the disposal of Treasure to Public Uses ; and laboured to pull off the common charge 60,000*l*. a-month, as you see. And if we had continued that charge that was left upon the Nation, perhaps we could have had as much money 'in hand,' as now we are in debt.— These things being thus, I did think it my duty to give you this account,—though it be wearisome even to yourselves and to me.

I have but one thing more to say. I know it is troublesome : —But I did read a Psalm yesterday ; which truly may not un-become both me to tell you of, and you to observe. It is the Eighty-fifth Psalm ;[1] it is very instructive and significant : and though I do but a little touch upon it, I desire your perusal at pleasure.

It begins : " Lord, Thou hast been very favourable to Thy
" Land ; Thou hast brought back the captivity of Jacob. Thou
" hast forgiven the iniquity of Thy People ; Thou hast covered
" all their sin. Thou hast taken away all the fierceness of Thy
" wrath : Thou hast turned Thyself from the fierceness of
" Thine anger. Turn us, O God of our salvation, and cause

---

[1] Historical : Tuesday, 16th Sept. 1656 ; Oliver Protector reading the Eighty-fifth Psalm in Whitehall. We too might read it ; but as his Highness recites it all here except one short verse, it is not so necessary.

"Thine anger toward us to cease. Wilt Thou be angry with
"us forever; wilt Thou draw out Thine anger to all genera-
"tions? Wilt Thou not revive us again, that Thy People may
"rejoice in Thee?" Then he calls upon God as "the God of
"his salvation,"[1] and then saith he: "I will hear what God
"the Lord will speak: for He will speak peace unto His People,
"and to His Saints; but let them not turn again to folly.
"Surely His salvation is nigh them that fear Him;" Oh—
"that glory may dwell in our land! Mercy and Truth are
"met together; Righteousness and Peace have kissed each
"other. Truth shall spring out of the Earth, and Righteous-
"ness shall look down from Heaven. Yea the Lord shall give
"that which is good, and our Land shall yield her increase.
"Righteousness shall go before Him, and shall set us in the way
"of His steps."

Truly I wish that this Psalm, as it is written in the Book, might be better written in our hearts. That we might say as David, "*Thou* hast done this," and "Thou hast done that;" "Thou hast pardoned our sins; Thou hast taken away our ini-"quities!" Whither can we go to a better God? For "He hath done it." It is to Him any Nation may come in their extremity, for the taking away of His wrath. How did He do it? "By pardoning their sins, by taking away their iniquities!" If we can but cry unto Him, He will "turn and take away *our* sins."—Then let us listen to Him. Then let us consult, and meet in Parliament; and ask Him counsel, and hear what He saith, "for He will speak peace unto His people." If you be the People of God, He will speak *peace*,—and we will not turn again to folly.

The latest of the Commentators expresses himself in reference to this Speech in the following singular way:

'No Royal Speech like this was ever delivered elsewhere in the
'world! It is,—with all its prudence, and it is very prudent,
'sagacious, courteous, right royal in spirit,—perhaps the most
'artless transparent piece of Public Speaking this Editor has ever
'studied. Rude, massive, genuine; like a block of unbeaten
'gold. A Speech not so fit for Drury Lane, as for Valhalla,
'and the Sanhedrim of the Gods. The man himself, and the
'England he presided over, there and then, are to a singular

---

[1] *Verse* 7, 'Show us Thy mercy, O Lord, and grant us Thy salvation.'

'degree visible in it; open to our eyes, to our sympathies.
'He who would see Oliver, will find more of him here than in
'most of the history-books yet written about him.

Speech being ended, the Honourable Members 'went to the
House,' says Bulstrode; and in the Lobby, with considerable
crowding I think, 'received, from the Chancery Clerk, Certificates in this form,'—for instance:

'COUNTY OF BUCKS. *These are to certify that*' Sir Bulstrode
Whitlocke '*is returned by Indenture one of the Knights to serve in
'this present Parliament for the said County, and approved by his
'Highness's Council.* NATH. TAYLER, *Clerk of the Commonwealth
'in Chancery.*'

Mr. Tayler has received Four-hundred 'Indentures' from
Honourable Gentlemen; but he does not give out Four-hundred
'Certificates,' he only gives Three-hundred and odd. Near One-
hundred Honourable Gentlemen can get no Certificate from Mr.
Tayler,—none provided for *you*;—and without Certificate there
is no admittance. Soldiers stand ranked at the door: no man
enters without his Certificate! Astonishing to see. Haselrig,
Scott and the stiff Republicans, Ashley Cooper and the turbulent
persons, who might have leavened this Parliament into strange
fermentation, cannot, it appears, get in! No admittance here:
saw Honourable Gentlemen ever the like?—

The most flagrant violation of the Privileges of Parliament
that was ever known! exclaim they. A sore blow to Privilege
indeed. With which the Honourable House, shorn of certain
limbs in this rude way, knows not well what to do. The Clerk
of the Commonwealth, being summoned, answers what he can;
Nathaniel Fiennes, for the Council of State, answers what he
can: the Honourable House, actually intent on Settling the
Nation, has to reflect that in real truth this will be a great
furtherance thereto; that matters do stand in an anomalous
posture at present: that the Nation should and must be settled.
The Honourable House, with an effort, swallows this injury;
directs the petitioning Excluded Members, 'to apply to the
Council.' The Excluded Members, or some one Excluded
Member, redacts an indignant Protest, with all the names
appended; prints it, privately circulates it, 'in boxes sent by
carriers, a thousand copies in a box·—and there it rests; his
Highness saying nothing to it; the Honourable House and the

Nation saying nothing. In this Parliament, different from the last, we trace a real desire for Settlement.

As the power of the Major-Generals, 'in about two months hence,' or three months hence, was, on hint of his Highness himself, to the joy of Constitutional England, withdrawn, we may here close *Part Ninth*. Note first, however, as contemporary with this event, the glorious news we have from Blake and Montague at sea; who, in good hour, have at last got hold of a Spanish Fleet, and in a tragic manner burnt it, and taken endless silver therein. News of the fact comes in the beginning of October: in the beginning of November comes, as it were, the fact itself,— some Eight-and-thirty wagonloads of real silver: triumphantly jingling up from Portsmouth, across London pavements to the Tower, to be coined into current English money there. The Antichrist King of Spain has lost Lima by an earthquake, and infinite silver there also. Heaven's vengeance seems awakening. 'Never,' say the old Newspapers 'never was there a more terrible 'visible Hand of God in judgment upon any People, since the 'time of Sodom and Gomorrah! Great is the Lord; marvellous 'are His doings, and to be had in reverence of all the Nations.' England holds universal Thanksgiving Day; sees Eight-and-thirty wagonloads of silver, sees hope of Settlement, sees Major-Generals abolished; and piously blesses Heaven.

PART X

SECOND PROTECTORATE PARLIAMENT

1657—1658

LETTER LIX

CARDINAL MAZARIN, the governing Minister of France in those days, is full of compliance for the Lord Protector; whom, both for the sake of France and for the Cardinal's sake, it is very requisite to keep in good humour. On France's score, there is Treaty with France, and War with its enemy Spain; on the Cardinal's are obscure Court-intrigues, Queen-mothers, and one knows not what: in brief, the subtle Cardinal has found, after trial of the opposite course too, that friendship, or even at times obedient-servantship to Cromwell, will be essentially advantageous to him.

Some obscure quarrel has fallen-out between Charles Stuart and the Duke of York his Brother. Quarrel complicated with open politics, with Spanish War and Royalist Revolt, on Oliver's side; with secret Queen-mothers, and back-stairs diplomacies, on the Cardinal's:—of which there flit, in the dreariest manner, this and the other enigmatic vestige in the night-realm of *Thurloe*; and which is partly the subject of this present Letter. A Letter unique in two respects. It is the only one we have of Oliver Cromwell, the English Puritan King, to Giulio Mazarini, the Sicilian-French Cardinal, and King of Shreds and Patches; who are a very singular pair of Correspondents brought together by the Destinies! It is also the one glimpse we have from Oliver himself of the subterranean Spy-world, in which by a hard necessity so many of his thoughts had to dwell. Oliver, we find,

cannot quite grant Toleration to the Catholics ; but he is well
satisfied with this 'our weightiest affair,'—not without weight
to *me* at least, who sit expecting Royalist Insurrections backed
by Spanish Invasions, and have Assassins plotting for my life
at present 'on the word of a Christian King!'—

Concerning the 'affair' itself, and the personages engaged in
it, let us be content that they should continue spectral for us,
and dwell in the subterranean Night-realm which belongs to
them. The 'Person' employed from England, if anybody
should be curious about him, is one Colonel Bamfield, once a
flaming Presbyterian Royalist, who smuggled the Duke of York
out of this Country in woman's clothes ; and now lives as an
Oliverian Spy, very busy making mischief for the Duke of York.
'Berkley' is the Sir John Berkley who rode with Charles First
to the Isle of Wight long since ; the Duke of York's Tutor
at present. Lockhart is Oliver's Ambassador in France. Let
us conceive, never so faintly, that their 'affair' is to maintain
in the Duke of York some Anti-Spanish notion ; notion of
his having a separate English interest, independent of his
Brother's, perhaps superior to it ; wild notion, of one or the
other sort, which will keep the quarrel wide :—as accordingly
we find it did for many months, whatever notion it was. We
can then read with intelligence sufficient for us.

'*To his Eminency Cardinal Mazarin.*'

'Whitehall,' 26th December 1656.

The obligations, and many instances of affection, which
I have received from your Eminency, do engage 'me' to
make returns suitable to your merits. But although I have this
set home upon my spirit, I may not (shall I tell you, I cannot ?) at this juncture of time, and as the face of my affairs
now stands, answer to your call for Toleration.

I say, I cannot, as to a public Declaration of my sense in that
point ; although I believe that under my Government your
Eminency, in the behalf of Catholics, has less reason for complaint as to rigour upon men's consciences than under the Parliament For I have of some, and those very many, had compassion ; making a difference. Truly I have (and I may speak
it with cheerfulness in the presence of God, who is a witness
within me to the truth of what I affirm) made a difference ;
and, as Jude speaks, "plucked many out of the fire,"—the raging
fire of persecution, which did tyrannise over their consciences,

and encroached by an arbitrariness of power upon their estates. And herein it is my purpose, as soon as I can remove impediments, and some weights that press me down, to make a farther progress, and discharge my promise to your Eminency in relation to that.

And now I shall come to return your Eminency thanks for your judicious choice of that Person to whom you have entrusted our weightiest Affair: an Affair wherein your Eminency is concerned, though not in an equal degree and measure with myself. I must confess that I had some doubts of its success, till Providence cleared them to me by the effects. I was, truly, and to speak ingenuously, not without doubtings; and shall not be ashamed to give your Eminency the grounds I had for much doubting. I did fear that Berkley would not have been able to go through and carry on that work; and that either the Duke would have cooled in his suit,[1] or condescended to his Brother. I doubted also that those Instructions which I sent over with 290 were not clear enough as to expressions; some affairs here denying me leisure at that time to be so particular as, 'in regard' to some circumstances, I would. If I am not mistaken in his 'the Duke's' character, as I received it from your Eminency, that fire which is kindled between them will not ask bellows to blow it, and keep it burning. But what I think farther necessary in this matter I will send 'to' your Eminency by Lockhart.

And now I shall boast to your Eminency my security upon a well-builded confidence in the Lord: for I distrust not but if this breach 'be' widened a little more, and this difference fomented, with a little caution in respect of the persons to be added to it,—I distrust not but that Party, which is already forsaken of God as to an outward dispensation of mercies, and noisome to their countrymen, will grow lower in the opinion of all the world.

If I have troubled your Eminency too long in this, you may impute it to the resentment of joy which I have for the issue of this Affair; and 'I' will conclude with giving you assurance that I will never be backward in demonstrating, as becomes your brother and confederate, that I am,

Your servant,
OLIVER P.

[1] His suit, I understand, was for leave 'to continue in France; an Anti-Spanish notion.

SPEECH V

SINDERCOMB

THE Spanish Invasion and Royalist Insurrection once more came to no effect : on mature judgment of the case, it seemed necessary to have Oliver Protector assassinated first ; and that, as usual, could not be got done. Colonel Sexby, the frantic Anabaptist, he and others have been very busy ; 'riding among his Highness's escort' in Hyde Park and elsewhere, with fleet horses, formidable weapons, with 'gate-hinges ready filed through,' if the deed could have been done ; but it never could. Sexby went over to Flanders again, for fresh consultations ; left the assassination-affair in other hands, with 1,600*l.* of ready money, 'on the faith of a Christian King.' Quartermaster Sindercomb takes Sexby's place in this great enterprise ; finds, he too, that there is nothing but failure in it.

Miles Sindercomb, now a cashiered Quartermaster living about Town, was once a zealous Deptford lad, who enlisted to fight for Liberty, at the beginning of these Wars. He fought strongly on the side of Liberty, being an earnest fierce young fellow ;— then gradually got astray into Levelling courses, and wandered ever deeper there, till daylight forsook him, and it became quite dark. He was one of the desperate misguided Corporals, or Quartermasters, doomed to be shot at Burford, seven years ago : but he escaped overnight, and was not shot there ; took service in Scotland ; got again to be Quartermaster ; was in the Overton Plot, for seizing Monk and marching into England, lately : whereupon Monk cashiered him : and he came to Town ; lodged himself here, in a sulky threadbare manner,—in Alsatia or elsewhere. A gloomy man and Ex-Quartermaster ; has become one of Sexby's people, 'on the faith of a Christian King ;' nothing now left of him but the fierceness, groping some path for itself in the utter *dark*. Henry Toope, one of his Highness's Lifeguard, gives us, or will give us, an inkling of Sindercomb ; and we know something of his courses and inventions, which are many. He rode in Hyde Park, among his Highness's escort, with Sexby ; but the deed could not then be done. Leave me the 1,600*l.*, said he ; and I will find a way to do it. Sexby left it him, and went abroad.

Inventive Sindercomb then took a House in Hammersmith ; Garden-House, I think, 'which had a banqueting-room looking into the road ;' road very narrow at that part ;—road from Whitehall to Hampton Court on Saturday afternoons. Inventive Sindercomb here set about providing blunderbusses of the due explosive force,—ancient 'infernal-machines,' in fact,— with these he will blow his Highness's Coach and Highness's self into small pieces, if it please Heaven. It did not please Heaven,—probably not Henry Toope of his Highness's Lifeguard. This first scheme proved a failure.

Inventive Sindercomb, to justify his 1,600*l.*, had to try something. He decided to fire Whitehall by night, and have a stroke at his Highness in the tumult. He has 'a hundred swift horses, two in a stable, up and down :'—set a hundred stout ruffians on the back of these, in the nocturnal fire ; and try. Thursday, 8th January 1656-7 ; that is to be the Night. On the dusk of Thursday, January 8th, he with old-trooper Cecil, his second in the business, attends Public Worship in Whitehall Chapel ; is seen loitering there afterwards, ' near the Lord Lambert's seat.' Nothing more is seen of him : but about half-past eleven at night, the sentinel on guard catches a smell of fire ;—finds holed wainscots, picked locks ; a basket of the most virulent wildfire, 'fit almost to burn through stones,'—with lit match slowly creeping towards it, computed to reach it in some half-hour hence, about the stroke of midnight !—His Highness is summoned, the Council is summoned ;—alas, Toope of the Lifeguard is examined, and Sindercomb's lodging is known. Just when the wildfire should have blazed, two Guardsmen wait upon Sindercomb ; seize him, not without hard defence on his part, 'wherein his nose was nearly cut off ; bring him to his Highness. Toope testifies ; Cecil peaches :—inventive Sindercomb has failed for the *last* time. To the Tower with him, to a jury of his country with him !—The emotion in the Parliament and in the Public, next morning, was great. It had been proposed to ring an alarm at the moment of discovery, and summon the Trainbands ; but his Highness would not hear of it.

This Parliament, really intent on settling the Nation, could not want for emotions in regard to such a matter ! Parliament adjourns for a week, till the roots of the Plot are investigated somewhat. Parliament, on reassembling, appoints a day of Thanksgiving for the Nation ; Friday come four weeks, which is February 20th that shall be the general Thanksgiving Day : and in the mean time we decide to go over in a body, and congratulate his Highness. A mark of great respect to him.

Parliament accordingly goes over in a body, with mellifluous Widdrington, whom they have chosen for Speaker, at their head, to congratulate his Highness. It is Friday, 23d January 1656-7; about Eleven in the morning; scene, Banqueting-house, Whitehall. Mellifluous Widdrington's congratulation, not very prolix, exists in abstract, but we suppress it. Here is his Highness's Reply;—rather satisfactory to the reader. We have only to regret that in passing from the Court up to the Banqueting-house, 'part of an ancient wooden staircase,' or balustrade of a staircase, 'long exposed to the weather, gave way in the crowding;' and some honourable Gentlemen had falls, though happily nobody was seriously hurt.

MR. SPEAKER,
I confess with much respect, that you have put this trouble on yourselves upon this occasion :—but I perceive there be two things that fill me full of sense. One is, The mercy on a poor unworthy creature; the second is, This great and, as I said, unexpected kindness of Parliament, in manifesting such a sense thereof as this is which you have now expressed. I speak not this with compliment! That which detracts from the thing, in some sense, is the inconsiderableness and unworthiness of the person that hath been the object and subject of this deliverance, to wit, myself. I confess ingenuously to you, I do lie under the daily sense of my unworthiness and unprofitableness, as I have expressed to you : and if there be, as I most readily acknowledge there is, a mercy in it to me, I wish I may never reckon it on any other account than this, That the life that is lengthened, may be spent and improved to His honour who hath vouchsafed the mercy, and to the service of you, and those you represent.

I do not know, nor did I think it would be very seasonable for me, to say much to you upon this occasion; being a thing that ariseth from yourselves. Yet, methinks, the kindness you bear should kindle a little desire in me; even at this present, to make a short return. And, as you have been disposed hither by the Providence of God, to congratulate my mercy; so give me leave, in a very word or two, to congratulate with you.

Congratulations are ever conversant about good, bestowed upon men, or possessed by them. Truly, I shall in a word or two congratulate you with good *you* are in possession of, and in some respect, I also with you. God hath bestowed upon you, and you are in possession of it,—Three Nations, and all that appertains to them. Which in either a geographical, or topical consideration, are Nations. In which also there are places of honour and consideration, not inferior to any in the known world,—without vanity it may be spoken. Truly God hath not made so much soil, furnished with so many blessings, in vain! But it is a goodly sight, if a man behold it *uno intuitu*. And therefore this is a possession of yours, worthy of congratulation.

This is furnished,—give me leave to say, for I believe it is true,—with the best People in the world, possessing so much soil. A People in civil rights,—in respect of their rights and privileges,—very ancient and honourable. And *in* this People, in the midst of this People, 'you have, what is still more precious,' a *People* (I know every one will hear 'and acknowledge' it) that are to God "as the apple of His eye,"—and He says so of them, be they many, or be they few! But they are many. A People of the blessing of God; a People under His safety and protection. A People calling upon the Name of the Lord which the Heathen do not. A People knowing God; and a People (according to the ordinary expressions) fearing God. And you have of this no parallel; no, not in all the world! You have in the midst of you glorious things.

Glorious things: for you have Laws and statutes, and ordinances, which, though not all of them so conformable as were to be wished to the Law of God, yet, on all hands, pretend not to be long rested-in further than *as* they are comformable to the just and righteous Laws of God.

And you have a Magistracy; which, in outward profession, in pretence, in endeavour, doth desire to put life into these Laws. And I am confident that among *you* will rest the true desire to promote every desire in others, and every endeavour, that hath tended or shall tend to the putting of these Laws in execution.

I do 'also' for this congratulate you: You have a Gospel Ministry among you. That have you! Such an one as,—without vanity I shall speak it; or without caring at all for any favour or respect from *them*, save what I have upon an account above flattery, or good words,—such an one as hath excelled itself; and, I am persuaded,—to speak with confidence before the Lord,—is the most growing blessing (one of the most growing blessings) on the face of this Nation.

ON DIVINE MERCY TO NATION

You have a good Eye 'to watch over you,'—and in that I will share with your good favours. A good God; a God that hath watched over you and us. A God that hath visited these Nations with a stretched-out arm; and borne His witness against the unrighteousness and ungodliness of men, against those that 'would' have abused such Nations,—such mercies throughout, as I have reckoned up unto you! A God that hath not only withstood such to the face; but a God that hath abundantly blessed you with the evidence of His goodness and presence. And He "hath done things wonderful amongst us," "by terrible things in righteousness." He hath visited us by "wonderful things!" In mercy and compassion hath He given us this day of freedom, and liberty to speak this, one to another; and to speak of His mercies, as He hath been pleased to put into our hearts. [*Where now are the Star-Chambers, High Commissions, Council-Chambers; pitiless oppressors of God's Gospel in this land? The Hangmen with their whips and red-hot branding-irons, with their Three blood-sprinkled Pillories in Old Palaceyard, and Four clean Surplices at Allhallowtide,—where are they? Vanished. Much has vanished; fled from us like the Phantasms of a Nightmare Dream!*]

Truly, this word in conclusion. If these things be so, give me leave to remember you but one word; which I offered to you with great love and affection the first day of meeting with you, this Parliament. It pleased God to put into my heart then to mention a Scripture to you, which would be a good conclusion of my Speech now at this time to you. It was, That we being met to seek the good of so great an Interest, as I have mentioned, and the glory of that God who is both yours and mine, how could we better do it than by thinking of such words as these, "His salvation is nigh them that fear Him," "that glory may dwell in our land!" I would not comment upon it. I hope I fear Him;—and let us more fear Him! If this 'present' mercy at all doth concern you, as I see it doth,—let me, and I hope you will with me, labour more to fear Him! Then we have done, 'that includes all;' seeing such a blessing as His salvation "is nigh them that fear Him,"—seeing we are all of us representatives of all the good of all these lands, 'to endeavour with our whole strength' "that glory may dwell in our land."

'Yes,' if it be so, "Mercy and Truth shall meet together, Righteousness and Peace shall kiss each other." We shall know, you, and I as the father of this family, how to dispose our mercies to God's glory; and how to dispose our severity. How to distinguish between obedient and rebellious children ;—and not to do as Eli did, who told his sons " he did not *hear* well of them," when perhaps he *saw* ill *by* them. And we know the severity of that. And therefore let me say,—though I will not descant upon the words,—that Mercy must be joined with Truth : Truth, in that respect, that we think it our duty to exercise a just severity, as well as to apply kindness and mercy. And, truly, Righteousness and Mercy must kiss each other. If we will have Peace without a worm in it, lay we foundations of Justice and Righteousness. And if it shall please God so to move you, as that you marry this redoubtable Couple together, Mercy and Truth, Righteousness and Peace,—you will, if I may be free to say so, be blessed whether you will or no ! And that you and I may, for the time the Lord shall continue us together, set our hearts upon this, shall be my daily prayer. And I heartily and humbly acknowledge my thankfulness to you.

On Monday 9th February, Sindercomb was tried by a jury in the Upper Bench ; and doomed to suffer as a traitor and assassin, on the Saturday following. The night before Saturday his poor Sister, though narrowly watched, smuggled him some poison : he went to bed, saying, " Well, this is the last time I shall go to bed ; " the attendants heard him snore heavily, and then cease ; they looked, and he lay dead. ' He was of that ' wretched sect called *Soul-Sleepers*, who believe that the soul falls ' *asleep* at death :' a gloomy, far-misguided man. They buried him on Tower-hill with due ignominy, and there he rests ; with none but Frantic-Anabaptist Sexby, or Deceptive-Presbyterian Titus, to sing his praise.[1]

Next Friday, Friday the 20th, which was Thanksgiving Day, ' the Honourable House, after hearing two Sermons at Margaret's ' Westminster, partook of a most princely Entertainment,' by invitation from his Highness, at Whitehall. ' After dinner his ' Highness withdrew to the Cockpit ; and there entertained ' them with rare music, both of voices and instruments, till the ' evening ;' his Highness being very fond of music. In this manner end, once more, the grand Assassination projects,

---

[1] ' Equal to a Roman in virtue,' says the noisy Pamphlet *Killing no Murder*, which seems to have been written by Sexby ; though Titus, as adroit King's-Flunkey, at an after-period, saw good to claim it. A Pamphlet much noised-of in those months and afterwards ; recommending all persons to *assassinate* Cromwell ;—has this merit, considerable or not, and no other worth speaking of.

Spanish-Invasion projects; unachievable even the Preface of
them ;—and now we will speak of something else.

LETTER LX

KINGSHIP

THIS Second Protectorate Parliament, at least while the fer-
menting elements or 'hundred Excluded Members' are held
aloof from it, unfolds itself to us as altogether reconciled to the
rule of Oliver, or even right thankful for it; and really striving
towards Settlement of the Nation on that basis. Since the First
constituting Parliament went its ways, here is a great change
among us: three years of successful experiment have thrown
some light on Oliver, and his mode of ruling, to all Englishmen.
What can a wise Puritan Englishman do but decide on complying with Oliver, on strengthening the hands of Oliver? Is
he not verily doing the thing we all wanted to see done? The
old Parchments of the case may have been a little hustled, as
indeed in a Ten-years Civil War ending in the Execution of
a King, they could hardly fail to be;—but the divine Fact of
the case, meseems, is well cared for! Here is a Governing Man,
undeniably the most English of Englishmen, the most Puritan
of Puritans,—the Pattern Man, I must say, according to the
model of that Seventeenth Century in England; and a Great
Man, denizen of all the Centuries or he could never have been
the Pattern one in that. Truly, my friends, I think, you may
go farther and fare worse!—To the darkest head in England,
even to the assassinative truculent-flunkey head in steeple-hat
worn brown, some light has shone out of these three years of
Government by Oliver. An uncommon Oliver, even to the
truculent-flunkey. If not the noblest and worshipfullest of
all English men, at least the strongest and terriblest; with
whom really it might be as well to comply; with whom, in
fact, there is small hope in not complying!—

For its wise temper and good practical tendency, let us
praise this Second Parliament;—admit nevertheless that its
History, like that of most Parliaments, amounts to little. This
Parliament did what they could; forbore to pester his Highness
with quibblings and cavillings and constitution-pedantries;
accomplished respectably the Parliamentary routine; voted,

what perhaps was all that could be expected of them, some needful modicum of supplies, 'debated whether it should be debated,' 'put the question whether this question should be put;'—and in a mild way neutralised one another, and as it were handsomely *did nothing*, and left Oliver to do.

This Parliament suppressed the Major-Generals; refused to authorise their continued 'Decimation' or *Ten-per-centing* of the Royalists; whereupon they were suppressed.

Blake even now is giving the Spaniards a terrible scorching in the Port of Santa Cruz!—Worth noting: In those very minutes while the Lord Protector is making a speech, there goes on far off, on the Atlantic brine, under shadow of the Peak of Teneriffe, one of the fieriest actions ever fought by land or water; this action of the Sea-king Blake, at the Port of Santa Cruz. The case was this. Blake cruising on the coast of Spain, watching as usual for Plate Fleets, heard for certain that there was a Fleet actually coming, actually come as far as the Canary Isles, and now lying in the Bay of Santa Cruz in Teneriffe there. Blake makes instant sail thither; arrives there still in time this Monday morning early; finds the Fleet fast moored in Santa Cruz Bay; rich silver-ships, strong warships, Sixteen as we count them; stronger almost than himself,—and moored here under defences unassailable apparently by any mortal. Santa Cruz Bay is shaped as a horse-shoe: at the entrance are Castles, in the inner circuit are other Castles, Eight of them in all, bristling with great guns; warships moored at the entrance, war-frigates moored all round the beach, and men and gunners at command: one great magazine of sleeping thunder and destruction: to appearance, if you wish for sure suicide to run into, this must be it. Blake, taking measure of the business, runs into it, defying its loud thunder; much out-thunders it,—mere whirlwinds of fire and iron hail, the old Peak never heard the like;—silences the Castles, sinks or burns every sail in the Harbour; annihilates the Spanish Fleet; and then, the wind veering round in his favour, sails out again, leaving Santa Cruz Bay much astonished at him. It is the last action of the brave Blake; who, worn out with toil and sickness and a cruize of three years, makes homewards shortly after; dies within sight of Plymouth.[1]

On the whole, the Spanish Antichrist finds his Highness a rough enemy. In these same April days, Six-thousand men

---

[1] 7th August 1657, in his Fifty-ninth year.

are getting mustered here, 'furnished with new red coats' and
other equipments, to join French Turenne in the Low Countries,
and fight the Spaniard by land too. For our French Treaty has
become a French League Offensive and Defensive,[1] to last for
one year; and Reynolds is to be Land-General, and Montague
to help him as Sea-General: of whom by and by there may be
tidings.

LETTER LXI

OFFICIAL Letter of Thanks to Blake, for his Victory at Santa
Cruz on the 20th April last. The 'small Jewel' sent herewith
is one of 500*l.* value, gratefully voted him by the Parliament;
among whom, as over England generally, there is great rejoicing
on account of him. Where Blake received this Letter and Jewel
we know not; but guess it may have been in the Bay of Cadiz.
Along with it, 'Instructions' went out to him to leave a Squadron
of Fourteen Ships there, and come home with the rest of the
Fleet. He died, as we said above, within sight of Plymouth, on
the 7th of August following.

'*To General Blake, at Sea.*'

Whitehall, 10th June 1657.

SIR,
    I have received yours of 'the 20th of April last;' and
thereby the account of the good success it hath pleased God to
give you at the Canaries, in your attempt upon the King of
Spain's Ships in the Bay of Santa Cruz.

The mercy therein, to us and this Commonwealth, is very
signal; both in the loss the Enemy hath received, and also in the
preservation of our 'own' ships and men;[2]—which indeed was
very wonderful; and according to the goodness and lovingkindness of the Lord, wherewith His People hath been followed in
all these late revolutions; and doth call on our part, That we
should fear before Him, and still hope in His mercy.

We cannot but take notice also how eminently it hath pleased
God to make use of you in this service; assisting you with
wisdom in the conduct, and courage in the execution 'thereof;'
—and have sent you a small Jewel, as a testimony of our own

[1] Signed 23d March 1656-7.
[2] '50 slain outright, 150 wounded, of ours.

and the Parliament's good acceptance of your carriage in this Action. We are also informed that the Officers of the Fleet, and the Seamen, carried themselves with much honesty and courage ; and we are considering of a way to show our acceptance thereof. In the mean time, we desire you to return our hearty thanks and acknowledgments to them.

Thus, beseeching the Lord to continue His presence with you, I remain,

Your very affectionate friend,
'OLIVER P.'

Land-General Reynolds has gone to the French Netherlands, with Six thousand men, to join Turenne in fighting the Spaniards there ; and Sea-General Montague is about hoisting his flag to co-operate with him from the other element. By sea and land are many things passing ;—and here in London is the loudest thing of all : not yet to be entirely omitted by us, though now it has fallen very silent in comparison. Inauguration of the Lord Protector ; second and more solemn Installation of him, now that he is fully recognised by Parliament itself. He cannot yet, as it proves, be crowned King ; but he shall be installed in his Protectorship with all solemnity befitting such an occasion.

Friday, 26th June 1657. The Parliament and all the world are busy with this grand affair ; the labours of the Session being now complete, the last finish being now given to our new Instrument of Government, to our elaborate Petition and Advice, we will add this topstone to the work, and so, amid the shoutings of mankind, disperse for the recess. Friday at two o'clock, 'in a place prepared,' duly prepared with all manner of 'platforms,' 'cloths of state,' 'and seats raised one above the other,' 'at the upper end of Westminster Hall.' Palaceyard, and London generally, is all a-tiptoe, out of doors. Within doors, Speaker Widdrington and the Master of the Ceremonies have done their best : the Judges, the Aldermen, the Parliament, the Council, the foreign Ambassadors, and domestic Dignitaries without end ; chairs of state, cloths of state, trumpet-peals, and acclamations of the people—Let the reader conceive it ; or read in old Pamphlets the 'exact relation' of it with all the speeches and phenomena, worthier than such things usually are of being read.

'His Highness standing under the Cloth of State,' says Bulstrode, whose fine feelings are evidently touched by it, 'the 'Speaker in the name of the Parliament presented to him : 'First, a *Robe* of purple velvet ; which the Speaker, assisted by

'Whitlocke and others, put upon his Highness. Then he,' the Speaker, 'delivered to him the *Bible* richly gilt and bossed,' an affecting symbolic Gift: 'After that, the Speaker girt the '*Sword* about his Highness; and delivered into his hand the '*Sceptre* of massy gold. And then, this done, he made a Speech 'to him on these several things presented;' eloquent mellifluous Speech, setting forth the high and true significance of these several Symbols, Speech still worth reading; to which his Highness answered in silence by dignified gesture only. 'Then Mr. Speaker gave him the Oath;' and so ended, really in a solemn manner. 'And Mr. Manton, by prayer, recommended 'his Highness, the Parliament, the Council, the Forces by land 'and sea, and the whole Government and People of the Three 'Nations, to the blessing and protection of God.'——And then 'the 'people gave several great shouts;' and 'the trumpets sounded; 'and the Protector sat in his chair of state, holding the Sceptre 'in his hand:' a remarkable sight to see. 'On his right sat the Ambassador of France,' on his left some other Ambassador; and all round, standing or sitting, were Dignitaries of the highest quality; 'and near the Earl of Warwick, stood the 'Lord Viscount Lisle, stood General Montague and Whitlocke, 'each of them having a drawn sword in his hand,'—a sublime sight to some of us!

And so this Solemnity transacts itself;—which at the moment was solemn enough; and is not yet, at this or any hollowest moment of Human History, intrinsically altogether other. A really dignified and veritable piece of Symbolism; perhaps the last we hitherto, in these quack-ridden histrionic ages, have been privileged to see on such an occasion.—The Parliament is prorogued till the 20th of January next; the new House of Lords, and much else, shall be got ready in the interim.

LETTER LXII

By the new and closer Treaty signed with France in March last, for assaulting the Spanish Power in the Netherlands, it was stipulated that the French King should contribute Twenty-thousand men, and the Lord Protector Six-thousand, with a sufficient Fleet; which combined forces were straightway to set about reducing the three Coast Towns, Gravelines, Mardike and Dunkirk: the former when reduced to belong to France, the two latter to England; if the former should chance to be the first reduced, it was then to be given up to England, and held as cautionary till the other two were got. Mardike and Dunkirk, these were what Oliver expected to gain by this adventure. One or both of which strong Haventowns would naturally be very useful to him, connected with the Continent as he was,—continually menaced with Royalist Invasion from that quarter; and struggling, as the aim of his whole Foreign Policy was, to unite Protestant Europe with England in one great effectual league. Such was the French Treaty of the 23d of March last.

Oliver's part of the bargain was promptly and faithfully fulfilled. Six-thousand well-appointed men, under Commissary-General Reynolds, were landed, 'in new red coats,' 'near Boulogne, on the 13th and 14th days of May' last; and a Fleet under Montague, as we observe, sufficient to command those seas, and prevent all relief by ships in any Siege, is actually cruising there. Young Louis Fourteenth came down to the Coast to see the English Troops reviewed; expressed his joy and admiration over them;—and has set them, the Cardinal and he have set them, to assault the Spanish Power in the Netherlands by a plan of their own! To reduce not 'Gravelines, Mardike and Dunkirk,' on the Coast, as the Treaty has it, but Montmédi, Cambray, and I know not what in the Interior;—the Cardinal doubling and shuffling, and by all means putting off the attack of any place whatever on the Coast! With which arrangement Oliver Protector's dissatisfaction has at length reached a crisis; and he now writes, twice on the same day, to his Ambassador, To signify peremptorily that the same must terminate.

Of 'Sir William Lockhart, our Ambassador in France' in these years, there were much more to be said than we have room for here. A man of distinguished qualities, of manifold adventures and employments; whose Biography, if he could find any Biographer with real industry instead of sham industry, and above all things with human *eyes* instead of pedant *spectacles*, might still be worth writing in brief compass. He is Scotch; of the 'Lockharts of Lee' in Lanarkshire; has been in many wars and businesses abroad and at home;—was in *Hamilton's Engagement*, for one thing; and accompanied Dugald Dalgetty or Sir James Turner in those disastrous days and nights at Preston, though only as a common Colonel then, and not noticed by anybody. In the next Scotch War he received affronts from the Covenanted King; remained angrily at home, did not go to Worcester or elsewhither. The Covenanted King having vanished, and Lockhart's connexions being Presbyterian-Royalist, there was little outlook for him now in Scotland, or Britain; and he had resolved on trying France again. He came accordingly to London, seeking leave from the Authorities; had an interview with Oliver, now newly made Protector,—who read the worth of him, saw the uses of him, advised him to continue where he was.

He did continue; married 'Miss Robina Sewster,' a Huntingdonshire lady, the Protector's Niece, to whom, in her girlhood we once promised 'a distinguished husband'; has been our Ambassador in France near two years now; does diplomatic, warlike, and whatever work comes before him, in an effectual and manful manner. It is thought by judges, that, in Lockhart, the Lord Protector had the best Ambassador of that age. Nay, in spite of all considerations, his merits procured him afterwards a similar employment in Charles Second's time. We must here cease speaking of him; recommend him to some diligent succinct Biographer of insight, should such a one, by unexpected favour of the Destinies, turn up.

'*To Sir William Lockhart, our Ambassador in France.*' [1]

Whitehall, 31st August 1657.

SIR,

I have seen your last Letter to Mr. Secretary, as also divers others: and although I have no doubt either of your diligence or ability to serve us in so great a Business, yet I am deeply sensible that the French are very much short with us in ingenuousness and performance. And that which increaseth our sense 'of this' is, The resolution we 'for our part' had, rather to overdo than to be behindhand in anything of our Treaty. And although we never were so foolish 'as' to apprehend that the French and their interests were the same with ours in all things; yet as to the Spaniard, who hath been known in all ages to be the most implacable enemy that France hath,—we never could doubt, before we made our Treaty, that, going upon such grounds, we should have been failed 'towards' as we are!

To talk of "giving us Garrisons" which are *inland*, as

[1] Now with the Court at Peronne (Thurloe, vi. 482, 487); soon after at Paris (*Ib.* 496).

Caution for future action! to talk of "what will be done next Campaign,"—are but parcels of words for children. If they will give us Garrisons, let them give us Calais, Dieppe and Boulogne;—which I think they will do *as* soon as be honest in their words in giving us any one Spanish Garrison upon the coast into our hands! I positively think, which I say to you, they are afraid we should have any footing on that side 'of the Water,' though Spanish.

I pray you tell the Cardinal from me, That I think, if France desires to maintain its ground, much more to *get* ground upon the Spaniard, the performance of his Treaty with us will better do it than anything appears yet to me of any Design he hath!—Though we cannot so well pretend to soldiery as those that are with him; yet we think that, we being able by sea to strengthen and secure his Siege, and 'to' reinforce it as we please by sea, and the Enemy 'being' in capacity to do nothing to relieve it,—the best time to besiege that Place will be *now*. Especially if we consider that the French horse will be able so to ruin Flanders as that no succour can be brought to relieve the place; and that the French Army and our own will have constant relief, as far as England and France can give it, without any manner of impediment,—especially considering the Dutch are now engaged so much to Southward [1] as they are.

I desire you to let him know That Englishmen have had so good experience of Winter expeditions, they are confident, if the Spaniard shall keep the field, As he cannot impede this work, so neither will he be able to attack anything towards France with a possibility of retreat.[2] And what do all *delays* signify but 'even this:' The giving the Spaniard opportunity so much the more to reinforce himself; and the keeping our men another Summer to serve the French, without any colour of a reciprocal, or any advantage to ourselves!

And therefore if this will not be listened unto, I desire that things may be considered-of To give us satisfaction for the great expense we have been at with our Naval Forces and otherwise; which out of an honourable and honest aim on our part hath been incurred, thereby to answer the Engagements we had made. And, 'in fine,' That consideration may be had how our

[1] Spain-ward: so much inclined to help the Spaniard, if Montague would let them; a thing worth Mazarin's consideration too, though it comes in irregularly here!

[2] You may cut off his retreat, if he venture that way.

Men may be put into a position to be returned to us ;—whom we hope we shall employ to a better purpose than to have them continue where they are.

I desire we may know what France saith, and will do, upon this point. We shall be ready still, as the Lord shall assist us, to perform what can be reasonably expected on our part. And you may also let the Cardinal know farther, That our intentions, as they have been, will be to do all the good offices we can to promote the Interest common to us.

Apprehending it is of moment that this Business should come to you with speed and surety, we have sent it by an Express.

Your very loving friend,

OLIVER P.

LETTER LXIII

SAME date, same parties; an afterthought, by the same Express.

'*To Sir William Lockhart, our Ambassador in France.*'

Whitehall, 31st August 1657.

SIR,

We desire, having written to you as we have, that the Design be *Dunkirk* rather than Gravelines; and much *more* that it be :—but one of them rather than fail.

We shall not be wanting, To send over, at the French charge, Two of our old regiments, and Two-thousand foot more, if need be,—if Dunkirk be the design.[1] Believing that if the Army be well entrenched, and if La Ferté's Foot be added to it, we shall be able to give liberty to the greatest part of the French Cavalry to have an eye to the Spaniard,—leaving but convenient numbers to stand by the Foot.

And because this action will probably divert the Spaniard from assisting Charles Stuart in any attempt upon us, you may be assured that, if reality may with any reason be expected from the French, we shall do all reason on our part. But if indeed the French be so false to us as that they would not have us *have* any footing on that side the Water,—then I desire, as in our other Letter to you, That all things may be done in order to the

---

[1] Gravelines is to belong to *them ;* Dunkirk to *us*: Dunkirk will be much preferable.

giving us satisfaction 'for our expense incurred,' and to the drawing-off of our Men.

And truly, Sir, I desire you to take boldness and freedom to yourself in your dealing with the French on these accounts.

Your loving friend,

OLIVER P.

This Letter naturally had its effect : indeed there goes a witty sneer in France, "The Cardinal is more afraid of Oliver than of the Devil ;"—he ought indeed to fear the Devil much more, but Oliver is the palpabler Entity of the two ! Mardike was besieged straightway ; girt by sea and land, and the great guns opened 'on the 21st day of September' next : Mardike was taken before September ended ; and due delivery to our General was had of Mardike. The place was in a weak state ; but by sea and land all hands were now busy fortifying and securing it.

LETTER LXIV

HERE has an old dim Letter lately turned up,—communicated, for new editions, by the distinguished General Montague's Descendant,—which evidently relates to this operation. Resuscitated from its dim Archives, it falls with ready fitness into rank here ; kindling the old dead Books into pleasant momentary light and wakefulness at this point, and sufficiently illuminating itself also thereby. A curious meeting, one of those curious meetings, of old Letterpress now forgotten with old Manuscript never known till now, such as occasionally cheer the learned mind !—Of 'Denokson,' clearly some Dutch Vauban, or war *timmerman* on the great scale, of him, or of 'Colonel Clerke,' whom I take to be a Sea-Colonel mainly, the reader needs no commentary; —and is to understand withal that their hasty work was got accomplished, and Mardike put in some kind of fencible condition.

For General Montague, on board the London, before Dunkirk: These.

Whitehall, 2d October 1657.

SIR,

This Bearer, Christian Denokson, I have sent to you,— being a very good artist, especially in wooden works,—to view the Great Fort, and the Wooden Fort, in order to the further strengthening of them.

I hope he is very able to make the Wooden Fort as strong as it is capable to be made ; which I judge very desirable to be done with all speed. I desire you will direct him in this view ; and afterwards speak with him about it, that upon his return I may have a very particular account about what is fit to be done, and what Timber will be necessary to be provided. I have written also to Colonel Clerke, the Governor of the Fort, about it. I pray, when he has finished his view, that you will hasten him back.

I rest,
Your very affectionate friend,
OLIVER P.

An attempt to retake Mardike, by scalado or surprisal from the Dunkirk side, was made, some three weeks hence, by Don John with a great Spanish Force, among which his Ex-Royal Highness the Duke of York, with Four English-Irish emigrant Regiments he has now got raised for him on Spanish pay, was duly conspicuous ; but it did not succeed ; it amounted only to a night of unspeakable tumult ; to much expenditure of shot on all sides, and of life on his Royal Highness's and Don John's side,—Montague pouring death-fire on them from his ships too, and 'four great flaming links at the corners of Mardike Tower' warning Montague not to aim *thitherward* ;—and 'the dead were carried-off in carts before sunrise.'

Let us add here, that Dunkirk, after gallant service shown by the Six-thousand, and brilliant fighting and victory on the sand-hills, was also got, next summer ;[1] Lockhart himself now commanding there, poor Reynolds having perished at sea. Dunkirk too remained an English Garrison, much prized by England ; till, in very altered times, his now Restored Majesty saw good to sell it, and the loyallest men had to make their comparisons.—On the whole we may say, this Expedition to the Netherlands was a successful one ; the Six-thousand, 'immortal Six-thousand' as some call them, gained what they were sent for, and much glory over and above.

These Mardike-and-Dunkirk Letters are among the last Letters left to us of Oliver Cromwell's :—Oliver's great heroic

[1] 13th June 1658, the fight; 15th June, the surrender; 24th, the delivery to Lockhart.

Dayswork, **and the** small unheroic pious one of Oliver's Editor, is drawing to a close.

Wednesday, 11*th November* 1657. 'This day,' says the old Newspapers, 'the most Illustrious Lady, the Lady Frances 'Cromwell, youngest Daughter of his Highness the Lord Pro- 'tector, was married to the most noble gentleman Mr. Robert 'Rich, Son of the Lord Rich, Grandchild of the Earl of War- 'wick and of the Countess-Dowager of Devonshire; in the 'presence of their Highnesses, and of his Grandfather, and 'Father, and the said Countess, with many other persons of 'high honour and quality.' At Whitehall, this blessed Wednesday; all difficulties now overcome;—which we are glad to hear of, 'though our friends truly were very few!'—And on the Thursday of next week follows, at Hampton Court, the Lady Mary's own wedding. Wedding 'to the most noble Lord, the Lord Fauconberg,' lately returned from his Travels in foreign parts: a Bellasis, of the Yorkshire kindred so named,—which was once very high in Royalism, but is now making other connexions. For the rest, a brilliant, ingenuous and hopeful young man, 'in my opinion a person of extraordinary parts;' of whom his Highness has made due investigation, and finds that it may answer.

And now for the new Session of Parliament which assembles in January next: the Second Session of Parliament, and indeed the last of this and of them all!

SPEECH VI

THE First Session of this Parliament closed, last June, under such auspicious circumstances as we saw; leaving the People and the Lord Protector in the comfortable understanding that there was now a Settlement arrived at, a Government possible by Law; that irregular exercises of Authority, Major-Generals and such like, would not be needed henceforth for saving of the Commonwealth. Our Public Affairs, in the Netherlands and elsewhere, have prospered in the interim; nothing has misgone. Why should not this Second Session be as successful as the First was?—Alas, success, especially on such a basis as the humours and parliamentary talkings and self-developments of Four hundred men, is very uncertain!

The new House of Lords was certainly a rather questionable

adventure. You do not improvise a Peerage :—no, his Highness
is well aware of that! Nevertheless 'somewhat to stand between
me and the House of Commons' has seemed a thing desirable, a
thing to be decided on : and this new House of Lords, this will
be a 'somewhat,'—the best that can be had in present circumstances. Very weak and small as yet, like a tree new planted ;
but very certain to grow stronger, if it have real life in it, if
there be in the nature of things a real necessity for it. Plant
it, try it, this new Puritan Oliverian Peerage-of-Fact, such as it
has been given us. The old Peerage-of-Descent, with its
thousand years of strength,—what of the old Peerage has Puritan
sincerity, and manhood and marrow in its bones, will, in the
course of years, rally round an Oliver and his new Peerage-of-
Fact,—as it is already, by many symptoms, showing a tendency
to do. If the Heavens ordain that Oliver continue and succeed
as hitherto, undoubtedly his new Peerage may succeed along
with him, and gather to it whatever of the Old is worth
gathering. In the mean while it has been enacted by the
Parliament and him ; his part is now, To put it in effect the
best he can.

The List of Oliver's Lords can be read in many Books ; but
issuing as that matter did, it need not detain us here. Puritan
Men of Eminence, such as the Time had yielded : Skippon,
Desborow, Whalley, Pride, Hewson, these are what we may
call the *Napoleon-Marshals* of the business : Whitlocke, Haselrig,
Lenthall, Maynard, old Francis Rouse, Scotch Warriston, Lockhart ; Notabilities, of Parliament, of Religious Politics, or Law,
Montague, Howard are there ; the Earls of Manchester,
Warwick, Mulgrave,—some six Peers ; of whom only one, the
Lord Eure from Yorkshire, would, for the present, take his seat.
The rest of the Six as yet stood aloof ; even Warwick, as near
as he was to the Lord Protector, could not think of sitting with
such a Napoleon-Marshal as Major-General Hewson, who, men
say, started as a Shoemaker in early life. Yes ; in that low
figure did Hewson start ; and has had to fight every inch of his
way up hitherward, doing manifold victorious battle with the
Devil and the World as he went along,—proving himself a bit
of right good stuff, thinks the Lord Protector! You, Warwicks
and others, according to what sense of manhood you may have,
you can look into this Hewson, and see if you find any manhood
or worth in him ;—I have found some! The Protector's List
compiled under great difficulties, seems, so far as we can now
read it, very unexceptionable ; practical, substantial, with an

eye for the New and for the Old ; doing between these two, with good insight, the best it can. There were some Sixty-three summoned in all ; of whom some Forty and upwards sat, mostly taken from the House of Commons :—the worst effect of which was, that his Highness thereby lost some forty favourable votes in that other House ; which, as matters went, proved highly detrimental there.

On the tenth day of the Debate, with its noise growing ever noisier, on the 4th of February 1657-8, 'about eleven in the morning,'—while peppery Scott is just about to attempt yelping out some new second speech, and there are cries of "Spoken ! spoken !" which Sir Arthur struggles to argue down,—arrives the Black Rod.—"The Black Rod stays !" cry some, while Sir Arthur is arguing for Scott.—"What care I for the Black Rod ?" snarls he : "The Gentleman" (peppery Scott) "ought to be heard."—Black Rod, however, is heard first ; signifies that " His Highness is in the Lords House, and desires to speak with you." Under way therefore ! "Shall we take our Mace ?" By all means, if you consider it likely to be useful for you !

They take their Mace ; range themselves in due mass, in the "Other House," Lords House, or whatever they call it ; and his Highness, with a countenance of unusual earnestness, sorrow, resolution and severity, says :

MY LORDS, AND GENTLEMEN OF THE HOUSE OF COMMONS,

I had very comfortable expectations that God would make the meeting of this Parliament a blessing ; and, the Lord be my witness, *I* desired the carrying-on the Affairs of the Nation to these ends ! The blessing which I mean, and which we ever climbed at, was mercy, truth, righteousness and peace,— which I desired might be improved.

That which I told you in the Banqueting-House 'ten days ago' was true, That there are preparations of force to invade us. God is my witness, it hath been confirmed to me since, not a day ago, That the King of Scots hath an Army at the water's side, ready to be shipped for England. I have it from those who have been eyewitnesses of it. And while it is doing, there are endeavours from some who are not far from this place, to stir up the people of this Town into a tumulting,—what if I said, Into a rebellion ! And I hope I shall make it appear to be no better, if God assist me.

It hath been not only your endeavour to pervert the Army

while you have been sitting, and to draw them to state the
question about a "Commonwealth;" but some of you have
been listing of persons, by commission of Charles Stuart, to join
with any Insurrection that may be made. And what is like to
come upon this, the Enemy being ready to invade us, but even
present blood and confusion?—And if this be so, I do assign
it' to this cause: Your not assenting to what you did invite
me to by your Petition and Advice, as that which might prove
the Settlement of the Nation. And if this be the end of your
sitting, and this be your carriage,—[*Sentence now all beautifully
blazing*], I think it high time that an end be put to your sitting.
And I DO DISSOLVE THIS PARLIAMENT! And let God be judge
between you and me!

Figure the looks of Haselrig, Scott and Company! 'The
'Mace was clapt under a cloak; the Speaker withdrew, and
'*exit Parliamentum*,' the Talking-Apparatus vanishes. "God
be judge between you and me!"—"Amen!" answered they,
thought they, indignantly; and sank into eternal silence.

It was high time; for in truth the Hydra, on every side,
is stirring its thousand heads. "Believe me," says Samuel
Hartlib, Milton's friend, writing to an Official acquaintance next
week, "believe me, it was of such necessity, that if their Session
"had continued but two or three days longer, all had been
"in blood both in City and Country, upon Charles Stuart's
"account."

His Highness, before this Monday's sun sets, has begun
to lodge the Anarchic Ringleaders, Royalist, Fifth-Monarchist,
in the Tower; his Highness is bent once more with all his
faculty, the Talking-Apparatus being gone, to front this
Hydra, and trample it down once again. On Saturday he
summons his Officers, his Acting-Apparatus, to Whitehall round
him; explains to them 'in a Speech two hours long' what kind
of Hydra it is; asks, Shall it conquer us, involve us in blood
and confusion? They answer from their hearts, No, it shall
not! "We will stand and fall with your Highness, we will
live and die with you!"—It is the last duel this Oliver has
with any Hydra fomented into life by a Talking-Apparatus;
and he again conquers it, invincibly compresses it, as he has
heretofore done.

One day, in the early days of March next, his Highness said
to Lord Broghil: An old friend of yours is in Town, the Duke
of Ormond, now lodged in Drury Lane, at the Papist Surgeon's

there: you had better tell him to be gone! Whereat his Lordship stared; found it a fact, however; and his Grace of Ormond did go with exemplary speed, and got again to Bruges and the Sacred Majesty, with report That Cromwell had many enemies, but that the rise of the Royalists was moonshine. And on the 12th of the month his Highness had the Mayor and Common Council with him in a body at Whitehall; and 'in a Speech at large' explained to them that his Grace of Ormond was gone only 'on Tuesday last;' that there were Spanish Invasions, Royalist Insurrections and Frantic-Anabaptist Insurrections rapidly ripening;—that it would well beseem the City of London to have its Militia in good order. To which the Mayor and Common Council, 'being very sensible thereof,' made zealous response by speech and by act. In a word, the Talking-Apparatus being gone, and an Oliver Protector now at the head of the Acting-Apparatus, no Insurrection, in the eyes of reasonable persons, had any chance. The leading Royalists shrank close into their privacies again,—considerable numbers of them had to shrink into durance in the Tower. Among which latter class, his Highness, justly incensed, and 'considering,' as Thurloe says, 'that it was not fit there should be a Plot of this kind every winter,' had determined that a High Court of Justice should take cognisance of some. High Court of Justice is accordingly nominated as the Act of Parliament prescribes: among the parties marked for trial by it are Sir Henry Slingsby, long since prisoner for Penruddock's business, and the Reverend Dr. Hewit, a man of much forwardness in Royalism. Sir Henry, prisoner in Hull and acquainted with the Chief Officers there, has been treating with them for betrayal of the place to his Majesty; has even, to that end, given one of them a Majesty's Commission; for whose Spanish Invasion such a Haven and Fortress would have been extremely convenient. Reverend Dr. Hewit, preaching by sufferance, according to the old ritual, 'in St. Gregory's Church near Paul's,' to a select disaffected audience, has farther seen good to distinguish himself very much by secular zeal in this business of the Royalist Insurrection and Spanish Charles-Stuart Invasion;—which has now come to nothing, and left poor Dr. Hewit in a most questionable position. Of these two, and of others, a High Court of Justice shall take cognisance.

The Insurrection having no chance in the eyes of reasonable Royalists, and they in consequence refusing to lead it, the large body of *un*reasonable Royalists now in London City or gathering thither decide, with indignation, That they will try it on their own score, and lead it themselves. Hands to work, then, ye unreasonable Royalists; pipe, All hands! Saturday the 15th of May, that is the night appointed : To rise that Saturday Night; beat drums for 'Royalist Apprentices,' 'fire houses at the Tower,' slay this man, slay that, and bring matters to a good issue. Alas, on the very edge of the appointed hour, as usual, we are all seized; the ringleaders of us are all seized, 'at the Mermaid in Cheapside,'—for Thurloe and his Highness have long known what we were upon! Barkstead Governor of the Tower 'marches into the City with five drakes,' at the rattle of which every Royalist Apprentice, and party implicated, shakes in his shoes :—and this also has gone to vapour, leaving only for result certain new individuals of the Civic class to give account of it to the High Court of Justice.

Tuesday, 25th May 1658, the High Court of Justice sat; a formidable Sanhedrim of above a Hundred-and-thirty heads, consisting of 'all the Judges,' chief Law Officials, and others named in the Writ according to Act of Parliament; sat 'in 'Westminster Hall at Nine in the morning, for the Trial of Sir 'Henry Slingsby Knight, John Hewit Doctor of Divinity,' and three others whom we may forget. Sat day after day till all were judged. Poor Sir Henry, on the first day, was condemned; he pleaded what he could, poor gentleman, a very constant Royalist all along; but the Hull business was too palpable; he was condemned to die. Reverend Dr. Hewit, whose proceedings also had become very palpable, refused to plead at all; refused even 'to take off his hat,' says Carrion Heath, 'till the officer was coming to do it for him;' had a Paper of Demurrers prepared by the learned Mr. Prynne,' who is now again doing business this way; 'conducted himself not very wisely,' says Bulstrode. He likewise received sentence of death. The others, by narrow missing, escaped; by good luck, or the Protector's mercy, suffered nothing.

As to Slingsby and Hewit, the Protector was inexorable. Hewit has already taken a very high line : let him persevere in it! Slingsby was the Lord Fauconberg's Uncle, married to his Aunt Bellasis; but that could not stead him,—perhaps that was but a new monition to be strict with him. The Commonwealth of England and its Peace are not nothing! These Royalist Plots every winter, deliveries of garrisons to Charles Stuart, and reckless 'usherings of us into blood,' shall end! Hewit and Slingsby suffered on Tower Hill, on Monday 8th

June; amid the manifold rumour and emotion of men. Of the City Insurrectionists six were condemned; three of whom were executed, three pardoned. And so the High Court of Justice dissolved itself; and at this and not at more expense of blood, the huge Insurrectionary movement ended, and lay silent within its caves again.

Whether in any future year it would have tried another rising against such a Lord Protector, one does not know,—one guesses rather in the negative. The Royalist Cause, after so many failures, after such a sort of enterprises 'on the word of a Christian King,' had naturally sunk very low. Some twelve-month hence, with a Commonwealth not now under Cromwell, but only under the impulse of Cromwell, a Christian King hastening down to the Treaty of the Pyrenees, where France and Spain were making Peace, found one of the coldest receptions. Cardinal Mazarin 'sent his coaches and guards a day's journey to meet Lockhart the Commonwealth Ambassador;' but refused to meet the Christian King at all; would not even meet Ormond except as if by accident 'on the public road,' to say that there was no hope. The Spanish Minister, Don Luis de Haro, was civiller in manner; but as to Spanish Charles-Stuart Invasions or the like, he also decisively shook his head. The Royalist Cause was as good as desperate in England; a melancholy Reminiscence, fast fading away into the realm of shadows. Not till Puritanism sank of its own accord, could Royalism rise again. But Puritanism, the King of it once away, fell loose very naturally in every fibre,—fell into *Kinglessness*, what we call Anarchy; crumbled down, ever faster, for Sixteen Months, in mad suicide, and universal clashing and collision; proved, by trial after trial, that there lay not in it either Government or so much as Self-government any more; that a Government of England by *it* was henceforth an impossibility. Amid the general wreck of things, all Government threatening now to be impossible, the Reminiscence of Royalty rose again, "Let us take refuge in the Past, the Future is not possible!"—and Major-General Monk crossed the Tweed at Coldstream, with results which are well known.

Results which we will not quarrel with, very mournful as they have been! If it please Heaven, these Two-hundred Years of universal Cant in Speech, with so much of Cotton-spinning, Coal-boring, Commercing, and other valuable Sincerity of Work going-on the while, shall not be quite lost to us! Our Cant will vanish, our whole baleful cunningly-compacted

Universe of Cant, as does a heavy Nightmare Dream. We shall awaken; and find ourselves in a world greatly *widened.*—Why Puritanism could not continue? My friend, Puritanism was *not* the Complete Theory of this immense Universe; no, only a part thereof! To me it seems, in my hours of hope, as if the Destinies meant something grander with England than even Oliver Protector did! We will not quarrel with the Destinies; we will work as we can towards fulfilment of them.

But in these same June days of the year 1658, while Hewit and Slingsby lay down their heads on Tower Hill, and the English Hydra finds that its Master is still here, there arrive the news of Dunkirk alluded-to above: Dunkirk gloriously taken, Spaniards gloriously beaten: victories and successes abroad; which are a new illumination to the Lord Protector in the eyes of England. Splendid Nephews of the Cardinal, Manzinis, Ducs de Crequi, come across the Channel to congratulate 'the most invincible of Sovereigns;' young Louis Fourteenth himself would have come, had not the attack of small-pox prevented With whom the elegant Lord Fauconberg and others busy themselves: their pageantry and gilt coaches, much gazed-at by the idler multitudes, need not detain us here.

The Lord Protector, his Parliament having been dismissed with such brevity, is somewhat embarrassed in his finances. But otherwise his affairs stand well; visibly in an improved condition. Once more he has saved Puritan England; once more approved himself invincible abroad and at home. He looks with confidence towards summoning a new Parliament, of juster disposition towards Puritan England and him. With a Parliament, or if extremity of need arrive, without a Parliament and in spite of Parliaments, the Puritan Gospel Cause, sanctioned by a Higher than Parliaments, shall not sink while life remains in this Man. Not till Oliver Cromwell's head lie low, shall English Puritanism bend its head to any created thing. Erect, with its foot on the neck of Hydra Babylon, with its open Bible and drawn Sword, shall Puritanism stand, and with pious all-defiance victoriously front the world. That was Oliver Cromwell's appointed function in this piece of Sublunary Space, in this section of swift-flowing Time; that noble, perilous, painful function: and he has manfully done it,—and is now near ending it, and getting honourably relieved from it.

LETTER LXV.

THE poor Protestants of Piedmont, it appears, are again in a state of grievance, in a state of peril. The Lord Protector, in the thickest press of domestic anarchies, finds time to think of these poor people and their case. Here is a Letter to Ambassador Lockhart, who is now at Dunkirk Siege, in the French King and Cardinal's neighbourhood: a generous pious Letter; dictated to Thurloe, partly perhaps of Thurloe's composition, but altogether of Oliver's mind and sense;—fit enough, since it so chances, to conclude our Series here.

'*To Sir William Lockhart, our Ambassador at the French Court: These.*'

'Whitehall,' 26th May 1658

SIR,
  The continual troubles and vexations of the poor people of Piedmont professing the Reformed Religion,—and that after so many serious instances of yours in the Court of France in their behalf, and after such hearty recommendations of their most deplorable condition to his Majesty in our name, who also has been pleased upon all such occasions to profess very deep resentments of their miseries, and to give us no small hopes of interposing his power and interest with the Duke of Savoy for the accommodating of those affairs, and for the restoring those poor distressed creatures to their ancient privileges and habitations,—are matter of so much grief to us, and lie so near our heart, that notwithstanding we are abundantly satisfied with those many signal marks you have always hitherto given of your truly Christian zeal and tenderness on their regard, yet the present conjuncture of their affairs, and the misery that is daily added to their affliction begetting in us fresh arguments of pity towards them, not only as men, but as the poor distressed Members of Christ,—do really move us at present to recommend their sad condition to your special care. Desiring you to redouble your instances with the King, in such pathetic and affectionate expressions as may be in some measure suitable to the greatness of their present sufferings and grievances. Which, the truth is, are almost inexpressible. For so restless and implacable is the malice and fury of their Popish Adversaries, that,—as though they esteemed

it but a light matter to have formerly shed the innocent blood
of so many hundreds of souls, to have burned their houses, to
have rased their churches, to have plundered their goods, and
to have driven out the Inhabitants beyond the River Pelice,
out of those their ancient Possessions which they had quietly
enjoyed for so many ages and generations together,—they are
now resolved to fill their cup of affliction up to the brim, and
to heat the furnace yet seven times hotter than before. Amongst
other things:

First,—They forcibly prohibit all manner of Public Exercises
at San Giovanni, which, notwithstanding, the Inhabitants have
enjoyed time out of mind: and in case they yield not ready
obedience to such most unrighteous orders, they are immediately
summoned before their Courts of Justice, and there proceeded
against in a most severe and rigorous manner, and some
threatened to be wholly destroyed and exterminated.

2. And forasmuch as, in the said Valleys, there are not found
among the Natives men fitly qualified and of abilities for
Ministerial Functions to supply so much as one half of their
Churches, and upon this account they are necessitated to entertain
some out of France and Geneva, which are the Duke of
Savoy's friends and allies,—their Popish Enemies take hold of
this advantage; and make use of this stratagem, namely, to
banish and drive out the shepherds of the flocks, that so the
wolves may the better come in and devour the sheep.

3. To this we add, their strict prohibition of all Physicians
and Chirurgeons of the Reformed Religion to inhabit in the
Valleys. And thus they attempt not only to starve their souls
for want of spiritual food and nourishment, but to destroy their
bodies likewise for want of those outward conveniences and
helps which God hath allowed to all mankind.

4. And as a supplement to the former grievances, those of
the Reformed Religion are prohibited all manner of Commerce
and Trade with their Popish neighbours; that so they may not
be able to subsist and maintain their families: and if they offend
herein in the least, they are immediately apprehended as rebels.

5. Moreover, to give the world a clear testimony what their
main design in all these oppressions is, they have issued out
Orders whereby to force the poor Protestants To sell their Lands
and Houses to their Popish neighbours: whereas the Papists are
prohibited upon pain of excommunication to sell any immovable
to the Protestants.

6. Besides, the Court of Savoy have rebuilt the Fort of La

Torre; contrary to the formal and express promise made by them to the Ambassadors of the Evangelical Cantons. Where they have also placed Commanders, who commit the Lord knows how many excesses and outrages in all the neighbouring parts; without being ever called to question, or compelled to make restitution for the same. If by chance any murder be committed in the Valleys (as is too-too often practised) whereof the authors are not discovered, the poor Protestants are immediately accused as guilty thereof, to render them odious to their neighbours.

7. There are sent lately into the said Valleys several Troops of Horse and Companies of Foot; which hath caused the poor People, out of fear of a massacre, with great expense and difficulty to send their wives and little ones, with all that were feeble and sick amongst them, into the Valley of Perosa, under the King of France his Dominions.

These are, in short, the grievances, and this is the present state and condition of those poor People even at this very day. Whereof you are to use your utmost endeavours to make his Majesty thoroughly sensible: and to persuade him to give speedy and effectual orders 'to' his Ambassador who resides in the Duke's Court, To act vigorously in their behalf. Our Letter, which you shall present his Majesty for this end and purpose, contains several reasons in it which we hope will move his heart to the performance of this charitable and merciful work. And we desire you to second and animate the same with your most earnest solicitations; representing unto him how much his own interest and honour is concerned in the making good that Accord of Henry the Fourth, his royal predecessor, with the Ambassadors of those very People, in the year 1592, by the Constable of Lesdiguières; which Accord is registered in the Parliament of Dauphiné; and whereof you have an authentic Copy in your own hands. Whereby the Kings of France oblige themselves and their Successors To maintain and preserve their ancient privileges and concessions.—Besides that the gaining to himself the hearts of that People, by so gracious and remarkable a protection and deliverance, might be of no little use another day, in relation to Pignerol and the other adjacent places under his Dominions.

One of the most effectual remedies, which we conceive the fittest to be applied at present is, That the King of France would be pleased to make an Exchange with the Duke of Savoy for

those Valleys; resigning over to him some other part of his
Dominions in lieu thereof,—as, in the reign of Henry the Fourth,
the Marquisate of Saluces was exchanged with the Duke for
La Bresse. Which certainly could not but be of great advantage
to his Majesty, as well for the safety of Pignerol, as for the
opening of a Passage for his Forces into Italy,—which 'Passage,'
if under the dominion, and in the hands of so powerful a Prince,
joined with the natural strength of these places by reason of their
situation, must needs be rendered impregnable.

By what we have already said, you see our intentions; and
therefore we leave all other particulars to your special care and
conduct; and rest,

'Your friend,'

OLIVER P.

Lockhart, both General and Ambassador in these months, is,
as we hinted, infinitely busy with his share in the Siege of
Dunkirk, now just in its agony; and before this Letter can
well arrive, has done his famous feat of Fighting, which brings
Turenne and him their victory, among the sandhills there.
Much to the joy of Cardinal and King; who will not readily
refuse him in any reasonable point at present.

DEATH OF THE PROTECTOR

THERE remain no more *Letters and Speeches of Oliver Cromwell* for us: the above is the last of them of either kind. As a Speaker to men, he takes his leave of the world, in these final words addressed to his Second Parliament, on the 4th of February 1657-8: "God be judge between you and me!"—So was it appointed by the Destinies and the Oblivions; these were his last public words.

Other Speeches, in that crisis of Oliver's affairs, we have already heard of; 'Speech of two hours' to his Officers in Whitehall: Speech to the Lord Mayor and Common Council, in the same place, on the same subject: but they have not been reported, or the report of them has not come down to us. There were domestic Letters also, as we still find, written in those same tumultuous weeks; Letters to the Earl of Warwick, on occasion of the death of His Grandson, the Protector's Son-in-law. For poor young Mr. Rich, whom we saw wedded in November last, is dead. He died on the twelfth day after that Dissolution of the Parliament; while Oliver and the Commonwealth are wrestling against boundless Anarchies, Oliver's own Household has its visitations and dark days. Poor little Frances Cromwell, in the fourth month of her marriage, still only about seventeen, she finds herself suddenly a widow; and Hampton Court has become a house of mourning. Young Rich was much lamented. Oliver condoled with the Grandfather 'in seasonable and sympathising Letters:' for which the brave old Earl rallies himself to make some gratefullest Reply;—" Cannot enough confess my "obligation, much less discharge it, for your seasonable and "sympathising Letters; which, besides the value they derive "from so worthy a hand, express such faithful affections, and "administer such Christian advices as renders them beyond "measure dear to me." Blessings, and noble eulogies, the outpouring of a brave old heart, conclude this Letter of Warwick's. He himself died shortly after; a new grief to the

HEALTH DECLINING

Protector.—The Protector was delivering the Commonwealth from Hydras and fighting a world-wide battle, while he wrote those Letters on the death of young Rich. If by chance they still lie hidden in the archives of some kinsman of the Warwicks, they may yet be disimprisoned and made audible. Most probably they too are lost. And so we have now nothing more; —and Oliver has nothing more. His Speakings, and also his Actings, all his manifold Strugglings, more or less victorious, to utter the great God's-Message that was in him,—have here what we call ended. This Summer of 1658, likewise victorious after struggle, is his last in our World of Time. Thenceforth he enters the Eternities; and rests upon his arms *there*.

Oliver's look was yet strong; and young for his years, which were Fifty-nine last April. The 'Three-score and ten years,' the Psalmist's limit, which probably was often in Oliver's thoughts and in those of others there, might have been anticipated for him: Ten Years more of Life; which, we may compute, would have given another History to all the Centuries of England. But it was not to be so, it was to be otherwise. Oliver's health, as we might observe, was but uncertain in late times; often 'indisposed' the spring before last. His course of life had not been favourable to health! "A burden too heavy for man!" as he himself, with a sigh, would sometimes say. Incessant toil; inconceivable labour, of head and heart and hand; toil, peril, and sorrow manifold, continued for near Twenty years now, had done their part: those robust life-energies, it afterwards appeared, had been gradually eaten out. Like a Tower strong to the eye, but with its foundations undermined; which has not long to stand; the fall of which, on any shock, may be sudden.

The Manzinis and Ducs de Crequi, with their splendours, and congratulations about Dunkirk, interesting to the street-populations and general public, had not yet withdrawn, when at Hampton Court there had begun a private scene, of much deeper and quite opposite interest there. The Lady Claypole, Oliver's favourite Daughter, a favourite of all the world, had fallen sick we know not when; lay sick now,—to death, as it proved. Her disease was of internal female nature; the painfullest and most harassing to mind and sense, it is understood, that falls to the lot of a human creature. Hampton Court we can fancy once more, in those July days, a house of sorrow; pale Death knocking there, as at the door of the meanest hut.

'She had great sufferings, great exercises of spirit.' Yes :—and in the depths of the old Centuries, we see a pale anxious Mother, anxious Husband, anxious weeping Sisters, a poor young Frances weeping anew in her weeds. 'For the last fourteen days' his Highness has been by her bedside at Hampton Court, unable to attend to any public business whatever. Be still, my Child ; trust thou yet in God : in the waves of the Dark River, there too is He a God of help ! On the 6th day of August she lay dead ; at rest forever. My young, my beautiful, my brave ! She is taken from me ; I am left bereaved of her. The Lord giveth, and the Lord taketh away ; blessed be the Name of the Lord !

'His Highness,' says Harvey,[1] 'being at Hampton Court, sick-
'ened a little before the Lady Elizabeth died. Her decease was
'on Friday 6th August 1658 ; she having lain long under great
'extremity of bodily pain, which, with frequent and violent con-
'vulsion-fits, brought her to her end. But as to his Highness,
'it was observed that his sense of her outward misery, in the
'pains she endured, took deep impression upon him ; who
'indeed was ever a most indulgent and tender Father ; his
'affections' too 'being regulated and bounded by such Christian
'wisdom and prudence, as did eminently shine in filling-up not
'only that relation of a Father, but also all other relations ;
'wherein he was a most rare and singular example. And no
'doubt but the sympathy of his spirit with his sorely afflicted
'and dying Daughter' did break him down at this time ; 'considering also,' innumerable other considerations of sufferings and toils, 'which made me often wonder he was able to hold-up
'so long ; except' indeed 'that he was borne up by a Super-
'natural Power at a more than ordinary rate. As a mercy to
'the truly Christian World, and to us of these Nations, had we
'been worthy of him !'

The same authority, who unhappily is not chronological, adds elsewhere this little picture, which we must take with us : ' At
'Hampton Court, a few days after the death of the Lady
'Elizabeth, which touched him nearly,—being then himself
'under bodily distempers, forerunners of that Sickness which
'was to death, and in his bedchamber,—he called for his Bible,

[1] A Collection of several Passages concerning his late Highness Oliver Cromwell, in the Time of his Sickness ; wherein is related many of his Expressions upon his Deathbed, together with his Prayer within two or three Days before his Death. Written by one that was then Groom of his Bedchamber.

'and desired an honourable and godly person there, with others,
'present, To read unto him that passage in *Philippians* Fourth ;
'"*Not that I speak in respect of want: for I have learned in
'whatsoever state I am, therewith to be content. I know both
'how to be abased, and I know how to abound. Everywhere,
'and by all things, I am instructed ; both to be full and to be
'hungry, both to abound and to suffer need. I can do all
'things, through Christ which strengtheneth me.*" Which read,—
'said he, to use his own words as near as I can remember
'them : "This Scripture did once save my life ; when my
'eldest Son"' poor Robert '"died : which went as a dagger to
'my heart, indeed it did." 'And then repeating the words of
'the text himself, and reading the tenth and eleventh verses,
'of Paul's contentation, and submission to the will of God in
'all conditions,—said he : "It's true, Paul, *you* have learned
'this, and attained to this measure of grace : but what shall *I*
'do ? Ah poor creature, it is a hard lesson for me to take
'out ! I find it so !" But reading on to the thirteenth verse,
'where Paul saith, "*I can do all things through Christ that
'strengtheneth me,*"—then faith began to work, and his heart
'to find support and comfort, and he said thus to himself, "He
'that was Paul's Christ is my Christ too !" And so drew
'waters out of the well of Salvation.'

In the same dark days, occurred George Fox's third and last
interview with Oliver. Their first interview we have seen.[1] The
second, which had fallen out some two years ago, did not prosper
quite so well. George riding into Town 'one evening,' with
some 'Edward Pyot' or other broadbrimmed man, espied the
Protector 'at Hyde Park Corner among his Guards,' and made
up to his carriage-window, in spite of opposition ; and was
altogether cordially welcomed there. But on the following day,
at Whitehall, the Protector 'spake lightly ;' he sat down
loosely 'on a table,' and 'spake light things to me,'—in fact,
rather quizzed me ; finding my enormous sacred Self-confidence
none of the least of my attainments ! Such had been our
second interview ; here now is the third and last.—George
dates nothing ; and his facts everywhere lie round him like the
leather-parings of his old shop : but we judge it may have been
about the time when the Manzinis and Ducs de Crequi were
parading in their gilt coaches, That George and two Friends
'going out of Town,' on a summer day, 'two of Hacker's men'
had met them,—taken them, brought them to the Mews.

[1] Omitted in text.—ED.

'Prisoners there a while :'—but the Lord's power was over Hacker's men: they had to let us go. Whereupon:

'The same day, taking boat I went down' (*up*) ' to Kingston, 'and from thence to Hampton Court, to speak with the 'Protector about the Sufferings of Friends. I met him riding 'into Hampton-Court Park; and before I came to him, as 'he rode at the head of his Lifeguard, I saw and felt a waft ' (*whiff*) ' of death go forth against him.'— — Or in favour of him, George? His life, if thou knew it, has not been a merry thing for this man, now or heretofore! I fancy he has been looking, this long while, to give it up, whenever the Commander-in-chief required. To quit his laborious sentry-post; honourably lay-up his arms, and be gone to his rest :—all Eternity to rest in, O George! Was thy own life merry, for example, in the hollow of the tree; clad permanently in leather? And does kingly purple, and governing refractory worlds instead of stitching coarse shoes, make it merrier? The waft of death is not against *him*, I think,—perhaps against thee, and me, and others, O George, when the Nell-Gwyn Defender and Two Centuries of all-victorious Cant have come in upon us! My unfortunate George— —'a waft of death go forth against him; and when 'I came to him, he looked like a dead man. After 'I had laid the Sufferings of Friends before him, and had 'warned him according as I was moved to speak to him, he 'bade me come to his house. So I returned to Kingston; and, 'the next day, went up to Hampton Court to speak farther 'with him. But when I came, Harvey, who was one that 'waited on him, told me the Doctors were not willing that 'I should speak with him. So I passed away, and never saw 'him more.'

Friday, the 20th of August 1658, this was probably the day on which George Fox saw Oliver riding into Hampton Park with his Guards, for the last time. That Friday, as we find, his Highness seemed much better: but on the morrow a sad change had taken place; feverish symptoms, for which the Doctors rigorously prescribed quiet. Saturday to Tuesday the symptoms continued ever worsening: a kind of tertian ague, 'bastard tertian' as the old Doctors name it; for which it was ordered that his Highness should return to Whitehall, as to a more favourable air in that complaint. On Tuesday accordingly he quitted Hampton Court;—never to see it more.

'His time was come,' says Harvey; 'and neither prayers nor tears could prevail with God to lengthen out his life and con-

'tinue him longer to us. Prayers abundantly and incessantly
'poured out on his behalf, both publicly and privately, as was
'observed, in a more than ordinary way. Besides many a secret
'sigh,—secret and unheard by men, yet like the cry of Moses,
'more loud, and strongly laying hold on God, than many spoken
'supplications. All which,—the hearts of God's People being
'thus mightily stirred up,—did seem to beget confidence in some,
'and hopes in all; yea some thoughts in himself, that God
'would restore him.'

'Prayers public and private:' they are worth imagining to
ourselves. Meetings of Preachers, Chaplains, and Godly
Persons; 'Owen, Goodwin, Sterry, with a company of others,
in an adjoining room;' in Whitehall, and elsewhere over
religious London and England, fervent outpourings of many a
loyal heart. For there were hearts to whom the nobleness of
this man was known; and his worth to the Puritan Cause was
evident. Prayers,—strange enough to us; in a dialect fallen
obsolete, forgotten now. Authentic wrestlings of ancient
Human Souls,—who were alive then, with their affections, awe-
struck pieties; with their Human Wishes, risen to be *transcendent*, hoping to prevail with the Inexorable. All swallowed
now in the depths of dark Time: which is full of such, since
the beginning!—Truly it is a great scene of World-History,
this in old Whitehall: Oliver Cromwell drawing nigh to his
end. The exit of Oliver Cromwell and of English Puritanism;
a great Light, one of our few authentic Solar Luminaries, going
down now amid the clouds of Death. Like the setting of a
great victorious Summer Sun; its course now finished. '*So
stirbt ein Held*,' says Schiller, 'So dies a Hero! Sight worthy to
be worshipped!'—He died, this Hero Oliver, in Resignation to
God; as the Brave have all done. 'We could not be more
desirous he should abide,' says the pious Harvey, 'than he was
content and willing to be gone.' The struggle lasted, amid
hope and fear, for ten days.—Some small miscellaneous traits,
and confused gleanings of last-words; and then our poor
History ends.

Oliver, we find, spoke much of 'the Covenants;' which
indeed are the grand axis of all, in that Puritan Universe of his.
Two Covenants; one of Works, with fearful Judgment for our
short-comings therein; one of Grace and unspeakable mercy;—
gracious Engagements, 'Covenants,' which the Eternal God has
vouchsafed to make with His feeble creature Man. Two: and

by Christ's Death they have become One: there for Oliver is the divine solution of this our Mystery of Life. "They were Two," he was heard ejaculating: "Two, but put into One before the Foundation of the World!" And again: "It is "holy and true, it is holy and true, it is holy and true!—Who "made it holy and true? The Mediator of the Covenant!" And again: "The Covenant is but One. Faith in the "Covenant is my only support. And if I believe not, He abides "faithful!" When his Children and Wife stood weeping round him, he said: "Love not this world. I say unto you, it is not good that you should love this world!" No. "Children, live like Christians:—I leave you the Covenant to feed upon!" Yea, my brave one; even so! The Covenant, and eternal Soul of Covenants, remains sure to all the faithful: deeper than the Foundations of this World; earlier than they, and more lasting than they!—

Look also at the following; dark hues and bright; immortal light-beams struggling amid the black vapours of Death. Look; and conceive a great sacred scene, the sacredest this world sees; —and think of it, do not speak of it, in these mean days which have no sacred word. "Is there none that says, Who will deliver me from the peril?" moaned he once. Many hearts are praying, O wearied one! "Man can do nothing," rejoins he; "God can do what He will."—Another time, again thinking of the Covenant, "Is there none that will come and praise God," whose mercies endure for ever!— —

Here also are ejaculations caught up at intervals, undated, in those final days: "Lord, Thou knowest, if I do desire to live, it is to show forth Thy praise and declare Thy works!"—Once he was heard saying, "It is a fearful thing to fall into the hands of the Living God!" 'This was spoken three times,' says Harvey; 'his repetitions usually being very weighty, and with great vehemency of spirit.' Thrice over he said this; looking into the Eternal Kingdoms: "A fearful thing to fall into the hands of the Living God!"— — But again: "All the Promises "of God are in *Him*: yes, and in Him Amen; to the glory of "God by us,—by *us* in Jesus Christ."— —"The Lord hath "filled me with as much assurance of His pardon, and His love, "as my soul can hold."—"I think I am the poorest wretch that "lives: but I love God; or rather, am beloved of God."—"I "am a conqueror, and more than a conqueror, through Christ "that strengtheneth me!"

So pass, in the sickroom, in the sickbed, these last heavy uncertain days. 'The Godly Persons had great assurances of a return to their Prayers:' transcendent Human Wishes find in their own echo a kind of answer! They gave his Highness also some assurance that his life would be lengthened. Hope was strong in many to the very end.

On Monday, August 30th, there roared and howled all day a mighty storm of wind. Ludlow, coming up to Town from Essex, could not start in the morning for wind; tried it in the afternoon; still could not get along, in his coach, for headwind; had to stop at Epping. On the morrow, Fleetwood came to him in the Protector's name, to ask, What he wanted here?— Nothing of public concernment, only to see my Mother-in-law! answered the solid man. For indeed he did not know that Oliver was dying; that the glorious hour of Disenthralment, and immortal 'Liberty' to plunge over precipices with one's self and one's Cause was so nigh!—It came; and he took the precipices, like a strongboned resolute blind gin-horse rejoicing in the breakage of its halter, in a very gallant constitutional manner. Adieu, my solid friend; if I go to Vevay, I will read thy Monument there, perhaps not without emotion, after all!——

It was on this stormy Monday, while rocking winds, heard in the sickroom and everywhere, were piping aloud, that Thurloe and an Official person entered to inquire, Who, in the case of the worst, was to be his Highness's Successor? The Successor is named in a sealed paper already drawn-up, above a year ago, at Hampton Court; now lying in such and such a place. The Paper was sent for, searched for; it could never be found. Richard's is the name understood to have been written in that Paper: not a good name; but in fact one does not know. In ten years' time, had ten years more been granted, Richard might have become a fitter man; might have been cancelled, if palpably unfit. Or perhaps it was Fleetwood's name,—and the Paper, by certain parties, was stolen? None knows. On the Thursday night following, 'and not till then,' his Highness is understood to have formally named "Richard;"—or perhaps it might only be some heavy-laden "Yes, yes!" spoken, out of the thick death-slumbers, in answer to Thurloe's *question* "Richard?" The thing is a little uncertain. It was, once more, a matter of much moment;—giving colour probably to all the subsequent Centuries of England, this answer!——

On or near the night of the same stormy Monday, 'two or three days before he died,' we are to place that Prayer his

Highness was heard uttering; which, as taken down by his attendants, exists in many old Notebooks. In the tumult of the winds, the dying Oliver was heard uttering this

PRAYER

Lord, though I am a miserable and wretched creature, I am in Covenant with Thee through grace. And I may, I will, come to Thee, for Thy People. Thou hast made me, though very unworthy, a mean instrument to do them some good, and Thee service; and many of them have set too high a value upon me, though others wish and would be glad of my death; Lord, however Thou do dispose of me, continue and go on to do good for them. Give them consistency of judgment, one heart, and mutual love; and go on to deliver them, and with the work of reformation; and make the Name of Christ glorious in the world. Teach those who look too much on Thy instruments, to depend more upon Thyself. Pardon such as desire to trample upon the dust of a poor worm, for they are Thy people too. And pardon the folly of this short Prayer: Even for Jesus Christ's sake. And give us a good night, if it be Thy pleasure. Amen.

'Some variation there is,' says Harvey, 'of this Prayer, as to 'the account divers give of it; and something is here omitted. 'But so much is certain, that these were his requests. Wherein 'his heart was so carried out for God and his People,—yea 'indeed for some who had added no little sorrow to him,' the Anabaptist Republicans, and others,—'that at this time he seems to forget his own Family and nearest relations.' Which indeed is to be remarked.

Thursday night the Writer of our old Pamphlet was himself in attendance on his Highness; and has preserved a trait or two; with which let us hasten to conclude. Tomorrow is September Third, always kept as a Thanksgiving day, since the Victories of Dunbar and Worcester. The wearied one, 'that very night before the Lord took him to his everlasting rest,' was heard thus, with oppressed voice, speaking:

'"Truly God is good; indeed He is; He will not"——Then 'his speech failed him, but as I apprehended, it was, "He will 'not leave me." This saying, "God is good," he frequently 'used all along; and would speak it with much cheerfulness,

'and fervour of spirit, in the midst of his pains.—Again he
'said: "I would be willing to live to be farther serviceable to
'God and His People: but my work is done. Yet God will
'be with His People."

'He was very restless most part of the night, speaking often
'to himself. And there being something to drink offered him,
'he was desired To take the same, and endeavour to sleep.—
'Unto which he answered: "It is not my design to drink or
'sleep; but my design is, to make what haste I can to be
'gone."

'Afterwards, towards morning, he used divers holy expres-
'sions, implying much inward consolation and peace; among
'the rest he spake some exceeding self-debasing words, *an-
'nihilating* and judging himself. And truly it was observed,
'that a public spirit to God's Cause did breathe in him,—as in
'his lifetime, so now to his very last.'

When the morrow's sun rose, Oliver was speechless; between
three and four in the afternoon, he lay dead. Friday, 3d
September 1658. "The consternation and astonishment of all
people," writes Fauconberg, "are inexpressible; their hearts
"seem as if sunk within them. My poor Wife,—I know not
"what on earth to do with her. When seemingly quieted,
"she bursts out again into a passion that tears her very heart
"in pieces."—Husht, poor weeping Mary! Here is a Life-
battle right nobly done. Seest thou not,

> 'The storm is changed into a calm,
> At His command and will;
> So that the waves which raged before
> Now quiet are and still!
>
> Then are *they* glad,—because at rest
> And quiet now they be:
> So to the haven He them brings
> Which they desired to see.'

'Blessed are the dead that die in the Lord;' blessed are the
valiant that have lived in the Lord. 'Amen, saith the Spirit'—
Amen. 'They do rest from their labours, and their works
follow them.'

'Their works follow them.' As, I think, this Oliver Cromwell's works have done and are still doing! We have had our
'Revolutions of Eighty-eight,' officially called 'glorious;' and
other Revolutions not yet called glorious; and somewhat has

been gained for poor Mankind. Men's ears are not now slit-off by rash Officiality; Officiality will, for long henceforth, be more cautious about men's ears. The tyrannous Star-chambers, branding-irons, chimerical Kings and Surplices at Allhallowtide, they are gone, or with immense velocity going. Oliver's works do follow him !—The works of a man, bury them under what guano-mountains and obscene owl-droppings you will, do not perish, cannot perish. What of Heroism, what of Eternal Light was in a Man and his Life is with very great exactness added to the Eternities; remains forever a new divine portion of the Sum of Things; and no owl's voice, this way or that, in the least avails in the matter.—But we have to end here.

Oliver is gone; and with him England's Puritanism, laboriously built together by this man, and made a thing far-shining miraculous to its own Century, and memorable to all the Centuries, soon goes. Puritanism, without its King, is *kingless*, anarchic; falls into dislocation, self-collision; staggers, plunges into ever deeper anarchy; King, Defender of the Puritan Faith there can now none be found;—and nothing is left but to recall the old disowned Defender with the remnants of his Four Surplices, and Two Centuries of *Hypocrisis* (or Play-acting *not* so-called), and put-up with all that, the best we may. The Genius of England no longer soars Sunward, world-defiant, like an Eagle through the storms, 'mewing her mighty youth,' as John Milton saw her do: the Genius of England, much liker a greedy Ostrich intent on provender and a whole skin mainly, stands with its *other* extremity Sunward; with its Ostrich-head stuck into the readiest bush, of old Church-tippets, King-cloaks, or what other 'sheltering Fallacy' there may be, and *so* awaits the issue. The issue has been slow; but it is now seen to have been inevitable. No Ostrich, intent on gross terrene provender, and sticking its head into Fallacies, but will be awakened one day,—in a terrible *à-posteriori* manner, if not otherwise!——Awake before it come to that; gods and men bid us awake! The Voices of our Fathers, with thousandfold stern monition to one and all, bid us awake.

CHRONOLOGY

FIRST PERIOD: BIRTH TO OUTBREAK OF CIVIL WAR (1599—1642)

A.D.	MONTH	AGE	FACTS
1599	April 25		Oliver Cromwell born at Huntingdon.
1599	April 29		Christened in St. John's Church, Huntingdon.
1603	Jan.	3	His grandfather, Sir Henry Cromwell, of Hinchinbrook, died.
1603	April 27		James I. visited Hinchinbrook.
1606 (?) – 1616		7-17	Educated at Huntingdon Grammar School, under Doctor Beard, a Puritan divine.
1616	April 23	16	Admitted Fellow Commoner at Sidney Sussex College, Cambridge.
1617	June	18	His father, Robert Cromwell, died.
1617		18	Went to London; made some study of law.
1618 – 1620		19-21	Probably living in London chiefly.
1620	Aug.	21	Married at St. Giles's Church, Cripplegate, London, to Elizabeth Bourchier, daughter of Sir James Bourchier, Knight, a City merchant.
1620 – 1630		21-31	Lived at Huntingdon with his mother, wife, and children.
1621	Oct.	22	His first child, Robert, born.
1623	Jan.	23	His second child, Oliver, born.
1624	July	25	His third child, Bridget, born.
1626	Oct. 4	27	His fourth child, Richard, born.
1627	June	28	Hinchinbrook estate sold by Sir Oliver Cromwell (his uncle) to Sir Sidney Montague, Knight, one of the King's Masters of the Court of Requests.
1628	Jan.	28	His fifth child, Henry, born.
1628	March	28	M.P. for Huntingdon. The *Petition of Right* confirmed by King.
1628	June 26	29	Parliament prorogued. Cromwell home to Huntingdon.
1628	Aug. 23	29	Duke of Buckingham assassinated at Portsmouth by Felton.
1629	March	29	Parliament dissolved. Cromwell home to Huntingdon.
1629	June	30	His sixth child, Elizabeth, born.
1630	July 8	31	Appointed (or confirmed) J.P. in new charter granted to Huntingdon.
1631	May	32	Sold his Huntingdon properties.

CHRONOLOGY

A.D.	MONTH	AGE	FACTS
1631	June (?)	32	Rented grazing-farm at St. Ives.
1631 } 1636 }		32-37	Lived at St. Ives.
1632	Jan.	32	Seventh child, James, born.
1633	May	34	King passed through Huntingdonshire on his way to Scotland to be crowned.
1634		35	The Writ of Ship-Money issued.
1636		37	Eighth child, Mary, born.
1636		37	Cromwell removed residence to Ely.
1637	July 23	38	The disturbance in St. Giles's Kirk, Edinburgh.
1637		38	Ninth (and last) child, Frances, born.
1638	April	39	Exchequer judgment against Hampden concerning "Ship-Money."
1638		39	Cromwell resists with success unjust action of King's commissioners concerning Drainage of Fens (the Bedford Level scheme).
1640	April 13 } May 5 }	41	Sat in the *Short Parliament* as M.P. for Cambridge borough.
1640	Aug. 28	41	King's forces defeated by Scots on the Tyne.
1640	Oct. 1	41	*Treaty of Ripon* made with Scots.
1640	Nov. 3	41	*Long Parliament* met. Cromwell again M.P. for Cambridge (town).
1641	May 12	42	Lord Strafford executed.
1641	Nov.	42	Parliament reassembled: a royalist reaction there.
1641	Dec.	42	Disturbances in London against Bishops.
1642	Jan. 4	42	King's attempt to seize the Five Members.
1642	Jan. 12	42	King left Whitehall Palace (to return no more till his execution).
1642	April 23	42	King refused admission to Hull by the Governor, Sir John Hotham.
1642	June	43	King finally rejects Parliamentary terms.
1642	Aug. 22	43	King sets up his standard at Nottingham.

SECOND PERIOD: OUTBREAK OF CIVIL WAR TO END OF SECOND CIVIL WAR (1642-1651)

A.D.	MONTH	AGE	FACTS
1642	Sept.	43	Cromwell commissioned as captain of a troop of horse.
1642	Sept. 9	43	Earl of Essex takes field with City train-bands.
1642 } 1643 }		43	In autumn and winter Cromwell raised his regiment of 1000 Horse (the "Ironsides"): created Colonel.
1643	March 14	43	Captured Lowestoft, with many influential royalists and large supply of warlike stores.
1643	May 13	44	Defeats royalists near Grantham.
1643	July 28	44	Appointed by Parliament Governor of Isle of Ely.
1643	July end of }	44	Routs royalists near Gainsborough.
1643	July	44	Earl of Manchester took command of forces of "the Eastern Association," Cromwell serving under him.

CHRONOLOGY

A.D.	MONTH	AGE	FACTS
1643	Oct. 9	44	Junction of Manchester's army with Fairfax at Boston.
1643	Oct. 11	44	Fairfax and Cromwell rout royalists at Winceby, near Horncastle.
1643	(winter of)	44	Cromwell busy in securing eastern counties, raising funds, and settling affairs in Ely district.
1644	April 10	44	Scottish Covenanted army, under Lesley, Earl of Leven, unite with Fairfax at Wetherby. They invest York.
1644	April	45	Cromwell (now lieutenant-general and second in command) and Manchester join Fairfax and Lesley.
1644	June	45	Prince Rupert relieves York.
1644	July 2	45	Parliamentary victory of MARSTON MOOR.
1644	July	45	York and Newcastle surrender to Parliament.
1644	Oct. 27	45	Cromwell at second battle of Newbury; indecisive, owing to lack of vigour in Earl of Manchester.
1644	Nov. 25	45	Cromwell, in House of Commons, censures conduct of Manchester.
1644	Dec 9	45	He urges need of remodelling army.
1645	April 3	45	"Self-denying Ordinance" passed, depriving members of Parliament of military command.
1645	April 23	45	Cromwell (dispensed from the ordinance) sent against Prince Rupert.
1645	April 24	45	Cromwell routs Rupert at Islip Bridge, near Oxford.
1645	April 26	46	Gains another victory at Radcot Bridge.
1645	May 31	46	King storms Leicester.
1645	Summer	46	Sir Thomas Fairfax made general-in-chief. "New Model" army raised.
1645	June	46	Cromwell appointed lieutenant-general (second in command) to Fairfax.
1645	June 13	46	Cromwell, with 6000 picked horsemen, joins Fairfax at Northampton.
1645	June 14	46	Royal army, under King in person, routed at NASEBY.
1645	July	46	Cromwell marches south-west against "Clubmen" (a new royal party) and makes an end of them at Shaftesbury.
1645	Sept. 11	46	Bristol taken by Fairfax and Cromwell.
1645	Oct.	46	Winchester surrenders to, and Basing House stormed by, Cromwell. *End of First Civil War.*
1646	April 22	46	Cromwell returns to his place in Parliament; takes strong part with the Independents against the Presbyterians.
1647	Jan. 30	47	King delivered by Scots to Parliamentary commissioners.
1647	June 10	48	Army-meeting on Triplow Heath, near Cambridge; great demonstration against Presbyterian majority in House of Commons.
1647	June	48	Army marches slowly on London.

CHRONOLOGY

A.D.	MONTH	AGE	FACTS
1647	June 25	48	Army reaches Uxbridge; Parliament grants demand for expulsion of eleven leading Presbyterians.
1647	July	48	Royalist and Presbyterian reaction in London; return of expelled members. Leading Presbyterians take refuge with army.
1647	Aug. 3	48	Army at Hounslow Heath.
1647	Aug. 6	48	Fairfax enters Westminster with four regiments; Independents triumphant.
1647	Aug. 8	48	Army marches through City to quarters in Surrey. King conducted to Hampton Court.
1647	Autumn	48	Fruitless negotiations with King, mainly conducted by Cromwell and Ireton.
1647	Nov. 12	48	King escapes from Hampton Court; is captured and taken to Carisbrook Castle, Isle of Wight.
1648	Jan. 3	48	Parliament resolves on no more "addresses to" (i.e. attempts at treaty with) King.
1648	Jan.	48	"Levellers" (mutinous section of army) under Lilburn put down by Cromwell.
1648	Spring	49	*Second Civil War begins.* Formidable risings against Parliament suppressed in London, Canterbury, Norwich, Exeter, etc. Revolt in Wales.
1648	May 3	49	Cromwell marches for Wales.
1648	May 11	49	He takes Chepstow.
1648	July 10	49	Pembroke Castle surrenders to Cromwell.
1648	July	49	He marches north against Scottish royalist army under Duke of Hamilton, joined by a Yorkshire force.
1648	Aug. 17 } Aug. 20 }	49	Cromwell and General Lambert rout Hamilton's army; the duke surrenders.
1648	Sept. 20	49	Cromwell enters Scotland by way of Berwick.
1648	Oct. 4	49	He enters Edinburgh.
1648	Oct. 7	49	Leaves Edinburgh for Carlisle, and receives its surrender.
1648	Oct.	49	Besieges Pontefract Castle; stubborn defence. He leaves Lambert in charge, and returns to London.
1648	Dec. 6	49	He reaches London.
1648	Dec. 7	49	Thanks of House accorded.
1648	Dec. 7 } Dec. 17 }	49	Presbyterian members expelled by "Pride's Purge"; Independents finally in power.
1649	Jan.	49	Cromwell sits on "High Court of Justice" at trial of King.
1649	Jan. 30	49	King executed at Whitehall.
1649	Feb.	49	Cromwell a chief member of the new "Council of State."
1649	March 15	49	He is nominated lord-lieutenant of Ireland.
1649	May 30	50	"Commonwealth" proclaimed in City.
1649	May } June }	50	Dangerous movement of "Levellers" in army quelled by Cromwell and Fairfax.
1649	July 10	50	Cromwell leaves London for Ireland.

CHRONOLOGY

A.D.	MONTH	AGE	FACTS
1649	July } Aug. }	50	Makes his preparations at Bristol.
1649	Aug. 13	50	Sails from Milford Haven.
1649	Aug. 15	50	Lands in Dublin.
1649	Sept. 10	50	Storms Tredah (Drogheda).
1649	Oct. 11	50	Storms Wexford.
1649	Dec. 2	50	Retires into winter quarters.
1650	Jan. 29	50	He takes the field again
1650	May	51	Kilkenny and Clonmel taken. [Ireton.
1650	May 31	51	Cromwell back in London, leaving Irish work to
1650	June 26	51	Appointed "Captain-general" of all forces of Commonwealth.
1650	June 29	51	Leaves London for north.
1650	July 22	51	Enters Scotland by Berwick.
1650	July 28	51	Encamps at Musselburgh. [repulsed.
1650	July 30	51	Sortie from Edinburgh by General David Lesley,
1650	Aug.	51	Manœuvring of Lesley's and Cromwell's forces; advantage rests with Lesley.
1650	Sept. 1	51	Cromwell retreats to Dunbar: is hemmed in near the town.
1650	Sept. 3	51	His great victory at DUNBAR. [there.
1650	Sept.	51	Edinburgh occupied by Cromwell. He winters
1650	Dec.	51	Edinburgh Castle surrenders.
1651	Feb.	51	Deputation from Oxford informs him of his election as Chancellor of the University.
1651	Spring	52	Cromwell dangerously ill; spends some days at Glasgow.
1651	June (end of) }	52	Marches for Stirling against Lesley.
1651	Aug.	52	Perth surrenders to Cromwell.
1651	Aug.	52	Charles the Second and Lesley march into England, followed by Cromwell.
1651	Sept. 3	52	The crowning victory of WORCESTER: second civil war ends.[1]

THIRD PERIOD: END OF SECOND CIVIL WAR TO CROMWELL'S DEATH

1651	Autumn	52	Scotland united to England by an Act. Navigation Act passed.
1652 } 1654 }		53-55	Dutch War begins; actions between Blake and Van Tromp, De Ruyter, and De Witt, with varied success. War ended by First Treaty of Westminster (April, 1654).
1652		53	Cromwell in London, managing Scottish and other affairs.
1653	April 20	53	Cromwell expels the remains ("Rump") of Long Parliament.
1653	July 4	54	New Parliament of one hundred and forty "persons of approved fidelity and honesty" (the "Little Parliament").

CHRONOLOGY

A.D.	MONTH	AGE	FACTS
1653	Dec. 12	54	Parliament resigns power into Cromwell's hands.
1653	Dec. 16	54	Cromwell proclaimed "Lord Protector" and solemnly installed in Westminster Hall.
1654	Jan. / Sept.	55	Cromwell and his Council issue eighty-two "Ordinances" for regulation of civil and religious affairs.
1654	Sept. 3	55	New Parliament met, elected under the "Instrument of Government." The Assembly wastes time in vain opposition to Cromwell.
1655	Jan. 22	55	Cromwell dissolves the Parliament.
1655		56	Ten "Major-Generals" appointed as executive.
1655	Summer	56	Cromwell effectively intervenes with the Duke of Savoy, Cardinal Mazarin (ruling in minority of Louis XIV.), and other sovereigns, in behalf of the persecuted Protestants in valleys of Piedmont.
1655 / 1656		56-57	Admiral Blake clears Mediterranean of pirates, and calls the Duke of Tuscany, the Pope, and the Deys of Tunis, Tripoli, and Algiers to account for wrongs done to British commerce.
1655 / 1658		56-59	War with Spain. Admirals Penn and Venables, repulsed at St. Domingo (Hispaniola), capture Jamaica.
1656	Sept. 17	57	New Parliament meets: Cromwell excludes at once over one hundred members as unsuitable.
1656		57	Blake captures Spanish galleons with silver.
1657	April 17	57	House of Commons, by large majority, desires Cromwell to assume royal title; he declines.
1657	April 20	57	Blake's great victory at Santa Cruz (Teneriffe).
1657		58	Six thousand English infantry aid French against Spain in the Netherlands.
1657	Spring	58	"Major-Generals'" rule ends.
1657	June	58	Under "Petition and Advice," he is permitted to name a successor and appoint a new House of Peers.
1657	June 26	58	Cromwell again solemnly invested with Protectorate at Westminster.
1657 / 1658		58-59	Various plots against Cromwell's life detected.
1658	Jan. 20	58	New Parliament meets; they refuse to sanction the new peerage.
1658	Feb. 4	58	Parliament dissolved.
1658	June	59	Cromwell's troops aid Turenne against Spaniards at Dunkirk.
1658	June 25	59	Dunkirk surrendered, and transferred to English rule.
1658	Aug. 6	59	Death of Cromwell's favourite daughter, Elizabeth Claypole.
1658	Sept. 3	59	Cromwell dies.

APPENDIX

THOMAS CARLYLE

ONE of the greatest British men of thought—essayist, historian, philosopher—the successful vindicator and champion of the greatest of English men of action in statesmanship and war—was born on December 4th, 1795, at the Dumfriesshire village of Ecclefechan, in Annandale. He was the eldest son in a family of eight, and his parents were of the best type of Scottish character in the class between laird and labourer, his father being first a stonemason and then a tenant farmer. The young Carlyle obtained a good basis of education, on the Scottish system, in Latin, French, mathematics, and other subjects, at the parish-school, the burgh-school of Annan, and the University of Edinburgh. He was, however, in the main, a man self-educated for the high calling of literature by his own omnivorous reading. In German he thus acquired a mastery which enabled him to make known to English readers some of the best work of Goethe and Schiller. His life for many years was a hard struggle in the vocations of a school-teacher, a writer of articles in the serials, and a translator from the German. He lived in Edinburgh for some years, ending in 1822, then for some months in London. In October, 1826, he married Miss Jane Welsh, a small landowner, and a lady of rare ability and force of character. After further residence in Edinburgh, where he wrote for the famous *Review*, his wife and he settled down, in 1828, on her little property at Craigenputtock, in his native county, where they mostly lived for about six years. Carlyle there wrote for the *Edinburgh* and other leading reviews and magazines, and produced his *Sartor Resartus*, a work which first displayed his new and peculiar style. During this period, they lived for a short time in Edinburgh, where he wrote one of his best things, the article on Queen Marie Antoinette's *Diamond Necklace*. It was his research for materials in this case that first led him to study the history of France in the later years of the eighteenth century. In June, 1834, the pair removed to London, and made a permanent abode of the house, No. 5 (now 24), Cheyne Row, Chelsea, a tenement which became a world-famous shrine, and is now public property as a permanent memorial. The author's future was now assured. In 1837, *The French Revolution*, the great prose-epic of the century, appeared. In that and some following years, he delivered courses of lectures, including those on *Heroes*, to audiences of distinguished position in the worlds of intellect and of fashion. In his *Chartism*, *Past and Present*, and *Latter-day Pamphlets*, he made fierce, scornful attacks on what he deemed to be false teachers and blind guides in legislation for social distresses and wrongs. We come now to the book here presented. In 1845 appeared *Oliver Cromwell's Letters and Speeches, with Elucidations*. Some estimates of this great work have already been given. It passed rapidly through several editions, or, as he wrote himself in his preface to the second issue, "spread itself abroad with some degree of impetus." It would have been wonderful had the result of his toilsome efforts been different. He had succeeded in fairly startling the world by a revelation of historical truth; he had triumphantly substituted fact for long-reigning falsehood; he had completely revolutionised the public estimate of the subject of his work. In 1851 his life of John Sterling was hailed as one of the most charming biographies in the language. The *History of Frederick the Great* appeared between 1858 and 1865, and closed his important literary work. In November, 1865, he was elected Lord Rector of Edinburgh University by a majority of 657 votes over 310 recorded for Mr. Disraeli, afterwards Lord Beaconsfield, and he was received with an extraordinary demonstration of enthusiasm on his installation in April, 1866, when he delivered to the students a famous address on "The choice of books." On his return home he suffered a terrible shock in finding that his wife had suddenly died during her carriage-drive. As regards public rewards for this illustrious writer, he had the distinction of declining, in 1874, the Grand Cross of the Bath (with the alternative of a baronetcy) and a good pension, offered by Disraeli, then Prime Minister. He had, earlier in the same year, accepted one of the highest rewards to which genius can aspire in the Prussian Order of Merit (Ordre pour le Mérite) bestowed in recognition of his life of the re-founder of the Order. This distinction has always been highly and justly prized. It is, compared to other honours, what Frederick the Great was to other Kings. This Order is not given by the Sovereign or the Minister, but by the Knights themselves, and the King can only confirm their choice. The number of the Knights is strictly limited to thirty German and thirty foreign, and thus every Knight knows who will be his peers. In 1853 the same distinction had been conferred on Macaulay. Thomas Carlyle died on February 5th, 1881, at his house in Cheyne Row. Burial in Westminster Abbey was offered; but according to his own desire, his body was laid beside those of his parents at Ecclefechan. The Craigenputtock property inherited from his wife was bequeathed to found "bursaries" for poor students at Edinburgh University. His books were left to Harvard College, Massachusetts. Of the literary and philosophical teacher of such men as Ruskin, Kingsley and Froude, *The Times*, in its leader, wrote, "The world seems duller and colder and darker that one gray old man at Chelsea has faded away from among us."

NOTES

MORE recent estimates of Oliver Cromwell may be found in Mr. Goldwin Smith's *Three English Statesmen* (1867); Mr. Frederic Harrison's *Cromwell* (1888); and Mr. John Morley's *Life of Oliver Cromwell* (1900).

P. 3. *Huntingdon.*—The town was in pre-Conquest days called "Huntantun," and in the Norman Survey (Domesday Book), "Huntersdune": the place was incorporated (made a municipal borough) in 1206.

P. 44. *Smectymnuus Hall.*—A "Carlylese" way of mentioning Dr. Joseph Hall, an able and witty preacher, controversialist, and satirist who, in 1641, when he was Bishop of Norwich (to which see he had been just "translated" from that of Exeter), published an answer to a Presbyterian work against Episcopacy, published under the name of *Smectymnuus*, a word composed of the initials of the five contributors, viz. *S. M*arshal, *E. C*alamy, *T. Y*oung, *M. N*ewcomen, *W. S*purstow.

P. 46. "*Attempting Hull Magazine* (arsenal) in vain."—An allusion to what was really the first overt act of rebellion against the King. Sir John Hotham, Governor of Hull, had been directed, by an "ordinance" of Parliament, to hold the garrison there "for King and Parliament," and to surrender the place to no one but under the orders of Parliament. Charles had now gone northwards, seeking support, and on April 23rd, 1642, he demanded admittance into Hull. Hotham went on the ramparts, and, falling on his knees, begged the King to excuse his refusal on the ground of his oath sworn to Parliament. Charles could do nothing but retire, denouncing him as a traitor, and a large store of arms and ammunition was thus secured for the popular cause.

Pp. 72 *sqq. Siege of Colchester.*—Early in June, 1648, the Earl of Norwich, driven out of Kent, fled across the Thames into Essex, and, being joined at Chelmsford by Lord Capel, Sir Charles Lucas, Sir George Lisle, and other leaders, with reinforcements collected in Hertfordshire and Essex, he seized Colchester, whose people were mainly for the Parliament, and was there besieged by Fairfax. The town was very strong in natural position, defended by the Colne on the north and east, and in its fortification by a parallelogram of walls seven or eight feet thick, of large flints imbedded in lime (as may yet be seen) with several courses of Roman bricks, the whole having become, in the course of centuries, one solid mass. The siege lasted from June 13th to August 28th, a close blockade being maintained after July 20th. Several attempts at sortie were repulsed, and surrender came at last through famine. The superior officers, by the terms agreed on, "surrendered to mercy," *i.e.*, without assurance of quarter, the victorious general being free to put them to the sword at once. With regard to the fate of Sir Charles Lucas and Sir George Lisle, the absurdly false inscription (cut deep on a slab of black marble), which describes them as "in cold blood barbarously murderd," is refuted by the following facts :—On March 23rd, 1646, Sir Charles Lucas, taken prisoner at Stow-on-the-Wold, and on June 24th, in the same year, Sir George Lisle, captured at Farringdon, had given their words of honour not again to take up arms against the Parliament. They had deliberately broken faith, and they received the punishment which, by the laws of civilised warfare, in these days as in those, was due to such an offence. Both these officers were well aware of the risk they were running, for on the night of July 15th they made a futile attempt to escape, repeated on several succeeding nights, until the discontent of their own followers was aroused. Again, on the night of August 25th, they were deterred from another effort to escape only by the mutinous attitude of the troops, who agreed to kill them if they attempted to stir. Sir George Lisle, and Sir Charles Lucas, therefore, died in obedience to a law, without the strict observance of which all honourable intercourse between hostile forces would be impossible. Lord Fairfax had proved himself, in the case of many surrenders in which he was on the victorious side, to be a most generous and lenient adversary, and it is calumnious to accuse him even of undue harshness in discharging, at Colchester, a most painful but necessary duty.

P. 166. *Catholics of the Pale.*—At the nominal Conquest of Ireland under Henry the Second, the districts really in possession of the English were confined to a small territory around the towns of Dublin, Waterford, Wexford, Drogheda, and Cork, known together as the *English Pale*; outside those limits the native chiefs were virtually independent. Under Henry VIII., the Pale included the country on the eastern coast from Dundalk to beyond Dublin, extending a few miles inland. In the time of Charles the First, "Catholics of the Pale" would mean the Anglo-Irish Catholics, or party of the "Lords of the Pale," as the landowners of the above districts, and of various confiscated territories, were called.

P. 253. *Barebones's Parliament.*—This derisive nickname was given by the royalists to Cromwell's "Little Parliament," because one of its members was a leather-merchant, named, in Puritan fashion as to his forename, "Praise-God" Barbon; his real surname being probably corrupted, by the paltry wit of the cavaliers, into "Barebone."

INDEX

'Adjutators,' (of army). *See* 'Agents'
'Agents' or 'Agitators' 113, 115 *sqq.*, 124
'Agreement of the People,' the (document), 247
Argyle, Marquis of, 154
Ashby-de-la-Zouch, 54, 86
'Association,' the, 49 *sqq.*, 69
Astley, Sir Jacob, 101

Baillie, General, 137, 140 *sqq.*, 149 *sqq.*
Barebones's Parliament. *See* 'Little Parliament'
Basing House, siege and final capture of, 95-9
Bastwick, Dr. John, 32
Beard, Dr. (Oliver's schoolmaster) 5, 16, 18
Bedford, Earl of, 48
Bedford Level, the, 34
Bishop's War, the, 39
Blake, Admiral, 87, 103, 181, 182, 249, 297-9, 303, 309, 313 *sq.*, 336 *sq.*
Bletchington House, capture of, 78, 80
Bradshaw, John, 157 *sq.*, 159, 271, 284, 288
Bristol, surrender of, 62
Buckingham, Duke of, 8, 15; his son, 134
Bulstrode. *See* 'Whitlocke'
Bunyan, John, 86
Burleigh House, 58
Burton, Rev. Henry, 32

Cambridge, 6, 50, 51
Capel, Lord, 50, 153, 160 *sq.*
Carisbrook Castle, 126
Charles the First, 13-8, 33, 38, 39, 43-6, 49, 52; (his queen) 53; 56, 62, 63, 64, 72, 73, 78, 83-7, 100, 101, 104, 108, 114-6, 122, 124-8, 157 *sq.*
Charles the Second, 193, 200, 201, 233, 236 *sqq*, 243, 248, 293, 311, 320 *sq*, 326, 345, 350
Clarendon, Lord, 25. *See* 'Hyde'
Claypole, Elizabeth (Cromwell's daughter) 106, 226, 359 *sqq.*
Clonmel, capture of, 188 *sq.*
Colchester, siege of, 131, 134, 153
'Committee of both Kingdoms,' the, 78, 79, 81
Cooper, Ashley (afterwards Earl of Shaftesbury), 263, 269, 271, 309, 316, 324
Cork, 181
'Council of State,' the, 159

Covenant, the Scottish, 192
Cromwell, Henry, 9, 71, 137, 227, 263, 272, 308, 311 *sq.*
CROMWELL, OLIVER, birth of, 1; his father's family and nearest relatives, 1-4; his mother and her family, 1-3; early life at Huntingdon, etc., 4-8; at Cambridge University, 6; in London, 8-10; his marriage, 10; becomes a Puritan, 11 *sq*; lives at Huntingdon, 10, 15; enters Parliament, 13; his first speech, 16; back to Huntingdon, 18; becomes J.P., 18; removes to St. Ives, 18, 19; his children, 20 *sq.*, 31; comments on his Letters and Speeches, 21-5; his life at St. Ives, 29-31; removes to Ely, 31; promotes fen-drainage, 34 *sq*; his supposed early wicked life, 36; his real character, 37; M.P. for Cambridge, 38, 40; royalist description of, 41; he signs the 'Protestation,' 43; prepares for war, 47 *sq*; takes the field, 48; fights at Edgehill, 48; in fen-country, 49; becomes Colonel, 49 *sq.*; at Cambridge, 50 *sq.*; raises siege of Croyland, 53; his rapid movements, 53; his victory at Grantham, 55, 56; at Nottingham, 57; takes Stamford, 57; his victory at Gainsborough, 58-60; his zeal for service, 61, 62; made Governor of Isle of Ely, 62; under Earl of Manchester, 63; raises his 'Ironsides,' 63; in Lincolnshire, 64; victorious at Winceby, 64, 65; his peril there, 66; at Ely, 66-8; in Parliament, 68; at MARSTON MOOR, 68-71; at second battle of Newbury, 73-4; attacks Earl of Manchester in Parliament, 73-4; speeches there, 74-5; marches to west, 76; victory at Islip, 78-80; made 'Lieutenant-General' for Eastern Counties, 81; at NASEBY, 83-6; at capture of Bristol, 87-93; at Winchester, 94, 95; captures Basing House, 95-100; in Parliament again, 101; in London, 106; historical attacks on him, 109-11; in Parliament-house, 114; receives thanks of Commons, 114; rejoins the army, 116, 117; signs army-letter to London Corporation, 121; his attitude towards King, 124; re-

ports King's escape from Hampton Court, 125; reports his attempted escape from Carisbrook Castle, 127; success in South Wales, 129-35; marches for Lancashire, 135; his victorious work there, 136-46; to Scotland, 154; in London, 156; signs death-warrant of King, 158; to Ireland, 162-5; his victorious course in Ireland, 166-89; returns to England, 190; starts for Scotland, 194; appointed 'Captain-General,' 194; operations in Scotland, 196-233; his illness, 224 *sqq.*; recovery, 230; marches into England in pursuit of Charles the Second and the Scots, 235 *sqq.*; his victory at WORCESTER, 237 *sqq.*; returns to London, 247 *sqq.*; turns out the 'Rump,' 249-51; summons new Parliament, 252 *sqq.*; becomes 'Lord Protector,' 265; his first installation 265 *sq.*; his personal appearance (1654) 266; his new 'Ordinances,' 269; his scheme for Church-government, 270; removes to Whitehall Palace, 270; at Westminster Abbey, 271; address to new Parliament, 272 *sqq.*; another speech, 285 *sqq.*; excludes some members, 287 *sqq.*, his accident in Hyde Park, 289; death of his mother, 289 *sq.*; continental estimate of him, 290; dissolves the Parliament, 291; his resolute attitude, 292; plots against his power, 293 *sqq.*, 312; intervention for Savoy Protestants, 296 *sq.*, 299 *sq.*; his foreign policy, 297, 340; receives embassy from Sweden, 301 *sq.*; makes alliance with France, 307; his encouragement of learning, 309 *sq.*; calls a new Parliament, 315 *sqq.*; his speech, 316 *sqq.*; his relations with Cardinal Mazarin, 326 *sqq.*; Sindercomb's plot against his life, 329 *sq.*; his love of music, 334; solemnly inaugurated (as 'Protector') in Westminster Hall, 338 *sq.*; his new House of Lords, 346 *sqq.*; dissolves Parliament, 348-9; trial and execution of new plotters, 350 *sq.*; his position at home and abroad, 353; his noble efforts for persecuted Protestants, 354 *sqq.*; death of his favourite daughter, 359 *sq.*; his illness and death, 359-368

Cromwell, Oliver, the younger, 20, 31, 48, 70
Cromwell, Robert, (Oliver's father) 1, 3, 4, 7, 8
Cropredy Bridge, fight at, 72
Dalbier, Colonel, 95, 100, 134
Danes, the, 280
'Declaration,' the, 112
Derby, Earl of, 235, 236
Desborow, Captain (Colonel, and General), 50, 89, 121, 263, 269, 294, 304, 347
Doon Hill, 203 *sqq.*
Drogheda, capture of, 168 *sqq.*
Dublin, 163, 165
Dunbar, 196, 202 *sq.*; battle of, 202-17
Dundee, storming of, 243
Dunkirk, 339, 343, 345, 353, 357
Dutch, war with, 248 *sq.*, 277
'Eastern Association,' the, 49, 53, 62, 63
Edgehill, battle of, 48, 53
Edinburgh, 32, 33, 154, 222
'Eleven Members', the, 121
Eliot, Sir John, 17
Essex, Earl of, 48, 51, 52, 54, 57, 62, 64, 72, 73, 76, 106
Fairfax, Lord, 51. *See* 62, 64, 68-71
Fairfax, Sir Thomas (and Lord), 76, 80, 81, 84, 85, 91, 100, 101-3, 106-8, 112, 115, 116, 121, 123, 129, 131, 132, 134, 159, 190, 194, 271
Falkland, Lord, 64
Fiennes, Colonel, 62
'Fifth Monarchy' men, the, 274 *sqq.*
Finch, Speaker of Commons, 17, 40
Five Members, affair of the, 45 *sq.*
Fleetwood, Captain (Colonel and General) 50, 114, 215, 237 *sqq.*, 269, 271, 305, 365
Fox, George, the Quaker, 361 *sqq.*
France, Cromwell's policy with, 277, 281, 307, 337, 339 *sqq.*. *See* 'Mazarin'
Gainsborough, 58, 61
Geddes, Jenny, 33
Gell, Sir John, 54, 81
Glasgow, 33, 38, 221
Gloucester, royalist siege of, raised, 63, 64
Goring, Lord, 76, 77, 93, 153
Grantham, Cromwell's victory at, 55, 56, 58
Grey, Lord, 49, 54, 57, 150
Hamilton, Duke of, 134, 137, 138-48 150-3, 160
Hammond, Colonel, 89, 90, 94, 97, 126, 127

INDEX

Hampden, John, 12, 34, 44, 45, 47-9, 52, 57
Hampton Court, 124, 125, 358 *sqq.*
Haselrig, Mr., M.P., 45, 203, 271, 284, 288, 316, 324, 347
Hinchinbrook House, 1, 3, 5, 7, 12, 115
Hispaniola, attack on, 305 *sq.*
Holland, Earl of, 124, 134, 160
Holles, Denzil, M.P., 17, 45, 112, 114, 118, 121
Holmby House, 115
Hopton, Sir Ralph, 51, 93, 100, 101
Hotham, Sir John, 53, 57, 62
Hull, 46, 62, 64, 66
Huntingdon, town of, 3, 4
Hyde (afterwards Lord Clarendon), 293, 311

'Independents,' rise of the, 107, 109
'Instrument of Government,' the (document), 259, 265, 267 *sqq.*, 287
Ireland, 166 *sqq.*
Ireton, General, 88, 101 *sqq.*; 103, 105-106, 114, 121, 163, 189, 190, 227
Irish Rebellion, the, 43 *sq.*
Ives, St. (Hunts), 29, 30

Jamaica, conquest of, 305 *sqq.*
James the First, 5, 7
Jones, General, 163
Joyce, Cornet, 115

Kilkenny, capture of, 185 *sqq.*
Kimbolton, Lord. *See* 'Manchester, Earl of.'

Lambert, General, 121, 131, 135, 156, 194, 197, 206-209, 231, 235, 237 *sqq.*, 269, 271 *sq.*, 305
Lammermoor Hills, 203, 205, 207
Lancashire, warfare in, 131, 136-145
Langdale, Sir Marmaduke, 131, 134, 136, 138, 139, 140 *sqq.*, 151
Lansdown Heath, Waller's defeat at, 62
Laud, Archbishop, 8, 16, 18, 25, 32, 39, 40, 45
Leicester, 86
Lenthall, the Speaker. *See* the Letters *passim*, also 251, 271, 284, 347, 352
Lesley, Field-Marshal, 38, 68-71, 154
Lesley, General David, 100, 154, 199-211
'Levellers,' the, 124, 125, 273 *sq.*
Leven, Earl of. *See* 'Lesley, Field-marshal.'
Lilburn, Colonel Robert, 121, 132, 236, 241, 305
Lilburn, John, 40
Lincoln, 61
Lincolnshire, warfare in, 53, etc., 64

Lisle, Sir George, 153
'Little Parliament,' the, 253 *sqq.*, 262 *sqq.*
Lockhart, the diplomatist, 327 *sq.*, 340, *sq.*, 347, 354, 357
LONDON, zeal for Parliament, 14, 15, 32, 40, 42, 44, 45, 46, 63, 64, 72; movement in, for King. 107, 109, 114, 118-24, 154-155
'Long Parliament,' the, 40
Louis XIV., 340, 353
Lucas, Sir Charles, 153
Ludlow, Edmund, 114, 160, 190, 249, 365
Lunsford, Colonel, 44
Lynn, 64

'Major-Generals,' the, 294 *sqq.*, 304 *sq.*, 325, 336
Manchester, Earl of, 45, 63-65, 66, 68-71, 72-74, 76
MARSTON MOOR, battle of, 69-71
Massey, General, 121, 123, 156, 230, 237 *sqq*
Maurice, Prince, 79, 102, 181
Mazarin, Cardinal, 326 *sqq*, 342 *sqq*, 352
Milton, John, 10, 161 *sq.*, 268, 269, 296 *sq.*
Monk, General, 194, 208, 215, 234, 235, 243, 249, 352
Montague family and Montague, Colonel (afterwards Earl of Sandwich), 12, 13, 82, 88-91, 94, 95, 96, 115, 263, 269, 271, 300, 307, 309, 313 *sq.*, 338, *sq.*, 340, 344, 347
Montrose, Lord, 39, 100, 193
Musselburgh, 197 *sq.*, 200, 202

NASEBY, battle of, 82-86
Navigation Act, the, 248
New Model army, the, 72, 76, 78, 83-87
Newark-on-Trent, 53, 54, 57, 101
Newburn, fight at, 39
Newbury, first battle of, 64, second, 73
Newcastle (on-Tyne) 38, 39, 40
Newcastle, Earl (Marquis) of, 46, 51, 53, 60, 61, 66, 68-71
Northampton, Earl of, 79, 80

Ormond, Marquis (and Duke) of, 162 *sqq.*, 175, 179, 349 *sqq.*
Oxford, 56, 78, 101, 102, 115

Pembroke Castle, siege of. *See* 'Poyer, Colonel'
Penn, Admiral, 290, 303, 305 *sq.*, 307
Peters, Hugh, 82, 94, 97-9, 124, 129, 156, 163
'Petition and Advice,' the (document) 338

INDEX

Petition and Remonstrance, the Grand, 44
PETITION OF RIGHT, the, 14, 15
Pickering, Colonel, 89, 91, 95, 96
Piedmont, persecution of Protestants in. *See* 'Savoy'
Portugal, dealings with, 277, 281
Poyer, Colonel, 128, 130, 132, 135, 161
Poyntz, General, 123
Presbyterianism (in England), 107-9, 112
PRESTON, battle of, 136-46
Pride, Colonel, 121, 144, 147, 155 *sq.*, 194, 206, 215, 216, 347
'Pride's Purge,' 156
Protectorate Parliament, the First, 267 *sqq.*, 271 *sqq.*, 291; the Second, 335 *sqq.*, 348 *sq.*
'Protestation,' the, 42, 43
Prynne, William, 32, 62, 156, 351
Puritans, the, 25-7; and *passim*
Pym, John, 45, 57

Rainsborough, Colonel, 88-90, 121, 136
Reading, taken by Lord Essex, 57
Ripon, Treaty of, 40
Ross (Ireland), capture of, 180
'Rump,' the (Parliament), 245 *sq.*, 248, 251
Rupert, Prince, 50, 52, 62, 63, 64, 69-71, 77, 78, 83-85, 87-93, 102, 181, 277

Saffron Walden, 112, 114, 115
Sandwich, Earl of. *See* 'Montague.'
Savoy, Duke of, 295 *sqq*; persecution of Protestants in, 295 *sqq*, 354 *sqq.*
Scots, the, 32, 33, 38-40, 68-71, 101, 104, 105, 106-108, 114, 128, 134, 137 *sqq.*, 151, 153-154, 191-240, 243
Selden, John, 17
'Self-Denying Ordinance,' the, 72, 76
'Seven Associated Counties,' the, 51, 67
Sexby, Colonel, 329 *sq.*, 334
Shakespeare, 6
'Short Parliament,' the, 38
Sindercomb, Miles, 329 *sqq.*
Skippon, General, 72, 88, 106-108, 113, 114, 116, 269, 271, 305, 347
SPAIN, Cromwell's policy concerning, 297 *sq*, 306 *sq.*, 311, 313 *sqq.*, 317 *sqq.*, 321, 337 *sq.*
Spalding, 55
St. John, Oliver, 34, 40, 246, 248

Stamford, Earl of, 51, 62; town, 52, 54, 57
Steward, Elizabeth (Cromwell's mother), 1, 2; 8, 19, 32, 289 *sq*
Strafford, Earl of, 14, 38, 39, 40, 42, 43
Strode, William, M.P., 17, 45
Surrey, insurrection in, 134; 'Surrey Petition,' the, 131
Sydney (Sidney), Algernon, 82, 103, 249

Thurloe, Secretary, 268; 269, 289, 301, 313, 365
Titus, Colonel, 115, 127
Tredah. *See* 'Drogheda'
'Triers,' the, 269 *sq*, 279
Triploe Heath, army-meeting at, 116
Tunis, Dey of 297 *sq.*
Turenne, Marshal, 337 *sq*, 357
Turner, Sir James, 136 *sqq.*

Vane, Sir Harry, 160, 161, 246, 251
Venables, General, 290, 303, 305 *sq.*, 307

Wales, royalist insurrection in, 128-35
Waller, Sir Hardress, 89, 95, 96, 121
Waller, Sir William, 62, 72, 73, 77, 112, 118, 121
Walton, Colonel, 70, 71
Warrington, 149
Warwick, Sir Philip, 35, 41, 118
Wentworth. *See* 'Strafford, Earl of'
West Indies, expedition to, 290, 297
Wexford, capture of, 182
Whalley, Captain (Colonel), 50, 59, 60, 61, 115, 124, 125, 194, 197, 215, 217, 232, 285, 305, 347
'Whiggamore Raid,' the, 154
Whitlocke, 301 *sq.*, 324, 339, 347
Wigan, 148, 149
Williams, Archbishop (of York), 44
Willoughby, Lord, 58, 59, 60, 61, 68
Wilmot, Lord, 80
Winceby, battle at, 64-6
Winchester, 94-5; Marquis of, 95-100
Windebank, Colonel, 78, 80
WORCESTER, 78, 235-40; battle of, 237 *sqq.*; its effect, 243

York, 46, 69, 71
York, Duke of (afterwards James II.), 326 *sq.*, 345